AF505809

Gender and Sexuality in 1968

Gender and Sexuality in 1968

Transformative Politics in the Cultural Imagination

Edited by
Lessie Jo Frazier
and
Deborah Cohen

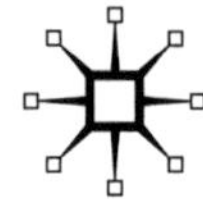

GENDER AND SEXUALITY IN 1968

First published in 2009 by
PALGRAVE MACMILLAN®
in the United States—a division of St. Martin's Press LLC,
175 Fifth Avenue, New York, NY 10010.

Where this book is distributed in the UK, Europe and the rest of the world,
this is by Palgrave Macmillan, a division of Macmillan Publishers Limited,
registered in England, company number 785998, of Houndmills,
Basingstoke, Hampshire RG21 6XS.

Palgrave Macmillan is the global academic imprint of the above companies
and has companies and representatives throughout the world.

Palgrave® and Macmillan® are registered trademarks in the United States,
the United Kingdom, Europe and other countries.

ISBN: 978–0–230–61871–8

Library of Congress Cataloging-in-Publication Data

Gender and sexuality in 1968 : transformative politics in the cultural
imagination / edited by Lessie Jo Frazier and Deborah Cohen.
   p. cm.
  ISBN 978–0–230–61871–8 (alk. paper)
   1. Sex—Cross-cultural studies. 2. Social change—Cross-cultural
studies. 3. Nineteen sixty-eight, A.D.—Social aspects. I. Frazier,
Lessie Jo, 1966– II. Cohen, Deborah, 1968–

HQ16.G45 2009
306.709′046—dc22   2009006896

A catalogue record of the book is available from the British Library.

Design by Newgen Imaging Systems (P) Ltd., Chennai, India.

First edition: November 2009

10 9 8 7 6 5 4 3 2 1

Printed in the United States of America.

CONTENTS

Part 2 Spirit, Awakenings, Imaginaries, Beyond '68

FOREWORD

Luisa Passerini

This book is an innovative contribution to the literature on 1968 in numerous ways. First of all, the selection of geopolitical spaces examined in this volume is particularly audacious: France, the Czech Republic, the United States, Africa, and Mexico constitute a wide range of different situations, and their choice does not try to be systematic or straightforwardly representative. Coupled with differing analytic and disciplinary approaches, this geographic range amounts to a very diverse set of chapters that make us reflect on the multiple points of view that are required to understand the complex phenomena that are associated with 68 as a phenomenon.

Second, the volume gives primary place to gender and sexuality, which even when considered important, are not generally seen as critical, and it does so in the context of relations between different social actors and institutions, including states. The perspective adopted here affirms not only that practices of the 1960s intertwined gender, sex, and sexuality with political projects, but also that all movements, including those that did not attend to gender, found their context in assumptions about gender and sexuality.

Third, the volume posits the view that the roots of 1968 can be found in anticolonial and anti-imperial movements throughout Asia, Africa, and Latin America, grounded in undercurrents about the racialized and gendered body that largely remained unarticulated in earlier versions of these movements. Such roots have not been fully studied; nor have 1960s transnational communications. Forgetting or marginalizing all this has dehistoricized and depoliticized 68, consigning to the oblivion a long prior period of political radicalism and with it, the Eurocentricism or Westernocentricism of particular approaches. In contrast, this volume explicitly states that the 1968 movements contributed to the establishing of postcoloniality as a whole. In fact, from 68 on, the large number of intellectual works produced in the course of these struggles was articulated with critical and dissident Western discourses and used against hegemonic forms of power. This political conjunction produced a form of theoretical intervention that came to be called postcolonialism.

One example of the volume's contribution in this vein is the inclusion of sub-Saharan Africa, which makes postcolonial territories visible within the landscape of the 60s. The chapter on this topic by Steven Pierce presents a seeming conundrum: the absence of a widespread counterculture in 1968 Africa, at the very moment that African liberation movements and African socialist societies appeared as the source of inspiration for a broader new world. Pierce's chapter demonstrates that this situation can be interpreted as evidence of dramatically differing configurations of politics and desire, suggesting that a multiplicity of idioms existed in sub-Saharan Africa, from progressive to religious, that testified to the range of affective relationships and structures of desire in the area.

The main point of this volume is to take seriously the idea that there is no politics that is disconnected from desire. Of course, the explicit foregrounding of desire in the volume implies the centrality of the body for politics, while expanding this concept to that of a gendered body. The series of essays presented here confirms and widens an assumption that must be put at the center of the understanding of the history of radical feminism in the 1970s: that the international outlook and the international networks developed in that decade were centered on the body and on body relations. It suffices to merely look at some of the photographs of feminist international meetings in Europe in the 1970s, from Femø in Denmark to Varigotti in Italy, to recognize that the new ways in which bodies were situated, collectively and reciprocally (including the practice of collective nudity), had a particular political value.

This political of valence that bodies cast had already been manipulated, in the occupation of public spaces practiced by 1968 movements, although with scarce awareness of gender oppression. It was precisely the presence and attitude of bodies in such political occasions that broke down the traditional barriers between public and private spheres. Thus, we see in those occasions one of the origins of the idea developed by radical feminism—and later by queer theory—that private feelings always have a public dimension. The slogan "the personal is political" was simply one of the expressions of a general attitude toward the body, both physical and mental, in intersubjective relations. The body itself was an expression of this new intersubjectivity, grounded in the general framework of new forms of subjectivity that involved attention to daily life and the relationship between the individual and the collective.

In the volume, the new attention to the body is presented through an extreme and dramatic case: Charles Sabatos' analysis of the literary representation—as well as that in oral memory—of Jan Palach, who burned himself in Prague to protest the growing apathy toward the Soviet occupation. Sabatos argues that this young male body became an icon for activists around the world. This image, gendered and aged, acquired in many places a double valence, as a symbol both of local challenges to and of the international protest against this Soviet repression in Eastern Europe.

The chapters in this volume offer many suggestions for the study of subjectivity and intersubjectivity, considered as intrinsically involving the body in its gendered dimensions. This implies attention to intersubjective relationships between movements, including both reciprocal influences and conflicts. Intersubjectivity also concerns derivations; for example, situating Gay liberation in the complex context of the Vietnam era helps understand why and how gay movements emerged after 1969 as a community claiming a distinct identity. The first chapter in the book, that of Justin Suran, shows how the configuration of sexual identity and political solidarity that was the basis of Gay Liberation derived much of its meaning and force from the contemporary culture of antiwar protest.

Another step of this itinerary concerns the conflicts between movements, beginning with Julian Bourg's analysis of the French debate between feminists and gay male activists on the constraints of desire, and more specifically, the political split that occurred as a result of two divergent directions: the radicalization and masculinization of the gay liberation movement, on the one hand, and the women's movement's shift from abortion activism to campaigning for a law against rape, on the other. This was a process of particular importance for the realization that the fantasy of total liberation ignores the limits that are the conditions for any partial but real liberation. Along a similar line of thought, Michael Sibalis' chapter shows how demonstrations and occupations in May 68 gave rise to encounters that led to the gay movement, and how activists of the French gay movements defined themselves (albeit at times oppositionally) in relation to the spirit of 68.

The connections between gender, sexuality, and the Cuban revolutionary project are explored, in Emily Maguire's piece, as the basis of Cuban cinema in 1968. Its revolutionary ideology was gendered, a gendering that at the same time situated 1968 as the starting year of a period of cultural repression in Cuba. This approach allows us to see the contradictions between the image of Cuban society projected to the world and its reality on the island, where the revolution required sacrifices from women and ambivalence toward the ideals of traditional femininity—as is the case for the female protagonists of the films considered. Another chapter, that of Susan Lord, is dedicated to Cuban cinema, more precisely, to the film-maker Sara Gómez, writer of documentaries in which the Afro-Cuban woman appears as a figure representing the revolution, as a foil against an explicated gendered and raced imperialist oppression.

Autobiographical subjectivities are also taken into account in the book. Oral histories of women activists from the 68 Mexican student move-ment, in the chapter of Cohen and Frazier, juxtaposed to narratives of men leaders, situate the story of 1968 in the context of radical changes in practices of sexuality and the body, critiques of domestic and state patri-archies, and a wider sense of the nation, especially in terms of class and ethnicity. From male leaders the chapter draws evidence of the space of the prison as a place for the formation of male activists' political subjectiv-ity, while it derives a description of the broader political practices in the movement and of its potential for transformation from women's narra-tives. The Mexican scene, illustrated in terms of the general dynamics of power and masculinity, which Elaine Carey's chapter shows, is revisited by yet another chapter, that of Michelle Joffroy, which is dedicated to the comparison between a Mexican 1983 novel and the so called *novelas of 68*, that is, the representative autobiographies of that period. According to the Joffroy, the novel depicts 68 as a ghost that haunts the present, compelling us to read 68 beyond the limits of its traditional actors and to imagine it as a contemporary cultural moment.

As Deborah Cohen and Lessie Jo Frazier argue in the Introduction, the gendering and sexualization of *all* key political spaces and demands that took place in the 1960s are critical to understanding the period's broader political and cultural transformations. Thus, this volume is a step on the road toward a historical understanding of what a politics of desire might have meant in the 1960s even as it at the same time poses, with great earnestness, the question of what a politics of desire could mean today, through a perspective capable of articulating the local and the global dimensions.

CONTRIBUTORS

Julian Bourg is Assistant Professor of History at Bucknell University where he teaches European intellectual history. He is the author of *From Revolution of Ethics: May 1968 and Contemporary French Thought* (2007); translator of Claude Lefort, *Complications: Communism and the Dilemmas of Democracy* (2007); and editor of *After the Deluge: New Perspectives on the Intellectual and Cultural History of Postwar France* (2004). His current research examines the intellectual history of terrorism.

Elaine Carey is an Associate Professor at St. John's University in Queens, New York. Her research and teaching interests include Latin American social movements, international human rights, globalization, history of narcotics, and gender studies. Elaine has received numerous grants, including Fulbright-García Robles fellowships 1996–1997 and 2007–2008 and funding from the National Endowment for the Humanities. She is the author of *Plaza of Sacrifices: Gender, Power, and Terror in 1968 Mexico* (2005). From 1998 to 2002, she taught Latin American and women's history at the University of Detroit Mercy where she cofounded the James Guadalupe Carney Latin American Solidarity Archive (CLASA). Currently, she is completing a book entitled *Selling Is More of a Habit: Women and Drug Trafficking in North America, 1900–1970.*

Deborah Cohen brings questions of race, gender, imperialism, modernity, labor, and immigration to bear on nation-state formation and other political projects. Her first book *Transnational Subjects: Braceros, Nation, and Migration (United States and Mexico, 1942–1964)*. Does this work by revealing the paradoxes of modernist political economies and the predicaments of transnational subjects; whereas her new project *Sex and Betrayal* delves more deeply into the intimacies of migratory laboring life. She and Lessie Jo Frazier are completing a duo-graph *Beyond '68: Gender and Political Culture in the Mexican 1968 Student Movement and Its Legacies* and beginning a project on the racialized erotics of Zorro.

Lessie Jo Frazier researches political culture including nation-state formation, violence, memory, movements, particularly engaging with cultural, gender, queer, and transnational feminist theories. She has published *Salt in the Sand: Memory, Violence and Political Culture in Chile, 1890–present* and the coedited *Gender's Place: Feminist Anthropologies of Latin America*. She is finishing *Desired States: Gender, Sex, and Political Culture* that, like her first monograph, explores the culturally and historically specific ways people come to relate affectively and ideologically and in practice to political projects. She has considered this by looking at, in the first book, changing temporalities and modes of memory and, in the second, desire broadly conceived.

Michelle Joffroy is Associate Professor of Spanish at Smith College, where she teaches courses on twentieth-century Latin American literature, film, and culture, and the U.S. Mexico Borderlands. She has done research on the intersection of gender, history, and literature in the representation of 1968 in Mexico, and has published on Mexican women's literature and feminist theory. She has also published articles on contemporary Chicana narrative and *fronterista* feminist thought and literary theory, with an emphasis on the deconstruction of borders, nationalism, and gender identity. Her current research focuses on Chinese communities on the Mexican frontier in the early twentieth century and on migration and environmental justice in a transborder context.

Susan Lord teaches at Queen's University (Kingston, Ontario), where she is Associate Professor in the Department of Film and Media, with cross-appointments to Women's Studies, Cultural Studies, and Art. Her research projects are currently focused on Cuban visual culture and cultural studies of media and technology. She codirects with Janine Marchessault the Visible City Archive and Project. She is coeditor of three collections of essays: with Janine Marchessault, *Fluid Screens, Expanded Cinema* (2007); with Annette Burfoot, *Killing Women: The Visual Culture of Gender and Violence* (2006); and with Karen Dubinsky, Catherine Krull, Sean Mills, and Scott Rutherford, *New World Coming: The 1960s and the Shaping of Global Consciousness*. She is completing a manuscript on the Cuban filmmaker Sara Gómez, and is working on a project entitled "An Archive in Fragments: The Black Public Sphere of 1960s Cuba." She is a member of the Public Access Collective and has edited several issues of *Public,* including the recent *Digipopo: Digital Poetics and Politics.*

Emily A. Maguire is an Assistant Professor in the Department of Spanish & Portuguese at Northwestern University. Her research focuses on the Hispanic Caribbean, and she has written and published on issues of race and gender in Caribbean Literature. She is presently at work on a book manuscript entitled *Fieldwork for the Nation: Negotiating Race in Cuban Literature and Ethnography.*

Luisa Passerini recipient of the 2002–2004 Research Prize of the Land of Nordrhein-Westfalen, is Director of the research group "Europe: Emotions, Identities, Politics" at the Kulturwissenschaftliches Institut, Essen, Professor of Cultural History at the University of Turin and External Professor of History of the Twentieth Century at the European University Institut, Florence. Among her recent publications are *Changing Cultural Tastes: Writers and the Popular in Modern Germany* (Berghahn 2009) *Europe in Love, Love in Europe: Imagination and Politics in Britain between the Wars* (New York Univeristy Press, 2000). On 1968, see her *Memory and Utopia: The Primacy of Intersubjectivity* (Equinox Publishing, UK, 2007) and *Autobiography of a Generation: Italy 1968* (Wesleyan 1996).

Steven Pierce teaches African history at the University of Manchester. He is the author of *Farmers and the State in Colonial Kano: Land Tenure and the Legal Imagination* and (with Anupama Rao) is editor of *Discipline and the Other Body: Correction, Corporeality, Colonialism.* He is currently completing a manuscript on corruption and a series of articles on gender and sexuality, both in northern Nigeria.

Charles Sabatos received his Ph.D. in Comparative Literature at the University of Michigan. His main fields of research include modern Czech, Slovak, Turkish, and American literary and cultural history. He has published articles in such journals as *Comparative Literature Studies, Middle Eastern Studies,* and *Europe-Asia Studies.* He currently teaches in the English language and literature department at Yeditepe University, Istanbul, Turkey.

Michael Sibalis is Professor of History at Wilfrid Laurier University in Waterloo, Ontario, Canada. He has published numerous articles and essays on the French nineteenth-century labor movement, the political police of Napoleon I, and the history of male homosexuality in France. He is currently writing a history of the male homosexual community of Paris since 1700.

Justin David Suran taught History at the University of California, Berkeley, the University of California, San Francisco, and Modesto Junior College (California). He currently teaches English at Marlborough School in Los Angeles.

Michelle Zancarini-Fournel is an internationally recognized expert on 1968, with an academic appointment at the University of Lyon. She is on the editorial board of the premiere French feminist journal, *Clio: Histoire, femme et société*. Her recent books include *Le Moment 68. Une histoire contestée* (Paris: Seuil, Collection Univers Historique, 2008); *Histoire des femmes en France: XIXe-XXe siècle* (Paris: PU Rennes, 2005); and *Femmes et fières de l'être: Un siècle d'émancipation féminine* (Paris, 2001); and she has numerous edited volumes, among them: *68: Une histoire collective, 1962–1981* with Philippe Artières (Paris: La Découverte, 2008); *Les années 68: Le temps de la contestation*, with Geneviève Dreyfus-Armand, Robert Frank, and Marie-Françoise Lévy (Paris: Editions Complexe, 2008); and *Genre et événement : Du masculin et du féminin en histoires des crises et des conflits*, with Marc Bergère and Luc Capdevila (Paris: PU Rennes, 2006).

Love-In, Love-Out: Gender, Sex, and Sexuality in '68

DEBORAH COHEN AND LESSIE JO FRAZIER

Nineteen sixty-eight was a pivotal year on a global scale. In cities throughout the globe, young people took over streets. They blockaded buildings, verbally and symbolically attacked state political apparatuses and projects, and challenged conventional imperialist world orderings. Patriarchal states made investments in youthful masculinities, and representations of youthful male martyrs took on symbolic importance that crossed national borders. Some movements embraced an incommensurable politics of desire, and organic relationships sprung up between movements usually thought of as disparate. Above all, the possibilities and limitations for political agency were intrinsically gendered. Yet despite the role of gender and sexuality in political agency in '68, the growing scholarship on the period still underestimates their importance.

The chapters in this volume begin to fill in this lacuna. Bringing together literary and film critics, historians, and anthropologists working on gender and sexuality in Europe, Africa, and the Americas, this volume offers new understandings of the ongoing power of '68 as a year, as a longer historical moment, and as an idea.[1] We foreground "'68" because it evokes those events clearly marked as political struggles whereas the term "the sixties" often evokes counterculture and generational experiences. In this volume we bring these two senses together. Our authors, who explore struggles in the United States, Mexico, the Czech Republic, Cuba, France, and Africa, collectively point to the multiple ways that gender and sexuality (as axes of power and, for some, movement goals) framed even movements not explicitly organized around these power configurations. Taken together, they show how gender and sexuality, as analytical lenses, can illuminate questions of memory, subjectivity, agency, political cultures of the state and contestatory social movements, and how the personal was (and still remains) political.

Our central motif for the volume is the love-in, a mass gathering likely involving dancing, singing, illicit substances, and sensual physical contact. The love-in became emblematic of the sixties countercultural scene and its ludically ambivalent relationship to arenas of formal politics and respectable public spaces as well as to contestatory political movements with their sit-ins and teach-ins. For us, the love-in epitomizes the intersection of bodies, desires, and politics.

Indeed, this volume's cover incorporates a 1968 poster of a flower child, seated amid a psychedelic field of orange and blue, announcing a love-in in Amsterdam's Vondel Park, a famous node of countercultural activity.[2] The poster's perspectival plane has three layers: closest to us is the half-naked flower child whose twiggy-esque Art Nouveau style harkens to the nineteenth century origins of the park as a privileged public space; in the middle is a giant Corinthian column that also forms the vertical axis of the image as the flower child's hand and gaze are raised seemingly to caress the column; both are backlit by a giant blue sun bathing them and the lush gardens and lagoons that perhaps echo nineteenth-century pastoral romanticism. The text across the top and bottom invites us to a "love-in" featuring love, flowers and grass (presumably of various sorts) at the speakers' corner, and clearly linking free love, expression, nature, and poetry. The flower child's love-in instantiates the erotics of political and countercultural movements, offering an archtype for how to be in that moment, and illustrating (albeit problematically for feminist politics) the sexual rewards accrued to those who heeded the call.

This image of a flower child beckoning us to a love-in was, as imagery of women often is, an icon for an affective nexus of practices and values extolling idealism, passion/love, and collectivity. Taking this image as symbolic not of a specific year (i.e. "1968"), but of "the sixties" as a historical moment, we suggest that "'68" as an imaginary involved shared and contested values and practices that interpellated (called into being) new subjectivities (senses of oneself and one's positionings) in pursuit of an array of political objectives. The image resonates with meanings assigned to the political upheavals of '68 and how these upheavals radiated through and were lived in multiple places, from Berkeley to Paris and Mexico City to Dakar. It does so because aesthetics and models of countercultural mobilization and political change not only circulated (albeit unevenly) across continents but because, like this image, they were themselves gendered and sexualized. Juxtaposing political processes with gender and sexuality, here condensed in the icon of the flower-child's love-in, allows us to tease out the ways in which the often contradictory practices of the sixties relied on gender, sex, and sexuality, intertwined with liberatory political projects. This juxtaposition simultaneously foregrounds the specific configurations of power (such as colonial and imperial projects) that these particular sixties projects sought to expose and unravel. Moreover, we contend that all movements, even those that did not overtly center on or contest questions of gender, sex, and sexuality, were undergirded by and grounded in particular gender and sexual assumptions and practices. Put differently, women's participation in sixties movements not strictly defined as women's movements or advocating so-called women's issues is a window onto the gendering and sexualization of all key political spaces and demands of the time. Gender and sexuality not only undergirded countercultural movements, but were critical to the period's broader political and cultural transformations.

Gender, sex, and sexuality are central to understanding relations between states and multiple social actors. We do not equate gender, sex, and sexuality with ideologically marked categories, such as *women* or *homosexuals*; nor are these categories anchored in notions of mere difference. Instead, our authors interrogate the institutionalized hierarchies of power undergirding these markers of difference. Following feminist theorist Chandra Mohanty, they refuse to understand these markers as a priori transhistorical or translocational, a point that becomes clear when looking at multiple contexts in conjunction.[3] Instead, gender, sex, and sexuality were produced in nuanced ways in particular contexts across this historical moment.

Our authors use gender and sexuality as analytic tools to tackle struggles over education, intimate relationships, consumption, revolutionary ideologies, conflicts between gays and feminists over the nature of desire, and the intersections of labor, anti-imperialist, and peace activisms. They have a broad appreciation for the geographic extent and contribution of the specific struggle examined, while still referencing current scholarly efforts to link the multiple dimensions of sixties political and cultural struggles as they entangled with issues of love, sex, and political desire. Of critical importance here, each author uses an expanded notion of what constitutes political struggle, drawn from the very movements in question. In so doing, contributors directly question the analytic bifurcation still present in the literature—between so-called political movements (student movements, labor movements, anti-imperialist and antiwar movements) and social movements often seen as precursors to identity politics (feminist, LGBTQ, and racial/ethnic movements). Hence, the title of this introduction: "love-in," but also "love-*out*."

Yet this is not to say that all struggles were the same at their core or could be reduced to similar issues or problems. To the contrary, they were often rife with internal contradictions and incommensurable interests. Still, they clearly shared an ethos, and while their protagonists were unable to use today's current organizing tool of choice—the Internet—they nonetheless participated in cross-national communication not always recognizable today. Just as many late-sixties lesbian and gay activists celebrated "coming out" as a collective and emergent process whose resulting subjectivities and configurations of sexuality could not be known in advance, in pushing our thinking on the place of gender and sexuality in emancipatory projects around the globe, we hope to participate in ongoing re-imaginings of a more just, yet still passionate, politics to come.[4]

This volume grapples with '68 through interdisciplinary methodologies and theoretical frameworks. We aim here not for a comprehensive account either of the events of 1968 or of the period in general; instead, authors sample the range of events that spanned so many regions of the world.[5] These included major North Vietnamese military offenses and setbacks for the United States in Vietnam; the quashing of vibrant political reimaginings in Czechoslovakia; the struggle for sovereignty in what is today Bangladesh; and the dramatic student mobilizations that met with state repression, most infamously in Senegal, Mexico, France, West Germany, and the United States. The volume, then, attends to cultural transformations—including issues of identity, agency, worldview, and desire—in relation to social and political movements in varied geopolitical contexts.[6] These historians, anthropologists, and literary/film scholars collectively draw on wide-ranging scholarship, such as postcolonial studies, feminist geography, practice theory, and queer theory. This volume nevertheless unites very different approaches. As editors, we have consciously sought out multiple approaches so as to build a cross-disciplinary framework and practice that, like the movements analyzed, pull on different strands of thinking and research. Thus, we ask the reader to remember, first, that the individual movements were broadly engaging with each other, even as each contributed to the larger international dialogue then underway, and, second, that movements operated at multiple registers, each with a different set of priorities and resonances.

We seek to generate a theoretical lens that emerges from the examined struggles precisely because, we insist, all politics are about desire and the lenses of gender and sexuality best articulate the workings and structures of these erotics.[7] Although gender was articulated differently in the various struggles, our authors recognize it as a vector of social and cultural hierarchies of power relations that involve changing meanings, practices, and performances enacted through societal ideas about the body and normative social roles. Gender, as a category of difference, is constituted in relation to multiple axes of power, such as race, class, age, and sexuality. To write generally about "men" and/or "masculinity" tells us little when we turn our attention to more finely tuned categories, such as "gentleman" or "gigolo." More to the point, writing *about* women or men does not constitute a gendered analysis. We join other scholars who think beyond gender as a binary system (male and female) based on some concrete, measurable, physical difference. Like gender, sexuality must also be understood vis-à-vis relations of power grounded in supposedly essential desires, qualities, and practices that are, in turn, naturalized in defining the social person (to "be" straight, for example). The authors here engage sexuality to think about how particular power relations are manifested and shape fields of desire and practices across a variety of arenas. In much the same way that Joan Scott argued for gender, the volume begins to show how sexuality can be a useful category of analysis for thinking about power dynamics in places other than those where sexual acts (conventionally understood) take place.[8]

The volume's international dimension suggests the multidirectional forms in which struggles spoke to each other and brought out overarching practices, logics, and symbolisms. This interchange between movements not only energized individual struggles; it also made individual movements more threatening to the states in question, increasing the likelihood that they would (attempt to) silence them, through repression, violence, and—over time—cooptation. These movements did not threaten the immediate overthrow of regimes, but rather their hegemonic projects. Such challenges were all the more potent because the middle-class and elite youth who often played a central role in them were likely to be seen as (eventually) taking over the reins of state and society. That is, the very universities preparing youths for such posts—and thus involved in the reproduction of class privilege—would become movement hotspots in challenging state projects. To gauge the impact of individual struggles on such projects, the chapters look for transformations and continuities in quotidian practices of power and in the deep structures of culture and politics. Integrating gender, sex, and feminist inquiry into thinking about '68 in its widest arenas, we gain a broader conceptualization of polity and of the nature of political desire. Furthered by this reconceptualization is a reading of the struggles analyzed in this volume—both vis-à-vis other movements *and* as part of larger social and political projects and ethics being formulated in '68.

Sixties Gender and Sexuality: The State of the Field

To date, the literature on gender and sexuality in the sixties is strongest in looking at its countercultural aspects, albeit within a narrow definition of culture. In contrast, those quite solid works that examine social movements and activists attempting to reshape institutions and state policies largely take for granted the ways in which protagonists were gendered—let alone the gendering of institutions, policies, and ideologies.[9] New research that brings these two strands of scholarship into dialogue reveals the multiple dimensions of sixties struggles and expands notions of who and what constituted their political struggles, protagonists, and polities. Such research highlights the gendered and sexualized dynamics at the heart of these movements, institutions, and social relations, as well as the gendered transformations in the political subjectivities of the activists themselves.

We have used Pierre Bourdieu's model of doxa (society's unarticulated presuppositions), orthodoxa (explicitly accepted ways of thinking and feeling), and heterodoxa (explicit challenges to these ways of thinking and feeling) as a heuristic template to map the various ways researchers have approached this tumultuous era and the intellectual gains we can achieve by incorporating gender and sexuality into our analyses. This synergy of research subject and theoretical question thus explains, in part, why research on the sixties represents some of the most exciting scholarship on gender and sexuality.[10]

Expanding Orthodoxa: New Actors in Movements, Institutions, and Official Histories

Scholarship on gender during the sixties is particularly strong—even groundbreaking—in considering unseen, forgotten, or underestimated movements and actors and their roles in challenging and reshaping key social and political institutions. Work in this area specifically broadens the scope of who counts as protagonists of social movements and who therefore merits a place in official histories of the period (an expansion of who counts in orthodoxa). The recent literature on welfare politics demonstrates such a broadening of the scope of protaganism. This work has shifted the conception of feminism by claiming struggles over welfare as examples of feminist struggles, and their protagonists, predominantly black and poor, as feminists.

Looking at particular sets of women activists, authors such as Rhonda Williams, Premilla Nadasen, and Felicia Kornbluh show how struggles for safe and affordable housing produced these activists as certain kinds of political actors with particular claims to rights as citizens, even though the rights these women fought for were not explicitly articulated as citizenship rights.[11] These researchers do so by first carefully depicting the women they study as political actors and then elaborating on their relationships with government officials at all levels, from local to federal. This line of thinking not only pushes us to see that women were at the helm of these struggles but requires us to acknowledge that their presence shook and reconfigured the foundations of power. That is, framing women welfare-policy activists as political actors unsettles our understanding of them as solely "local" actors and forces us to see them, and their movements, as directly challenging existing parameters of the feminist literature, especially its definition of feminism's protagonists.

In expanding which activists and movements are considered agents of feminism in their own right, scholars examining struggles over welfare have effected an important shift; this new sixties scholarship pushes the feminist mainstream to recognize and incorporate a broader set of political actors and projects. The notable examples of this trend in the literature, such as Benita Roth's work, reveal the vast space in which movements and actors maneuvered to come out of the periphery and gain recognition in the national center.[12] Principal actors in these movements were forced to navigate political landmines and choose between the struggle for gender rights and the struggle for the rights of their supposedly natural communities, defined in terms of race, ethnicity, or nationality.

This new scholarship insists not only that the goals of sixties movements, as well as their protagonists (not previously recognized as feminists), had a racial and ethnic dimension, but also that class dynamics undergird these same movements and activists. For example, feminist groups at times dismissed the needs of white working-class women, which were not seen as central to women's so-called real priorities. For women of color, class, race, and ethnicity were often conflated, such that to be recognized as "being" fully Chicana (in particular, by Chicano leaders), a woman had to hold a particular set of class and race- and ethnicity-based interests.[13] That is, in groups organized around issues of race and ethnicity, demands put forth by a male leadership were made synonymous with assumed shared class interests and heteronormative sexual orientation. Women activists of color who challenged entrenched hierarchical gender practices and heterosexual orientation within such organizations confronted the charge that they were not full members of their racial or ethnic community. That is, only white or whitened girls could fall prey to a feminist, especially lesbian, project, and activists of color who adopted feminist stances had their commitment to racial and ethnic political projects called into question. In the end, women of color were often forced to choose between—or at least hierarchize—priorities of gender and sexuality, on the one hand, versus those based on race, ethnicity, and class, on the other. There was no legitimate space or way to "be" both, as if the axes of social positioning were not always already intertwined.

The experiences of black and Chicana activist women, marginalized within so-called feminist groups *and* those dedicated to their presumed racial or ethnic interests, have been a focal point for scholarship exploring the clash between feminism and racial and ethnic activism. For example,

Kimberly Springer's *Living for the Revolution: Black Feminist Organizations, 1968–1980* foregrounds the ways activists combated the choices they were required to make and creatively maneuvered the in-between spaces that resulted from their marginalization. Taken together, this kind of work shows how activists powerfully articulated their relationship to other movements and challenged a framing of interests and issues from which they did not stand to gain. More important still, because such activists and groups emerged in relation to previously defined axes and left a legacy on subsequent organizations, we see how crucial it is to connect sixties movements with both earlier and subsequent struggles.[14] Newer work on gay liberation follows a similar line of analysis, spinning from it a queer geography in which drag queens, homeless queer youth, and other gender transgressors played leading roles precisely because their super-subordinate positions enabled and induced radical action.[15]

Taken as a whole, this trend in the scholarship significantly raised the demands made by nonwhite women and gays—and the activists themselves—to a more prominent place within the sixties literature, as the authors cast a grander vision of what could and should count as feminist projects. It puts into dialogue those actors who knowingly argued for their place as feminists (white women) and radicals (heterosexual white men) and those whose history as racially and sexually marked subjects had made this connection less recognizable or publicly palatable. In so doing, this kind of work exemplifies the strength of scholarship on gender and sexuality: it incorporates new actors and struggles. It also adds texture and complexity to the political and social world of the sixties and frames as explicitly feminist struggles those movements and actors formerly considered outside this realm.

While this line of research has been important in broadening the consequences of these struggles and the actions of their activists, there are limits to what it can do to move the field beyond its current focus. Part of this limit may be due to the "social history" approach that predominates in this type of work. Social history—itself a product of the incorporation of former sixties activists into the academy—brought an activist, ground-level orientation into a historiography that had previously viewed so-called great men as the only actors worthy of historical examination. It validated long-excluded actors such as workers, students, women, and peasants, and folded the nuances of their daily lives and struggles into the historical narrative. Publications in this tradition not only incorporate a greater range of protagonists and movements but also beautifully convey the texture and tension of protagonists' lives. Yet this approach has been less successful in addressing the changes that these struggles wrought at the level of broad social relations and structures. That is, although it has done an admirable job of recovering the lives and legacies of social actors, social history has yet to analyze the shifting subject positions of movement protagonists with respect to the social categories around which activists couched their activism, such as "woman," "black," "gay," and "black woman."

This is not to say that social history does not incorporate race, class, or sexuality, in addition to gender, as social categories of experience through which we might understand the lives of its protagonists. Rather, to the extent that social history focuses on gender (or race or class) as an ongoing, lived process, it does so taking these arenas as already determined categories. Though the best recent social histories hint at changes in activists' subjectivities, we would encourage future researchers to delve into the transforming subjectivities of movement protagonists more directly, and to concern themselves with the complex processes through which activists "become" activists. That is, we encourage social historians to follow the approach that Justin Suran and Michael Sibalis take in this volume, tracing out how their subjects grew to see themselves as critical actors occupying certain kinds of subject positions in their respective movements. In the end, failing to foreground the complex and problematic remaking of subjectivity that occurs around particular political projects reduces gender (and class and race, for that matter) to a matter of activists' bodies; this leads us to overlook how these subjectivities shape the ways in which relevant social institutions, policies, and cultural practices structured the types of claims these activists could and would make over the course of the movement and the ideological impact of these movements on broader society.

More critically, there are explicit consequences when scholars prioritize and attend to actors and movements at the expense of structures, ideologies, and processes of transformation, both collective and individual. An inattention to subjectivity and gendered structures and ideologies tends to reproduce in the scholarship itself what has been labeled "identity politics," with its creation of certain kinds of authentic political actors and their attendant political spaces. Within the scope of identity politics, actors are reduced to specific categories marked by gender, sexuality, race, or ethnicity; scholars whose identities match those whom they are studying can investigate, write, or speak about these actors or communities without a hint of cultural imperialism and with a presumed special epistemological access. Ultimately, the failure to incorporate an analysis of the gendering of structures, institutions, and ideologies obscures the very epistemological projects advocated by these sixties activists, and to which they themselves were wedded.

We do not suggest the abandonment of scholarship on women, on ethnically and racially marked communities, or on the distinct struggles of lesbian, gay, bisexual, transgendered, or queer activists. Clearly, there is a continued need for such work. Yet new scholarship must be attentive to the historical and cultural specificities and operation of these social categories. It should heed the call to look at such categories within their particular context, as conjunctural alliances always in formation—insights made by Chandra Mohanty, for whom alliances are never based on (scholars' assumptions of) the salient preexisting positionalities and identities of actors, but rather, always forged in struggle.

It is a challenge to not reproduce movement actors' (and their allied scholars) march to identity politics as inevitable—toward a teleological set of goals, priorities, and outcomes. However, reading the social in relation to the cultural (understood in the broadest sense of worldviews and practices) helps get at the structures that shaped and were shaped by each movement and set of actors, rather than treating the two as discreet arenas. An example of a book that successfully links the two is Beth Bailey's *Sex in the Heartland*.[16] She argues that those ideas about sex we usually associate with sixties countercultural movements were nascent everywhere, even in small towns. Valerie Korinek similarly argues, in *Roughing It in the Suburbs: Reading Chatelaine Magazine in the Fifties and Sixties*, that a seemingly normative and very popular Canadian women's magazine did, upon closer inspection, raise issues in ways that facilitated later feminist alternative cultural imaginaries.[17] Together, Bailey and Korineck offer a longer-term perspective on the transformations in social and cultural life that made the so-called sexual revolution possible. Dagmar Herzog takes a similar approach in looking at German sexuality, though the account she tells is a much more sinuous one than the U.S. case, replete with intergenerational misperceptions.[18] These books offer a helpful bridge between the social history approach grounded in an examination of particular actors, institutions, and social movements, and one that pays rigorous attention to the systemic logics—or doxa—that both made certain actors and relations imaginable, and, in part, generated conflicting cultural worldviews or imaginaries.

Celebrating Heterodoxa: Countercultural Experimentations

Before discussing other works that explore culture in the sense of doxa, we should consider the prevailing way of thinking about cultural history in U.S. and Canadian scholarship—that is, in terms of arenas marked as cultural (such as music, literature, fashion)—and the ways that the sixties are associated with the widespread flourishing of countercultural, ludic arenas. Scholars of gender and sexuality in the sixties have been deeply interested in the countercultural. The term *countercultural* generally indexes issues and movements that pressed for an opening up and reorienting of major social institutions—such as family, religion, educational organizations, economy, and the state—or, at a minimum, that opted out of the realm of the normative. This area of inquiry has been promising in no small part because scholars working in this area have not been tied so literally to fixed definitions and social categories and are instead willing to explore the abstract and contingent.

Not surprisingly, cultural criticism offers important tools for such work—in part because this line of research draws not only historians, generally cultural and intellectual, but also cultural critics and media and communications scholars as well. Of interest along these lines are two edited volumes—Patricia Juliana Smith's *The Queer Sixties* and Avital Bloch and Lauri Umansky's *Impossible to Hold: Women and Culture in the 1960s*—along with a newly released analysis by musicologist Annie J. Randall, *Dusty! Queen of the Postmods,* which positions singer Dusty Springfield as a master of sixties gender and racial sensibility and camp.[19] Smith's collection brings together essays by (mostly) literary critics who analyze a variety of cultural forms, including novels, Andy Warhol paintings, and Dusty Springfield songs, in search of a sixties queer sensibility. A queer sensibility does not refer to the presumed gayness of the artistic content or the artist. Rather, it indicates a way of reading cultural forms that neither reproduces heteronormative binaries nor merely inverts them but instead plays with those binaries, makes them visible, and proposes other possible organizing principals. Thus, for example, Andy Warhol paintings do not automatically contribute to a queer sensibility because this painter was identified as gay; nor is a supposedly straight film with a linear romance plot precluded from being read for its queer elements, as the Smith collection's chapters on the Beatles and Jim Morrison demonstrate. Hence, the realm of queer is broadly read in these popular artistic expressions.

Impossible to Hold foregrounds particular celebrity women as symbolic of the way that women's lives changed more generally. The essays cover and go beyond such key representations as "hippie chicks and Weatherwomen," Judy Chicago and "Hanoi Jane," in a concerted effort to unite women's history and cultural history. The editors contrast this approach with what they argue has been the scholarly overshadowing of the sixties cultural revolution by precisely the kind of social-historical works discussed previously in this introduction. And yet, the essays in *Impossible to Hold* are very much like that social history. Just as social historians sought to recover the agency of lost heroines, Bloch and Umansky seek to insert neglected actors back into the official history of the era, actors unproblematically labeled as "women." Thus, this volume misses an opportunity to use the cultural revolution as a lens through which to examine contestations over the category "women" and instead offers a rousing celebration of women roaring.[20]

Randall's *Dusty! Queen of the Postmods* is a penetrating examination of Dusty Springfield's life and music. Born in Britain and initially part of the London pop scene, Springfield is best known in the United States for her 1964 hit "I Only Want to Be with You." While Randall analyzes the artist's music, stage presence, and her public persona (most notably marked by a blond beehive wig and heavy black mascara) to deem her a sixties icon, the author also paints Springfield as a particularly gendered representation whose appeal crosses musical genres and national boundaries. Yet Randall's analysis goes further, seeing Springfield as an actor whose complex incarnations provide an apt lens through which to explore critical struggles of the period, such as those around (post)colonialism and identity.

All of these works employ close readings and textual analysis to examine actors too often seen as outside the purview of the sixties: for the first volume, the queer at the heart of the period; for the second, the women who are still not recognized as central to its impact and legacies. The focal actor of the third book, though a previously recognized sixties pop icon, is now positioned as part of the broader countercultural scene; and in so doing, Dusty Springfield stands in for other issues in play. These works argue that the cultural—specifically the *counter*cultural—is key to understanding the influence that these icons possessed and the cultural changes that transpired.

These books, and the many others that rely on this approach, bring much that is beneficial and novel to the study of the sixties as a field. They apply a deep analysis to diverse, and at times wild, subject matter, capturing the playfulness of some sixties scenes. Randall's monograph and Smith's edited volume examine gender as a broad and diverse set of changing relations, practices, and ideas, and not just "women" or "queers" as already constituted and stable categories and social positions. This approach reveals the complexity of the sixties as a particular historical moment, complete with its own distinct cultural sensibilities.

Yet analysis from the perspective of cultural criticism often leaves social historians cold, for the questions these scholars ask and the approach that they take largely remove cultural shifts from the particular social struggles of which they are part and product; in other words, they run the risk of divorcing culture with a capital C from its broader context. As we think through ways we might bridge this gulf, we again call attention to Bailey's *Sex in the Heartland*. This author locates the changes too often assumed to be associated with the countercultural—sexual practices and rites, ideas about birth control, sexually transmitted diseases, co-ed college dorms, and homosexuality—in an array of social struggles and shifts, with nuanced descriptions and analysis that give these spectacular changes depth, grounding, and context. Though not a direct or overt response, Bailey has in fact heeded the caution of sixties scholars such as Doug Rossinow and Julie Stephens, who have warned against a romanticization of the politics of sixties countercultural actors.[21] According to them, too often scholars have presumed that sixties cultural politics were automatically or ultimately emancipatory; they instead argue that the political beliefs and projects pushed by sixties actors and activists may have unintentionally reconfigured the social terrain in ways that realigned the conditions of possibility and made feasible the neoliberal conservatism that came fully onto the U.S. scene in the eighties with the election of Ronald Reagan.

However, there are productive points of dialogue between the research of (social) historians interested in social actors and movements, and that of intellectual and cultural historians, literary critics, and media scholars. Such a conversation could take ideas and methods now applied largely to the countercultural and use them to analyze the heteronormative. That is, instead of merely focusing on what has been considered non-normative, the work of literary and media critics would be enhanced if they could turn their analytic lens to see the wild heterodoxa behind "the establishment"—to use a term fashionable in the sixties to describe those with the power to make orthodoxa—as well as the mundane and quotidian world of doxa.

Interrogating Doxa: Making Gender and Sexuality Central

If scholarship in this field is to move in this direction, we must first understand the implications of separating social actors and the movements to which they belong from culture, battles over culture, and the larger impact of those clashes. We must address the ways in which the sociopolitical struggles and the countercultural movements and transformations have been treated as existing in isolation, rather than being coeval: that is, sharing the same time, space, and broad experiences. Thus, regardless of whether scholars define the shifts demarcated by the sixties (as a historiographical category) as either cultural or social, these changes were part of the broad moment in which the personal was seen as, and made, political; when there was a call to "make love, not war"; and when racism was being challenged on many, often competing, fronts. These shifts, in other words, were coeval.

Out of this intricate mix of the social and the cultural emerges a gendered understanding and reading of the complexities of the body politic. An interesting pairing with Julian Bourg's chapter in this volume is Marianne DeKoven's reading of Shulamith Firestone's influential _The Dialectic of Sex_ (1972) in _Utopia Limited: The Sixties and the Emergence of the Postmodern_.[22] DeKoven argues that radical utopias ran up against competing political values and desires. Second-wave feminism becomes an exemplary space of contention that reveals, for DeKoven, the collision between modernist radical utopias (for example, the second-wave women's movement) and nascent postmodern diffusions of political energies. While feminist imaginaries, then, constitute a case study in DeKoven's argument, Diana Sorensen's cultural history of the sixties, *A Turbulent Decade Remembered: Scenes from the Latin American Sixties*, uses gender as a central category for her cultural critique.[23] Sorensen, who like DeKoven looks at the sixties as a nodal point, argues that "male discourse and authorship" fettered the long-term impacts of political and cultural engagements, even as this historical moment ushered a broadly shared, transcontinental sensibility into the Americas. Sorensen moves from looking at gender as a key aspect of sixties struggles to using a gendered analysis to interrogate the sixties at its core, in particular with regard to the radical—and perhaps ultimately limited—imaginings of polity.

Painting broad pictures of political culture and the body politic can link social struggle with cultural transformation, as we see in Margo V. Perkins's *Autobiography as Activism: Three Black Women of the Sixties*. This book examines the individual autobiographies written by Angela Davis, Assata Shakur, and Elaine Brown, all of whom were involved in the black power movement.[24] Yet *Autobiography as Activism* is not so much an exploration of the work of these women as it is an examination of the ways that these activists use their writing to link their particular life circumstances to those of other sixties activists. Perkins contends that by placing gender at the forefront of their experience of the movement and linking the personal with the political in these women's push for a transformative action, they construct an alternative, gender-inflected epistemology that challenges established ways of knowing. She links the production of a particular kind of alternative knowledge with the process of coming to a non-normative position of knowing, anchored in and constituted by the gendered practice of activism, thus offering a glimpse at possibilities we might find when we bring these two strands, the social historical and the cultural-political, together. Similarly, Pamela Barnett, in *Dangerous Desire: Literature of Sexual Freedom and Sexual Violence since the Sixties*, looks at the cost of radical cultural imaginaries in her analysis of key texts in U.S. culture, showing the prevalence of rape as a response to assertions of sexual freedom.[25] Not surprisingly, rape emerges from a particularly racialized erotic economy. Barnett and Perkins take seriously the power that narrative exerts, as the terrain on which agency is enacted and the counterrevolutionary is disciplined, and they explore this power in very nuanced ways.

It should be clear by now that gender and sexuality, as lenses of analysis and not merely social categories, do more than flesh out what scholars already know, and that connecting the sociopolitical and the cultural does more than add to or broaden existing analyses. Rather, doxic, orthodox, and heterodox understandings of gender and sexuality undergirded—in varying forms or registers—*all* sixties struggles. Thus, they are central to discovering the full implications of the vast array of political projects, movements, and confrontations of the moment.[26] A book that perhaps best fulfills this promise is Peter Ling and Sharon Monteith's edited volume *Gender and the Civil Rights Movement*. Especially strong are Belinda Robnett's chapter on the Student Nonviolent Coordinating Committee (officially in existence from 1960 to 1969), Peter Ling's essay on manhood in the Southern Christian Leadership Conference, and Brian Ward's analysis of male rhythm and blues and sexual politics in the black freedom movement.[27] Similarly, Steven Estes's monograph *I Am a Man!: Race, Manhood and the Civil Rights Movement* shows how the question of manhood reveals fundamental ideologies and worldviews that explain key practices and episodes in the U.S. civil rights movement.[28]

Like Estes's book, Laurie Green's *Battling the Plantation Mentality: Memphis and the Black Freedom Struggle* turns its lens to the gendered dynamics inherent in the civil rights movement.[29] Covering a longer period than does Estes—from World War II to the Memphis sanitation workers' strike at which Martin Luther King Jr. delivered his "I've been to the mountaintop" speech on the day before he was assassinated—Green uses gender (and race and class) as social categories for understanding how civil rights activists saw the daily instantiations of these struggles. She transcends this level of gendered analysis, however, examining the fundamental role of freedom—as discourse and sets of practices—in activists' understandings of and struggles against ingrained power relations. Green's use of gender (and race and class) allows her to get at freedom's deeper meanings, some of which are articulated in the realm of doxa and contested in heterodoxa, revealing for her reader the deep cultural imaginaries (doxa) that shape worldviews and practices. For Green, then, there was a gendering of activists and their lived experiences, as well as (and maybe more importantly) of the conceptual framework through which activists understood and power relations and fought to subvert them.

As we have seen in the discussion of the state of the field in terms of sixties gender and sexuality, the impact of sixties protagonists—from movements and seemingly individual gestures of solidarity, to songs, love-ins, activists, and ideological proclamations and concepts—are revealed in critical ways through an examination of their gender and sexual configurations. Michele Zancarini's afterword for this volume brings French '68 scholarship to the table; in so doing, Zancarini interrogates the tensions we have outlined here between social and cultural approaches. She concludes that analyses grounded in gender and sexuality as analytical tools, and as theoretical frameworks—such as queer theory, cultural/social theory, and feminist theory—are more important than methodological distinctions between social and cultural when it comes to addressing the core historiographical challenges of working on the sixties.

Gender, sex, sexuality, and contests over sexism broadly undergirded '68 movements, as norms and quotidian practices shifted dramatically in public discourse and beneath the surface. By using them not just as social categories but as analytic categories and lenses to understand dispositions, processes, institutions, and polities in the broadest senses, we expose the often contradictory practices and imaginaries integral to the moment's liberatory political projects and its cultural experiments. It is to this end that we offer this collection.

Contributors

Gender and Sexuality in 1968 contains two parts. Contributors to part 1, "'68 in Movement and 'Others,'" explore social movements of the 1960s and early 1970s. These essays draw upon dramatic nodal points in these movements while expanding the frames of reference with which these movements engage. Justin Suran's article opens this section, connecting two 1960s movements too rarely linked—the anti–Vietnam War movement and Gay Liberation. He insists on the centrality of the former for the emergence of the latter. In so doing, he not only challenges the implicit divide between antiwar and identity politics but shows why, as he puts it, "antiwar organizing was, for many, sexually liberating."

Elaine Carey examines the Mexican student movement, situating its struggle between students and state as a rift between fathers and sons within the Mexican revolutionary family. In a reading of newspaper cartoons and movement propaganda, she shows how both sides mobilized images and rhetoric of a deviant masculinity to depict the other and substantiate their claims to represent the broader interests of the Mexican family. Thus, Carey elucidates the gendered and sexed heart of these state-student contestations.

Shifting to consider issues of sexuality and desire, broadly conceived as dimensions of political action, Julian Bourg looks to the women's and gay liberation movements in France to examine debates over sexuality and politics: in particular, those *between* feminists and gay male activists over the necessary constraints of desire. These two movements ultimately diverged over what he calls "an ethics of sexuality," which pitted those who adhered to the notion of unfettered desire against those who recognized that society might have a need for enforced limits.

Contesting the flow of global political desire that rendered, paradoxically, certain revolutionary places like Vietnam the (passive and idealized) objects of political solidarity, Emily Maguire puts Cuba in an agentive spotlight, positing that the revolutionary ideology at work in its cinema was, at its core, a gendered ideology. For many students and left-leaning activists throughout the world engaged in reimagining society in '68, the Cuban Revolution served as an exemplar of transformative change. Yet in Cuba '68 was not a year of social upheaval; rather, it witnessed the continued consolidation of changes begun in 1959. Even as Cuba stood in solidarity with many of the postcolonial and independence struggles in developing nations, it strengthened its ties with the Soviets and in 1968 also began the infamous "five-year gray period" that entailed widespread repression of all forms of cultural expression on the island. Maguire finds that two particularly important films from 1968 each dealt with the question of commitment to the revolution in gendered terms, complicating the situating of particular places, marked as already revolutionary, in a panorama of transformative political ferment.

Steven Pierce departs from the case study format to provide a synthetic analysis of a region completely neglected in studies of the sixties: sub-Saharan Africa. He challenges the conflation of the sixties with explicitly countercultural movements, especially with respect to gender and sexuality scholarship. This tendency, he claims, has resulted in the erasure of colonial/postcolonial territories from the map of the "global sixties." Pierce, signaling arenas for future research, uses a regional perspective to critique theories of "de-repression and libidinal politics," revealing the possibilities and limits of global interpretations of the era.

Part 1, then, reveals how gender and sexuality were rubrics for theorizing '68, a theorizing that itself was a central feature of many movements that took gender and sexual practices and identities as terrains of struggle. Contending political movements were, in other words, influenced by, and themselves shaped, fields of political desires.[30]

Part 2, "Spirit, Awakenings, Imaginaries: Beyond '68," examines the legacies of the '68 movements vis-à-vis other kinds of social movements and processes of political formation. In our chapter, we explore the gendered framing of political agency as a window onto the legacies of the Mexican student movement. We (i.e. Cohen and Frazier) draw on men and women's distinct readings of leaders' and activists' participation as a map of gendered terrains of expertise, authority, and impact, and suggest new understandings of both historical agency and the spaces in which we can see the long-term impacts of '68.

Likewise, seeing the importance of struggle over collective imaginaries of historical agency, Susan Lord argues that the documentary films of sixties Cuban filmmaker Sara Gómez auto-ethnographically situate the Afro-Cuban woman as a pivot for decoding revolutionary visual allegories of gendered and racialized imperialist oppression. She, like Maguire, offers a new collective imaginary, and her own body is a "significance-saturated figure for the revolution." Whereas Maguire and Pierce challenge a priori cartographies of '68, Lord situates Cuba squarely in a global affective economy as a site of encounter—for example, Stokely Carmichael's 1967 visit, the World Cultural Congress of early 1968—albeit a problematic one, particularly in the ways in which the Cuban state by the late sixties was only willing to see racism as a problem "over there" (that is, the United States) and actively silenced Afro-Cuban artists and intellectuals' efforts to shape a revolutionary agenda capable of grappling with racism and a decolonized Afro-Cuban culture. Moreover, Lord reads the films as working in direct relation to newsreel and Left Bank film, international decolonizing networks, black power, and feminist activism. This is a revolutionary convergence through which Gómez remapped the city as a space of both global citizenship and localized memory, of contestation and love, and remapped anticolonial revolutions as necessarily transpersonal and transnational.

Charles Sabatos explores the ways that the figure of Czech activist Jan Palach, as a martyred youthful male body, became mobilized iconographically by activists around the world as a means of mounting local challenges and critiquing Soviet repression in Czechoslovakia and Cold War militarization in general. Sabatos analyzes a range of cultural texts to draw out the symbolics of Palach's act and body, and the legacies of these representations around the world.

Michelle Joffroy examines a genre of the literature produced in a post-'68 Mexico, when the student movement was underground, public activists were in jail, and the state had been robbed of its moral authority as a result of its repression of these activists. The *novela del 68*, as this genre was called, engages theoretical and philosophical questions over the representation of history, culture, and state subjects. Drawing on our (i.e. Cohen and Frazier's) piece, Joffroy argues that the '68 novel configures the autobiographical subject of '68, making visible a gendering of the historical experience of '68 and its literary articulations, and with them, the possibilities for political subjectivities.

Michael Sibalis shows that, although homosexuality was not on most activists' radars during the uprisings of May '68 in Paris, this moment did trigger nascent homosexual movements in France. Building on Suran's discussion of the mutual constitution of U.S. antiwar and gay rights movements and Bourg's analysis of tensions between French feminist and gay activists over sixties ideas of sexual freedom, Sibalis's essay traces the French gay movement forward in time as activists defined themselves in relation to "the spirit" of May '68. In the end, he argues that the history of gay liberation in France makes clear the *insignificance* of May '68 to French politics narrowly defined, even as he reveals the centrality of this movement as an axis of moral—sexual and gender—revolution. Thus, part 2 explores the forms and voices through which the impact of these oppositional movements in diverse sectors was both promoted (through narrative and performative acts) and stifled (through complex forms of silencing—in particular, subsequent political and cultural debates).

In sum, this volume attends to cultural dynamics and develops the analytic vectors of gender and sexuality as interlinked with class and race in interrelated kinds of movements to contextualize the study of gender and sexuality within a broadly international perspective. Thus, it places student and other (so-called) political movements within an expansive frame of social actors and issues as a way of constructing a more nuanced sense of the struggles and possibilities that constituted the '68 historical conjuncture.

Notes

With Palgrave, we thank Brigitte Shull, Lee Norton, Matt Robison, and the three anonymous readers. For help in preparing the manuscript and index, we thank Stacy Wieda and Cierra Thomas-Williams. Some of this introduction material appeared previously in *Clio: Histoire, Femmes, et Société* 29: May 2009. For feedback on this introduction we thank Ellen Moodie, Emily Maguire, Laura Westhoff, Andrea Friedman, Flannery Burke, Kathryn Litherland, and Rebecca Rogers. Ageeth Sluis helped us interpret the cover image. We appreciate conceptual feedback from Jeff Gould, Patrick Barr-Melej, and the other participants of "1968 in Latin America: Events, Impacts, Legacies Symposium," Indiana University Center for Latin American and Caribbean Studies; likewise, we thank Eileen Boris, Jeffrey Stewart, George Lipsitz, and participants of "'68, A Global Year of Student Driven Change Conference," University of California—Santa Barbara Black Studies Department.

1. Here we use 1968 to refer to the specific calendar year, '68 to refer to the phenomenon or historical conjuncture, and the sixties to refer to an era. Sara Evans marks the lacuna in attention to gender in her tour de force article "Son's, daughters, and patriarchy: gender and the 1968 generation" *American Historical Review* April 2009: 331–347. Recently published volumes on the sixties include a number of excellent broad overviews; however, most deal predominantly with the United States such as David R. Farber, ed., *The 60s: From Memory to History* (Chapel Hill: University of North Carolina Press, 1994); Maurice Isserman and Michael Kazin, *America Divided: The Civil War of the 1960s* (New York: Oxford, 2000); Dominick Cavallo, *Fiction of the Past: The Sixties in American History* (New York: St. Martin's, 1999); M.J. Heale, *The Sixties in America* (Chicago: Fitzroy, 2001); and Peter Braunstein and Michael William Doyle, *Imagine Nation: The American Counterculture of the 1960s and '70s* (New York: Routledge, 2002). There are a number of extended studies of specific U.S. cases such as William J. Billingsley, *Communists on Campus: Race, Politics, and the Public University in Sixties North Carolina* (Athens: University of Georgia Press, 1999); Mike Marqusee, *Redemption Song: Muhammad Ali and the Spirit of the Sixties* (London: Verso, 2000); Barry Laffan, *Communal Organization and Social Transition: A Case Study from the Counterculture of the Sixties and Seventies* (New York: Peter Lang, 1997); Craig Cox, *Storefront Revolution: Food Co-Ops and the Counterculture* (New Brunswick, NJ: Rutgers University Press, 1994); Timothy Miller, *The 60s Communes: Hippies and Beyond* (Syracuse, NY: Syracuse University Press,1999); and Dan Georgakas and Marvin Surkin, *Detroit, I Do Mind Dying* (Cambridge: South End Press, 1998). Fine examples of non-U.S. case studies include Luisa Passerini, *Autobiography of a Generation: Italy, 1968* (Middletown, CT: Wesleyan University Press, 2004), which brings an innovative mix of memoir and historical scholarship and feminist critique to consider the student movement in Italy.

Diana Sorenson, *A Turbulent Decade Remembered. Scenes from the Latin American Sixties* (Stanford: Stanford University Press, 2007), integrates gender intrinsically into her rendition of the '60s; Eric Zolov, *Refried Elvis* (Berkeley: University of California Press, 1999), discusses Mexican youth culture as reflecting international tensions and cultural flows. Some recent volumes that broaden the focus of scholarship around issues of race, ethnicity, gender, and sexuality, mostly focusing on the United States, are Patricia Juliana Smith, ed., *The Queer Sixties* (New York: Routledge, 1999); Carlos Muñoz, ed., *Youth, Identity, Power: The Sixties Chicano Movement* (London: Verso, 2002); and August Meier, Elliot M. Rudwick, John H. Bracey eds., *Black Protest in the Sixties* (New York: Markus Wiener, 1991). Few scholarly books bring an international, comparative perspective to the topic. Exceptions are Arthur Marwick *The Sixties: Cultural Revolution in Britain, France, Italy, and the United States, c. 1958–c.1974* (New York: Getty, 1999), a helpful monograph for thinking about change in "the West," and Gerard DeGroot, ed., *Student Protest: The Sixties and After* (London: Longman, 1998), an anthology that covers a rather different and more specific emphasis (solely on student activism) than our own. For a forthcoming edited volume, see Belinda Davis, W. Mausbach, M. Klimke, and C. MacDougall, eds., *Changing the World, Changing Oneself: Political Protest and Transnational Identities in the 1960s/70s West Germany and U.S.* (New York: Berghahn Books forthcoming, 2010).

2. "Vondel Park Love-in," by Willem De Ridder. Thanks to Willem De Ridder for permission to use the image and the International Institute for Social History (IISG), Amsterdam, for facilitating access to the image.

3. Chandra Mohanty, *Feminism without Borders: Decolonizing Theory, Practicing Solidarity* (Durham: Duke University Press, 2003).

4. Robert McRuer, "Gay Gatherings: Reimagining the Counterculture" *Imagine Nation*, Peter Braunstein and Michael William Doyle, eds., (New York: Routledge, 2002), 215–240.

5. For a more comprehensive account see Tariq Ali and Susan Watkins, *1968 Marching in the Streets* (London: Free Press, 1998); Mark Kurlansky, *1968, The Year that Rocked the World* (New York: Ballantine Books, 2004).

6. We explore the global dimensions of '68 in "More than Mojo: Gender and the Racialized Erotics of the Global '68," *Kalfou, A Journal of Comparative and Relational Ethnic Studies*, forthcoming 2010.

7. See, for example, Lessie Jo Frazier, *Desired States* ms.

8. Joan W. Scott, *Gender and the Politics of History* (New York and London: Columbia University Press, 1999). Jennifer Doyle makes a cogent case for analytically centering sex using, among other examples, Andy Warhol's films in her *Sex Objects: Art and the Dialectics of Desire* (Minneapolis: University of Minnesota Press, 2006).

9. The exception to this is in terms of intersectionality, the notion that one's gender position is mitigated by other social categories, such as class, race, ability, and language, and age.

10. For a provocative overview of this terrain, see the editorial mission statement for the new scholarly journal dedicated to research on the sixties, Jeremy Varon, Michael S. Foley, and John Mcmillian, "Time is an ocean: the past and future of the Sixties," *The Sixties: A Journal of History, Politics, and Culture* Vol. 1, No. 1, pp. 1–7, 2008.

11. Rhonda Williams, *Politics of Public Housing: Black Women's Struggles against Urban Inequality* (New York: Oxford University Press, 2005); Premilla Nadasen, *Welfare Warriors: The Welfare Rights Movement in the United States* (New York: Routledge, 2004); and Felicia Kornbluh, *The Battle for Welfare Rights: Politics and Poverty in Modern America* (Philadelphia: University of Pennsylvania Press, 2007).

12. See Benita Roth's *Separate Roads to Feminism: Black, Chicana, and White Feminist Struggles in America's Second Wave* (New York: Cambridge University Press, 2003), and Enriqueta Vasquez, with Dionne Espinoza and Lorena Oropeza, eds., *Enriqueta Vasquez And the Chicano Movement: Writings from El Grito Del Norte*, a collection of columns that Vasquéz wrote for the newspaper *El Grito del Norte* (Albuquerque: Arte Público Press, 2006). Also

see Winifred Breines, *The Trouble Between Us: An Uneasy History of White and Black Women in the Feminist Movement* (New York: Oxford, 2006).

13. For example, see Gloria Anzaldúa, *Borderlands/La Frontera, The New Mestiza* (San Francisco: Aunt Lute Books, 3rd edition, 2007); Alma M.García, *Chicana Feminist Thought: The Basic Historical Writings* (New York: Routledge, 1997); Patricia Hill Collins, *Black Feminist Thought: Knowledge, Consciousness, and the Politics of Empowerment* (New York: Routledge Press, revised 10th Anniversary 2nd Edition, 2000); Cherrie Moraga and Gloria Anzaldúa, eds., *The Bridge Called My Back, Writings by Radical Women of Color* (New York: Kitchen Table/Women of Color, 1984).

14. Barbara Ransby makes a similar point in connecting the sixties to prior activism in her beautiful biography, *Ella Baker and the Black Freedom Movement: A Radical Democratic Vision* (Chapel Hill: University of North Carolina Press, 2003).

15. David Carter, *Stonewall: The Riots That Sparked the Gay Revolution* (New York: St. Martin's Press, 2004); Stonewall was preceded by the similarly diverse 1966 Compton's Cafeteria Riot, a watershed for the San Francisco LGBT movement, see Susan Stryker, *Transgender History* (Berkeley: Seal Press, 2008).

16. Beth Bailey, *Sex in the Heartland* (Cambridge: Harvard University Press, 1999).

17. Valerie Korinek, *Roughing it in the Suburbs: Reading Chatelaine Magazine in the Fifties and Sixties* (Toronto: University of Toronto Press, 2000).

18. Dagmar Herzog, *Sex after Fascism: Memory and Morality in Twentieth-Century Germany* (Princeton: Princeton University Press, 2005).

19. Patricia Juliana Smith, *The Queer Sixties* (New York, Routledge Press, 1999); Avital Bloch and Lauri Umansky, *Impossible to Hold: Women and Culture in the 1960s* (New York: New York University Press, 2005); and Annie J. Randall, *Dusty! Queen of the Postmods* (New York: Oxford University Press, 2009). Also of interest is Hilary Radner and Moya Luckett, eds., *Swinging Single: Representing Sexuality in the 1960s* (Minneapolis: University of Minnesota Press, 1999), an important volume that analyzes pop culture in a theoretically sophisticated way.

20. As in Canadian singer Helen Reddy's well-known feminist anthem, "I am woman, hear me roar."

21. Julie Stephens, *Anti-Disciplinary Protest: Sixties Radicalism and Postmodernism* (New York: Cambridge University Press, 1988); Peter Braunstein and Michael William Doyle, eds., *Imagine Nation: The American Counterculture of the 1960s and '70s* (New York: Routledge Press, 2002); Doug Rossinow, *The Politics of Authenticity* (New York : Columbia University Press, 1998).

22. Marianne DeKoven, *Utopia Limited: The Sixties and the Emergence of the Postmodern* (Durham: Duke University Press, 2004); Julian Bourg, *From Revolution to Ethics: May 1968 and Contemporary French Thought* (Montreal: McGill-Queens' University Press, 2007).

23. Diana A. Sorensen, *Turbulent Decade Remembered: Scenes from the Latin American Sixties* (Palo Alto: Stanford University Press, 2007).

24. Margo V. Perkins, *Autobiography as Activism: Three Black Women of the Sixties* (Jackson: University of Mississippi Press, 2000); Elaine Brown, *A Taste Of Power: A Black Woman's Story* (New York: Anchor Books, 1992); Angela Davis, *Angela Davis: An Autobiography* (Oakland: International Publishers, 2006 [1974]); and Assata Shakur, *Assata: An Autobiography* (Chicago: Lawrence Hill Books, 2001 [1987]).

25. Pamela Barnett, *Dangerous Desire: Literature of Sexual Freedom and Sexual Violence Since the Sixties* (New York: Routledge, 2004). Among the texts she examines are: Eldridge Cleaver, *Soul on Ice* (Berkeley: Ramparts Press, 1970); Susan Brownmiller, *Against Our Will: Men, Women, and Rape* (New York, Simon and Schuster, 1975); Marilyn French, *The Women's Room* (New York: Jove/HBJ Book, 1978); Gloria Naylor, *The Women of Brewster Place, A Novel in Seven Stories* (New York: Penguin Group, 1983); Alice Walker, *Meridian* (New York: Pocket Books, 1976); and James Dickey, *Deliverance* (Holt, U.K.: Laurel Books, 1994).

26. See Elaine Carey, *Plaza of Sacrifices: Gender, Power, and Terror in 1968 Mexico* (Albuquerque: University of New Mexico Press, 2005).
27. Peter J. Ling and Sharon Monteith eds., *Gender and the Civil Rights Movements* (New Brunswick: Rutgers University Press, 2004).
28. Steve Estes, *I Am a Man!: Race, Manhood, and the Civil Rights Movement* (Chapel Hill: University of North Carolina Press, 2005).
29. Laurie B. Green, *Battling the Plantation Mentality: Memphis and the Black Freedom Struggle* (Chapel Hill: University of North Carolina Press, 2007).
30. For a somewhat kindred reflection on the "mythology" of Stonewall in the U.S. see John Rechy, "The outlaw sensibility in the arts: from drag and leather to prose, the mythology of Stonewall, the defense of stereotypes," in *Queer Frontiers: Millennial Geographies, Genders, and Generations,* ed., Joseph A. Boone (Madison: University of Wisconsin Press, 2000), 124–132.

P A R T   1

———

'68 in Movement and "Others"

"Out Now!": Antimilitarism and the Politicization of Homosexuality in the Era of Vietnam

JUSTIN DAVID SURAN

Since the 1970s, commentators on the history of sexuality (following the lead of Michel Foucault) have written extensively on the emergence of "the homosexual" as a clinical category and social type in the North Atlantic West. In contrast, there has been little academic inquiry into the more recent emergence of other identity-naming keywords such as *gay, straight,* and *queer.* The mode of cultural studies invites us to view even our most contemporary-sounding categories as both ideologically conditioned and historically contingent. The full spectrum of meanings covered by these identity-naming keywords is sometimes easy to read, as it is in present-day usage of the once pejorative *queer*—a term that has now come to be associated not only with a heavily politicized field of antihomophobic academic discourse, but with the self-conscious adoption of an antagonistic stance toward "mainstream" culture. Less easily perceptible today, thirty years after Gay Liberation, is the palpable ideological force-field that once surrounded (and to some extent, continues to surround) the signifier "gay." This chapter insists on the centrality of both the Vietnam War experience and the antiwar movement to the emergence of the Gay Liberation movement in the United States. Situating Gay Liberation squarely in the context of the Vietnam years not only helps explain the force with which gay people emerged after 1969 as an assertively identity-affirming community and aboveground interest group. It also connects the familiar student-led movements of the 1960s to the liberationist initiatives of the 1970s.

Historians of the Vietnam War and American antiwar movement have missed almost entirely that conflict's unique relevance to homosexual men and the homosexual rights movement.[1] More surprising, however, is the fact that historians of Gay Liberation have consistently overlooked evidence of the war's considerable impact on the lives of homosexual men and women.[2] Focusing on events in the city of San Francisco, I argue in this chapter that the emergence of the modern gay rights movement was tightly bound up with the mobilization of people and resources nationwide both in compliance with U.S. policy toward Indochina and in opposition to it. Because the war meant different things to different people and because it affected men and women differently—for example, women were not drafted—my argument is based primarily on the experiences of gay men in one city and the significance attached to male homosexuality in the context of the war. By foregrounding certain dramatic experiences shared by homosexual men (in particular, experiences with the Vietnam draft and antiwar movement), this chapter recalls forgotten aspects of both the Vietnam experience and the social origins of Gay Liberation.[3]

My narrative begins in the decades after World War Two, when the problems of homosexual servicemen became a major focus of newly formed "homophile" organizations in San Francisco such as the Mattachine Society and, later, the Society for Individual Rights. In the mid- to late 1960s homophile groups fought to secure the right of homosexual servicemen to serve discreetly in uniform. At the same time, the Vietnam draft was confronting increasing numbers of young homosexual men with a peculiar quandary, one that forced them to choose between revealing or concealing their sexual orientation. Militant youth and their allies in the movement soon rebelled against older homophile groups that refrained from taking a public stance against the war. In this way, the Vietnam War politicized countless gay men while polarizing homosexual politics. In San Francisco, Gay Liberation made its full-scale debut in 1969, when gay radicals joined protestors nationwide in observing the Vietnam Day Moratorium. From 1969 to 1971 mass antiwar protests in San Francisco and other cities played a crucial role in bringing Gay Liberation politics out of the closet and into the streets.[4] After an antiwar march that drew a sizable gay contingent in the spring of 1971, one Gay Liberationist in San Francisco marveled: "Vietnam helped to bring thousands of gay people together in the strongest show of gay power in the history of the world.... Indeed, Vietnam has awakened life in the midst of death."[5]

Situating Gay Liberation in the crucible of 1960s radicalism casts new light on Gay Liberation's 1969 debut (generally evoked by historians with a few picturesque sentences about drag queens rioting at the Stonewall Inn[6]) and on the larger story of social protest with which we associate the Vietnam years.[7] Nearly every available version of the Gay Liberation story begins or ends at the Stonewall Inn, the legendary Greenwich Village bar where a midnight police raid ignited a weekend of angry street protests. The Stonewall uprising provides the climactic conclusion to John D'Emilio's 1983 monograph on the making of a homosexual minority in the United States, a still-definitive study that interprets Stonewall in 1969 as the combustion-point in "a much longer historical process through which a group of men and women came into existence as a self-conscious, cohesive minority."[8] In D'Emilio's account, Stonewall is the end of a long-burning fuse, a fuse lit in the immediate postwar decades when a small number of homophile agitators, inspired by the successes of the civil rights movement, resisted their own subordination with ever-increasing militancy. To D'Emilio, Stonewall epitomizes the triumph of a radical social vision and militant approach to politics, a "liberation impulse" with antecedents in the small but heroic acts of homosexual resistance that came before it.

The problems inherent in a Stonewall-centered version of gay history are increasingly clear to students of the homosexual rights movement, who have begun to argue that Stonewall ought to be put into perspective. This chapter contributes to the reconsideration of Stonewall's historical importance by shifting the focus of the Gay Liberation story from New York to San Francisco and by highlighting deep interconnections between Gay Liberation and the radical antimilitarism of the Vietnam years. Unlike the mostly East Coast–centered narratives that emphasize the formative influence of homophile organizations and the civil rights movement on the emergence of Gay Liberation in New York, this version explores the formative influence of the antiwar movement on gay solidarity and urban protest in the San Francisco Bay Area. Unlike D'Emilio's story, which posits a vital continuity between the "homophile" 1960s and "gay" 1970s, this story sees Gay Liberation as *an abrupt departure from the homophile and civil rights traditions, a rupture most clearly evident in Gay Liberation's aggressive disavowal of the long-standing homophile demand for integration into the armed services.* This chapter explores a nexus of arguments about the meaning of sexual freedom and the merits of military service, arguments that have been at the heart of homosexual politics since World War Two.

A new look at Gay Liberation raises larger questions as well about the way historians have portrayed the protest movements of the 1960s. Historical narratives regularly place Gay Liberation at or near the end of a chronological series of more-or-less sequential 1960s movements, beginning with civil rights, moving on to campus-based student politics and the New Left, bringing in feminism and Women's Liberation, and ending with a kaleidoscope of identity-based initiatives such as Gay Liberation in the early 1970s. However, a closer look suggests that this sequential understanding of the 1960s is overly schematic: it obscures the most intriguing points of contact *among* these various movements.[9] In the present study, it appears that homophile activism and Gay Liberation did not exactly "follow" these other movements; rather, homosexual freedom was a constitutive part of the 1960s all along.[10] Much remains to be learned about the historical interactions among the various, seemingly distinct, yet frequently overlapping and simultaneously occurring elements of 1960s and 1970s protest. Local studies are one way to reveal these connective tissues, as well as the distinctive patterns of regional variation and specificity, which more sweeping narratives obscure. This is not to say that we should abandon large-scale narratives of the 1960s—only that we might better incorporate a sense of simultaneity, interaction, and local specificity into the big picture.

Last, exploring the social origins of Gay Liberation advances our understanding of the intricate linkages among identity, politics, and culture in High Sixties protest. Although "lifestyle choices," "culture," and "identity politics" are often seen as distinct alternatives to more traditional forms of political activity such as antiwar organizing, this chapter suggests that identity-based solidarities were a crucial factor in antiwar organizing and that antiwar activities played a critical role in the formation of identity-based movements such as Gay Liberation. Though commentators on the 1960s often make decisive analytic distinctions between identity-based forms of cultural politics and more conventional forms of Left organizing, this distinction tends to dissolve upon close inspection of the political history of the 1960s. In fact, a militant antiwar ethos was absolutely central to the formation of a specifically "gay" identity in the United States. Indeed, Gay Liberation and the antiwar movement were closely related examples of a style of political protest invented in the 1960s, a style that has been characterized as "personal" or "personalist," "prefigurative," and "antidisciplinary."[11] Deemphasizing distinctions between "antiwar" and "identity" politics, this essay begins to explain not only how homosexual liberation became a political force in the 1960s, but why antiwar organizing was, for many, sexually liberating.

Homophile Liberalism and the Homosexual Soldier

Since mid-century, critical transformations in the homosexual rights movement have occurred alongside major wars. Historians have described World War Two, for instance, as a national "coming-out experience," when homosexual men and women far removed from their hometowns formed new friendships and sometimes fell in love in the sex-segregated institutions of the military and war industries.[12] Though numbers are hard to gauge, one recent study has claimed that homosexual men were about as likely as other men to serve in the armed forces between 1941 and 1954;

lesbian women were ten times more likely than other women to have served.[13] After World War Two, but before the *Brown v. Board of Education* decision and Montgomery bus boycott ushered in the civil rights movement, homosexual men and women founded the first "homophile" organizations, discreet associations established to combat discrimination and integrate homosexuals into mainstream American society. Among this generation of postwar homophile activists were veterans of World War Two and the Korean War, former service members who knew firsthand the often life-shattering consequences of a "less than honorable" discharge and other sanctions imposed against homosexual soldiers.[14]

By the late 1950s, chapters of the San Francisco-based Mattachine Society, a homophile organization for men, had formed in cities across the country; Phyllis Lyon and Del Martin, two San Francisco lesbians, had organized the Daughters of Bilitis (DOB) for women. Aggressively polite in their campaign for equal rights, homophile groups pursued a strategy of militant respectability and tactics of protest comparable to those adopted simultaneously by the civil rights movement. Though assiduously respectable, homophile activism presented a forceful critique of federal policies and prevailing Cold War stereotypes of homosexual degeneracy. In 1950 the U.S. Navy alone issued undesirable discharges for homosexuality to 483 enlisted men; in 1952, 1352 men were so expelled. An executive order issued by President Eisenhower in 1953 listed "sexual perversion" among the sufficient grounds for dismissing a federal employee.[15] Classified as "security risks" and suspected as agents of communism, known and suspected homosexuals were fired from government jobs without a public hearing and discharged from the military without benefits.[16] Men with less than honorable discharges from the armed services had difficulty finding jobs, barred not only from government employment but also from any position requiring a security clearance. Stigmatized as "deviants," such men were more likely than others to attempt suicide.[17]

As military purges resulted in the annual discharge of hundreds, even thousands, of enlisted men in the 1950s and 1960s, the nation's mass media circulated forbidding images of homosexuality. *Time* magazine declared homosexuality "a pernicious illness" in the mid-1960s, and *Life* revealed to its readers the "sad and often sordid" subculture of the urban homosexual.[18] One 1965 Harris Survey determined that an overwhelming majority of Americans considered homosexuals "harmful to American life," along with other nonconformists such as civil rights and antiwar demonstrators.[19] In this hostile climate, a relatively small and loosely coordinated network of homophile organizations first began to defend the civil liberties of homosexuals by opposing antisodomy laws, discrimination in federal employment, and the use of plainclothes policemen to patrol bars and bathhouses. Conscientiously constructing a collective identity compatible with mainstream American values and established institutions, homophile groups put a respectable face on the pitied and reviled homosexual. "Responsible action by responsible people in responsible ways" went the motto of the San Francisco-based Society for Individual Rights (SIR), a group founded in 1964 "to present the true image of the homosexual to the community."[20]

From 1961 to 1966, therefore, some degree of synergy existed between the relatively small, decentralized homophile movement and the interracial civil rights movement. Homophile rhetoric reflected obvious analogies to the civil rights movement, which embraced the same social ideal of integration into a national community of equal rights and shared responsibilities. On the East Coast, especially in New York and Washington, D.C., the accomplishments of civil rights organizers inspired homophile activists like World War Two army veteran Frank Kameny, who argued that the Washington Mattachine should adopt a similarly "vigorous civil liberties, social action approach."[21] During this mid-1960s civil rights chapter in homosexual politics, homophile agitators added direct-action protest to their political repertoire. In 1964 eleven members of the New York Mattachine, calling attention to the military ban on homosexuals and practice of releasing draft records to employers, picketed lower Manhattan's Whitehall Street Induction Center in the first public protest for homosexual rights.[22] In April 1965 seven men and three women paraded at the White House for homosexual rights. As it happened, Students for a Democratic Society drew twenty thousand antiwar protestors to the Washington Monument on the same day.[23]

If a civil rights ethos and the example of the Civil Rights Movement informed homosexual politics between 1961 and 1966, the late 1960s were dominated by the Vietnam War. After 1966, military service and antiwar protest emerged as the pivotal issues in homosexual politics. At the first National Planning Conference of Homophile Organizations (NACHO) held in 1966 in Kansas City, delegates from East and West Coast homophile organizations agreed to elevate military service to the top of their first national agenda. At the center of their action-oriented plan was an agreement to hold coordinated demonstrations in several major cities across the country on Armed Forces Day. Supporters of the plan argued that an Armed Forces Day event would demonstrate patriotism while highlighting instances of discrimination. But some delegates objected to the proposal, arguing that it might be misconstrued as an endorsement of American intervention in Indochina. Others pointed out that the problems stemming from military service and the draft affected only a fraction of NACHO's constituents, primarily men. The proposal was nevertheless approved by the conferees, many of whom were veterans with a visceral understanding of the historical connection between military service and citizenship rights. The May demonstrations would "protest the moral dilemma with which homosexual men are confronted because of the draft and the risk of getting a less-than-fully-honorable discharge if discovered in the armed forces."[24]

The objections raised in Kansas City suggest that American intervention in Vietnam had already begun to weaken a foundational plank of the homophile platform. Though spokesmen insisted the coordinated protests were not a comment on the war in Indochina, some observers found it hard to separate the issues. One San Francisco paper sought support for the upcoming demonstrations by exploiting fears about the war: *Cruise News* directed an appeal to "parents whose [drafted heterosexual] sons are serving in the armed forces because some homosexuals have not been allowed to serve." On May 21 in a scene that invited comparison to recent student-led antiwar demonstrations, a respectably attired crowd of several hundred (mostly) men in overcoats, suits, and ties gathered in front of the Federal Building in downtown San Francisco. The Reverend Cecil Williams, a veteran of the Civil Rights Movement, began the afternoon with the Pledge of Allegiance. Speakers at the rally criticized the Defense Department not for waging war, but for preventing homosexuals from serving in the military and government jobs. Signs declared "Sexuality Does Not Determine Patriotism" and "Every Man Has a Right to Serve His Country." As organizers had hoped, two local TV stations covered the protest on the evening news, carrying the issue of federal discrimination against homosexuals into Bay Area living rooms.[25]

Armed Forces Day, 1966, was in retrospect the apex of homophile liberalism and epitome of militant respectability. For the women and men who came of age between 1941 and 1954, homosexuality was an aspect of identity thought to be compatible with a broad array of other ideals, commitments, and solidarities, including the civic ideal of military service. Affirming one's homosexuality, they believed, should not interfere with one's ability to participate in the public culture of the nation and its dominant institutions. But by 1966, members of a younger generation had begun to see their homosexuality in a different light, and once again, mobilization for war contributed to that transformation. Seeking to avoid the Vietnam draft, a new generation of young gay men found themselves turning for advice to the same organizations then fighting to secure a homosexual's right to be drafted. In the summer of 1966, one University of California student who opposed the war but faced induction on account of his late registration with the selective service worried that if he admitted his "homosexual tendencies" to an army psychiatrist he would never be eligible for employment in state or local government. In his letter to the *Mattachine Review*, "Mr. C." from Los Angeles expressed legitimate concern about future "security checks" into his background as well as the confidentiality of his draft board records.[26]

Unlike their heterosexual peers, young men with "homosexual tendencies" faced a special quandary in relation to the draft, a complex dilemma normally reduced to the simple terms of whether or not to "check the box." The box in question was the last item on the standard medical survey given to all prospective draftees when they appeared for mandatory physicals. "Have you ever had or have you now…homosexual tendencies?" was the question posed to every American male reporting to his local draft board for preinduction screening. In 1966 *The New Republic* described how the selective service system "boxed in" the draft-age male: "If a homosexual checks the 'no' box, he violates a federal law and risks fine and imprisonment. If he checks 'yes,' he is disqualified and he may be permanently handicapped in getting or holding a job."[27] If inducted after checking "no," a man risked both death in Vietnam and the possibility of being ferreted out in an antihomosexual purge. In the eyes of the Defense Department, gay men and lesbians were security risks and "rejects"; seldom were they kindly treated in the humiliating process of separation. If on the other hand a prospective draftee checked "yes," he became instantly ineligible for millions of civil service jobs, and his name went on record with the FBI. Moreover, since draft boards were locally staffed, declaring one's homosexuality often meant coming out to one's family, friends, and neighbors.[28]

To help gay men navigate the military bureaucracy, homophile organizations published numerous articles and informational brochures. In 1967, SIR's Community Services Committee produced a widely distributed pamphlet entitled "What Should I Do About the Draft?" that advised draftees not to sign waivers giving administrative personnel access to induction files. The brochure's intent was neither to dissuade nor to persuade young men to "check the box." Instead, it hoped to promote an informed and conscientious choice.[29] Ubiquitous "draft counseling" centers in the Bay Area also handled inquiries from men confronting the selective service. Draft Help in San Francisco reminded its counseling staff that a man's decision to declare or conceal his homosexuality depended on many factors, including his occupation, his family and social circle, and his "philosophic outlook" on life.[30] Allan Bérubé has argued that the military during World War Two "reinforced" the homosexual identities of gay GIs "by managing them as homosexual persons in its screening, antivice, and discharge policies."[31] The same is true of the Vietnam draft, which enforced at least the appearance of excluding homosexuals from its ranks. In coming to terms with the draft, many gay men between the ages of eighteen and twenty-six were compelled to come to terms with their homosexuality.

Heterosexual men as well were forced to grapple with homosexuality: to convince the army one was gay was one way to beat the draft.

Inadvertently the Vietnam War intensified interest in the military's anti-gay policies as, for the first time in history, countless heterosexual men assumed a homosexual identity to avoid being drafted. The problem of the "gay deceiver"—heterosexual men pretending to be gay—plagued the selective service, which soon realized it was in many cases being duped. As the war dragged on and manpower needs increased, it became more and more difficult for men to dodge the draft by claiming homosexual tendencies, however real.[32] In March 1968, the Stanford Anti-Draft Union informed its counselors: "[I]t is very difficult to 'queer out' at certain experienced induction centers, such as Oakland [California]. One must have a record of homosexuality, evidenced by an arrest record, letters from doctors, or letters from psychiatrists."[33] Sparrow Robinson, a gay man coming to terms with his sexual orientation, was asked by his draft board to provide "proof" from a doctor. After obtaining a referral to a psychiatrist who wrote letters for draftees, Robinson was reclassified, following two psychiatric consultations at thirty-five dollars per session.[34] As a consequence of such requirements, homosexual men were sometimes disbelieved and drafted, while heterosexual men able to obtain the appropriate letters or mimic homosexual stereotypes were deferred.

The state of California acquired a reputation for laxity in its enforcement of draft regulations. Home to sympathetic psychiatrists and ACLU lawyers, the San Francisco Bay Area became a haven for draft resisters.[35] Still, proving one's homosexuality to the draft board was frequently an ordeal. In part, the problem stemmed from the military's inability to provide a clear definition of "a homosexual." Apart from vague guidelines outlining grounds for rejection—namely, "Character and behavior disorders, as evidenced by overt homosexuality or other forms of sexual deviant practices [*sic*] such as exhibitionism, transvestism, voyeurism, etc."—army psychiatrists had no standard criteria upon which to base their judgments. As one Draft Help memo put it, military psychiatrists relied on "their own preconceptions of the psychological makeup and behavior of homosexuals," an observation that helps to explain why military doctors required written "evidence" of a draftee's homosexuality. Bisexual men only further bewildered the military. "Bisexuality," noted Draft Help, "particularly if the man is presently living with or married to a woman, may confuse the psychiatrist who may reject the claim unless the homosexual component is documented."[36]

Because induction interviews were more about seeming gay than being gay, one Berkeley manual for draft resisters advised men to "[p]lay the homosexual bit": "Besides flicking your wrist, move your body like chicks do-hold cigarette delicately, talk melodically, act embarassed [*sic*] in front of the other guys when you undress." The same circular suggested not only that men ask their girlfriends for lessons, but that men "watch the Frisco North

Beach Crowd" on a weekend night or visit a gay bar in the city's Tenderloin district.[37] Frequently, army interviewers ignored the testimonies of gay men who were not effeminate or did not fit (as *One* magazine put it) "the extreme androgyne type."[38] A twenty-one-year-old San Francisco man was drafted after presenting a psychiatrist's letter and repeatedly acknowledging his homosexuality. Terry Barnard recalled that his induction center interviewer "never contested my being gay, but stated that since I wasn't effeminate, he wouldn't grant me a deferment." Only after spending six hours in an army stockade, hiring a lawyer, contacting legislators and homosexual organizations, and asking his lover of one and a half years to sign a statement saying the two had engaged in homosexual conduct, was Barnard finally granted an honorable discharge three months later.[39] By raising the standard of proof that homosexual men had to meet to avoid breaking federal law and entering the service, the Vietnam draft forced gay men not merely to admit their homosexuality, but to assert a homosexual identity.

For many Americans, Vietnam was a political awakening; for many gay men, it was also a sexual awakening. Sparrow Robinson described the experience with his draft board as "a major breakthrough" in his life: "it was the first time I had to take total responsibility for my life and accept the consequences....In order to come to terms with the draft...I had to come to terms with [being] gay."[40] Mobilization for war confronted soldiers and civilians alike with questions of sexual identity as the draft pushed the issue of homosexuality, particularly *male* homosexuality, from the margins to the center of the nation's public discourse. Though opinions about homosexuality were often based on prejudicial stereotypes, public discussion of the draft nevertheless promoted widespread recognition of "the homosexual" as a sexual identity and social type.[41] By creating a life-or-death incentive for heterosexual men to claim to be gay despite legal sanctions and long-standing taboos against doing so, the draft even had the unintended consequence of *rendering normal* to some degree the public acknowledgment of homosexual conduct. Moreover, to the extent that the draft's unpopularity heightened the appeal of countercultural values, the Vietnam War produced an ethical climate of radical dissent in which homosexuality could be more readily embraced. In opposing but mutually reinforcing ways, both wartime mobilization and the mobilization of radical dissent created a unique set of conditions inviting men to "come out" as homosexuals.

Toward Liberation

In the course of the High Sixties, Gay Liberation revolutionized homosexual identity in the United States and in the process, Americans came to be sorted into the mutually exclusive, ideologically marked categories "gay" and "straight." Other historians have commented on the radical ethos of Gay Liberation and its exuberant repudiation of homophile/civil rights politics. But no account has adequately described how opposition to the Vietnam War accelerated the consolidation of a specifically *radical* homosexual identity in the United States. Adopting a gay identity in 1969 or 1970 meant more than simply affirming one's same-sex orientation. It meant situating oneself in a matrix of ideals and initiatives associated at the time with radical politics. First and foremost, adopting a gay identity in 1969 or 1970 meant being both out of the closet and against the Vietnam War. In the United States, the convergence of antimilitarist protest and homosexual discontent created political opportunities for Gay Liberation. Antimilitarism was central to the formation of gay identity; resistance to the Vietnam War was at the heart of Gay Liberation's rupture with homophile liberalism.

In San Francisco, Gay Liberation was founded on a rift between two generations divided over the Vietnam War. Although many of the leading figures in San Francisco's homophile community personally opposed the Vietnam intervention, homophile organizations chose not to adopt a public stance on the war.[42] Homophile liberals believed that adopting an antiwar position would only further marginalize their already marginal constituencies. Furthermore, organization leaders recognized that many of their constituents approved of U.S. policy, and they did not wish to antagonize the prointervention segment of the homosexual community. SIR's president Larry Littlejohn believed an antiwar stance would be "damaging to the homosexual's chances of being accepted as a person." Moreover, he argued, sexual orientation did not determine one's position on Vietnam. SIR's vice president reminded his colleagues: "Conservatism is, unfortunately, in vogue, and this is a poor time to test the heterosexual community on its love for the rights of the homosexual."[43] As spokesmen for the nation's largest homosexual organization, the leadership of SIR made an effort to accommodate the spectrum of positions represented by its nearly seven hundred members.[44]

Homosexual youth and their special concerns had never been part of the homophile consensus. By the mid-1960s, homophile organizations had adopted rules limiting membership to persons twenty-one years of age and over, largely because they feared charges of pedophilia and "contributing to the delinquency of minors."[45] Beyond the formal exclusions against the "juvenile homosexual," a cultural divide separated middle-aged men from homosexual youth. Gay teenagers felt little connection to the common culture of their elders, many of whom frequented the downtown gay bars and shared a playful "inside" idiom of campy histrionics. Though "middle-aged bitchery," "high camp and sequins," and "Garland and

Monroe" might delight a room of older men, most teenagers were, as one SIR member put it, "[q]uickly bored back onto the streets" by the culture of their elders.[46] Indeed, "the streets" of San Francisco—especially the streets of the Tenderloin district, where many of the city's gay bars, prostitutes, drug dealers, and late-night eateries were located—had become home to some of the city's most underprivileged gay youth. For them, the homophile groups had little to offer.

It was among San Francisco's homosexual youth, outsiders to the homophile consensus, that homosexual orientation and a radical ethos began to coalesce in a distinctly new understanding of homosexual identity, an identity different from and in many respects incompatible with the ideals of homophile liberalism. In 1966 some Tenderloin youth formed an organization of their own to alleviate problems of the neighborhood's addicts, hustlers, and homeless.[47] Led by president "Jean-Paul Marat," the group known as Vanguard displayed a distinctly countercultural style at odds with the staid decorum and liberal nationalism of the homophiles. Nowhere was that difference more apparent than in Vanguard's position on the Vietnam War. Whereas the members of SIR tended to view the armed services as an institution to which homosexuals should have equal access, the members of Vanguard associated the military exclusively with senseless deaths in Vietnam. Thoughts of dying in Vietnam loomed large in the minds of men such as Mark Miller, whose poem "For Ken, the Soldier" appeared in the October 1966 issue of *Vanguard*. "His name is gone / lost somewhere in the jungle," Miller wrote, "his gun rusted and voiceless / in the warm, killing rains....It does not matter / if he was lifted up / on a chariot of gold."

The following year, Vanguard member Keith St. Clare denounced the war in print, suggesting that everyone "Fuck for Peace." After the city's first antiwar rally, one *Vanguard* columnist ridiculed the Society for Individual Rights: "All those 'responsible' people refused to organize any public display of feelings about 'Johnson's' war." Mocking SIR's members as "Sissies in Revolt," the column attacked that organization's leadership. "At best," jabbed *Vanguard*'s column, "[SIR] will remain a private dancing club unless some teeth are put into those busy gums."[48] Indeed, many homosexual men found radical political voices in the midst of antiwar protest. After organizing the Dow Action Committee against chemical and biological warfare, Morris Kight turned to the struggle for homosexual rights. Founder of the Gay Community Services Center in Los Angeles, Kight later recalled: "I felt emancipated when I marched in the first antiwar rally in San Francisco on March 15, 1967."[49] Groups that once had concentrated their efforts on fighting homosexual exclusion from the military sometimes found themselves working even harder to prevent men from being inducted. When inductions surged after the 1968 Tet offensive, Don

Slater's Los Angeles-based Committee to Fight Exclusion of Homosexuals from the Armed Forces blasted the military for its blatant hypocrisy: even as it declared homosexuals unfit for service, the army drafted men it knew to be gay simply to fill manpower quotas.[50]

Nowhere was the war's radicalizing effect on homosexual politics more evident than in a dramatic rift that opened between the Society for Individual Rights and the San Francisco Bay Area's first "Gay Liberation" group. Organized in the spring of 1969 (before the Stonewall uprising) by lovers Leo Laurence and Gale Whittington, the Committee for Homosexual Freedom (CHF) adopted a militant political style characteristic of other late-1960s liberation groups. Though he did not fit the standard profile of the counterculture rebel, the thirty-six-year-old Laurence identified with the New Left and hip culture. In 1968 he covered the Democratic convention in Chicago as a reporter and identified with the antiwar protesters clubbed by police.[51] After Chicago, Laurence went to work for an alternative newspaper in the East Bay, the *Berkeley Barb,* and was hired to edit *Vector,* SIR's newsletter. In both publications, Laurence bluntly criticized the "timid" leadership of SIR, whom he ridiculed as "a bunch of middle-class, uptight, bitchy old queens." When he and Whittington appeared, stripped to the waist and embracing, on the *Barb's* front page, Whittington lost his job at States Steamship Lines, and Laurence was relieved of his editorial duties at the Society for Individual Rights.[52]

In April, the two men formed the CHF and organized a picket outside Whittington's former employer. Quickly the CHF found itself in the vanguard of homosexual groups forming partnerships with antiwar activists. That spring, members of the CHF conducted weekly business at The Cabaret, a Movement hangout in San Francisco on whose "colorfully tawdry premises," according to one Gay Liberationist, "for the first time in the homosexual freedom movement [a] true integration of homosexuals and heterosexuals occurred." When The Cabaret closed in the summer of 1969, the CHF moved its meetings to the Haight Street office of the War Resisters League (WRL), with whose activists the CHF had been collaborating from its inception. That spring, the WRL joined the States Steamship picket line and mailed CHF literature to its members. Shortly thereafter, the CHF joined the War Resisters League in a picket line at Safeway supermarkets, an event that Gay Liberationists viewed as "a small but significant step toward joining the [larger] Movement."[53]

Mingling with antiwar activists on picket lines and in Movement hangouts, San Francisco's CHF aspired to move gay politics out of the relatively insular world of the homophile organizations and into the rushing currents of 1960s radicalism. Even before Stonewall, the elements of a new phase in homosexual liberation were present among this small cadre committed to "fucking for peace" and "joining the Movement." Whereas the city's homophile groups had opted to exclude youth while accommodating a wide spectrum of political commitments among its members, the youthful members of the Committee for Homosexual Freedom did not seek to accommodate a wide spectrum of opinion: the group aligned itself closely with the antiwar movement and other youth-driven agendas. Members of the CHF began to articulate a new perspective on sexual identity, including the point of view that homosexual liberation was inextricably linked to a larger process of social transformation. At the beginning of 1969, only a marginal group of homosexual militants endorsed this "revolutionist" approach; by year's end, Gay Liberation revolutionaries had overturned the homophile consensus. How did a radical perspective on gay identity politics move from the fringe of the homosexual rights movement to its center in a matter of months? The June Stonewall riot and October Vietnam Day Moratorium accelerated a process already in motion.

When the patrons of the Stonewall Inn resisted a routine raid by New York City police in the summer of 1969, they touched off a riot that has become, in D'Emilio's words, "a kind of queer shorthand for a larger historic phenomenon: 'the sixties.'"[54] Indeed, the Stonewall riot as a discrete event has claimed a remarkable hegemony in the history of the homosexual rights movement, a notoriety that far exceeds its power to explain Gay Liberation's rapid consolidation. To be sure, the remarkable news of gay rebellion in Greenwich Village spread like fire through the information networks of Movement activists.[55] Gays and lesbians in New York, imagining their struggle as an extension of third world wars for independence, organized themselves as the Gay Liberation Front (GLF), specifically invoking the National Liberation Fronts of Algeria and Vietnam.[56] The news of gay rebellion on the East Coast inspired West Coast homosexuals: soon afterward, Bay Area students formed their own Gay Liberation Fronts on college campuses including the University of California at Berkeley and San Francisco State. But Stonewall did not touch off San Francisco riots, nor did it occupy a uniquely privileged place in political discourse on the West Coast. In fact, the first time large numbers of gay people took to San Francisco's streets was not in June 1969 but months later, as participants in an antiwar demonstration.

As part of the Vietnam Day Moratorium held on October 15, 1969, a group calling itself Gay Liberation Theater (GLT) made its debut on the University of California campus. Performing in front of several hundred Berkeley undergraduates, the gay "freaks" of GLT presented the original play "No Vietnamese Ever Called Me a Queer." On the same day that Stanford University's Susan Haldeman (daughter of Nixon's chief of staff) and Peter Ehrlichman (son of the President's chief domestic adviser) joined thousands of other students nationwide in opposition to the war, GLT declared it "queer, unnatural and perverse" to send soldiers to Vietnam "while we torment, rape, jail and murder men for loving their brothers here." The brainchild of Konstantin Berlandt, former editor of the campus newspaper, GLT provoked the crowd's response by explicitly connecting the repression of homosexual Americans to the suppression of third world revolutions. "If Ladybird [Johnson] had been a better lay," GLT proclaimed, "we might not be fucking Vietnam. Sexual repression is basic, sexual revolution is essential."[57]

For the members of GLT and the allied Committee for Homosexual Freedom, one thing was self-evident: to be a gay activist in 1969 meant to be against the Vietnam War.[58] Although the words "homophile" and "Gay Liberation" are no longer used to describe the spectrum of positions represented by today's gay rights organizations, in 1969 that distinction was central to Gay Liberation's self-definition.[59] Decisions made by San Francisco's homophile organizations neither to endorse nor participate in the Vietnam Day Moratorium incensed Gay Liberationists. "Paradoxically," declared CHF's Whittington one week before October's protest march, "the enemy of gay progress is now the up-tight, authoritarian bureaucracy of SIR."[60] Gay Liberationists (seen as naïve and confrontational by veterans of the homophile movement) lambasted the Society for Individual Rights as a "Society for Idle Rap."[61] Withholding its official endorsement of the Vietnam Day Moratorium, SIR held an open membership meeting on October 15 to which the public was invited; gay folksinger Don Burton was scheduled to perform. That evening, political differences between homophile veterans and Gay Liberationists erupted in a familiar High Sixties drama.

When Don Burton took the stage at SIR, he was already something of a local celebrity in the San Francisco counterculture. The charismatic Burton was a native of Torrance, California, a town thirty miles south of Los Angeles where napalm was manufactured. Inspired in his youth by the music of Joan Baez, Burton aspired to become an antiwar folksinger. Later he recalled: "[I]n the middle of it all, I felt empty....I was singing about peace, when I was sick to my stomach with fear...the fear every homosexual learns." On one occasion Burton was performing at a meeting of the Elk's Club when he diverged from his antiwar repertoire. To the Elks' astonishment, Burton declared his homosexuality and proceeded to deliver what he considered his "first honest performance." When he finished the last stanza of a gay protest song, the audience rose to a standing ovation. After that performance Burton began singing in Hollywood's gay bars and clubs, where he earned a reputation as "the Joan Baez of the Gay World." A romance with CHF cofounder Leo Laurence, whom Burton met one Sunday in a gay Los Angeles church, brought the folksinger to San Francisco and, subsequently, to SIR's auditorium the night of the Moratorium.[62]

What happened next in San Francisco illustrates how disagreements over the war inflamed a generational conflict between gay "freaks" and established homophile groups, as Gay Liberation declared war on the homophile movement and condemned its political reticence. On a cue from Burton, the Gay Liberation Theater altered the evening's agenda by rushing the stage. After their brief performance received scattered applause from a bewildered audience, the meeting deteriorated into a volley of recriminations between irate SIR members and inflamed Gay Liberationists. Don Burton resumed the stage, charging SIR with attempting to co-opt the radical thrust of Gay Liberation, before inviting those assembled to join him in a walkout. In the street Burton and other Liberationists rallied against SIR. As cameras flashed, several men burned their SIR membership cards in a ritual reminiscent of antidraft protests.[63] Gay Liberation's political theater made use of a familiar set of rhetorical gestures and disruptive tactics favored by the counterculture. But the hyperbole and recriminations dramatized an important difference between hippies and homophiles. At the heart of escalating disputes between the two groups were very different understandings of the meaning of gay identity.

A countercultural ethos of radical antimilitarism was central to the creation of a specifically "gay" identity. For Gay Liberationists, homosexual acts were revolutionary acts: to claim a gay identity meant to rebel against the very system waging war in Vietnam. Almost universally, "liberated" gays denounced the American intervention as an effect of the same repressive apparatus that alienated homosexuals from their own desires. Jim Rankin, a Gay Liberationist from Berkeley known by the alias "Elijah," declared alienation from one's body to be "the first imperialism." "For this reason," he concluded, "we gay (powerless) males must of necessity of our condition be anti-war, and anti-imperialist. We are already a conquered territory."[64] Moreover, being gay meant rejecting social norms of masculinity and coming to terms with "the woman in one's self." "That's what it means to be a faggot," declared Elijah on Berkeley's KPFA radio, "to be a man without balls, a man who is not a man." As a politics of identity, Gay Liberation construed sexual orientation as so fundamental to one's personality that it necessarily entailed particular political commitments and an oppositional relation to conventional norms of masculinity. Exclusion from the military or federal civil service meant little to Gay Liberationists, for whom the Vietnam-bound soldier was the antithesis of "be[ing] a faggot."[65]

To be sure, homophile men had also felt constrained by conventional norms of masculinity, but as a group they had not defied those norms as strenuously and as publicly. No doubt, the social imperative to conform had suppressed many "queer" expressions of gender. A March 1967 article in the *Citizens News* once suggested that "[whereas] the hippie glories in his rejection and frankly could not be less interested [in the opinion of others]; the homosexual is sensitive about society's rejection of him and strives for that respectability."[66] For homophile men, homosexual identity was neither in conflict with certain conventional forms of masculine identification nor incompatible with military service. Even at the height of the Vietnam War, *Vector* magazine reinforced conventional images of masculinity as it fed readers' fantasies about men in uniform. Pictured on one of its covers was a wholesome muscled soldier, his chest pinned with medals, who according to the caption had "just returned from Vietnam." This kind of erotica not only reinforced conventional images of masculinity; it reflected homophiles' persistent attempts to *depoliticize* the Vietnam War, to keep it from becoming a divisive political issue for homosexual men.

Antiwar Organizing as Identity Politics

Gay Liberation's alignment with 1960s radicalism found its highest expression in the culture of antiwar protest. Here the correlative radical imperatives of coming-out-as-gay and opposing-the-Vietnam-War could be realized simultaneously in political practice: antiwar demonstrations were in fact instrumental in bringing homosexual politics out of the closet and into the streets. In sheer numbers, antiwar-connected Gay Liberation events dwarfed even the largest of the homophile actions held before 1969. Shrewd organizing tactics accounted in large part for the high turnout of gay-identified protesters at major peace marches. In San Francisco, Gay Liberationists planned parties, rallies, and conferences to coincide with major antiwar mobilizations; at antiwar rallies Gay Liberation groups circulated flyers and petitions, made speeches, and sought alliances with other segments of the Movement. By piggybacking their protests on antiwar events, Gay Liberationists insured not only a reassuring strength-in-numbers and the partial anonymity of a crowd, which were conducive to coming out. They guaranteed themselves a relatively welcoming and open-minded audience as well.[67] Indeed the radical phase of Gay Liberation flowered in the shadow of the antiwar movement.

In the High Sixties, Gay Liberation endorsed a worldview that characterized the nonparticipation of homosexuals in the American military as a positive good. Its critique of military service consisted of several interrelated assertions: (1) *It is politically and morally inadmissible to pursue the right to serve in the military.* Not only did Gay Liberationists demand the immediate exemption of all homosexuals from the draft; they rejected long-standing homophile calls for "the equal right of Homosexuals to be drafted and serve in the Armed Forces" as "giv[ing] aid and comfort to the war machine of imperialist Amerika."[68] (2) *War is the result of socialization to*

conventionally masculine roles; both are inherently alien and oppressive to gay men.
Gay Liberationists viewed war as a game in which men were forced to "play
a 'Macho' role" in order to "prove [their] masculinity." "As homosexuals,"
argued a Gay May Day Tribe in 1971, "it is especially ludicrous to ape
this non-homosexual role playing."[69] In the Bay Area, Gay Liberationists
Nick Benton and Jim Rankin made the case for an "effeminist" ethos of
anti-imperialism in a series of manifestos drawing on feminist discourse
and Fanon's analysis of Third World liberation.[70] (3) *Imperialism and other
forms of domination are extensions of heterosexuality and/or repressed homosexuality.* Gay Liberation attributed the Vietnam War to white heterosexual male
"fantasies of domination." Homosexual self-loathing explained why "[m]
any high ranking militarists [were] homo."[71] (4) *Homosexuality itself is antiwar, antiestablishment, and anti-imperialist from an objective political perspective.*
Gay Liberationist Jim Rankin explained why gay men "must of necessity
of [their] condition be anti-war, and anti-imperialist." Such claims ranged,
however, from Rankin's elaborate theories of self-determination to the
unelaborated assertion that "homosexual acts are revolutionary acts."[72]

After claiming the political stage both literally and figuratively the night
of the Vietnam Day Moratorium, Gay Liberation looked to future antiwar
events as occasions to mobilize a local constituency. At a November 15
march sponsored by the New Mobilization Committee, for instance, the
Committee for Homosexual Freedom hoped to "impress homosexuality on the minds of straight revolutionaries as a legitimate social issue"
while collecting signatures in the park on a fair-employment petition.[73]
After a Gay Liberation party held the night before in Berkeley, four hundred people met in San Francisco the next morning, some with mimeographed flyers, others with signs, and lined up behind a large banner
reading "Homosexuals Against the War."[74] At such events Gay Liberation
achieved an important display of solidarity alongside other segments of
the antiwar movement. At the same time, antiwar demonstrations could
be sites of controversy where ideological tensions within Gay Liberation
(between lesbian feminists and male Gay Liberationists, for example) were
exposed or enacted. During a speech by Black Panther David Hilliard,
for instance, some Gay Liberationists joined other pacifists in shouting
Hilliard down, while others raised a clenched fist in defiant salute.[75] As
one faction upheld the radical ideal of Movement solidarity, another registered its principled objection to masculine aggression and chauvinistic
violence.[76]

Despite their occasional disagreements, Gay Liberationists were
committed to the pursuit of public visibility: they believed strongly in
coming-out-as-gay as a political means and end. Whereas older men generally preferred to socialize in bars, Gay Liberationists preferred dance
parties, love-ins, and public "happenings."[77] On November 15 the CHF's

Whittington expressed some chagrin that a number of his comrades had avoided the gay contingent so as not to identify themselves as gay. He compared the openness of Gay Liberation's tactics at the peace march with what he considered the furtiveness of "Gay ghetto bars," which he dismissed as "walk-in closets."[78] Since antiwar events were ideal occasions for Gay Liberationists to speak out and be acknowledged, gay activists lobbied antiwar organizers to be included on speakers lists. On October 31, 1970, Nick Benton of the Berkeley GLF became the first Gay Liberation spokesman to address a major antiwar demonstration. When rally monitors attempted to prevent folksinger Don Burton from singing after Benton's speech, gay freaks started a disruptive chant, forcing monitors to relent.[79] As eager partners in the antiwar coalition, Gay Liberationists insisted they be allotted time at the microphone. By doing so, they facilitated their own integration into the antiwar movement.

Gay antiwar organizing reached its climax in April 1971, when the People's Coalition for Peace and Justice (PCPJ) and National Peace Action Coalition (NPAC) sponsored simultaneous protests in Washington, D.C., and San Francisco. In the weeks leading up to April 24, Gay Liberation groups publicized the event in gay-oriented newspapers and arranged local accommodations for out-of-town visitors. Activists such as Nick Benton reached out to gay readers by writing articles for the *Berkeley Barb* and other alternative newspapers.[80] Community services such as the Peninsula Gay Switchboard, run on donations and staffed by volunteers, served as a clearinghouse for information about joining antiwar contingents. Even in the flood of new gay weeklies—the explicitly "nonpolitical" *Adz Gayzette,* for example, featuring bar guides, personal ads, and pictures of "Hunky Guys" undressing—gay readers found telephone numbers to contact for information about the April demonstration.[81] One number directed gay men to Emmaus House, a nonprofit community center offering group therapy and social events that had arranged an overnight "crash pad" for visitors at a nearby Catholic church.[82]

Planning for April 24 involved not only coordination among local institutions, but also collaboration among Gay Liberationists from across California and the United States. Emmaus House members attended organizing sessions and sat on committees with other West Coast activists including students from campus-based Gay Liberation groups. San Franciscans anticipated the arrival of sizable delegations from cities as far-flung as Sacramento, Fresno, and San Diego and as far away as Portland and Seattle. The Los Angeles GLF coordinated rides for what was expected to be "the biggest show of force of the Gay Liberation movement yet": one GLF flyer urged southern Californians to "Truck on up to San Francisco" for April 24.[83] Moreover, Gay Liberation groups in fourteen states and over fifty cities endorsed antiwar contingents. They collaborated in the drafting of "gay preambles" to a May Day "People's Peace Treaty," the PCPJ's formal declaration of solidarity with the people of Southeast Asia. In Berkeley, a committee calling itself "Gay May Day West" crafted its own text. In the name of Gay Liberation, Gay May Day West rejected the "masculine ideology of war and conquest" and repudiated "[white male] power over peoples of the Fourth and Third World."[84] On both coasts, Gay Liberationists broke with homophile liberalism by adopting a strong public stance on an issue other than civil rights for homosexuals and by making radical declarations on behalf of all gay men.[85]

A flurry of organizing activity occurred on both coasts. In Washington, D.C., Gay May Day Tribes arranged housing for out-of-town visitors and handed out buttons reading "May Day Is Gay Day."[86] The Student Mobilization Committee (SMC), an organ of the Young Socialists, made a Gay Liberation contingent one of its top priorities.[87] At the grassroots, members of the San Francisco GLF distributed leaflets, venturing even into the downtown gay bars whose patrons they had often criticized as conservative "closet queens." At The Trap, a Tenderloin bar with a "dingy, locker-room" atmosphere inviting "frantic, blatant cruising," nervous GLF activists entered in a broad, determined phalanx, distributing flyers quickly from back to front. Continuing their rounds, the group left flyers with bathhouse desk clerks and stopped to educate cruising "street queens." Some men with whom they spoke had never heard of the Gay Liberation Front. One patron at The Trap asked whether "Gay People Against the War and Sexism" meant the GLF was against war and sex; another man asked about AA groups for homosexuals. "We finished up on Polk Street," the activists reported, "after the bars had closed, leafleting the solitary figures pacing the sidewalks in the drizzle still searching for someone to spend the rest of the night with."[88]

April 24 was a watershed in gay organizing. An estimated three thousand people turned out for the gay march in San Francisco, the largest Gay Liberation demonstration yet held on the West Coast.[89] On Friday evening, three hundred people—including the androgynous Cockettes, a local "genderfuck" performance group—attended an Emmaus House dance; the next morning, thousands rallied at Union Square and Civic Center before parading to Golden Gate Park. As public spectacle, the San Francisco parade set a new standard of visibility for West Coast gays. Lavender armbands and "Gay Is Good" buttons identified participants, as did lavender Viet Cong flags.[90] Signs reading "Pull Out Now Dick" skewered Richard Nixon in the raunchy idiom of homosexual camp. And a gay male aesthetic informed the musical selections blaring from a Gay Liberation Front sound truck: arm in arm, gay men paraded through the streets to "Good Ship Lollipop" and the Triumphal March from *Aida*. Later that evening, activists met in the Basement Hall of Sacred Heart

Church for a West Coast Gay Liberation Conference, where they agreed to conduct a California Gay Liberation Symposium in Los Angeles the weekend of Hollywood's Christopher Street West parade.[91]

Antiwar parades put Gay Liberation on the map of San Francisco politics. As participants in the antiwar coalition, Gay Liberationists asserted a collective identity as gay people alongside members of other politically recognized interest groups. One flyer mapping the April 24 parade route indicated Civic Center Plaza as the "Gay People's" rally site. In November, parade organizers distributed a map designating rendezvous sites for "GI," "Student," "Women," "Raza," "Ecology," "Native American," and "Gay" contingents.[92] And while homosexual men differed in their degree of commitment to antiwar politics, Gay Liberationists believed the two movements to be inextricably linked. They agreed with NPAC's Dan Rosenshine when he suggested that "Third World and gay people are especially oppressed by the military system and by the war." One protester declared: "Coming out publicly as a gay person is a great act against the war itself."[93] For many, simply marching in an antiwar parade among Gay Liberationists was psychologically liberating. Said one man: "You don't know what it means for a homosexual who has spent his whole life actively trying to hide his identity, to march down an avenue in broad daylight waving a gay lib banner."[94]

By coming out against the war, gay people overcame private feelings of isolation. At the same time, they became influential actors in public life. Two gay activists from Oakland commented that April 24 had "demonstrated to ourselves and everyone else…by our numbers that we are, next to blacks, the largest minority in this country." Nor was the significance of "an orderly and well organized [gay] bloc" missed by the editors of the *Bay Area Reporter*. "It is hoped," wrote the *B.A.R.,* "that these same persons who marched proudly as Gay People [on April 24] also march proudly to their polling places in the Fall and vote."[95] Though wearied by years of antiwar coalition politics, Gay Liberationists were buoyed by a sense of their collective strength as an identity-based "community." "In retrospect," said some Gay Liberationists, "the leafleting of the Gay community beforehand and the Gay Dance the following night are more important to the creation of a strong, independent Gay movement than participation in yet another ineffectual peace march." Typical as well were the comments of Doug Brown of Emmaus House, who remarked that gay antiwar protesters had exhibited "the true Emmaus spirit, [through] the building of a dignified and joyous Gay community."[96] For many gay men, the rhetoric of community corresponded with their experience of a new social reality.

By 1971, organizations such as the Student Mobilization Committee had begun to recognize the untapped potential of the gay community, and some gay men were already flexing their muscles in electoral politics.[97] Tenderloin activist and *Vanguard* editor Keith St. Clare (who had once urged readers to "Fuck for Peace") was nominated for State Assembly in February 1970 by the California Peace and Freedom Party, which adopted a Homosexual Liberation plank calling for an end to "all laws and practices that discriminate against any person because of actions expressive of their sexual natures."[98] Gay Liberationists held political rallies in San Francisco to support candidates for mayor, sheriff, and city supervisor.[99] One group, the Gay Activists Alliance, hosted a successful "candidates night" attended by all but one of the city's mayoral contenders.[100] Homophile agitator Frank Kameny, cofounder of the Washington Mattachine, became the first openly homosexual person to run for Congress when he sought election as the District of Columbia delegate to the House of Representatives in 1971. Urging a "Vote for Personal Freedom," Kameny called for an immediate withdrawal of troops from Southeast Asia and an end to the "oppressive and discriminatory draft system."[101] On the West Coast, liberal antiwar Democrat George McGovern met with SIR's political director to discuss gay rights.[102]

As Gay Liberationists found a bolder public voice in the context of antiwar activism, they grew impatient with coalition politics. "We're planning marches of our own," said two Bay Area activists in the summer of 1971, "expressions of our gay militancy, Gay-organized, Gay-directed, against the war and against our own oppression." At the same time that gay men became aware of their own power, old doubts about weighing in on "nongay" issues began to resurface. SIR, which from the outset had refrained from aligning itself with antiwar radicalism, continued throughout the war to question the utility of cross-issue alliances.[103] But even Gay Liberationists who had been active in the antiwar movement began to reassess that commitment. Disagreements within the antiwar movement became increasingly apparent as gays and others bridled under the leadership offered by socialist organizations such as the National Peace Action Coalition. Following the April 1971 peace march, the GLF's Nick Benton, an antiwar partisan, conceded that "had everyone [at the march] not had their heads pointed forward toward the common issue of the war, it wouldn't have taken long for conflicts to emerge among obviously incompatible groups."[104] In the 1970s an independent politics of gay identity emerged from the scattering elements of the 1960s antiwar coalition.

Contingency, Identity, and Solidarity

The dream of an "independent Gay movement" in the 1970s expressed a wish among many Gay Liberationists for a community of homosexual solidarity removed from the frustrations and constraints of antiwar coalition politics. The movement for gay rights would indeed become relatively freestanding, due in no small part to the disintegration of the antiwar coalition by the end of the Vietnam War. In another sense, however, the dream of an independent gay movement would remain a dream. If the gay rights movement of the 1970s would no longer aspire to "fuck for peace" or "join the Movement," it would remain deeply situated in the surrounding matrix of American political culture and therefore subject to powerful social forces originating outside the gay community. Politics became personal for homosexual men in the High Sixties in part because the state inquired insistently into the sexual lives of American men in the process of determining whom to send to Vietnam. The politicization of homosexuality in the era of Vietnam reveals the extent to which sexual identity and political solidarity were configured not only in relation to established institutions such as the military but within the contingent parameters of the surrounding political culture.

In the 1980s Jeffrey Escoffier offered an important analysis of the political emergence of homosexuals and the politicization of sexual identity. "The sex/gender system is not an isolated system of institutions and practices," he argued, "it interacts with the economy and the state as well as other social ensembles such as those devoted to racial formation, class structure, or generations."[105] Escoffier's groundbreaking essay was oddly silent on the Vietnam War and antiwar movement, making little more than passing reference to these contemporary events. But to understand how homosexuality became not merely a social fact but a political identity in the United States, I believe it is essential to know why many gay people chose to oppose the Vietnam War *as gay people*. Not even the most intimate aspects of life escaped the vortex of Vietnam, and sexual identity offered many Americans a powerful way to understand the relationship between politics and personal experience. Seeing Gay Liberation in the context of the Vietnam War therefore helps explain why and in what way homosexuality came to function as a political identity in the late 1960s and early 1970s.

The unique configuration of sexual identity and political solidarity that powered the radical phase of Gay Liberation derived much of its meaning and force from the contemporary culture of antiwar protest. Situating Gay Liberation in the context of the antiwar movement helps explain why (according to D'Emilio) "politics came to infuse the very essence of [gay] souls" in the High Sixties.[106] First, the culture of antiwar protest created favorable conditions for a dramatically heightened publicity in the practice of homosexual politics.[107] Homosexuals had once occupied a sad and sordid underworld in the American imagination. During antiwar protests, heterosexuals encountered untold numbers of "out" gay men for the first

time in urban public spaces. Second, Vietnam-era demonstrations transformed the political culture of the homosexual rights movement as Gay
Liberationists appropriated the antidisciplinary tactics of the counterculture in the context of antiwar parades. With chants of "one, two, three,
four, we don't want your macho war" modulating easily into "two, four,
six, eight, gay is just as good as straight," Gay Liberation expanded the
repertoire of tactics available to the homosexual rights movement. Finally,
antiwar protest sustained a high level of solidarity among an extended network of gay radicals in cities across the United States, a solidarity based on
a decidedly "revolutionist" construction of gay identity.

Histories of the 1960s tend to assume that civil rights and other protest movements "inspired" Gay Liberationists in self-evident ways to
"embrace" an identity that had been privately acknowledged but previously hidden from public view. In reality, a socially constructed persona
was central to the initiation of Gay Liberation as a mass protest movement;
Gay Liberationists constituted an identity as revolutionist-homosexuals in
the culture of antiwar protest. Even as some (no doubt large) proportion
of homosexual men quietly eschewed the more radical ambitions of Gay
Liberation, the signifier *gay* nonetheless attached itself to them: a person
of homosexual orientation, whatever his or her politics or self-perception,
soon discovered in the High Sixties that he or she actually possessed a
"gay" identity. To be sure, the Gay Liberation movement offered many
men a powerful way to understand the relationship between politics and
personal experience. Even as Gay Liberationists spoke out loudly on behalf
of all gay men, they could not and did not preclude alternative understandings of the relationship between sexual identity and political solidarity.

At the height of the Vietnam War, some gay men continued to articulate and defend an alternative political discourse advancing distinctly
"homophile" objectives and ideals. In San Francisco, for instance, the
Society for Individual Rights continued to contest discrimination in federal employment and to act as advocates for homosexual veterans and service members, even as Gay Liberationists criticized SIR's preference for
working within established institutions.[108] Two incompatible positions
had thus become clearly established in the discourse on gay rights, one
seeking to uphold the High Sixties ideals of Gay Liberation, another seeking to reinstate a politics identified with mainstream professionalism and
liberal pragmatism. "Homophile" and "Gay Liberation" discourses offered
alternative visions of gay politics. Each nevertheless advanced a distinctly
politicized understanding of gay identity.

A dialectic between homophile and Gay Liberation approaches defined
only one axis of the 1970s gay rights movement, however. Advancing a
depoliticized configuration of gay solidarity, the cultural politics of gay pride

offered a third alternative to the homophile and Gay Liberation agendas and to the ideological antagonisms associated with the High Sixties culture of protest. In the 1970s, Gay Pride rallies and Gay Freedom Day parades commemorating Stonewall took the place of antiwar demonstrations as the principal venue for public expressions of gay solidarity. Hoping to include "radical as well as conservative Gay organizations and all of those in between," organizers of the San Francisco parade scrupulously insisted on the subordination of political objectives to the creation of a nonconfrontational forum "for all Gay persons to re-affirm their various life styles and take pride in their homosexuality."[109] "We are confident," announced boosters in advance of the 1975 parade, "that participants in the fair will participate in a non-sectarian manner, focusing on the theme of gay solidarity and unity."[110] Whereas antiwar demonstrations had tapped the radical gay enthusiasm of the High Sixties, Gay Freedom Day parades embraced the depoliticized zeitgeist of the "life style"-affirming 1970s.

Gay Pride parades enlarged the circle of the gay-identified community in the 1970s. The cultural politics of gay pride thus succeeded in extending the boundaries of gay solidarity beyond the relatively circumscribed homophile and Gay Liberation communities of "the Sixties." At the same time, by subordinating politics to the celebration of identity, the cultural politics of gay pride tended to create solidarity without a purpose larger than the celebration of gay identity itself. No single configuration of gay solidarity—homophile liberalism, Gay Liberation, or the cultural politics of gay pride—emerged after Gay Liberation as a dominant paradigm for the gay rights movement. When a technical sergeant named Leonard Matlovich came out to his superior officer in 1975 to defy the military's ban on homosexuals and to contest his discharge from the Air Force, his case appeared to highlight not only a deep ambivalence toward politics but a deep dissensus in the 1970s gay rights movement.[111] In San Francisco, one faction of gay activists refused to defend Matlovich because he had served in the Vietnam War.[112] When the National Gay Task Force hosted a Fire Island champagne party on his behalf, partygoers donated only eighty-five dollars to his legal fund.[113]

Homophile politics had addressed the welfare of the stigmatized homosexual soldier; Gay Liberation politics addressed the problems of the antiwar draft resister but echoed the Cold War military doctrine that declared homosexuality incompatible with military service. Matlovich might therefore seem an appropriately ambivalent icon for the post–1960s gay rights movement: his coming out against the military ban seemed to occupy a political no-man's-land between homophile liberalism and Gay Liberation. An alternative candidate for the role of 1970s gay-rights icon is Alexander Briley, who wore the "military man" costume as part of the

Village People's six-member gay male disco act.[114] Whereas Matlovich and the politics of military service called attention to persistent disagreements within the gay rights movement over the objectives of gay solidarity, the Village People found mainstream acceptance in macho drag while establishing a beachhead in the popular-culture consensus. "Where can you begin to make your dreams all come true?" asked the Village People in their 1979 hit single "In the Navy." As gay men in real uniforms struggled in the wake of Gay Liberation to overturn the military's ban on homosexuals, they faced hostility and suspicion inside the gay rights movement and beyond it.

Notes

1. Tom Wells, *The War Within: America's Battle over Vietnam* (Berkeley: University of California Press, 1994); Fred Halstead, *Out Now!: A Participant's Account of the American Movement Against the Vietnam War* (New York: Monad Press, 1978); Nancy Zaroulis and Gerald Sullivan, *Who Spoke Up? American Protest Against the War in Vietnam, 1963–1975* (Garden City, NY: Doubleday, 1984); and Charles DeBenedetti, *An American Ordeal: The Antiwar Movement of the Vietnam Era* (Syracuse, NY: Syracuse University Press, 1990).
2. Some writers have commented on connections between the Vietnam War and Gay Liberation, but that relationship has never been discussed in depth. See Donn Teal, *The Gay Militants* (New York: Stein and Day, 1971); John D'Emilio, *Sexual Politics, Sexual Communities: The Making of a Homosexual Minority in the United States, 1940–1970*, 2nd ed. (1983; Chicago: University of Chicago Press, 1998); Randy Shilts, *Conduct Unbecoming: Lesbians and Gays in the U.S. Military, Vietnam to the Persian Gulf* (New York: St. Martin's Press, 1993).
3. In the past decade, American historians have given us vivid pictures of homosexual life before Gay Liberation, yet the Gay Liberation movement itself remains poorly understood. See Allan Bérubé, *Coming Out Under Fire: The History of Gay Men and Women in World War Two* (New York: Free Press, 1990); George Chauncey, *Gay New York: Gender, Urban Culture, and the Making of the Gay Male World, 1890–1940* (New York: Basic Books, 1994); Lillian Faderman, *Odd Girls and Twilight Lovers: A History of Lesbian Life in Twentieth-Century America* (New York: Columbia University Press, 1991); and John D'Emilio's groundbreaking *Sexual Politics*.
4. Scholars routinely overlook the Vietnam-era antiwar protests as formative demonstrations of gay pride and solidarity. In one recent book that is part of a series in gay and lesbian studies, Lauren Berlant reiterates a commonly held but mistaken view; she claims that the "genealogy" of Queer Nation's politics "extends from the Gay Pride parades of the 1970s, when, for the first time, gay bodies organized into a visible public ritual." Lauren Berlant, *The Queen of America Goes to Washington City: Essays on Sex and Citizenship* (Durham, NC: Duke University Press, 1997), 159.
5. Letters to the Editor, San Jose State College newspaper, no date [1971], Box 1, File 29, Charles Thorpe Papers, San Francisco Public Library. The *Advocate* described the homosexual contingent at the San Francisco March as "[o]ne of the largest concentrations of gay power ever assembled" and "[the] third largest gay demonstration yet held, surpassed only by the Christopher Street parade in New York and the recent Albany March [of March 14]." For the April 1971 protest, see D. Beardslee and J. Kepner, "Thousands Protest War: Gay Lib Marches in S.F.," *Advocate*, May 26–June 8, 1971, 1, 6; Tom Wells, *The War Within*, 497–498; Fred Halstead, *Out Now!*, 611–617.

6. For example, see the paragraph on Gay Liberation in Maurice Isserman and Michael Kazin, *America Divided: The Civil War of the 1960s* (New York: Oxford University Press, 2000), 275–276.

7. For other recent overviews, David Farber, *The Age of Great Dreams: America in the 1960s* (New York: Hill and Wang, 1994); David Farber, ed., *The Sixties: From Memory to History* (Chapel Hill, NC: University of North Carolina Press, 1994); David Burner, *Making Peace with the 60s* (Princeton: Princeton University Press, 1996); Howard Brick, *Age of Contradiction: American Thought and Culture in the 1960s* (New York: Twayne, 1998). For perspectives on the New Left, see Van Gosse, *Where the Boys Are: Cuba, Cold War America and the Making of a New Left* (New York: Verso, 1993); and Doug Rossinow, *The Politics of Authenticity: Liberalism, Christianity, and the New Left in America* (New York: Columbia University Press, 1998).

8. D'Emilio, *Sexual Politics*, 4, 231–239.

9. Studies have begun to describe an array of complex interactions between and among the various constitutive elements of the 1960s, movements and constituencies that have often been viewed in isolation from one another. For interaction among different elements of the 1960s, Sara Evans, *Personal Politics: The Roots of Women's Liberation in the Civil Rights Movement and the New Left* (New York: Vintage Books, 1979); David Farber, "The Counterculture and the Antiwar Movement," and Alice Echols, "'Women Power' and Women's Liberation: Exploring the Relationship Between the Antiwar Movement and the Women's Liberation Movement," both in *Give Peace a Chance: Exploring the Vietnam Antiwar Movement*, ed. M. Small and W. D. Hoover (Syracuse, NY: Syracuse University Press, 1992). For an original study of the relationship between postwar lesbian and gay communities, see Marc Stein, *City of Sisterly and Brotherly Loves: Lesbian and Gay Philadelphia, 1945–1972* (Chicago: University of Chicago Press, 2000).

10. For a New York–centered argument along similar lines, Terence Kissack, "Freaking Fag Revolutionaries: New York's Gay Liberation Front, 1969–1971," *Radical History Review* 62 (Spring 1995): 104–134.

11. On the transformation of political culture in the 1960s, Julie Stephens, *Anti-Disciplinary Protest: Sixties Radicalism and Postmodernism* (New York: Cambridge University Press, 1998). For a related discussion of a different period, Nan Enstad, "Fashioning Political Identities: Cultural Studies and the Historical Construction of Political Subjects," *American Quarterly* 50 (December 1998): 745–782.

12. D'Emilio, "Gay Politics, Gay Community: San Francisco's Experience," in *Making Trouble: Essays on Gay History, Politics, and the University* (New York: Routledge, 1993), 76–77; Bérubé, *Coming Out Under Fire*.

13. Dan Black, Gary Gates, Seth Sanders, and Lowell Taylor, "Demographics of the Gay and Lesbian Population in the United States: Evidence from Available Systematic Data Sources," *Demography* 37 (May 2000): 139–154.

14. Allan Bérubé has described how the Second World War gave rise to new homosexual communities and fostered the postwar homophile movement. "World War II was as crucial to these women and men," wrote Bérubé, "as the 1969 Stonewall Rebellion would be to a later generation." See Bérubé, "Marching to a Different Drummer: Lesbian and Gay GIs in World War II," in *Hidden from History: Reclaiming the Gay and Lesbian Past*, ed. M. Duberman, M. Vicinus, and G. Chauncey (New York: NAL Books, 1989), 384. For homophile politics, see D'Emilio, *Sexual Politics*, 63–70, 101–103; Neil Miller, *Out of the Past: Gay and Lesbian History from 1869 to the Present* (New York: Vintage Books, 1995), 333–339. Even before the homophile movement, a group of New York veterans formed the Veterans Benevolent Association, the first major membership organization for homosexuals. Its social events sometimes attracted up to five hundred men. D'Emilio, *Sexual Politics*, 32; Bérubé, *Coming Out Under Fire*, 249.

15. Bérubé, *Coming Out Under Fire*, 260–270.

16. H. Johnson, "And a Red Too…," *One*, September 1953, 2–3. *One* parodied the logic supporting the government's persecution of gays: "[C]ommunists are bad. Homosexuals are bad. Therefore communists are homosexuals." See also R. Noone, "You Are a Public Enemy," *One*, May 1953, 5–7, and M. Prentiss, "Are Homosexuals Security Risks?," *One*, Dec. 1955, 4–6.

17. Colin J. Williams and Martin S. Weinberg, *Homosexuals and the Military: A Study of Less Than Honorable Discharge* (New York: Harper & Row, 1971), 49, 181.

18. "The Homosexual in America," *Time*, January 21, 1966, 40–41; "Homosexuality in America," *Life,* June 26, 1964, 66–74.

19. "Public Registers Strong Disapproval of Nonconformity," *Washington Post,* September 27, 1965, A2. For a discussion of the "countersubversive" tradition in American politics, see Michael Rogin, *Ronald Reagan, the Movie, and Other Episodes in Political Demonology* (Berkeley: University of California Press, 1987).

20. *Vector,* February 1965, 6; *Ladder,* February 1963, 13; *Citizens News,* 4:14 (1965): 8. For a history of these and other publications, Rodger Streitmatter, *Unspeakable: The Rise of the Gay and Lesbian Press in America* (Boston: Faber and Faber, 1995).

21. For back-to-back chapters contrasting the East and West Coast scenes, see D'Emilio, *Sexual Politics*, 149–195.

22. Miller, *Out of the Past*, 349.

23. D'Emilio, *Sexual Politics*, 165.

24. *Ladder,* April 1966, 4; Minutes from 1966 National Planning Conference of Homophile Organizations (NACHO), (February 19, 1966); Lyon/Martin Papers, Gay and Lesbian Historical Society of Northern California; Larry Littlejohn, interview by Paul Gabriel, video recording, (San Francisco, September 17, 1996).

25. *Vector,* June 1966, 5; *Citizens News,* July 1966, 1; Larry Littlejohn interview; "Homosexuals to Demand Right to Serve Their Country," *Cruise News,* April 1966, 10. In *Citizens News,* July 1966, Guy Strait commented on the homophile strategy of protesting exclusion from the military: "It is difficult for many…to divorce the idea of the plight of the homosexual from national foreign policy" (1). Of interest is Strait's 1967 essay "What Is a Hippie?" in *"Takin' it to the streets": A Sixties Reader,* ed. Alexander Bloom and Wini Breines (New York: Oxford Univ. Press, 1995), 310–312.

26. Letters, *Mattachine Review* July 1966, 31.

27. D. Sanford, "Boxed In," *New Republic,* May 21, 1966, 8–9.

28. At the time, this dilemma was widely recognized. For example, see R.E.L. Masters, *The Homosexual Revolution* (New York: Julian Press, 1962), 132–139; "Viet Nam: Quandary for Homosexuals Up for Draft," *Town Talk,* January/February 1966, 1; "A Gay Guide: Beating the Draft," *Gay Sunshine,* January 1971, 12; and even a misinformed Dear Abby column in response to nineteen-year-old "Patriotic But Gay," repr. in W. Beardemphl and T. Parker, "The Dilemma of Being a Gay Soldier," *Vector,* April/May 1968, 5.

29. Flyer, "What Should I Do About the Draft?" SIR Community Services Committee, 1967–1968, Box 8, File 34, Social Protest Collection, Bancroft Library, Univ. of California, Berkeley, Calif.; *Vector,* May 1968, 22.

30. Memo, "Homosexuality: The Draft and Armed Forces," Draft Help, S.F., p. 1, Box 1, File 23, Charles Thorpe Papers.

31. Bérubé, *Coming Out Under Fire*, 228.

32. Shilts, *Conduct Unbecoming*, 64–68.

33. Guide to Draft Counseling prepared by Leonard Siegel, Stanford Anti-Draft Union, Mar. 1968, Box 2, File 7, Social Protest Collection.

34. Sherry Gershon Gottlieb, *Hell No, We Won't Go: Resisting the Draft During the Vietnam War* (New York: Viking, 1991), 104. Robinson was the only gay man Gottlieb interviewed who

actually received a deferment for being gay (105). Gottlieb notes: "There are no figures on how many of the men who got out for being homosexual were actually gay; but my impression while doing interviews for this volume is that the percentage of actual gays was very small. One draft counselor recalled, 'All of my clients who faked it got their exemptions, but they drafted the one fellow who was really gay'" (93).

35. For the Bay Area's reputation as a haven for draft resisters, see *S.F. Free Press,* Sept. 1969, 7; and *Gay Sunshine,* June/July 1971, 7. *S.F. Free Press* and the following publications can be found in the San Francisco Bay Area Gay and Lesbian Serial Collection, Doe Library, University of California, Berkeley, CA: *Agape and Action, Committee for Homosexual Freedom Newsletter, Dykes and Gorgons, Effeminist, I Am, Vanguard.*

36. Memo, "Homosexuality: The Draft and Armed Forces," 1–2.

37. Flyer, "Brief Notes on the Ways and Means of 'Beating' and Defeating the Draft," 2407 Fulton St., Berkeley, Calif., Box 1, File 30, Social Protest Collection.

38. "The Serviceman's Dilemma," *One,* January 1966, 22.

39. "Army Won't Believe He's Gay," *Advocate,* 14–27 April 1971, 14; "Lover, Lawyer Finally Convince Army He's Gay," *Advocate,* April 28–May 11, 1971, 9.

40. Gottlieb, *Hell No,* 105.

41. Lillian Faderman makes a similar argument in *Odd Girls and Twilight Lovers* about McCarthyite persecution, which she says inadvertently fostered a sense of homosexual identity even as it pushed some women deeper into the closet (190).

42. In 1967, San Francisco became the first major city to vote on a local measure calling for an end to the war. Larry Littlejohn of SIR was one of the signatories to a full-page ad urging passage of the measure. Other prominent endorsements from the homophile community included Al Alvarez, Herbert Donaldson, Dorr Jones, Bill Plath, Evander Smith, Guy Strait, and Chuck Thayer. *Vector,* November 1967, 11.

43. *Vector,* November 1967, 11. In a breach of homophile protocol, former SIR president Bill Beardemphl once compared Lyndon Johnson to the leader of Hells Angels. One angry letter to the editor accused SIR of political "extremism." "'[R]esponsible people' do not justify their actions by invective," the letter argued in defense of Johnson. See *Vector,* November 1965, 10; *Vector,* December 1965, 13.

44. Neil Miller quotes SIR's 1967 membership as twelve hundred (*Out of the Past,* 349), but statistics given in *Vector* magazine place the organization's membership at 581 in December 1966 and 850 in July 1968.

45. Not until 1971 did SIR members vote to lower the membership age to eighteen. *Vector* (July 1971): 38.

46. B. Hazelrigg, "The Youth Scene and S I R.," *Vector,* April 1970. For 1960s youth culture, see George Lipsitz, "Who'll Stop the Rain?: Youth Culture, Rock 'n' Roll, and Social Crises," in Farber, ed., *The Sixties,* 206–234.

47. D. Martin, "History of S.F. Homophile Groups," *Ladder,* October 1966, 13, 26; *Vanguard,* 1966 [first issue], 1–2; *Vanguard,* October 1966, 4–5.

48. *Vanguard* 1:5, 1967, 4; *Vanguard* 1:6, 1967, 20.

49. *Gay Pride* [S.F.], June 25, 1972, 1.

50. Shilts, *Conduct Unbecoming,* 66, 75.

51. Gay Liberationists gleefully appropriated the words of the chief government prosecutor in the Chicago Seven conspiracy trial, who referred to the protests as a "freaking fag revolution." Barry D. Adam, *The Rise of a Gay and Lesbian Movement,* rev. ed. (New York: Twayne, 1995), 84.

52. *Vector* April 1969, 11; *Berkeley Barb* April 11–17 1969, 11; D'Emilio, *Sexual Politics,* 230–31; Streitmatter, *Unspeakable,* 99–100; Teal, *Gay Militants,* 45–47.

53. *CHF Newsletter,* April 29, 1969, 2; *CHF Newsletter,* May 6, 1969, 2; *CHF Newsletter,* May 13, 1969, 1; *CHF Newsletter,* July 31, 1969, 1.

54. D'Emilio, "Afterword, 1998," *Sexual Politics*, 260. For Stonewall, Martin Duberman, *Stonewall* (New York: Dutton, 1993).
55. D'Emilio, "Gay Politics," 84–86.
56. For the New York origins of the GLF, see Martha Shelley's oral history in Eric Marcus, *Making History: The Struggle for Gay and Lesbian Equal Rights 1945–1990* (New York: HarperCollins, 1992), 175–186.
57. Wells, *War Within*, 371, 374; *Tribe,* October 10–16, 1969), 11; *Tribe*, October 24–30, 1969, 13; Flyer, "No Vietnamese Ever Called Me a Queer!" October 15, 1969, Box 8, File 21, Social Protest Collection; *Free Particle*, April 1970, Box 8, File 26, Social Protest Collection. For obscenity and incivility in 1960s protest, see Kenneth Cmiel, "The Politics of Civility," in Farber, ed., *The Sixties*, 263–290.
58. Carl Wittman expressed a minority opinion, arguing that the CHF should not commit itself to issues other than homosexual rights; he feared disagreements over Vietnam would tear the group apart. *CHF Newsletter*, April 22, 1969, p. 2. On sex and politics, Beth Bailey, "Sexual Revolution(s)," in Farber, ed., *The Sixties*, 235–262.
59. After 1969 the euphemistic *homophile* fell out of use. In 1971 the Society for Individual Rights claimed to be not only "inside the gay liberation movement," but "leaders in that movement." That same year a *Newsweek* report on "The Militant Homosexual" identified New York's Gay Activist Alliance and San Francisco's SIR as the "largest and most important of the gay lib groups." *Newsweek*, August 23, 1971, 47.
60. *Tribe*, October 10–16, 1969, 22.
61. *San Francisco Free Press*, October 16–31, 1969, 1; *S.F. Free Press*, November 1–14, 1969, 7; *Tribe*, October 10–16, 1969, 22.
62. "From Torrance With Love," *S.F. Free Press* (October 16–31, 1969), 11.
63. *S.F. Free Press*, November 1–14, 1969, 7; Teal, *Gay Militants*, 69–70.
64. *The Effeminist* (Fall 1971), 5.
65. "A Conversation between Cy Schoenfield and Elijah," KPFA radio, Berkeley, CA, September 1971, Box 8, File 36, Social Protest Collection; *Barb*, January 7–13, 1972, 10. For the use of "faggot" as an all-purpose put-down among Movement activists, see Kissack, "Freaking Fag Revolutionaries," 111–113.
66. *Citizens News*, March 1967, 9.
67. In *Out Now!* Fred Halstead comments: "It still wasn't easy in most places for gays to demonstrate by themselves. But on antiwar demonstrations during this period…they could come out in full force without fear of harassment and show themselves to be a significant part of the population" (612).
68. Flyer, "Resolution on the War and Draft passed May 4, 1970" [Gay Liberation Front, Berkeley, CA], Box 8, File 41, Social Protest Collection.
69. *Barb*, April 9–15, 1971, 6.
70. *The Effeminist*, May 1971, 1–2; "Our Bodies," *The Effeminist* (Fall 1971), 5.
71. *Tribe* January 9–15, 1970, 6; *Agape and Action*, October 28, 1970, 5.
72. Lesbian feminists framed the antimilitarist position in different terms. Whereas gay male effeminists denounced war as an expression of heteronormative *masculinity*, lesbian feminists defined themselves in opposition to a "*male* propensity for violence." "War is a male chess game, defined by males, initiated by males, and performed by males for male rewards," argued transsexual feminist Angela Keyes Douglas. "War will only be ended when feminist consciousness prevails on this planet." Condemning "prick-war politics," lesbian feminists linked their criticisms of American military aggression to the problem of male violence against women. "Certainly these senseless crimes in dark streets and lonely apartments," wrote one contributor to the *Ladder* in an essay on rape and domestic violence, "equal the atrocities at My Lai." "One indeed shudders," she continued, "to think what the Viet Nam veterans who are now stringing human ears on their gun belts will do for fun and games when they come home." "Almost every war waged on earth," declared one writer in the

Dykes and Gorgons collective, "was attempted gynocide under the guise of men killing men.... We are full in the midst of a war waged upon women." "Peace Banner Helps Sisters Bridge Sex," *Barb*, November 12–18, 1971, 7; "Gay Fem," *Barb*, May 12–18, 1972, 3; Clue Dennis, "Atrocities at Home: Who Speaks for Women?" *Ladder* 16:7–8, April/May 1972, 12; *Dykes and Gorgons*, Berkeley, CA, May–June 1973, 7.

73. *CHF Newsletter*, October 16, 1969, 1.

74. "Berkeley Gay Movement," *Tribe*, November 14–21, 1969, 25.

75. *Barb*, November 21–27, 1969, 5; *S.F. Free Press*, December 7–21, 1969, 8–9.

76. Eldridge Cleaver, Black Panther minister of information and field marshal, was notorious for calling James Baldwin a faggot and referring to King as Martin Luther Queen. It was Jean Genet who reportedly convinced Huey Newton to release an August 1970 statement endorsing Gay Liberation. Burner, *Making Peace*, 69–76; Kissack, "Freaking Fag Revolutionaries," 113, n. 27.

77. Students for Gay Power at the University of California held their first full-scale public dance (billed as "a revolutionary act") on May 22, 1970, in Berkeley's Pauley Ballroom. See *DOB Newsletter*, S.F., May 1970; Flyer, "Students for Gay Power," May 1970, Box 8, File 35, Social Protest Collection.

78. *Barb*, November 21–27, 1969, 5. Gay Liberationists howled when a writer for the *San Francisco Examiner* characterized the city's gay bars as "sad, dreary after-hours traps." Nevertheless, Gay Liberationists often criticized the "plastic world of the gay ghetto bars." *S.F. Free Press*, October 16–31, 1969, 14; "The Dreary Revels of S.F. 'Gay' Clubs," *San Francisco Examiner*, October 25, 1969, 5.

79. *Tribe*, October 30–November 6, 1970, 20; *Barb*, November 6–12, 1970, 5, 8.

80. "Gays for Peace," *Barb*, April 16–22, 1971, 4; "Gay Group," *Barb*, April 23–29, 1971, 2.

81. *Adz Gayzette*, S.F. ed., April 22, 1971, 3.

82. "Emmaus Chatter," *I Am* [Emmaus House], no. 3 [1971], 4.

83. "Gay Group," *Barb*, April 23–29, 1971, 2; Flyer, "Truck on Up to San Francisco" [1971], Box 1, File 30, Charles Thorpe Papers.

84. Wells, *War Within*, 480; "Gay May Day," *The Effeminist*, Berkeley, CA, May 1971, 2; *Barb*, March 26–April 1, 1971, 2; *Barb*, April 9–15, 1971, 6; *Barb*, April 16–22, 1971, 4; *Barb*, April 23–29, 1971, 2.

85. In whose name Gay Liberation spoke was itself a matter of contention between East and West Coast delegations. Gay May Day West criticized east coast gays for presuming to speak for all "gay women, males, transvestites, and transsexuals." By contrast, the Gay May Day West preamble began "We gay men of North America." See *The Effeminist*, May 1971, 2, for the text of both preambles.

86. *Barb*, April 9–15, 1971, 6.

87. Laura Miller, "Gay Liberation Task Force," *The Organizer* [Young Socialists Alliance], April 2, 1971, Young Socialists File, Anson Reinhart Papers, Gay and Lesbian Historical Society of Northern California. Participants at a SMC conference voted in February 1971 to organize a gay contingent for April 24. The Socialist Workers Party and Young Socialists Alliance had played a major role in the antiwar movement since the 1967 creation of the Student Mobilization Committee to End the War in Vietnam, or SMC, and the creation of the New Mobilization Committee to End the War in Vietnam, or New Mobe, in 1969.

88. *Barb*, April 23–29, 1971, 2; "Gays Against War," *Gay Sunshine*, June/July 1971, 5; Flyer, "Gay People Against the War and Sexism," April 1971, Box 1, File 42, Bois Burk Papers, Gay and Lesbian Historical Society of Northern California.

89. The *Advocate* reported that only two recent gay rights protests in New York State had drawn larger crowds. *Advocate*, May 26–June 8, 1971, 1, 6; Halstead, *Out Now!*, 612. Approximately two hundred thousand others participated in the San Francisco March, which *Newsweek* called the largest West Coast demonstration in history. DeBenedetti, *American Ordeal*, 304.

90. Frank Kameny, cofounder of the Washington, DC, Mattachine, first adopted the slogan "Gay Is Good" in the early 1960s. SIR's Larry Littlejohn sold some of the earliest gay paraphernalia, including "Gay Is Good" buttons, from a shop in North Beach. Larry Littlejohn interview.

91. *Advocate*, May 26–June 8, 1971, 1, 6; Flyer, "Gay People Against the War and Sexism"; "Gays Against War," *Gay Sunshine*, June/July 1971, 5; "Emmaus Chatter," *I Am* 3:4.

92. Flyer, "Gay People Against the War and Sexism"; Flyer, November 6 [1971] March and Rally, Box 1, File 55, Social Protest Collection; Flyer, "Join the Gay Pride Contingent, November 6" [1971], Box 1, File 42, Bois Burk Papers. According to the *Student Mobilizer*, June/July 1971, over 140 gay groups nationwide endorsed the April 24 gay contingent.

93. *Advocate*, May 26–June 8, 1971, 1, 6; *Gay Sunshine*, June/July 1971, 5; *I Am* 3:4; *Barb*, April 30–May 6, 1971, 10.

94. "Peace March," *Barb*, April 30–May 6, 1971, 10.

95. *Gay Sunshine*, June/July 1971, 5; Editorial, *B.A.R.* 1:3, May 1, 1971, 1.

96. *I Am* 3, 4.

97. In 1961 José Sarria, a drag performer and waiter at a popular North Beach bar, became the first openly homosexual San Franciscan to run for political office. He received fifty-six hundred votes after campaigning for a seat on the city's Board of Supervisors. Stryker and Van Buskirk, *Gay by the Bay*, 42; D'Emilio, *Sexual Politics*, 188.

98. "Homosexual Liberation Plank," *S.F. Free Press* 1:9 (1970): 10.

99. *Barb*, October 1–7, 1971, 16.

100. *Gay Pride*, June 25, 1972, 5. The city's homophile organizations had held candidates' nights since 1967, which (D'Emilio notes) "tended to attract aspirants to elective office in need of votes rather than incumbents." A significant homosexual voting bloc had not yet materialized in San Francisco. *Sexual Politics*, 203–204.

101. "Vote for Personal Freedom," Kameny for Congress brochure [1971], "Kameny for Congress campaign, 1971" File, Anson Reinhart Papers.

102. *Vector*, Jan. 1972, 15.

103. In Feb. 1970, such alliances were the topic of discussion at one of SIR's Friday night meetings, where participants were asked, "Should Gay Group Support Non-Gay Social Causes?" SIR Gold Sheet, Feb. 1970, Box 1, File 31, Bois Burk Papers.

104. *Barb*, April 30–May 6, 1971, 2; *Gay Sunshine*, June/July 1971, 5.

105. Jeffrey Escoffier, "Sexual Revolution and the Politics of Gay Identity," *Socialist Review* 15 (July–October 1985): 121. Also of interest is John D'Emilio, "Not a Simple Matter: Gay History and Gay Historians," *Journal of American History* 76 (September 1989): 435–442.

106. This phrase is from D'Emilio's 1998 preface to *Sexual Politics*, 9.

107. For mainstream media reports, "The Militant Homosexual," *Newsweek*, August 23, 1971, 45; "Gays on the March," *Time*, September 8, 1975, 32.

108. "S.I.R. Sues Govt.!" *Times Kalendar*, February 2, 1972, 1; *Barb*, August 13–19, 1971, 4; *Adz Gayzette*, August 12, 1971, 1; "Gay GI Releases 'Certain,'" *Barb*, September 8–14, 1972, 23; Press release on Discharge Upgrading Project [S.F.], September 18, 1973, Box 1, File 19, Pacific Counseling Service Papers, Bancroft Library, University of California, Berkeley, CA.

109. "Christopher Street Parade," *B.A.R.*, June 28, 1972, 1–2; "A Fabulous Gay Freedom Celebration in Sunny San Francisco," *B.A.R.*, June 27, 1973, 1.

110. "Gay Freedom Day Fair," *B.A.R.*, June 26, 1975, 6.

111. "Armed Forces: Homosexual Sergeant," *Time*, June 9, 1975, 19; "The Sergeant v. The Air Force," *Time,* September 8, 1975, 34; "Armed Forces: 'No' to Matlovich," *Time*, September 29, 1975, 32; Martin Duberman, "The Case of the Gay Sergeant," *New York Times Magazine,* November 9, 1975, 16.

112. "BAGL…?" *B.A.R.*, February 6, 1975, 4–6; David C. Goldman, "A Letter from B.A.G.L.," *B.A.R.*, April 3, 1975, 12–13; *BAGL Newsletter*, August–October 1976, Gay

and Lesbian Historical Society of Northern California; Tim Corbett and rama [Charles Hinton], "Practice Makes Powerful: Can Gays Get It Together in San Francisco? A Political Analysis of Bay Area Gay Liberation," *Magnus*, Summer 1977, 37–47, in Box 8, File 39, Social Protest Collection.
113. Clendinen and Nagourney, *Out for Good*, 243.
114. For the Village People, see http://www.villagepeople-official.com.

CHAPTER TWO

Los Dueños de México: Power and Masculinity in '68

ELAINE CAREY

In the midst of the Mexican Economic Miracle that had begun in the 1940s, Mexico, the first Spanish speaking nation to host the Olympics, appeared to be at a critical juncture to enter the developed world without the student troubles that had plagued developed nations in the late 1960s. By hosting the Olympics, Mexico planned to introduce the world to its culture but also to its entrance into the modern world.[1] In July of 1968, President Díaz Ordaz welcomed international journalists, arriving to report on the time trials, to a country with stadiums, metro lines, international hotels, and luxury tourist spots. Despite all the preparations to showcase Mexican culture and modernity, a crisis brewed in the city.

In the shadow of the new hotels and metro lines, street battles between young men and police broke out on July 22, and again on July 26, 1968 shattering the illusion of a tranquil modern life. Key political figures—Díaz Ordaz, Secretary of Interior Luis Echeverría, Regent of Mexico City Alfonso Corona del Rosal, and Minister of Defense Marcelino García Barragán—responded with violence that has been well-documented.[2] From these initial skirmishes in El Centro (the old colonial center), a mass student-led social movement emerged that questioned the authority of the Mexican leaders and the existence of democracy. Those young middle-class men and women who challenged Mexican leaders were from the sector of Mexican society that was assumed to have benefited the most from the modernization of the nation.[3] Unlike their international counterparts who criticized bureaucratic communism or Western capitalism, Mexican youth took to the streets to challenge the authoritarian one-party system and to demand respect for the Mexican constitution. As suggested by Lessie Jo Frazier and Deborah Cohen in the introduction to this volume, the desire for change inscribed in gender and sexuality serves as an analytical window to examine political life.[4] That desire as it translated into action demonstrated students' status as a newly constituted political collective body that sought to challenge those in positions of power.[5] While both young men and women mobilized in the summer of '68, the Mexican government responded ferociously to young male activists.[6] Through his criticism of the regime, his actions on the street, and his embracing of revolutionary icons such as Ernesto "Che" Guevara, Fidel Castro, and Ho Chi Minh, the Mexican male student activist was a danger to political authority and to the ideals of the Mexican Revolution. Not because he was ever in a position to overthrow the government, but because he rejected the illusion of the metaphoric revolutionary family put forth by the *Partido Revolucionario Institucional* (Party of the Institutional Revolution, or PRI).

Recent studies of reveal that gender is more than simply masculinity and femininity; instead, it is an analysis of power.[7] Within the study of masculinity principle power struggles emerge between powerful versus powerless, dominant versus submissive, and influential versus insignificant. Keeping in mind the ability of those in power to define and construct the "other," I consider how tensions between young educated, middle-class men in the streets and more mature men of the same background but in control of the government that emerged through the summer of '68. This type of confrontation was not new. During the railroad workers strike of 1958 and the medical doctors' strike of 1965, the government acknowledged the economic demands of the workers and doctors, but balked at their attempts to union democracy and self-organizations. As mentioned by Cohen and Frazier, sexuality serves as a tool to examine heteronormative forms of power. The case between young Mexican men and the political oligarchy in '68 speaks to the sexualized nature of political and social control whether through rhetorical manipulation or direct violence. Both students and the government used sexualized language to undermine the agency and power of their opponents.

On the streets of Mexico City in '68, young male students exerted their power to define themselves as influential political, but also cultural, actors. In turn, the movement was an attempt to chart a new political path for the country. By challenging the power structure, young men endured the ruthless responses from the paternal powers of the PRI and the Díaz Ordaz administration. The response from the government was twofold: direct and indirect confrontation. The direct response included police and military action on the streets of Mexico City. The indirect assault on the students came in the form of antistudent rhetoric that circulated in the government-controlled press. In turn, a war of words and discourse emerged between the government and the students of Mexico City, and this battle was waged in the press and on the streets.

As noted by contemporary scholars of Mexico, the PRI and the president—the patriarch—defined and represented the Mexican revolutionary family.[8] As parents acculturate their children into the family, the society, and the culture, the PRI political machine served a similar process acculturating young men into politics.[9] For the generation of '68, they, like their predecessors, were to learn from their elders, and later, take their places within the power structures. When challenged by young, educated, middle-class men on the streets of Mexico City in July and August, the Díaz Ordaz administration and its protagonists employed gendered language and images to construct a dangerous enemy of the nation. In turn, students adopted their own gendered and revolutionary rhetoric to undermine the government's attacks. The language and images that both the government and the students adopted reflected a generational cultural clash that had spread throughout the world in the 1960s. This essay considers the clash between students and the government as a struggle between fathers and sons within the metaphoric Mexican revolutionary family.[10] Young men who were influenced by the Cuba Revolution, Vietnam, and the international student protests, as well as youth culture, undermined certain established Mexican gender constructs.[11] On one hand, the Mexican government deemed politicized young male activists as deviant, suspicious, seditious, and dangerous. On the other hand, the Mexican government continued to negotiate with the students offering their prodigal and disobedient children a path of potential reconciliation with the revolutionary family. Conversely, the students replied with their own constructions of male deviancy: blood-thirsty, power-hungry, authoritarian traitors who freely administered violence to maintain absolute control of the Mexican people. At the same time, they continued to press for dialogue with the government, but particularly with Díaz Ordaz.[12] Despite the iconography and rhetoric, both the students and the government continued to remain in a dialogue with one another hoping to reach an agreement whereby the students would return to the revolutionary family and the patriarchs would yield to the political demands of their children. Nonetheless, the students' revolutionary and idealistic zeal and their misinterpretation of politicized language and the potency of power had dire consequences.

The Eruption

The movement began in an unlikely scenario. On July 26, the *Federación Nacional de Estudiantes Técnicos* (National Federation of Technical Students, or FNET) planned a demonstration to protest police violence against the students at vocational schools affiliated with the *Instituto Politécnico Nacional* (National Polytechnic Institute, or IPN) that had previously occurred. FNET was a student organization with close ties to IPN, vocational students, nonautonomous institutions, and to the Secretariat of Public Education, SEP. The FNET march went from the plaza de La Ciudadela in the Casco de Santo Tomás to the Plaza of the Constitution (the *zócalo*). Meanwhile in the south of Mexico City, groups affiliated with the *Universidad Nacional Autonóma de México* (National Autonomous University of Mexico, UNAM) also prepared to march. Some UNAM student groups and members of the *Central Nacional de Estudiantes Demócraticos* (National Center of Democratic Students, CNED) organized a demonstration to protest U.S. involvement in Vietnam and to commemorate the fifteenth anniversary of Fidel Castro's July 26, 1953 attack on the Moncada Barracks. Both groups of marchers obtained permits for their protests from the Federal District offices.[13] While the FNET demonstration was to end before the CNED march, the two groups numbering approximately 5,000 protesters met in the street surrounding the main plaza.[14]

As the two demonstrations merged, street fighting broke out between the students and the *granaderos* (riot police). The government version of the FNET and CNED demonstrations insisted that the students became violent, breaking downtown shop windows and looting jewelry stores. By all accounts, students, mostly young men, met the police in the streets of Tacuba and 5 de Mayo.[15] Mysteriously, in the garbage cans that lined the avenues, students found rocks that they hurled at the police.[16] Raúl Mendiolea Cercero, subdirector of the police, coordinated the actions of his men in this violent clash between three thousand students and two hundred granaderos and police.

What followed the July 26 clash were three days of intense fighting that culminated in a police and Army bazooka attack on a preparatory school affiliated with UNAM on July 28–29. After firing on the students who sought shelter behind the colonial doors of San Idelfonso, the military and granaderos entered the school. They reported that they detained 126 young men, 10 molotov cocktails, 2 cans of gasoline, a 5-liter bottle of nitric acid, a bottle of ammonia, and a box of propaganda from the *Partido Comunista de México* (Mexican Communist Party, PCM).[17]

Unsure of who was responsible and unwilling to accept an internal student problem in the climate of '68, what followed the street battles could be described as a cascade of blame. The Mexican government declared that the students were manipulated by "foreign interests," and denounced the PCM. These foreign interests included the PCM and the *Juventud Comunista Mexicana* (Mexican Communist Youth, JCM), as well as foreign "interlopers" seeking another Prague in spring or Paris in May. On

July 26, 1968, government officials invaded the PCM Central Committee headquarters. The police justified their attack on the PCM headquarters by insisting that foreign influences were contributing to the student unrest.[18] The newspapers also provided names of other individuals who were detained, particularly those who were not Mexican citizens or had French or anglicized names, and who, according to information provided by the newspapers, had entered Mexico illegally.[19]

While the battles raged on the streets of the city, the *Cámara de Diputados* (House of Deputies), just minutes from the sites of the student unrest, debated modifying Article 34 of the Mexican Constitution to lower the voting age to eighteen. President Díaz Ordaz championed this change. Lowering the voting age to eighteen was a nod from Díaz Ordaz to the influences of modernity and also his recognition of the potential influence of youth in the political process. Moreover with the Olympics, Diaz Ordaz administration embraced youth as their cultural ambassadors that served to showcase Mexico modernity.[20] The government painted this illusion of modernity and youth as clean-cut and respecting of its elders and in turn the state.[21] The participation of young people as ambassadors and athletes in the Olympics demonstrates how their bodies and presence served as an embodiment of national identity and modernity.

In an editorial cartoon from the newspaper *Excélsior* published the day before the first street skirmish, Díaz Ordaz is portrayed as a barber cutting hair and shaving beards of young men under the watchful eyes of prominent Mexican forefathers: Venustiano Carranza, Benito Juárez, Miguel Hidalgo y Costilla, José María Morelos y Pavón, and Francisco I. Madero (figure 2.1).[22] To the left of the barber Díaz Ordaz, the young men who enter under the sign "Articulo 34" represent the youth culture of the 1960s. The sign next to the doorway lists the services that will be performed by the citizen-making barber: hair, beard, sideburns, and style. All the young men have longish hair, some are wearing hippie emblems such as sandals and jewelry with flowers or crosses. One is carrying a guitar representing rock-n-roll, while two have beards and one has long sideburns. The client hidden by the Barber Díaz Ordaz sits in the chair surrounded by his hair—the remnants of his youthful follies. To the barber's left, three clean-cut young men exit the "shop" into the respectable world of "citizen of the Mexican nation." One newly minted citizen straightens his tie as if preparing to take his rightful place as a bank teller. Another dons a suit dashing out to his new executive position. And finally, the last one wears a letterman's jacket reveling in his school spirit. Díaz Ordaz literally has converted hippies into productive, functional, and respectably middle-class citizens. All the citizens represent the middle class rather than workers and peasants. And yet, the young people whom

Figure 2.1 *Rac y Roc, "Los Debutantes"* in *Excélsior,* July 21, 1968

Díaz Ordaz was modifying and creating would be in the streets in the following days protesting police violence.

In the image, Díaz Ordaz, posing as a barber, is the architect of the Mexican nation, the revolution, and the citizen. Through his haircuts and shaves he continues the PRI traditional that through the party one achieves success.[23] He embodies the final arbiter of what it is to be a proper Mexican male. As cultural critics Samuel Ramos and Octavio Paz noted and other scholars have continued to reveal, the president is the embodiment of power and legitimacy in Mexico, and he is both the wise and benevolent patriarch and also the unyielding and violent macho.[24] Díaz Ordaz did not fit the image of the unyielding macho, he was described by his contemporaries as skinny, awkward, and "ugly."[25] However, Díaz Ordaz argued that his personal shortcomings were a political asset since his ugliness could inspire fear.[26] As the benevolent head of state offering haircuts, he is creating the type of citizen that will follow his rule and respect his absolute legitimacy, but one of his most powerful assets, his face, is hidden from the viewing public but not from the young men entering the barbershop.

During the first days of the movement, Díaz Ordaz maintained his position as the paternal father figure to the Mexican nation that until then seemed untainted by the events that transpired in late July. The press, however, jumped upon the government's rhetorical bandwagon rooting out the culprits, foreigners, and leftists, which led certain young men astray. From the 1930s, the Mexican press operated as the media mouthpiece of the government and the party.[27] Moreover, the press facilitated the creation of the imagined nation of a revolutionary family that was the basis of PRI domination.[28] In the first few weeks of the movement, the press portrayed the activists as street thugs, gang members, or overindulged, spoiled brats. It also created a furor over foreign interlopers, perhaps looking for another May, and communists' inciting the students to riot combined with attitudes that young men were impressionable and violent. In the Mexican newspapers, government officials continued to insist that foreigners who had come to Mexico to disrupt the Olympics or communists who wished to humiliate the nation controlled the students.[29] These attitudes played out in the comics.

In an editorial cartoon published in *El Universal* on July 29, two slovenly dressed young men hide behind a shield that is reflecting an image of a well-groomed, if not stunned, student with books in his hand (figure 2.2). In this representation, the young student's good reputation is being tarnished by outsiders who use the students as their "shield." The young men from behind the shield are unshaven, with longish hair, and sheepishly grimacing at the chaos they have concocted. One young man wielding a club wears a shirt that reads "Professional Agitator," and the other student with a scraggy beard wears a shirt that reads *Vendepatrias* (Traitors). At their feet are stacked papers identified with the words "Propaganda" across the one stack, just beneath an image of the hammer and sickle. The captions reads: "How many crimes do they commit in your name."[30] Thus, the "foreign" students with longish hair and facial hair are traitors and communists. The clean-cut Mexican student contrasts as studious and patriotic, while the "foreign" young men engage in dissent and violence. The Mexican student respects his elders and himself as evident by his clean-cut appearance.

In the July 31 edition of the major newspaper *Excélsior*, caricaturist Marino published a cartoon entitled "Yo Acuso (bis)" in which two students are denouncing one another with the same phrase: "*El es el culpabale* (He is guilty)" (figure 2.3). Again, juxtapositions of good versus evil, citizen versus foreign interloper take place. One student is clean-cut, carrying a book, and wearing a sweater with a "U" for *Universidad* on it. The other young man has long hair and a beard. He is wearing a vest and hippie-style clothing. On his arm is an arm-band with an image of the hammer and sickle.[31] Again, communism and foreign influences upon youth culture are portrayed as to blame for the student unrest.

ESTUDIANTE

Figure 2.2 *"Cuántos crímenes se cometan en su nombre …"* (How many crimes they commit in your name) in *El Universal*, July 29, 1968

All three political cartoons, the barber Díaz Ordaz and the two comics denouncing students, depict the enemy of students and the nation as young men who are caught up in the contaminating influences of youth culture and the left.[32] In the first image of Díaz Ordaz as the barber, the only method by which young men may become citizens is to leave behind the growing youth culture and become part of the established system. Merely with a few snips, Barber Díaz Ordaz as the patriarch of the Mexican Revolution and nation creates his own citizens to work within his system. In this image, manhood is linked to a prescribed and preexisting category of "citizen" constructed by Díaz Ordaz. If masculinity is "a stylized repetition of acts," that is learned, adopted, and adapted, then it is also a creation that is malleable and changeable.[33] As the barber and the president, Díaz Ordaz is in the position to influence, to alter, to interpret, and to construct proper Mexican manhood for youth.

In the last two comics, caricaturists portray a face off between young men. Young men, imprinted with emblems of popular culture, defied the bourgeois sentimentality of manhood constructed by Díaz Ordaz and the Mexican revolutionary family. The young men who are clean cut, well-dressed, and carrying books are portrayed to be true students and true Mexican young men. In contrast, those young men contaminated by foreign influence are responsible for the violence, they are traitors, communists, and professional agitators. The characterization of certain young men as hippies and Communists also asserts that they are political, social, and sexual deviants; they exist as aberrations of modernity and Mexican national goal.[34] Indeed, the comics question the nationalism of the young men; how could these young men support the ideals of the Mexican Revolution when they are contaminated by negative foreign influences? Thus, the rhetoric from the government is intertwined casually with the sort of message suggested by these cartoons; that the students were being incited by some other influences, whether French students, Fidel Castro, or the Communist International. Some other force or agent was influencing the constructions of Mexican masculinity that countered the national goals of Mexico. Those agents of deception and change had to be challenged to preserve the revolutionary family.

The problem of Mexican masculinity and youth was further complicated by the mobilization of Javier Barros Sierra. The continued attacks on college preparatory schools affiliated with the UNAM were egregious violations of university autonomy. In response, Rector of UNAM Barros Sierra held a meeting at the campus protesting the government's violation of university autonomy on August 1, 1968. After the meeting, students and faculty from Politécnico and UNAM with Barros Sierra at the front marched in the rain from University City to their planned destination of the Plaza of the Constitution. Marching north on Insurgentes Boulevard

Figure 2.3   Marino, "*Yo Acuso (bis)* (I accuse you)" in *Excelsior*, July 31, 1968

in the presence of the police, the demonstrators met the National Army at Felix Cuevas Boulevard in between the Del Valle and Napoles districts. Newspapers reported that the communities and district chiefs of Del Valle and Napoles feared outbreaks of violence and destruction of business and property. In turn, the communities had requested police protection. Rather than continuing on Insurgentes as planned, the march turned east heading toward Coyoacán to return to University City.

Although the National Army halted the march to the *zocálo*, it was a public relations success. The newspapers reported upon the orderly nature of the march. Journalists also discussed the festive atmosphere. Besides its jubilance, María Luisa Mendoza reported on the "dignity" by which the students demonstrated citizenship.[35] A journalist for *El Universal* agreed that the demonstration was "An example of order and sanity that will pass into the history of the student movements was the gigantic demonstration that happened yesterday, approximately 100,000 students marched in defense of university autonomy, civil liberties, and law."[36] The photos of the march show Barros Sierra and upper administrators and faculty leading the march.[37] This high-ranking government official was not a dupe for the PCM, Castro, or Daniel Cohn-Bendit. Photos depict the actual physical existence of the masculine archetype of citizen that the barber Díaz Ordaz was trying to create leading a march protesting the very same government. Barros Sierra was a prominent Mexican politician and PRI insider, not some young man caught up in the youth culture of the 1960s. Although Barros Sierra was not of the generation that would ultimately lead the mass social movement of '68, he ignited the movement and gave it respectability. The war of words heightened.

The Batman

By early August, students from IPN, UNAM, the National Agriculture School, and other institutions were calling for a general strike. With students on strike, professors and teachers protesting, and the Rector of UNAM calling for a public discussion, Díaz Ordaz had to respond to the emerging crisis. All his plans and all his hard work could be undermined by a student protest in front of many people who were arriving daily to Mexico for the Olympic trials. On August 1, 1968 the same day as the UNAM march led by Barros Sierra, Díaz Ordaz published a statement from Guadalajara calling for harmony and an end to the violence. In it, he stated:

Peace and calm must be restored in our country. A hand has been extended; it is up to the Mexican citizens to decide whether to grasp this outstretched hand. I have been greatly pained by these deplorable and shameful incidents. Let us not widen the gap between us; let us all refuse to heed the prompting of our false pride, myself included, naturally.[38]

Díaz Ordaz, as the patriarch of the Mexican revolutionary family, appealed to the Mexican people on the basis of nationalism. He did not single out the students for criticism; instead he asserted the capabilities of the Mexican leadership and nation to meet the needs of the people. Díaz Ordaz never criticized the students, but he also never mentioned them explicitly. In his veiled comments, the growing student problems seemed inconsequential to the president as if they were happening in France rather than waiting his return to the Federal District. Later, Díaz Ordaz viewed this paternalistic gesture as a reaching out to the students, who in his perception, defied his authority by continuing to organize.[39]

Juxtaposed with the speech, Barros Sierra and the march did not question the legitimacy of the PRI and the president; instead, his march undermined the construction of the deviant male student activist. Consequently, Barros Sierra legitimized the students concerns, and offered the people of Mexico City another model of the male university activists: one that was a mature PRI insider.[40] On August 1, 1968, the discussion of the problems that plagued Mexico appeared to be a discourse of power between the upper echelons of authority.

The students, however, shattered the illusion of an internal political rapport between influential players cast from the same lot, as represented by Barros Sierra and Díaz Ordaz. Due to the continued police violence and the rage students felt after July 26, students from UNAM, Chapingo National Agriculture School, IPN, and the vocational and preparatory schools gathered at the Poli campus to organize to combat the police.[41] This was unprecedented. The students from Poli, UNAM, and Chapingo had rarely joined for anything except sporting competitions. The students came from two different worlds. UNAM hosted Mexico's top research institutions and top scholars. Future politicians and business leaders were plucked from the ranks of its student organizations.[42] On the basis of socioeconomic divisions, UNAM was the house of the elite. Poli, on the other hand, was the technical school. From its ranks came technical and middle management professionals. While not entirely, many students from Poli and Chapingo were the children of the Mexican economic miracle, which allowed more parents the opportunity to send their children to an institution of higher learning. Poli was the ticket to the middle class; UNAM was a ticket to even more.

With the escalation of hostility, the students broke down the barriers that had previously separated them—socioeconomic differences and physical space—to work together. Following the August 1 march led by Barros Sierra, students from IPN held a march on August 4 in which students from other institutions participated. In the days following the UNAM and IPN marches, the students developed a sophisticated student movement. They voted on and elected representatives from the secondary schools and colleges and universities to the *Consejo Nacional de Huelga* (National Strike Council, or CNH), the umbrella organization of the student strike. The CNH had approximately 210 members of that only an estimated 20–30 percent had ties to any leftist party or organization.[43] Some CNH members had direct ties to the same party as Díaz Ordaz, the PRI.

On August 8, 1968, the CNH released its first set of demands to the press. The demands included that democratic liberty be respected; that certain police officials be terminated from their positions; that the corps of granaderos be disbanded; that families of injured or murdered students be given an indemnity; that student prisoners be released immediately; and that Article 145 of the Penal Code (an article of sedition) be abolished.[44] These demands became known as the Six Point Petition. Besides the petition, the CNH called for a public dialogue with the government, or it would extend the strike.

With the demands being circulated in the press, government officials needed to respond. With the CNH, the students developed their sense of power and politics. As the clock ran down in regard to the students' demand for dialogue and their demands defined in the Six Point Petition, Alfonso Corona del Rosal, the Regent of the Federal District (Mexico City), sent a public letter to IPN Director Dr. Guillermo Massieu. Perhaps Corona del Rosal hoped to assist Massieu's efforts to return students to the classrooms at IPN. In the letter, Corona del Rosal responded to the Six Point Petition. Taking a bureaucratic stance, he argued that he was unable to respond to the students' demand to terminate officers Cueto Ramírez, Raúl Mendiolea Cueto, and Alfonso Frías without proper procedure in the police department.[45] In response to the students' demands for indemnities to the families of those murdered or injured, Corona del Rosal argued, his department needed to have precise information regarding those individuals who had died or were injured in the riots. He stressed that the demands could not be acted upon without further investigation. By August 11, the CNH succeeded to position itself as the leader of a mass student movement; and it had finally provoked some form of public dialogue, though it was directed to an university official.

On the same day as his letter to Massieu was published, Corona del Rosal addressed a government sponsored-demonstration of ten thousand people in Lázaro Cárdenas park. He took the opportunity to directly criticize the students and justify the government's actions in order to maintain peace.

Falling upon the continued mantra that outside agitators and supporters of the foreign "Cuban Revolution" were responsible for the violence, Corona del Rosal declared that the government was simply maintaining peace. In his speech, Corona del Rosal disputed student claims by focusing his attention on the circulation of rumors and documents saying that students and others lost their lives since July 26. He argued that "There has not been one death."[46]

The following day, the CNH issued a public statement disputing Corona del Rosal's letter and speech. The CNH contested Corona del Rosal's paternalistic response that seemed to malign the students' assumed lack of knowledge surrounding things political. As far as Corona del Rosal was concerned, political discussions fell in the domain of mature men, not kids. Thus, the CNH clarified its position and authority:

> The *Consejo Nacional de Huelga*, the representative of more than 150,000 students on strike, considers it necessary to clarify before the public and students and professors of the country, some points that derived from the letter of Lic. Corona del Rosal, chief of the Federal District, to Doctor Guillermo Massieu, director of the National Polytechnic Institute, which have been interpreted by the national press as a response to the students' petition.[47]

The CNH countered statements made by Corona del Rosal by publicly retaking their own demands and rhetoric. The CNH stated that the idea to form a commission to investigate those who were responsible for the violence was part of the students' initial petition. It criticized the fact that Corona del Rosal sent the letter only to Massieu offering his suggestions and answers, completely ignoring the students from the universities, the technical schools, the normal schools, and the private institutions. By speaking specifically to Massieu and ignoring the students, Corona del Rosal appeared as the disapproving adult requesting parental intervention between bickering children. Thus, the CNH closed their response to Corona del Rosal with a call to demonstrate, and for all Mexicans to join them for the march to be held on August 13, 1968.[48]

The August 13 march represents the escalation of the movement in which the students countered the government's rhetoric. As outlined by the CNH, the march was orderly with students marching in their respective schools and departments.[49] Professors and teachers affiliated with the Teachers Coalition led the march from the Casco de Santo Tomás.[50] The 150,000–200,000 demonstrators wound their way from the Casco de Santo Tomás, passed the Hospital of the Green Cross, and continued to the Plaza of the Constitution, about five kilometers in distance. The streets were lined with military and police, and most of the shops closed early to avoid trouble. The newspapers reported that the march was fairly orderly and peaceful with students marching and insisting that the Six Point Petition be addressed.

As the students wound their way through the streets, they challenged the authority of the government through their own political language and images. They marched with images of their heroes, such as Che Guevara and they chanted "HO-HO-HO CHI MINH." Their placards referred to the international student movement, particularly focusing on Vietnam. One banner read, "Hitler 1939, Johnson 1968," while another read, "Hitler 1940, GDO (Gustavo Díaz Ordaz), 1968."[51] Thus, United States' President Lyndon B. Johnson and Mexican President Díaz Ordaz are one in the same as Hitler: violent, imperialistic, and authoritarian. Student placards also targeted their own experiences: ¡Respeto a la Constitución! (Respect the Constitution); and Los verdaderos agitadores son el hambre, la ignorancia, y la injusticia (The true agitators are hunger, ignorance, and injustice).[52]

The following day, certain journalists reported on the students and professors and political analysis and criticism. Other journalists, however, found some of the students to be aggressive and confrontational. They pointed out "brigades" of students who used megaphones to coordinate chants that were deemed offensive to the armed forces and the police. Newspapers also published photos of two male students marching with a coffin with a message painted on the side: "The Army burns cadavers."[53] This image resulted in Secretary of Defense Marcelino García Barragán's disavowal of the students' references to deaths. As Regent Corona del Rosal had done the week before, García Barragán "categorically denie[d] that there were deaths that resulted from the confrontations between the students and soldiers."[54] In his statement, he went on to claim that the military had nothing against the students and that many officers have children at the UNAM and IPN.[55] García Barragán offered activists a path to reconcile with parents, who may or may not have been in the military, and also a path to return to the revolutionary family. To further illustrate his and the state's parental concern, García Barragán minimized and downplayed the role of the army. He argued that the army of Mexico was not that powerful, and, that was the reason that Mexico has enjoyed peace and stability compared to other countries.[56] Mexico was not like the United States, the Soviet Union, or even France.

The interview with García Barragán was an attempt to subvert the goals of the students by portraying the government, represented by García Barragán, as the defender of the ideals of the Mexican revolution. García Barragán was introduced as a Mexican revolutionary hero who fought alongside General Monclovio Herrera beginning in 1913. In '68, He was portrayed as a fatherly figure concerned with maintaining the goals that he fought for during the Revolution and offering young men a place in the revolutionary family. Of course, he, a true Mexican revolutionary who put his life in danger for the struggle, was the living embodiment of the Revolution and the nation. Like the president, García Barragan represents both the benevolent patriarch and the strong man. The General earned his stripes because he was a soldier in the Mexican Revolution, and within the revolutionary family he continued to hold a central place of authority and esteem. The use of the general as the model of Mexican manhood and citizen was an attempt to delegitimize the young male activists and their movement.[57] Thus, the young male students never could attain the position of a war-scarred veteran of the real struggle; the struggle of the students was imagined and created. They and their movement were on the institutional fringe of politics, society, culture, and revolution; both were illegitimate.[58]

Despite the attempts to undermine the students' purpose and due to the success of the August 13 march, students and government officials dueled over who held the position to define democracy and the ideals of the Mexican revolution. Since the students did not have the level of access to the press as did the government, they had to develop their own propaganda machine. During the entire movement, students produced their own publicity and commentary. As the students physically occupied the various campuses around the Federal District, they had supplies—poster paper, paint, markers, and so on—and equipment—mimeograph machines—at their disposal.[59] Consequently, students told their side of the story through representations of their own choosing and design. Their posters, placards, and flyers undermined the paternalistic depictions that government officials used to portray themselves. With the students garnering growing support, they further employed their own images to counter the government's portrayal of the students as communist-inspired, out of control, dangerous, and traitorous. Instead, the students positioned the government as dangerous and violent. Although Díaz Ordaz tried to remain the benevolent and paternal defender of the ideals of the Mexican Revolution during his speech of August 1 and the annual presidential speech of September 1, the students targeted and depicted Díaz Ordaz as the deviant and power-thirsty politician. Rather than seeing Díaz Ordaz's physical appearance as an asset, they found it an easy target for ridicule. Díaz Ordaz was portrayed as a bat or a vampire, which played on his apparent overbite. One that circulated displayed Díaz Ordaz's with fangs that dripped with blood and depiction reads, "The Beast of 68 is thirsty for blood" (figure 2.4).[60] In others, Díaz Ordaz is represented by a bat, and is referred to as the Batman.

The student's use of a vampire or bat suggests that Díaz Ordaz and his administration were sucking the life out of the Mexican Constitution and the nation. To the students, Díaz Ordaz did not represent true democracy

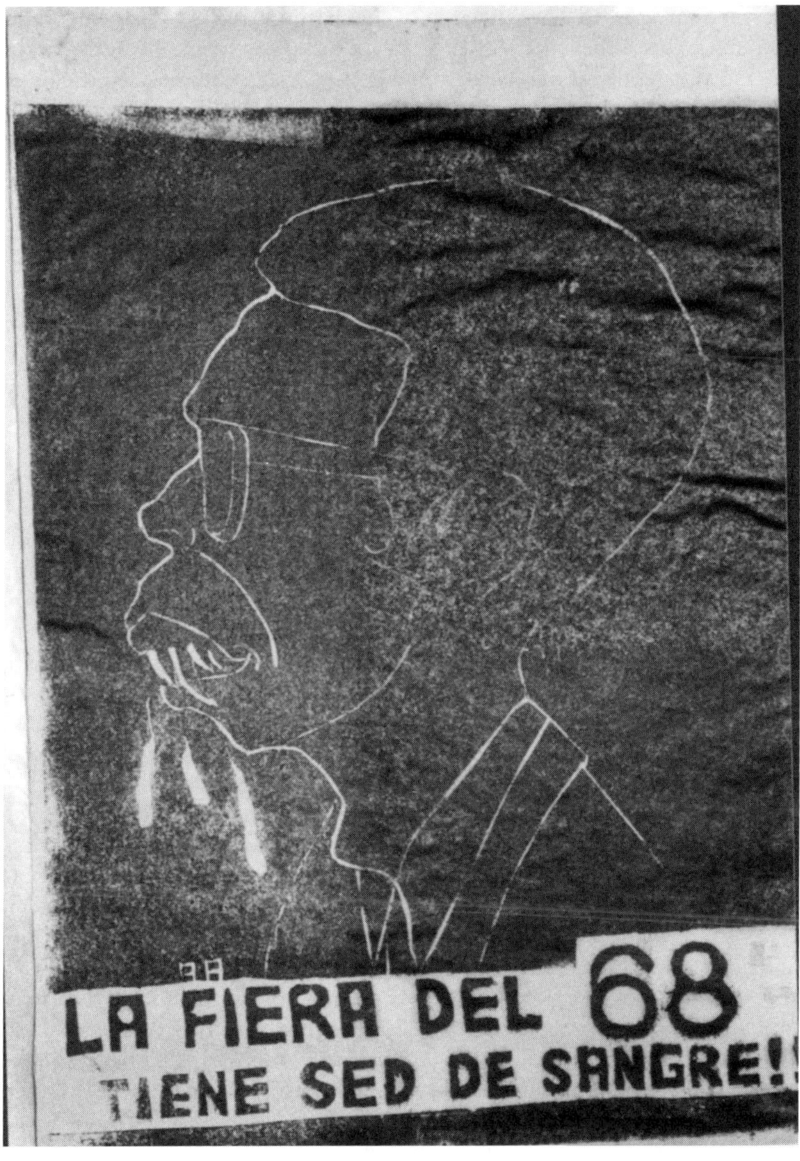

Figure 2.4 *Colección de impresos Esther Montero, Instituto de Investigación Sobre la Universidad y la Educación, Archivo Histórico de Universidad Nacional Autónoma de México-* (IISUE/AHUNAM) Biblioteca Nacional, México, D.F.

and freedom; instead, the patriarch of the nation was a bloodsucking beast who sustained himself at the expense of those with whom he came in contact: the people of the nation. The government characterized the male activists as deviant and criminal, and the students depicted the president as animalistic and parasitic. He was sneaky, cruel, and manipulative; the embodiment of masculine deviancy and treachery. At the same time, they continued to implore him to meet with them and engage in a public debate.

Díaz Ordaz was not the only figure of the administration that received attention by the students. The granaderos (riot police) became the out-of-control males, usually represented by the hypermasculine image of an ape. The flipside of the students as mindless pawns of the PCM or foreign interlopers from May in Paris, the granaderos were hapless thugs following the orders of a corrupting Mexican government. Díaz Ordaz represented a blood-sucking manipulative beast and the granadero apes, his henchmen. Student activists ridiculed the young men that comprised the granaderos; many of who did not have the luxury or resources to attend the university. To the activists, they were mindless drones simply cracking heads on command without argument. One student-produced poster shows an ape wearing riot gear holding a gingerbread man cookie on a stick with a U on its chest. The caption reads: "Persuasion is our job."[61] Obviously, peaceful persuasion was far from students' conceptualization of the *granaderos*.

In other images, the granaderos' and police weapons were juxtaposed with the image and icons designed for the '68 Olympics. The ironic theme for the '68 Olympics held in Mexico City was "The Year of Peace." Students manipulated the symbol of the Olympics, a dove. In one piece of student-produced propaganda, a bayonet pierces the dove drawing blood. In these depictions, the doves represented the people of Mexico, the bayonet portrayed the violence of government, and the blood symbolized the death of the revolution and the people.[62] Students used the icon of "Mexico '68" created for the Olympics, and replaced letters or "'68" with images of tanks, apes in riot gear beating students, or other violent depictions. In all cases, they undermined the position of the government as a defender of democracy and the people. Instead, Mexico was violent, bleeding, struggling, and consequently, slowly dying. In the hands of the students, the representations of Mexico's modernity, the dove and "Mexico '68," became emblems of authoritarianism.

The slogans and images that the students created did not remain stagnant; they changed as the movement unfolded. The students designed and circulated their own propaganda to challenge the rhetoric of the government-supported press. As the movement developed, the students grew more astute in challenging the government's portrayals of the movement. The CNH organized lightning brigades to spread the message of the movement to the streets.[63] These brigades became the propaganda arm of the movement, and they circulated the political messages of the movement.

As the student movement progressed through the summer months, it became a mass social uprising. Students from the provinces continued to express solidarity with those in Mexico City.[64] The movement reached its nexus on September 13, 1968, the day of the Great Silent March. Held on a Friday to ensure the presence of people in the city, the march silently made its way through the city. During this march, students carried banners of Mexican historical heroes to counter the government's charges that they were controlled by Castro or foreign interests. The students and their supporters marched through the streets gagged and silent. The marchers did not chant or yell slogans. Their silence marked the silent suffering of those political prisoners who languished in jail. It also marked the prohibition of freedom and democracy by an authoritarian government; 500, 000 people joined the students in their march, while thousands of bystanders yelled their support for the students. The students appeared to have the upper hand in defining the revolution.

Batman Returns

By the Great Silent March, the students had learned a great deal about rhetoric and imagery. To combat the idea that the students were led by foreigners and communists, the CNH issued a call to use only Mexican images rather than those of Ernesto Che Guevara or Ho Chi Minh. Similar to the Mexican government that used the Mexico City newspapers to circulate the myth of a revolutionary family, the students recognized the importance of creating their own propaganda that kept to these themes that showed their own devotion to Mexican heroes and nationalism. With attention to Mexican themes, the students held a counter*grito* in University City on September 15 to commemorate Mexican Independence.[65] The jubilation that the students sensed after their successful September 13 march and the counter*grito* dramatically changed on September 19 when government forces invaded University City. The government violated its own laws but later justified its actions in the press.[66] For the students, they lost their strong-hold, and access to resources needed to maintain the movements' momentum. Barros Sierra denounced the invasion, but the government forces were not stopped. Six days after the UNAM invasion, the military engaged in street battles with secondary students to occupy other campuses. In both cases, the government justified violating university autonomy by denouncing the students. Furthermore, Secretary of Interior Luis Echeverría argued that since the campuses were not being used for purposes of education, autonomy was not an issue.

In the wake of the attacks, The CNH refused to end the strike and called for another important meeting to be held on October 2, 1968 in the Plaza of Three Cultures in the Nonoalco-Tlatelolco housing project where much of the earlier fighting had taken place. That day, hundreds if not thousands of students and bystanders died in the plaza when government and police forces opened fire. *El Año de la Paz* (the Year of Peace), the XIX Olympiad, opened without incident from students, but government forces continued to arrest and persecute students. In the wake of this brutal massacre, the movement continued despite the growing threats. The government sought, arrested, and detained leaders of the movement. With the leaders being arrested and others fleeing Mexico and with the continued violence frightening many potential activists, the strike ended and students returned to classes on December 4, 1968.

On October 2, 1968, the government had chosen violence to prove that in fact it was *el dueño de México* or the ruler of Mexico; however, the students were never completely quieted. Instead, their voices and actions represented growing dissent. The student propaganda machine continued through the years reflecting the crisis of power and the Mexican Revolution that began in the summer of '68. To this day, on the campuses of UNAM and Poli in September and October, propaganda commemorating the movement is found. If one takes a walk around the Plaza of Three Cultures in Tlatelolco, one sees a plague that commemorates those who died in the plaza on October 2, but one also sees graffiti: *Nunca Olvidamos* (We will never forget). The government's sexualized depiction of young men as dangerous, seditious, leftist, and foreign and the students' portrayal of the government as violent, brutal, castigating, and out-of-control reflected the gendered generational clash that marked the 1960s.

The brutal clash between the Díaz Ordaz administration and young Mexican men remains indicative of the inability of the Mexican government to respond to criticism or demands for change. In '68, students were never in a position to overthrow or oust the government, but they and their adoption and adaptation of rhetoric that challenged the illusion of the revolutionary family was a threat. The student activists were the emerging educated, but also disillusioned, elite. More importantly, these young men displayed their potential for power by occupying physical spaces and engaging in public dialogue with the rulers. In a few short months, student activists had built their own propaganda machine, organizations, and mass social movement. Moreover, they rejected the traditional path to political success. This prospective power that the students demonstrated was what threatened the Díaz Ordaz administration and what contributed, in part, to the massacre on October 2, 1968. The world in '68 was far different from that of the 1940s and 1950s. The students, beneficiaries of the Mexican Economic Miracle, but the birth control pill, were not content with the politics of their elders. The violence that took place in the summer of '68 on this newly constituted political body marked the generation for the next forty years.[67]

Despite the official cleaning of the blood from Tlatelolco in '68 and the metaphorical cleansing of the historical record in the late 1960s and early 1970s, the physical and political violence that the generation of '68 endured ensured a continued search for answers.[68] That continued struggle for truth challenges the impunity of the state that developed a rhetoric that portrayed the young male activist of '68 as an aberration and a deviant of the modern nation.[69]

Notes

This essay draws on material in my book *Plaza of Sacrifices: Gender, Power, and Terror in 1968 Mexico* (Albuquerque: University of New Mexico Press, 2005). Excerpts used with the permission of the publisher. I would like to thank Raúl Álvarez Garín, Sandra Peña, Marcelino Perelló, Lucía Rayas Velasco, and José Agustín Román Gaspar,

1. See Ariel Rodriguez Kuri, "Hacia México 68: Pedro Ramírez Vázquez y el proecto olímpico," *Secuencia* 56, May–August 2003, 37–73; "El otro 68: Politica y estilo en la organización de los juegos olímpicos de la ciudad de México," *Relaciones* 19, Fall 1998, 109–129; Eric Zolov, "Showcasing the `Land of Tomorrow': Mexico and the 1968 Olympics, " *The Americas* 61:2 (October 2004): 159–188; and Kevin Witherspoon, *Before the Eyes of the World: Mexico and the 1968 Olympic Games* (Deklab: Northern Illinois University Press, 2008).

2. See Raúl Alvarez Garín, Gilberto Guevara Niebla, Hermann Bellinghausen, Hugo Hiriart, eds., *Pensar del 68* (México, DF: Cal y Arena, 1988); Cesar Gilberto, *Él habito de la utopía: Analisis del imaginario sociopolitico en el movimiento estudiantil de Mexico, 1968* (México, DF: Instituto Mora: Miguel Angel Porrua, 1993); Gilberto Guevara Niebla, *La democracia en la calle: Crónica del movimiento estudiantil mexicano UNAM* (México, DF: Instituto de Investigaciones Sociales, 1988); *La luchas estudiantiles en México,* 2 vols. (México, DF: Linea, 1983); *La crisis de la educación superior en México,* (México, DF: Nueva Imagen, 1981); Elena Poniatowska, *Massacre in Mexico,* trans. Helen Lane (Columbus: University of Missouri Press, 1992); Eduardo Valle, *Escritos sobre del movimiento del 68* (México: Universidad Autónoma de Sinaloa, 1984); and Sergio Zermeño, *México: Una democracía utópica, el movimiento del 68* (México, DF: Siglo Vienturno Editores, 1978).

3. Stephen Niblo, *Mexico in the 1940s: Modernity, Politics, and Corruption* (Wilmington: Scholarly Resources Press, 1999); and John Sherman, "The Mexican 'Miracle' and Its Collapse," in *The Oxford History of Mexico,* ed. Michael Meyer and William Beezley (New York: Oxford University Press, 2000).

4. Deborah Cohen and Lessie Jo Frazier, "Introduction," in *Gender and Sexuality in 1968: Transformative Politics in the Cultural.* See also, Carole S. Vance, ed., *Pleasure and Danger: The Politics of Sexuality* (New York: Harper Collins, 1993).

5. Enrique Semo, "Mexico: The Roots of 1968" presented at conference 1968 in the Global South, November 7, 2008.

6. For a discussion on the role of women in the movement, see Carey, *Plaza of Sacrifices;* Lessie Jo Frazier and Deborah Cohen, "Defining the Space of Mexico '68: Heroic Masculinity in the Prison and `Women' in the Streets," *Hispanic American Historical Review* 83:4

(2003): 617–680; and Julia Sloan, "The 1968 Student Movement and the Crisis of Mexico's Institutionalized Revolution" (Ph.D. diss., University of Houston, 2001).

7. Joan W. Scott, "Gender: A Useful Category of Historical Analysis," *American Historical Review* 91 (December 1986): 1053–1075; Sandra McGee-Deutsch, "Gender and Sociopolitical Change in Twentieth Century Latin America," *Hispanic American Historical Review* 71 (1991): 259–306; and Ana María Alonso, *Threads of Blood: Colonialism, Revolution, and Gender on Mexico's Northern Frontier* (Tucson: University of Arizona Press, 1995), 74–90.

8. See Ilene Malloy, *The Myth of the Revolution: Hero Cults and the Institutionalization of the Mexican State, 1920 to 1940* (New York: Greenwood Press, 1986); Ann Rubenstein, *Bad Language, Naked Ladies, and Other Threats to the Nation: A Political History of Comic Books in Mexico* (Durham: Duke University Press, 1998); Eric Zolov, *Refried Elvis: The Rise of the Mexican Counter-Culture* (Berkeley: University of California Press, 1999). See also Marit Melhuus and Kristi Anne Stølen, eds., *Machos, Mistresses, and Madonnas: Contesting the Power of Latin American Gender Imagery* (New York: Verso Press, 1996).

9. For a discussion of the co-option of university student leaders into the PRI, see Donald Mabry, *The Mexican University and the State, 1910–1971* (College Station: Texas A&M Press, 1982).

10. Arturo Warman, "Secreto de familia," in *Pensar el '68*, 132–133. In a brief analysis, Warman, a 1968 activist, sees the student movement as a struggle within the family. He uses the Mexican family as a category for geopolitical analysis. See also Frank Brandenburg, *The Making of Modern Mexico* (Englewood Cliff: Prentice Hall, 1967).

11. José Agustín , *La contracultura en México: La historia y el significado de los rebeldes sin causa, los jipitecas, los punks, y las bandas* (México, DF: Editorial Grijalbo, 1996); Carlos Monsiváis, *Días de guardar* (México, DF: Bibliotecas Era, 1970); and Zolov, *Refried Elvis*.

12. Herbert Braun, "Protests of Engagement: Dignity, False Love, and Self-Love in Mexico During 1968." *Comparative Studies in Society and History* 39 (July 1997): 511–549. The students continued to press for a public dialogue with the president. Three days before the Great Silent March, the pinnacle of the movement, the CNH appealed directly to the president asking for a dialogue. See, Marcelino Perelló and the CNH to President Díaz Ordaz, September 10, 1968, reprinted in *El Día,* September 18, 1968. Although the Díaz Ordaz administration did have representatives negotiating with the students, Díaz Ordaz argued throughout the movement that the students must correspond and reach an agreement with Luis Echeverría, the Secretary of Interior.

13. While FNET was an active participant in the July 26, 1968 marches, student activists in August demanded that the FNET disband. In part, this was due to the FNET ties to the Mexican government. By early August, students active in FNET issued public statements that supported the government's actions. Escuela Nacional Preparatoria Plantel, No. 8, Comité de lucha, Comunicado núm 1. De los estudiantes al pueblo, July 28, 1968, box 1, document 112, Impresos Sueltos del Movimiento Estudiantil Mexicano, 1968 (hereafter CME); Biblioteca Nacional Mexico City, Mexico. Instituto Politécnico Nacional, ESIA (Ingeniería), Comité de Huelga, Boletín Informativo, August 3, 1968, box 9, document 892, CME.

14. See *El Día*, July 26, 1968; *El Sol*, July 26, 1968; *El Universal*, July 27, 1968. The *zócalo* is the main plaza in Mexico City.

15. "Violentos choques entre estudiantes y la Policía," *El Día*, July 27, 1968; "La policía exculpa a los estudiantes de los alborotos," *El Sol*, July 27, 1968; and "El foco de la agitación," *El Universal*, July 27, 1968.

16. Luis González de Alba, *Los días y los años* (México, DF, 1971), 26–28.

17. Informa las actividades realizados con motivo de la Misión encomendada a esta unidad, July 30, 1968, Secretaria de la Defensa Nacional, México, DF, reprinted in Julio Scherer García and Carlos Monsiváis, *Parte de Guerra Tlatelolco 1968* (México, DF: 1999).

18. *El Universal*, July 28, 1968.

19. Ibid.

20. Ariel Rodríguez Kuri, "Hacia México 68," and Eric Zolov, "Showcasing the Land of Tomorrow," 159–188.

21. Jorge Castañeda, interview, " Mexico 1968: A Movement, a Massacre, and the 40 Year Search for Truth," Radio Diaries and National Public Radio, aired December 1, 2008.

22. "Los Debutantes" in *Excélsior*, July 21, 1968.

23. Héctor Aguilar Camín and Lorenzo Meyer, *In the Shadow of the Mexican Revolution: Contemporary Mexican History 1910–1989*, trans. Luis Alberto Fierro (Austin: University of Texas Press, 1993).

24. Octavio Paz, *The Labyrinth of Solitude and the Other Mexico, Return to the Labyrinth of Solitude, Mexico, and the United States, The Philanthropic Ogre* (New York: Grove Press, 1985); Samuel Ramos, *Profile of Man and Culture in Mexico*, trans. Peter G. Earle, (Austin: University of Texas Press, 1962); and Ana Maria Alonso, *Thread of Blood*, 82–84.

25. See Luis M. Farías, *Así lo recuerdo: testimonio político* (México, DF: Fondo de Cultura Económica, 1992), 56–57; and Julio Scherer, *Los presidentes* (México, DF: Grijaldo, 1986), 15.

26. Farías, *Así lo recuerdo*, 56–57. For an analysis of Díaz Ordaz, see Enrique Krauze, *Mexico: A Biography of Power: A History of Modern Mexico, 1810–1996* (New York: Harper Perennial, 1997), 665–738.

27. Chappell Lawson, *Building the Fourth Estate: Democratization and the Rise of the Free Press in Mexico* (Berkeley: University of California Press, 2002). Lawson examines the media shifts that took place in Mexico in the 1990s. He argues from 1930 to 1990, the Mexican regime manipulated the news that was printed and broadcast through subsidies, bribes, and corruption, thus creating a docile tool for its propaganda. In 1968, there were exceptions. *El Día*, the left-of-center newspaper carried many of the student statements and announcements. *El Día*, however, had a much more limited distribution compared to other Mexico City based newspapers.

28. Benedict Anderson, *Imagined Communities: Reflections on the Origin and Spread of Nationalism* (New York: Verso Press, 1991); and Doris Sommer, *Foundational Fictions: The National Romances of Latin America* (Berkeley: University of California Press, 1993), 30–51.

29. See *El Universal*, July 28, 1968. This newspaper provided names of people who were detained by authorities, particularly those who were not Mexican citizens. According to information provided by the newspapers, had all allegedly entered Mexico illegally.

30. *El Universal*, July 29, 1968.

31. *Excélsior*, July 31, 1968.

32. Beginning in the 1960s, a split began to emerge in the Mexican Communist Party. Young activists pushed for a more direct action within the party. It is from these early confrontations, that students would break away to form their own organizations such as the reorganized *Juventud Comunista Mexicana* (Communist Youth) in the early 1960s and later the *Central Nacional de Estudiantes Democráticos* (National Democratic Students Committee, CNED). Although Communist Youth were active, the CNED was comprised of students of various ideological backgrounds, who embraced the ideals of the telephone, teachers, and railroad and telephone workers, and their purpose was to fight for a program of reasserted democracy. See Raúl Alvarez Garín, "Los años de gran tentación" en *Pensar del 68*, ed. by Raúl Alvarez Garín,et. al. (México, DF: Cal y Arena, 1993), 25–32. It was in these "new" left, that young men and women could chart their own course outside of the traditional left and PRI dominated student organizations.

33. Judith Butler, *Gender Trouble: Feminism and the Subversion of Identity* (New York: Routledge Press, 1990), 140.

34. Jeffrey Weeks, *Sexuality* (New York: Routledge Press, 2003), 70–86. The Mexican government response to activists was not dramatically different than how young men were perceived in the other nations. See George Katsiaficas, *The Imagination of the New Left: A Global Analysis of 1968* (Boston: South End Press, 1987); and Robert V. Daniels, *Year of the Heroic Guerrilla: World Revolution and Counterrevolution in 1968* (New York: Basic Books, 1989).

35. María Luisa Mendoza, "La O o el Redondo," *El Día*, August 2, 1968.

36. "Un ordenada manifestación, *El Universal*, August 2, 1968.

37. For the photos, see *El Universal*, August 2, 1968. Also see *Novedades*, August 2, 1968,; *El Día*, August 2, 1968; and *Excélsior*, August 2, 1968.

38. For a complete transcript of the speech, see *Excélsior* and *El Día*, August 2, 1968. Translation in Elena Poniatowska, *Massacre in Mexico*, 328.

39. Díaz Ordaz referred to the so-called outstretched hand in his annual address to the nation on September 1, 1968. For a discussion and partial transcriptions of the speech, see *El Heraldo de México, Novedades*, and *El Universal,* September 2, 1968.

40. Javier Barros Sierra was rector of UNAM from 1966 to 1970. His role in '68 is viewed as a legitimizing act. See Gastón García Cantú, *1968: Javier Barrios Sierra: Conversaciones con Gastón García Cantú* (México, DF: Siglo Veintiuno Editores, 1972). Also see *1968: Universidad y cultura*, Nexos TV (August 15, 1993), 60 mins., videocassette.

41. One of the few documents reflecting the earliest meetings between Poli and UNAM is a statement discussing police and government violence issued at the end of July. "A la opinión pública," July 1968, box 5, document 492, CME.

42. For a discussion of Mexican student politics at UNAM, see Donald Mabry's *The Mexican University and the State: Student Conflicts, 1910–1971*(College Station: Texas A&M Press, 1982).

43. Raúl Jardón, "1968: El fuego y la esperanza" (unpublished manuscript in possession of author, 1996); Raúl Jardón, interview with author, Mexico City, March 6, 1997. Jardón and Adriana Corona, both CNH members, accounted for 128 CNH members.

44. The demands were published in several newspapers. See *El Universal,* July 30, 1968; and *El Día,* July 30, 1968.

45. "Carta de Corona del Rosal a Massieu," *El Día*, August 9, 1968.

46. "Llamado a la Concordia, en bien de México, formuló Corona," *Excélsior,* August 9, 1968.

47. "A la opinión pública," *El Día*, August 10, 1968.

48. Ibid.

49. *Gaceta: Boletín Informativo del Comité Coordinador de Huelga de UNAM*, No. 1, August 13, 1968. box 7, no. 787, CME.

50. The *Coalición de Profesores de Enseñanza Media y Superior Pro Libertades Democráticas* (the Coalition of Secondary and University Teachers for Democratic Liberties) formed on August 8. Led by engineer Heberto Castillo, the Coalition comprised teachers, researchers, and professors from IPN, UNAM, and their institutes and national schools, as well as Chapingo, IPN's technical and vocational schools, various UNAM preparatory schools, and the Association of Administrative workers at UNAM.

51. See Leobardo López Arteche and CUEC, *El grito*, 1969, 120 mins. Videocassette. Also, see images in García Cantú, *1968: Javier Barros Sierra*.

52. Listed in Ramón Ramírez, *El movimiento estudiantil de México*: 2 volumes (México: Ediciones Era, 1969). Also can be seen in *El grito*.

53. *El Heraldo de México*, August 14, 1968.

54. "Insultos al ejército y las autoridades," *El Heraldo*, August 14, 1968.

55. A comic published in the newspaper *Novedades* portrayed a similar statement. In this comic, a granaderos in his riot gear relaxes in an easy chair as his son, wearing a Poli sweater, waves to his father on his way out the door to the August 13 march. *Novedades*, August 13, 1968.

56. Ibid.

57. Christian Krohn-Hansen, "Masculinity and Political Among Dominicans: The Dominican Tigre," in *Machos, Mistresses, and Madonnas*. Krohn-Hansen contemplates how masculinity plays a central role in political legitimacy.

58. Butler, *Gender Trouble*, 118–123.

59. See Leobardo López Arteche and CUEC, *El grito*, 1969, 120 mins. Videocassette. In the film, students are shown making fliers and posters. There is also a scene where a father is showing his young children the student propaganda at UNAM

60. Colección de impresos Esther Montero, Instituto de Investigación Sobre la Universidad y la Educación, Archivo Histórico de Universidad Nacional Autónoma de México- (IISUE/ AHUNAM) Biblioteca Nacional, México, DF.

61. Colección de impresos Esther Montero, IISUE/AHUNAM.

62. See Grupo Mira, *La gráfica del '68: Homenaje al movimiento estudiantil* (México, DF: El Juglar, Ediciones Zurda, 1988).

63. See Comité de lucha, Facultad de Ciencias Políticas y Sociales, "La formación y funcionamiento de brigadas políticas estudiantiles de secundaria, preparatoria, UNAM, e IPN," August 26, 1998, box 3 document 213, CME. Also republished in Leopoldo Ayala, *Nuestra Verdad: Memorias popular del movimiento estudiantil popular y el dos de octubre de 1968* (México, DF: Joaquín Porrúa, 1989), 106.

64. From early August and the organization of the CNH, activists from outside of Mexico City mobilized. The *Universidad Autónoma de Chihuahua* (Autonomous University of Chihuahua) and the *Universidad Autónoma de Puebla* (Autonomous University of Puebla) had representatives on the CNH. Activists from the states of Mexico, Morelos, and Hidalgo were also represented. After the invasion of UNAM on September 18–19, students other states occupied buildings and went on strike, including northern states of Nuevo León and Baja California and in the southern state of Yucatan. "Impedirán mítines estudiantiles en Oaxaca; paros in Monterrey, Mérida, y otros lugares," *Excélsior*, September 23, 1968.

65. The *grito* refers to the call for independence that Father Miguel Hidalgo made on September 15–16, 1810. On Mexican independence day, the president issues the *"grito"* calling out the names of Mexico's forefathers.

66. "La CU se entregará a las autoridades universitarias en cuanto estas lo soliciten, declara Echeverría," *El Día*, September 20, 1968.

67. For a scholarly documentation of the continued struggle, see Comité 68 Pro Libertades Democráticas, *México: Genocidio y delitos de lesa humanidades documentos básicos 1968–2008* 10 vols. (México, DF: Comité 68 Pro Libertades Democráticas, 2008), in possession of author. This collection includes early publications regarding the movement as well as recent documents from the special prosecutor and the Comité's ongoing investigation.

68. Elaine Carey and José Agustín Román Gaspar, "Carrying on the Struggle: El Comité 68," with, *NACLA Report on the Americas* special issue "Against Impunity: The Decline of the Mexican Social Pact," May/June 2008, 20–21.

69. See Sergio Aguayo Quezada and Javier Treviño Rangel, "Neither Truth Nor Justice: Mexico's Deafacto Amnesty," *Latin American Perspectives* 33:2 (March 2006): 56–68.

CHAPTER THREE

"Your Sexual Revolution Is Not Ours": French Feminist "Moralism" and the Limits of Desire

JULIAN BOURG

The sexual revolution and the social movements of gender contestation associated with it—feminism and gay liberation—were never unified phenomena. Although feminists and some male activists often had great reason to find common cause with one another in attacking the sexual and gender "old order," such solidarity did not always materialize. Advocates of sexual and gender liberation certainly encountered limits to their intentional projects from without (religious, middle class, and/or patriarchal). They also encountered limits within generally consonant and sometimes conflicting sexual and gender liberation movements, as various parties struggled among themselves to define what the sexual revolution promised and what it could deliver. Ironically, sexual politics sometimes fought other sexual politics all in the name of liberation.

In this essay, I discuss conflicts in France *between* certain feminists and certain male leftists over what the liberation of desire was supposed to mean. Though the story of feminist/male leftist conflict should not for a moment be taken as exemplifying or summing up relationships that were otherwise often conciliatory and strategically linked, such antagonisms could be felt even as the French women's and gay liberation movements were founded in 1970–1971. Simmering for several years, those tensions came out into the open, especially between 1976 and 1978, around the specific questions of sexual violence and the law. Disagreements on these questions often broke down along lines of sex difference. Some men on the French far-left—associated with gay liberation and the "revolutionary" appeal of criminality—were incapable of appreciating the limits of liberation and desire. Debate ultimately turned on the promises and risks of participation/collusion with French law, courts, and prisons. As in the earlier history of French feminism, 1970s sexual politics also had "only paradoxes to offer" not simply between difference and equality but also between "revolution" and "reform."[1] Such paradoxes emerged when good questions were raised about the limits of legal limits (incarceration as an end) and also when feminists who said that the sexual revolution had limits (violence against women) were accused by some men of "moralism."

This essay begins by examining the widespread displacement of gender during the revolts of May '68 and the tensions between women and men in the gay and women's liberation movements founded in the late 1960s and early 1970s. In the context of gay male liberation, the activist and theorist Guy Hocquenghem articulated a vision of sexual liberation that focused on the negation of limits on male desire, limits understood in the complementary forms of patriarchal familialism, psychoanalytic normalization, and bourgeois legality. This last category—law—is of particular interest, and in the subsequent section of this essay I consider how the attitudes of some feminists toward the French legal system evolved during the mid-1970s, as mobilizations around the issue of sexual violence came to supplant earlier campaigns against the illegality of abortion. There was no shortage of controversy on the French far-left as to how one ought to regard the legal institutions of the Fifth Republic. Acrimony often departed from and could be assessed according to lines drawn between "revolutionaries" and "reformists," between gays and straights, or what interests us here, between males and females. I thus examine one particularly heated series of debates between men and women in the newspaper *Libération*, and I conclude by suggesting that 1970s French feminist mobilization around the law culminated in a fruitful, paradoxical vision: while cautionary tales about the law's normalizing force remain useful, the law is one site where the gains of sexual and gender liberation are instantiated. The charge of "feminist moralism" coalesced in large measure around the question of how the far-left—men and women, gay and straight, mobilized around questions of gender or indifferent to them—would relate to the law, grapple with its normalizing tendencies, and involve it in the project of liberation. It took a number of years for some of the liberational contradictions of May '68 to work themselves out. Gender, sex difference, and sexuality were some of the terms involved in this sorting. I do not mean to suggest that phenomena of the *sexual revolution* and *gender* can be reduced one to the other. Rather, since in 1970s France they combined in fascinating and sometimes conflicting ways, it is their relationship I will examine in greater detail.

This chapter in the story of the sexual revolution and social movements of gender contestation is intended to complement other analyses, two of which can be found in this volume.[2] Justin David Suran draws attention to the tensions between "homophile and civil rights traditions," on one hand, and radical gay liberation, on the other hand. I take as my point of departure some of the "points of contact" and "sites of controversy" among men and women to which he alludes but does not explore in detail. Concerned as he is with linking American male gay liberation to protests against the Vietnam War—women were not drafted—conflicts between feminism and gay liberation and between lesbians and gay men are backgrounded. Suran cannot be reproached for not making claims outside the scope of his analysis. Similarly, my essay is meant to supplement that of Michael Sibalis, who succinctly recounts the shifts in French gay liberation from '68 through the early 1980s. He mentions the "ambient misogyny" of the early gay liberation movement, but does not explore its later consequences. Though I more explicitly treat Hocquenghem's differentialist sexual politics as somewhat of a dead end, if for immediate rhetorical efficacy, my account nevertheless complements the overall picture he paints— from "provocation" to "reformism." As will be clear in what follows, some of the positions maintained by men of the French far-left indicate the era's moral ambiguities.

Gender and '68: Tensions from the Start

Gender concerns were not highlighted during the famous events of May '68 in France. Revisionist historians will no doubt continue to find evidence to the contrary,[3] but accounts of the French women's and gay liberation social movements generally contend that widespread leftist mobilization around and contestation of gender matters developed only later, around 1970.[4] To be sure, the group *Féminin, masculin, avenir* (Female, Male, Future) had formed in 1967, and inasmuch as gender was linked to questions of sexuality and desire, signs of this kind of cultural ferment abounded in the student milieu. The May movement could be traced to agitation the previous year (April 1967) at the Nanterre campus of the University of Paris when male students had demanded the right to visit the dorm rooms of female students. That right was granted on the condition that they procure signed permission slips from their parents. Also at Nanterre, in January '68 the student leader Daniel Cohn-Bendit had been told by the Minister of Sports, François Missoffe, that if he was sexually frustrated then he could jump in the newly completed university swimming pool.[5]

Some celebrated graffiti of the May days captured the liberational/ libertine ethos of the moment—*Take one's desires for reality*; *The more I make love, the more I make revolution*—but aphoristic expressions did little to systematize or strategize a "desiring revolution," even if such slogans helped seal the reputation of May '68 as a festival where the rules of everyday life had been suspended and speech had been taken up and proliferated (*prendre la parole*). While the Freudo-Marxist works of Herbert Marcuse and Wilhelm Reich would be devoured in the early 1970s, few people during May had read them, including the "leaders" of the movement.[6] The group, *Mouvement jeune révolutionnaire* (Young Revolutionary Movement), admitted its own isolation when it claimed in one of its tracts that it "alone frankly approaches the problem of women."[7] However, the *Mouvement démocratique feminine* (Female Democratic Movement) circulated a tract addressed to "women students" that declared "the society to be built must be the work of women as well as of men; it must give all women equal opportunity with men."[8] In the occupied Sorbonne, the two-person *Comité d'Action Pédérastique Révolutionnaire* (Committee for Revolutionary Pederastic Action) put up fliers that were immediately ripped down, and a day-care center was organized for women trying to strike a balance between the demands of motherhood and those of radical agitation.[9] Groups and efforts such as these were hardly coordinated, and further evidence for gender and sexuality being taken up in the maelstrom of the May revolts is similarly anecdotal. It was true that sex was viewed as some kind of challenge to repressive bourgeois society, but critical energies were turned to work and speech and generally not focused on gender and sexuality.[10] If for at least a generation afterward the French terms *jouissance* (pleasure, enjoyment, orgasm) and *épanouissement* (flowering, opening out onto) would be associated with May '68, it was not because sexuality had immediately become political, but because politics had suddenly seemed sexy. The problematization of sexuality—and with it as a historical companion piece, the problematization of gender—did not take place until the French far-left stopped expressing itself, as it still had in '68, in the mono-language of class.

The Early 1970s: *Vive la Révolution* and Tout!

During the extended period of radical agitation in early 1970s the French far-left began to face the challenge of diversifying the sites and terms of its liberational projects. It is important, first of all, to underscore the relevance of this focus on French radicals. Though the evolution of sexual and gender social mores during the 1960s and 1970s owed much to anonymous demographic, economic, and cultural forces, there is little doubt that the women's and gay liberation movements, small in number and often initially ignored, contributed mightily to those changes. The margin led and the masses followed. The era certainly saw the astonishing demise of avant-garde politics, but such politics did not die without bringing certain parts of the "old world" down with them. Furthermore, many of the actors and actresses at the forefront of the post–'68 French far-left turned out to be, for better or worse, some of the most influential political and cultural leaders in France during subsequent decades.

Among post–'68 far-left groups open to the sexual revolution and to shifting the focus from class war to the transformation of daily life, the most important was the Maoist group *Vive la Révolution!* (Long Live Revolution! or VLR) formed in the fall of 1969 under the leadership of Roland Castro and Tiennot Grumbach.[11] Castro tried to welcome groups organized around specific identities—women, gays, immigrants, youth movements—into the organization. These groups, which Alain Touraine popularized as the New Social Movements, were still framed for VLR within a Marxist-Leninist scaffolding.[12] In a 1970 text whose title borrowed a line from the poet Arthur Rimbaud, *Change Life*, Castro wrote:

> The people oppose on all fronts of social life tit-for-tat responses against oppression, exploitation, anarchy, boredom, and capitalist manipulation. To begin to oppose on every front, everywhere, popular legality against bourgeois legality: this is the conducting wire for *changing life.*[13]

The suspicion of "bourgeois legality," whose corollary was found in talk of "prolonged armed struggle," continued to haunt the far-left for sometime thereafter. Castro's strategy was to organize autonomous groups in the form of a union, directed by a Leninist structure but preserving the autonomy of specific parties. "It didn't work like that," he admits.[14] The contradictions of Marxism-Leninism and the New Social Movements came to a head with the publication of the infamous issue number twelve of the VLR newspaper, *Ce que nous voulons: Tout!* (What do we want? Everything!), published on April 23, 1971. In the wake of increasing dissension following that issue, Castro abruptly dissolved the group several months later.

The editors of the paper had given responsibility for the contents of the twelfth issue to a group of male homosexual and feminist activists. Many of the articles were signed by members of the *Front Homosexuel d'Action Révolutionnaire* (Homosexual Front for Revolutionary Action or FHAR), which had begun meeting the previous month.[15] The front page of the newspaper captured aspects of the agenda, as well as some of the dilemmas, of gay and feminist activists working together:

> Yes, our bodies belong to us.
> - free abortion and contraception
> - right to homosexuality and all sexualities

- right of minors to the freedom of desire and to its accomplishment

These exigencies raise questions about the limit points of life: about incest, rape, euthanasia, suicide... They have their extensions: refusal to submit one's body to the census, to pollution, to daily rhythms, to work accidents... They exceed themselves: the free disposition of my body cannot exercise itself against those of others. This freedom only really exists in the blossoming [*l'épanouissement*] of all. They designate the ends of the revolution: the perfection of happiness.[16]

The side-by-side appearance of reproductive rights, "all sexualities," and the sexuality of minors was significant. Such terms would not again be so easily invoked together. Similarly, the question of limits, the extension of sexual matters into biopolitical and knowledge-power regimes (e.g., the census), and the conjunction of a happy liberal vision of self-delimiting freedoms with the utopian forecast of revolutionary beatitude—these very different judgments of "our bodies belong to us" were also worked over in the coming years. The remainder of the articles in issue number twelve demonstrated how collaborative strategizing between feminists and homosexuals was already leading to a number of divergent emphases.

Differences emerged in the respective agenda and perceptions of feminists and gay men. For women, the reclamation of reproductive rights and the question of the women's movement becoming *non-mixte*, or separatist, figured prominently. For men, the sexuality of minors seemed important—first of all, minors had a right to express their sexuality; second, amorous relations between adults and minors ought to be permitted. Programmatic contrasts spilled over into attitudes. Whereas one male FHAR member wrote of the project of the "disruption of all mores, without restriction," a woman from the group spoke of how "our homosexual [male] friends are raised like others in the overestimation of pseudo-virile values," but noted optimistically that "they succeed in throwing off [those values] to the extent that they know better than anyone else the repressive significance of the hetero-cop morality [*la morale hétéro-flic*]." On the other hand, another man from FHAR decried the "legend" of gay male misogyny. Woman had "opened the way," and gay men found themselves in the position of "desiring men" and "despising virility": "We claim our 'femininity,' that which women reject, at the same time that we declare that these roles have no meaning." On the question of strategic allegiances between women and gay men, a certain Sylvie wrote that "their struggles seem incompatible." Gay men took themselves as the "elite of the male sex [*le race mâle*]" and lived in a "world of misogynist selection which is the very opposite of the liberation of the woman." Mentioning a position that would be popularized during debates on pornography in 1974–1975, she noted that lesbianism formed a key part of the "erotic commerce" of straight society, though she went on to say that even if lesbianism could bring a "disalienation" in consciousness, consciousness alone did little to change the "political and social situation of women."[17]

The twelfth issue of *Tout!* was, as the next number reported, a "paving stone in the leftist pond."[18] The issue certainly made a number of waves. Using a frostier metaphor, the editors wrote that an "avalanche of letters," laudatory and critical, had been received. The far-left press expressed dismay, especially over a printed statement by Jean Genet, who said in effect that if he had not slept with Algerian boys, then he may not have supported the Algerian insurgency during the 1956–1962 war. The *Tout!* staff also felt obliged to answer objections that issue number twelve had been "antiworker."[19] The real storm, though, came when, following the complaints by a member of the National Assembly, Michel Caldagùes, and the Mayor of Tours, Jean Royer, number twelve was confiscated by the police. Its nominal director of publication, Jean-Paul Sartre, was charged with *outrage aux bonnes moeurs*, or public indecency. This led Sartre to comment that "a new bourgeois offensive for moral order" had begun in which "market pornography is favored, but those who want to conquer freedom against sexual oppression are prosecuted."[20] Bad publicity on the far-left and from the government had the effect of boosting sales. Attendees at the FHAR's weekly meetings jumped from forty to around four hundred within the month.[21]

The predominance of male homosexuality in *Tout!* number twelve had been fairly evident even to those involved. The position of women in VLR was less obvious in April 1971. Matters were somewhat cleared up, if scandalously so, with the publication of issue fourteen on June 7.[22] As the introductory editorial note that accompanied the "Letter from Mohamed" explained, "This text is serious and even provocative.... For many of us, it is difficult to swallow."[23] The "Letter" accused French female radicals of an awful racism. The proof of this racism, Mohamed said, was that French girls refused to go to bed with him. Behind the pathetic argument was a larger, more serious point about race on the far-left and in the politics of everyday life: "You say that you aren't racist, that there are simply cultural and educational differences.... To make love you don't need a diploma in philosophy or science." But Mohamed added insult to injury by targeting what he called "leftist fascism": "French girls are rotten with racism; they have it in their blood like an almost incurable virus.... You incarnate all the evil of Europe, the bestiality of the filthy white." The editors of *Tout!*, admitting that "this text expresses a male racism at the same moment it denounces a racism of color," decided to publish it anyway since "today, Arab comrades speak of their life also... We don't care if we're full of contradictions. We assume them." Understandably, part of the reason why women would leave both far-left organizations and the newly born gay one was that the culture of masculinity—straight and gay—played itself on very broad bandwidths.

Needless to say, the text and *Tout!*'s decision to publish it provoked the ire of some VLR feminists. The following issue of *Tout!* (June 30, 1971) included both a "Response to the Letter from Mohammed," whose author said that she had slept with several Arabs without any significant problems, and, more significantly, a scathing criticism of the VLR-*Tout!* ambiance that had tacitly supported the more questionable aspects of Mohamed's polemic.[24] This latter piece, "Your Sexual Revolution Is Not Ours," was authored by two "militants from the Women's Liberation Movement [*Mouvement de libération des femmes*, or MLF]"—Françoise Picq and Nadja Ringart. "The numbers 12 and following of *Tout!* give a certain image of the 'sexual revolution,'" the essay said,

> by taking pleasure/enjoyment [*jouissance*] and the right to enjoy oneself/come more [*plus jouir*] for basic criteria. ...Since men and women are alienated, there is at present only an alienated conception of pleasure/enjoyment. It remains to find new forms of pleasure/enjoyment.

Even the "new image" of the liberated woman corresponded to this relational structure, since women in VLR were "fixed in this ['liberated'] role and made to feel guilty when they no longer corresponded to it." That was to say, promiscuity was a putatively revolutionary act. Picq and Ringart called for a prolonged "deconstruction" of power on many levels in order to "at last discover our totality of being human." The question of "love" could not be posed until women were "liberated." Picq and Ringart's text accompanied a mock study of the mores of the *Tout!* staff, in *faux* anthropological speak, entitled, "Life and Mores of the 'Tuot' Tribe, or May Your Bones Rot in the Moonlight."[25]

The controversy continued in the next issue of *Tout!*, which was the newspaper's last. Although a "group of girls" struck back at Mohamed's "aberrant generalization" and "infantile logic," the final word seems to have gone to several male FHAR members. One *Tout!* editor, responding to "Your Sexual Revolution is Not Ours," admitted that some "comrades" had tried to form "veritable harems" by telling women that any jealousy on their part was residual "bourgeois" sentiment. But, he went on to say, the phrase "enjoy oneself/come more" [*plus jouir*] could not be applied equally to straight and gay men. It was the "fault of women" if they did not challenge any "more subtle oppression...at the moment when this ideology was constituted." Even if women and gay men seemed to be "natural allies," the program of the FHAR was "rather different" than that of the MLF: "Sexuality occupies the principal place in the revolt of [male] homosexuals." Echoing this sentiment, several FHAR activists, drawing the "balance sheet" of the group's first few months, concluded that the "sensibilities" of lesbians and gay men were "frankly different and we have a bit too quickly cried for 'unity.'" After the summer holiday, when the group met again in September, it was likely that "two distinct movements" would be formed.[26]

The *Front Homosexuel d'Action Révolutionnaire* and Guy Hocquenghem

Alliances between lesbians and gay men in the FHAR were short-lived in 1971. The group's weekly Thursday night meetings at the Beaux-Arts school in Paris were often contentious, and before long, they turned into forums for sexual cruising as much as for political discussion. The infamous "sixth floor" was reputed for its shadowed encounters. It did not take long for the FHAR to collapse into a kind of gay male party and for women—lesbians in FHAR as well as other feminists more generally—to bemoan how the group fostered a certain kind of "machoism" sometimes summed up by the phrase "sex without love." In one representative example, Cathy Bernheim recounts how one weekend retreat in the country for lesbians and gay men from FHAR concluded with the men going into the local town to try to pick up boys, and the women staying at the group's lodging to discuss whether sexual liberation meant more than the right to have multiple sexual partners.[27]

One person—Guy Hocquenghem—did the most to represent and publicly express the male sensibility of the FHAR, and his writings on gay liberation give a glimpse at two important points in the FHAR/MLF constellation—"dark homosexuality" and its relation to feminism.[28] Hocquenghem's first major publication, *Homosexual Desire* (1972), was indebted to Gilles Deleuze and Félix Guattari's collaborative *Anti-Oedipus*, published several months earlier.[29] The latter had attacked psychoanalysis and the bourgeois family as two heads of the same repressive dragon, promoting in their place the notion of "desiring machines" as the basic elements in a "schizoanalytic" alternative. Hocquenghem's "homosexual desire" built directly on this model. The Oedipal complex represented a "double bind" for homosexuals: to be "normal" they had to give up their desire; to keep their desire, they had to accept identification as "perverse."[30] Normalization of any kind was Hocquenghem's general worry. Attempts to play the Oedipal games of identity and politics were rigged in advance. In his view, efforts to secure greater toleration, to reform antigay legislation, and even to cultivate gay "pride" were structurally skewed as no-win situations. The double bind assured that identity and politics—both phallic procedures in the way that their significations centered on the prime Signifiers of the self and the state—led only to "gilded bars" on homosexuals' social cages.[31] According to Hocquenghem, gay families, for example, would have been the worst form of bourgeois "recuperation" since they reduced gay difference to a "phallic" convention of bourgeois patriarchal society. Hostility to normalization, then, culminated in an antinomian rebellion against any reform or limit—against what he called the "lighted agora" of sexual politics. Law, whether psychoanalytic or republican-democratic, was suspect. In place of greater political recognition or social toleration, Hocquenghem asserted what he called "dark homosexuality"—the world of Jean Genet, of prostitutes, criminality, cruising, and public sex.[32] Against its canalization into reproductive heterosexual normalcy, desire was intended to circulate and achieve machine-like productivity. The Guattaro-Deleuzian term "desiring machines" was given new meaning in the claim that gay men were "orgasm machines."[33] The phallic identity politics of Oedipal desire were to be contrasted with "anal" sexuality—the realm of the private, the scatological, the transgressive, and the not-yet-sublimated.[34] Anonymous sexual encounters between gay men, the so-called "pick-up machine," modeled dark homosexuality's effort to escape the double-bind.

Hocquenghem's differentialist theory of homosexual desire exemplifies one moment of tension between women and men within the French sexual liberation/far-left movements of the early 1970s. At a certain extreme, his view of dark homosexuality culminated in a deep hostility toward anything resembling normalization, such as the plausible suggestion that the orgasm machine might itself have limits as a model of progressive sexual politics. In this register, Hocquenghem's attitude toward feminism is telling. While he acknowledged that gay men were indebted to feminists and that the FHAR had come into being on a "political terrain already cleared by the Women's Liberation Movement," Hocquenghem had little to say about or to women.[35] Homosexuality was implicitly masculine. There was no discussion of lesbianism in *Homosexual Desire*, and women's sexuality had only been mentioned to demonstrate the tyranny of the phallocratic Oedipus. From the summer of 1972 forward, Hocquenghem was dissecting the corpse of any gay male-feminist alliance. The gay movement had needed "independence" from the MLF.[36] The two movements had "totally different ideological bases," since the MLF "apparently needs to put itself in a position of relative strength with respect to male society."[37] In as much as Hocquenghem's orgasm machines were meant to make gay liberation an "antihumanist" movement, any concern for the contextual "psychology of relationships" was retrograde. In his judgment of what he heard around him, feminism was a humanism. That being said, the next step was to draw the full circle and connect feminism to the normalizing traps of identity, reform, and integration.

Feminists had criticized a special issue of the journal *Recherches*, entitled *Three Billion Perverts: Great Encyclopedia of Homosexualities* (March 1973), which had published a variety of articles on Arab gay sex, masturbation, pick-ups, pedophilia, sado-masochism, and institutions.[38] What bothered some feminists was likely the prominent display of male bodies and erect penises and the suspicion that some of the authors of the special issue were reverting to "phallocratism," perhaps of nontraditional shades, but masculinist nonetheless. In July, Hocquenghem responded somewhat bitterly to what he saw as the "moral rearmament" of "Mao-feminism":

> The movement is pulled between two extremes, a body with multiple organs (sado-masochist, crossing-dressing, etc.) and a new morality that aims to exclude diversity and the polymorphism of the new perverts in the name of a one and only law, that which distinguishes the friends and enemies of the People—excuse me—women.[39]

Hocquenghem could only see in feminist criticisms a "new law," a "new phallus," and a new norm. That a voice came from the Left was no guarantee that it was not normalizing. The crux of the matter was that feminist criticism and state censorship coincided accidentally and temporally, and Hocquenghem related them thematically and spatially. In his view, neonormalizations had to be met with the same ruthless critique directed against the traditional Oedipal system. As he had written in *Homosexual Desire*,

> [W]hy set a limit?—if there is to be an end to the sexual norm, this must come through the concrete disintegrative process which the gay movement has begun.... We shall therefore not accuse the gay movement of failing to relate to women, lest we reintroduce thereby the very guilt which we have worked to dissolve.... The danger for homosexuality, the trap of desire, lies elsewhere, in what we call its guilt-induced perversion.[40]

Hocquenghem could admit that "misogyny" existed, but he had little to say about it.[41]

Why is Hocquenghem's difficult theory important? To begin with, as a social actor in the gay liberation movement, his thought conveyed, albeit in abstract and indirect ways, one position within the sexual liberation movements. More specifically, Hocquenghem represented the current of "differentialist" cultural politics, born in the "cultural revolution" of the '60s and influential even in our day in cultural studies and identity politics. *The right to difference* has been a key demand and political stance for some time. But Hocquenghem's position raises some good questions about the moral and political coherence, usefulness, and worth of valorizing difference in contradistinction to the *universalism* now classically associated with bourgeois morality, law, and patriarchy. To take the example to which we now turn, does the right to difference apply to perpetrators of sexual violence? Of course not. But according to the right to difference, why not?

Feminism, Law, Rape, and Leftist Male Reaction

The MLF and 1970s French feminism included diverse tendencies. For the specific question of conflict between female and male activists and the emergence of the charge of feminist "moralism" one development merits close examination: the changing status of law among certain feminists during the 1970s, particularly the shift from the struggle for reproductive rights (1972–1974) to the struggle to have rape taken more seriously (1976–1978). These years witnessed the replacement of a feminist position *outside* the law (abortion was illegal) by a feminist position operating *within* the law (the criminalization and punishment of rape). From revolt against and defiance of a proscriptive law that forbade, many feminists moved toward a more positive evaluation of French Republican legal institutions as one site where feminists could agitate for rights and justice for women, by using, Picq says, "the judicial scene to drive rape out from clandestiny and insignificance" into the open.[42] There were, in fact, serious disagreements among feminists over the uses to which French justice could be put—the limits, so to speak, of legal limits. The focus on the positive relation to law advocated by some feminists is meant to draw a contrast with a particularly vicious, if generally short-lived strain of leftist antifeminism. During these years the MLF had to confront a distinctly far-left hostility to "bourgeois" legality, a hostility already expressed by Hocquenghem, but which ran much deeper. The often hysterical and sometimes pathetic entrenchment in a "revolutionary" view of French law by some male leftists—who decried feminist calls for penalizing rape—did much to mobilize feminists in a positive embrace of progressive legislation. To be sure, some men and women raised good questions about the limits of legal recourse, especially penalization. But the shift from "revolution" to "reform," otherwise known as "recuperation" among leftists, marked both the end of one post–'68 ambiance and also a generalized implementation of a certain spirit of '68 with regard to gender and sexuality.

The charge on the far-left that feminists were instigating new forms of moralism coalesced around the issue of rape. Beginning in the winter of 1975–1976 and concluding in the famous Aix-en-Provence trial of May 1978 and subsequent introduction of new legislation that June, the rape debate emerged in several distinct phases punctuated by a discrete series of controversies, most notably in the newspaper *Libération* in March and April 1977. From an initial and incremental mobilization throughout 1976, the *Libé* acrimony—limited to the far-left but during which some men made some outrageous statements—was followed in September and October 1977 by a true mass-media mobilization on the issue. By early 1978, some feminists were expressing real doubts that the French judicial system, though taking rape more seriously, could serve women's interests alongside its own. But such hesitations could not reverse the overall transformation, which culminated symbolically in late-spring and early-summer 1978 in the Aix trial and the introduction of new legislation (not passed, however, until 1980).

In February 1976, lawyers representing two Belgian tourists who had been raped in August 1974 succeeded in having the case transferred from the *Tribunal correctionel* to the *Cour d'Assises*—the equivalent of bumping the charge up from misdemeanor assault to felony rape.[43] Though the trial by jury in Aix-en-Provence would not take place until fifteen months later, in May 1978, the comment was made later in 1976 that "the campaign against rape truly began" with that appellate decision.[44] Meanwhile, throughout 1976, the issue of rape took on greater importance within the feminist movement and in public discourse. An International Tribunal of Crimes against Women was held in Brussels (March 4–8, 1976), at which the lack of juridical consequence for violence against women figured significantly.[45] The issue of female circumcision/genital mutilation first began to be taken seriously in France.[46] Susan Brownmiller's *Against Our Will* (1975) arrived in bookstores on November 23, 1976, translated as *Le Viol*, the same title as a book by Marie-Odile Fargier, also published in 1976.[47] Most significant, however, was the "Ten Hours Against Rape" held at the Mutualité meeting hall in Paris on June 26 and attended by close to five thousand women. The meeting was closed to men, a group of whom stood on the sidewalk asking women as they came out of the Mutualité what was happening inside.[48] In the form of a general speak-out, discussion ran from collective self-defense and vigilante justice to the recounting of tragic and painful personal experience. The fact that the Mutualité meeting concerned rape (apparently more than the fact that it was a closed-door event) seemed to provoke resentful reactions from some male leftists. The newspaper *Libération* published on several occasions letters from men who spoke of their incredulity toward the growing mobilization around sexual violence.[49] Male leftist reaction soon reached hysterical proportions, and it is difficult in retrospect to treat it with sympathy.

The *Libération* Debates

Throughout 1976 and early 1977, the debate on rape continued to mount in intensity, particularly as a number of court cases were given heightened publicity. However, the real moment of conflict between feminists and male leftists (as well as among some feminists) came in March and April 1977 when the newspaper *Libération* hosted a particularly contentious debate. The controversy would lead several women to ask: "At *Libération*, which sexual liberation are you for? Those of rapists? Is the war of the sexes the only solution you leave us with?"[50] The controversy began with a trial. Brigitte Ribaillier, twenty-six years old, had been raped in April 1976, and her aggressor had been brought before the *Tribunal correctionel* on assault charges. As in the case of the two Belgian tourists, Brigitte's lawyers had asked that the court declare itself incompetent and send the dossier to the *Cour d'Assises*. The court reached that decision on March 21, 1977. That same day, *Libération* published an interview with the defense attorney, Maître Koskas, a lawyer with the *Mouvement d'action judiciaire* (Movement for Judicial Action).[51] The thrust of his remarks addressed the fact that the accused, Youri Eshak, was a twenty-seven-year-old Egyptian student at the University of Vincennes. Koskas did not hesitate to play the terms of race, sexual violence, and "bourgeois" Republican justice off one another. Marie-Odile Fargier was not exaggerating when she wrote that this "trial will remain one of the hardest moments of a debate opened inside the Left, and above all on the far-left, on the approach to take with rapists."[52]

In his interview, Koskas distinguished between, on one hand, the desire to "repress" and punish the perpetrator of a crime, and, on the other hand, his own "political reaction" that attempted to contextualize and explain the crime. Ultimately, the social, in the form of male "sexual misery," was to blame.[53] Koskas went on to say that feminists were only hurting themselves by appealing to a repressive juridical system whose structures and interests were fundamentally at odds with any collective campaign for changing "the ensemble of social relations."

> I say thus that their action is wrong, reactionary, and that paradoxically, they discredit the fight they want to lead. Repressing this guy will not help the relations between men and women.... They don't see that men and women are in the same shit. To appeal to repression is to situate oneself in a traditional way of seeing things: that of the

weak woman who seeks protection from the code of men. What will they gain? Years in prison and exile. Nothing else.

Koskas thus used one politicized version of the trial, foregrounding race and class (the accused was a poor Egyptian immigrant persecuted by white bourgeois justice) to counter the feminist version of the political trial of rape. In the face off between rape politics and race politics, the Left stared itself down.

As if Koskas's statements in *Libération* were not inflammatory enough, the following day, newspapers published accounts of what he had said in the courtroom.[54] He had denounced certain "cultured women ready to sacrifice a poor guy for a debate of ideas.... In the name of the life, equality, and oppression of women, we pass lightly over the other victims of society.... Your struggle is abstract, as full of hate as that of the classic reactionaries. It's together that men and women will change society." The accused had been "begging for love, he committed a crime of love.... If she had consented, none of us would be here." Koskas's comments provoked such an uproar among those observing the trial that the judge cleared the courtroom. Fargier wrote of the experience of "feeling so much hostility in this voice that wanted to denounce hate." The lawyers for the plaintiff—Josyane Moutet, Colette Auger, and Monique Antoine—were completely surprised by the venomous tirade. Moutet responded, "The most oppressed and crushed man can still turn his aggressivity against women, the designated victims."[55] The rape of Brigitte and the charge of assault against Youri were symptomatic of the violence women faced every day and of the ineptness of the judicial system in defending women. "The judicial system is a means used in all times, even by revolutionaries," Moutet said. "The legal procedure is the only means at our disposal at the present moment. It only represents a step, a moment in our struggle. We use it with neither joy nor satisfaction and will only abandon it when we have other means."[56]

What those other means might be was not exactly clear in 1977 and 1978. There were, of course, serious divisions among feminists with respect to the question of rape and the French legal system, especially prison sentences. Writing of the lack of "unanimity" among feminists on the question, Michèle Solat commented in October 1977,

> We have trouble admitting that the women's movement, coming out of the oppositional Left which has denounced "bourgeois justice" since 1968, could use the current reigning institutions [*les institutions en place*]. Some go as far as saying that in dragging rapists in front of the *Assises* court, or even simply filing complaints, rape victims participate in "repression." It remains to be known if feminists have any other choice.[57]

Solat drew the parallel between the use of courts to dramatize the injustice of the law against abortion and the campaign against rape ("to sensitize public opinion and, through the occasion of a trial, to call into question a law and its application"). But she also noted that a shift had occurred: women were no longer defendants, but civil parties who "accuse." Though the "general tendency" had been to seek incarceration for rape perpetrators, there had yet to be consensus on that goal. Certain organizations mobilized around the legal representation of rape victims—*Choisir, S.O.S. Femmes,* and *La Ligues des droits des femmes* (Choose, S.O.S Women, and the League of the Rights of Women)—had fewer qualms about penalization, perhaps because they were also seeking reforms in rape law and trial practices. Moutet and her colleagues, Auger and Antoine, belonged to the *Collectif juridique de défense des femmes* (Women's Legal Defense Collective), a group generally suspicious about the effectiveness and political wisdom of seeking harsh prison sentences. They were not alone. In the midst of the Youri affair, on March 23, 1977, *Libération* published a letter from a group calling themselves the "Cassandras" in which they wrote that "the prison, a system of repression that reinforces the violence of men among themselves, is not for us the best solution."[58] On March 29, the "'Rape' Commission of the 18th Arrondissement" proposed the simple posting of the photo and name of the rapist in the neighborhood where he lived.[59] On April 30, Hélène Lanive wrote that women "must refuse to let themselves fall into the circle where we have been put" and that "to refuse *also* prison for rapists is elementary."[60] As we will see below, the contradictions of being for trials and against punishment came to a head, especially for Moutet et al., in early 1978.[61]

Three Inflammatory Articles

Despite the diversity of feminist positions, there was a clear closing of ranks when three inflammatory articles, written, as it were, in the spirit of Koskas, appeared in *Libération* in late March and early April. The articles reflected a far-left discourse of political criminality—valorizations of criminality, politicizations of violence—that had surfaced in the post–'68 era of radical agitation. If bourgeois justice was rotten, then there could be no compromises with it. Following the Youri Eshak trial, certain male leftists accused feminists of antirevolutionary complicity with legal institutions in their prosecution of sexual violence. The articles speak for themselves. The first, by Pierre Goldman, appeared on March 23, 1977—the same day as the "Cassandras'" unavailing plea mentioned above and also the day that Jean-Antoine Tramoni, who had famously murdered the militant Pierre Overney in 1972, was himself assassinated by leftists in an act of vigilante justice shortly after being released from a two-year prison sentence. A quixotic figure of the far-left, Goldman had made a reputation for himself as half-gangster, half-urban guerrilla by blending politics and crime.[62] His *Libération* article was entitled, "On Rape, the Correct Application of the Law, and Despair."[63] Though he carefully recounted the logic of leftist uses of the legal system, and even more carefully the rationale behind feminists' turn toward penal law, he went on to address the "tragic…contradictions" of this development. Though no society would likely do without law (it prevented "the savage reign of the law of the strongest, of lynching, of the vendetta," though one wonders if he had feminist vigilante justice in mind), there remained individuals such as himself who regarded "all legal justice, all legal judgment, all legal repression as an infamy." Goldman spoke for those few who saw themselves as "determined to remain, morally and not in the sense of the penal code, definitively and absolutely *outside the law* [*des 'horsla-loi' definitifs et absolus*]." It was a position of "marginality" and one of "despair" he was happy to reclaim.

The second article was written by Hocquenghem and published on March 29, four days after Jacques Chirac had been elected Mayor of Paris. Implying that he needed to spell things out, the piece was called simply, "R-A-P-E."[64] Attacking the idea that criminal penalization could serve as a deterrent, he said that the feminist pursuit of exemplary punishment was motivated by "vengeance" and that feminists were "ruthless" and had "become Amazons." In a crude and malicious contrast of feminist and gay male politics, he claimed that gay men did not ask the law to punish those who assaulted them. Gay men knew out of "good sense" that filing charges accomplished nothing; it could not undo a crime that had taken place—"justice helps them not at all."

> Because who in the end has ever seen a fag complain about being *raped*? To have been beaten up, yes. But raped…It certainly seems that the anus of the gay man is not endowed with the same transcendental qualities as the vagina. And the curious thing is, it is rape alone that makes calling on justice indispensable.

The indispensability, in Hocquenghem's mind, was proved by the fact that only in the case of rape, not the case in theft and physical assault, was some sort of postfacto realignment sought. Through judicial redress, vengeance would be assuaged and "a certain virginity, that of dignity" restored.

The final intervention was the transcript of a "dialogue of the deaf" between "Mohamed" and "Françoise," published on April 5.[65] This was the same Mohamed who had written the inflammatory letter in 1971 to *Tout!* in which he had suggested that French woman revealed their racism by refusing to sleep with him. He had contacted *Libération* in 1977 to comment on the absence of race from the rape debate. "My problem is not," he began, "to approve or disapprove that one sends a guy to the *Cour d'Assises*. My problem is to say that every immigrant, the day he arrives in France, is already in the hands of French injustice; he is already in a prison, in a vast prison." Mohamed said that the immigrant faced repression if he decided to rebel in any way: by striking, demonstrating, or—preposterously—"taking what he is refused, which could be a woman." Though in a fleeting moment he acknowledged that women were also victims in French society, he gave race priority over gender ("Who raped whom first? It is easy to forget that and to give oneself a good conscience.") and stressed the incommensurability of the positions of male immigrants and women ("Listen. We don't have the same problems. Our political, economic, and cultural interests don't converge."). He concluded his increasingly heated exchange with his interlocutor, Françoise, with the bitter statement,

> I am not waiting for anything from the West. I have no solution. I don't care. I say: You only speak of the rapist, never of the situation that surrounds him. I say: Don't clear yourselves [*Ne vous déculpabilisez pas*]. Assume your responsibilities. French imperialism did not fall out of the sky....I want you to know who we are and who you are, that's all.

These three overlapping attacks showed the fragmentation of the post–'68 far-left around revolutionary criminality and the identity politics of homosexuality and race—all of which were mobilized here to batter feminist mobilization on rape. Though *Libération* was not alone on the Left in giving prominence to such antifeminist views, the newspaper's editorial choices did not improve its image among some feminists, even if it did, however, make some room for debate. Responses to these attacks were understandably incensed. On March 28, Josyane Moutet posed a battery of "questions to Pierre Goldman."[66] To his embrace of despairing marginality, she replied that feminists were despairing of leftists unable to come to terms with sexual violence. The erroneous notion that feminists were engaged in antiliberational recuperation completely underestimated how their turn to law was strategic and occasional. Moutet specified that she and Brigitte's other lawyers had not asked for a particular penalty, had not opposed Youri being let out on bail (which the judge had in any case denied), and had refused to make use of police testimonies. Claiming that the "dialectic of relations of force applied also to the women's struggle," Moutet emphasized the coherence of a strategy that sent "men back to their own organized violence" and ensured that "the law did not dupe" women. As for the suggestion that feminists were playing into the hands of the powers-that-be, Moutet asked mockingly, "Do you fear we are so stupid as not also to denounce this [judicial] machine?," a machine structurally skewed, she acknowledged, along class lines. There was a qualitative difference between, on one hand, theft or attacks on institutions and, on the other hand, sexual violence against women, crimes that point "in the most archaic direction of the patriarchal system."

The real high point of the *Libération* acrimony followed Mohamed's intervention. The following two days, April 6–7, 1977, the newspaper published a dossier entitled, "Rape or Violences?" Elisabeth Salvaresi wrote that women avoided playing the role of "rapists of the rapists," by making two masculine regimes—sexual violence and criminal justice—confront one another "until they notice our absence from their game." The "violence" of the debate between feminists and "certain so-called leftist men" showed the "half-peace" that reigned between the sexes. "There is between them and us," Salvaresi concluded mournfully, "a gap [*un décalage*] of desire and of reality greater than at other times." Paul Roussopoulos wrote that the "editors of *Libération*" made a huge "error" in believing that the French justice was a monolithic block to be denounced out of hand. Pierre Goldman's acquittal attested to the self-corrective capacity of legal systems, and Goldman himself was caught between the *hors-la-loi* status he claimed for himself and the fact that he had participated in the system in order to seek his release (having appealed his case, relied on lawyers, and accused the police themselves of having acted *hors-la-loi*). Goldman's "despair" was thus "theoretical" and in performative contradiction with his actions. The *Libération* controversy, the Left's "crises of conscience," was in the end a "museum debate" over the dusty and dried idea that French justice needed to be attacked in its totality. Men on the Left needed to face up to the poverty of their own philosophy. Roussopoulos cautioned that "*Libération* not respond to me by saying that it is feminist because it sometimes grants a page to the problems of women. And the men's page? Don't look for it. It's the rest of the newspaper."[67]

On April 7, Odile Dhavernas, a lawyer with the same leftist legal defense fund as Koskas, the Movement for Judicial Action, attacked her colleague's "odious act" during the March 21 trial. To Koskas's question published in *Libération*, as to why women claimed the "privilege of indignation," Dhavernas shot back that she wondered why women were granted the "privilege of rape." Rape was not an "expedient means" of sexual satisfaction, it was an affirmation of "power over another," a "revenge" that had nothing to do with either desire or enjoyment/pleasure (*jouissance*). Koskas's suggestion that rape derived from the "irrepressible pulsions of men" was abhorrent. Dhavernas said that women wanted "to have the support of our male comrades" in the women's movement, but if, like Koskas, they acted like "enemies," feminists would appropriately defend themselves.[68] Thierry Lévy wrote that feminists "disqualified themselves as lawyers and militants" when they made a criminal defendant, already in a position of weakness with respect to the law, into the "physical target of a criminal politics of elimination." They had the "gall" to try to enforce a "repressive" law and then to say that they were not opposed to letting the accused out on bail. Worse still, the "stain" of rape on the victim "was nothing when compared to that which judicial debates inflict." The rape victim, already having suffered physical and emotional trauma, would be submitted to a "thorough auscultation" in the courtroom that would border on "dry pornography" and would call into question whether or not "her body, her pleasure, her secrets [*mystères*] belong to her."[69] Finally, Hélène, a judge "in training," said that she herself was outside-the-law (*hors-la-loi*), a feminist working within legal institutions in despair at the prospect of "one day [applying] this 'phallic law.'" At the bottom of this contradiction and despair was "a hole out of which only an infinite silence exits." Although other interventions followed throughout the rest of April and into the months that followed, one of the last comments on the Youri trial was made in late May by Brigitte herself in an open letter addressed to Koskas. After picking apart some of his more outrageous statements, she concluded that "if it is not repression that will improve relations between men and women, it is certainly not the actual state of things!"[70]

Popularization of the Campaign

The *Libération* debate had the effect of pushing the issue further onto the map of public discourse, and in the fall of 1977, the issue reached a certain popular critical mass. High-publicity trials continued; mainstream newspapers like *Le Matin* and *Le Monde* published multipart series on the issue of sexual violence; television documentaries and roundtables appeared.[71] Broader debate on rape forced to the surface many cultural a priori, or predispositions, which form even today part of the social imaginary: the presumed connection between rape and the permissive society (rape is more prevalent or more visible), rape as an "inevitable" consequence of irrepressible male instincts or as a socially overdetermined phenomenon, rape as one end of a continuum of daily sexual aggression and harassment, and rape as an age-old problem receiving long-overdo and, to say the least, appropriate attention.[72]

Such mainstream debates set the scene for the Aix trial in May 1978 and the subsequent introduction of new legislation in June. Significantly, also in early 1978 some feminists previously committed to bringing rape cases to trial were having second thoughts. The strategy of trying rape cases before the *Cour d'Assises* as a forum for getting the crime taken more seriously seemed to be getting out of hand. As the numbers of trials and severity of sentences both increased, the justice system showed that it had logics of its own that operated independently of feminist involvement. Feminists were upset by the usurpation of their discourse by the judicial establishment. For instance, a State prosecutor said at one trial "Think of your wives, your daughters"; as one woman noted, he had spoken "in the name of women and their dignity, in order to hold onto the most reactionary and repressive discourses." As Françoise Picq notes, "The judicial machine was launched. It could not be stopped. Women wanted to use justice, and it used them. The campaign against rape would be the alibi for repression, fueling the discourse of security."[73] *Libération* commented at the time, "No matter what the intentions or jurisdictions, the judicial machine never puts rape on trial. Only the rapist."[74] Martine Storti summed up her contradictory position following the sentencing of an Algerian immigrant, Lakdhadar Setti, to twenty years in prison for rape, a judgment feminists and their supporters had protested as too severe.

> I had neither the desire to renounce my and other women's fight, nor the desire to continue in the same fashion, faced with this double wall of repression and the reinforcing of institutions. [At Setti's sentencing] this was the wall I hit, and I no longer know today how to get out....It is also against incarceration that we are fighting. And nevertheless, would I have resented it on Wednesday if Setti had been freed? There's no lack of contradictions. In my head. In reality. In the movement taken up by feminists for their liberation. A struggle lived, precisely, as the most contradictory. But we have chosen to never leave ourselves shut up in a unilateral political line or discourse. Today, our struggle against rape, directed with seriousness and emotion, is at an impasse.[75]

Paradoxically, the moment of impasse from one point of view was also the moment at which rape was taken most seriously by mainstream society, a fact reflected in the Aix trial and in the new legislation that followed.[76] If 1978 showed fissures among feminists, it also marked the moment at which a certain discourse on rape achieved its fought-for and sought-after legitimacy.

Conclusion

The full charge of feminist moralism came in December 1978 in the midst of the so-called *Détective* affair.[77] In late November, the government had decided to ban the sale to minors of the marginal "true crimes" magazine,

Détective, which had since the early 1970s featured accounts of sex crimes in an effort to attract a broader readership. Several members of the National Assembly had pursued the interdiction of the publication on the grounds that it degraded women, and had appealed for censorship by the mysterious government "Commission Charged with the Surveillance and Control of Publications Destined to Children and Adolescents." In the almost predictable fallout in *Libération* and *Le Monde*, feminism in general was blamed (some feminists had torn down *Détective* posters the previous month). The participation by some feminists in the legal institutions of the Fifth Republic was conflated with government acts that were not necessarily supported by many feminists. As Liliane Kandel commented soon thereafter, "The autumn of 1978 and the *Détective* affair could well mark, after years of fascinated terror (or prudent muteness) another moment: the tentative resumption of the right of men (of the 'Left,' indeed 'feminists') to speak about and judge the women's movements. Sometimes at any price: there are old accounts to settle."[78] Serge July wrote an editorial in *Libération*—"It Is Forbidden to Forbid, Even for Women"—in which he asked rhetorically: "Are certain feminists on the way to constituting the new embryos of new moral leagues under cover of the denunciation of sexism?...Could they not become the pilot fish of a moral reaction?"[79] Bruno Frappat, long-time commentator on gay issues for *Le Monde*, published on the same day a reflection on "feminism and repression."

> Is the defense of the liberty of women and their dignity passing by an aggravation of repression? Certain French feminists give the impression to have responded in the affirmative. Two recent campaigns led in their care [*menées par leurs soins*] attest to it. It has been many months since rape cases are the object of a vigilante surveillance on the part of a group of women....More recently, a very short campaign against the biweekly *Détective*...ended in the interdiction of the magazine....It is a question of a change in strategy heavy in consequence.[80]

By "strategy" Frappat meant the shift from agitating outside the "law of men" to the turn toward the law as an "ally." "If we don't watch out," he concluded, "The third step in the strategy of feminist groups risks arriving at propositions to change laws, by arguing that they enable abuses, in the more radical sense of a restriction of certain liberties." This explosion of leftist antifeminism seemed to be the zenith of a certain post–'68 far-left incredulity toward law and the state.

The election of Mitterrand a year and a half later in May 1981 would force a new reckoning of various parties of the Left with the state, one that bore fresh contradictions and confronted other limits. On the cusp of the Mitterrand era a series of new legislative measures instantiated the shifts wrought by post–'68 sexual politics, reflecting the "dialectic between law and social mores," which Gisèle Halimi, the feminist lawyer most often associated with the French right to choice and rape campaigns, says she long tried to pursue.[81] The right to choose was reaffirmed in 1979, a new law on rape accepted in December 1980, homosexuality was decriminalized and the minimum age of consent lowered to fifteen in August 1982. A further analysis would discuss specific legislation.[82]

Françoise Picq has suggested that the 1970s witnessed the shift from the "pleasure principle" of May '68 to the "reality principle" of progressive politics working within the limits of existing political institutions.[83] Though she rightly cautions against taking such a description too far, Picq raises a good point. The negative-critical manner of relating to norms is not the same as a positive-constructive one. *Don't tell me what to do* is not the same kind or quality of statement as *How will we live?* Such "pleasures" and "realities" are analytically and politically distinct. Limits are one conceptual/ practical site where an ethics of sex and sexuality is worked out (the particular form of limit discussed in this essay is a legal one). This standpoint requires moving beyond the discourse of "moral panic" in which valorized transgressions are tragically integrated by monolithic, dominant systems (like religious or middle-class morality) and that tends to equate norms with normalization.[84] Precisely because the normative may be an inescapable social and conceptual field, negative-critical modes of relating to it need to be supplemented by positive-ethical ones. Against a negative "moral panic" view, I take normativity (in the form of *limits* and the *law*) in a positive sense as reflected in the ethical question: where and how did actors engaged in the liberational project of the sexual revolution draw limits on liberated desire—sexual desires but also desires for liberation?

One protagonist from this story, Cathy Bernheim—feminist, former member of FHAR, and friend of Hocquenghem—sees in the charges of feminist moralism during the 1970s a failure to appreciate what the sexual revolution promised women such as herself.[85] In her view, "antimoralism" discourse expressed male desires for limitless desire, a refusal to admit the ethical boundaries that began where power/desire attempted to extend over others. This power could take the form of explicit sexual violence. Desire had its ethical limits.

It was always very clear to me that social actors are moral actors. If not, we find ourselves in societies in which all is permitted and all is possible. For me it was extremely clear, and I think it was clear for many among us. But then we were taken up into the rhetoric that said, "You are moralists." For me, I was also clear that I was not going to bend over backwards in order to say that I was right. No, I knew that there must be a certain ethics [*morale*] in society and that we need to have certain actions and acts that we don't accept. I also had a strong perception of the constraints that society imposed on women. For example, when one spoke of sexual misery, I always recalled that the worst sexual misery faced by human beings in our society was that of women and not men.[86]

The tricky part, she concedes in reference to a book by Jean-Marie Domenach, is to articulate "an ethics [*morale*] without moralism," to find a way between a general order that is imposed on others and the articulation of an ethics/morality that "people give themselves."[87] Where such a challenge touches upon desire/power in the form of violence, it seems that at some point it must involve the state and politics in a mundane sense.

This is not to say that the law provides easy answers. On the contrary, it creates further dilemmas. Here, skepticism about juridical institutions by some feminists and male activists was well-placed. As Michel Foucault said at the time, everything is dangerous: certainly the knowledge-power regimes of law and justice, but also the fantasy of a total liberation that denies the constraints that themselves are the condition of possibility for any partial liberation.[88] The calculus of shifting dangers requires a vigilance against inflexibility and the courage to draw limits where such limits are required. One of the overall accomplishments of the sexual politics of the 1970s was to have sought out desire's possibilities within and against its perimeters. More specifically, the paradox of feminist "moralism" reached in two directions at once: the law as a limit and the limits of the law.

Notes

This chapter is a revised and reduced version of a section by the same name in my From Revolution to Ethics: May 1968 and Contemporary French Thought (Montreal: McGill-Queen's University Press, 2007). For a companion article see my "Boy Trouble: French Pedophiliac Discourse of the 1970s," in *Between Marx and Coca-Cola: Youth Cultures in Changing European Societies, 1960–1980,* ed. Axel Schildt and Detlef Siegfried (New York: Palgrave Macmillan, 2005).

1. Joan Wallach Scott, *Only Paradoxes to Offer: French Feminism and the Rights of Man* (Cambridge, MA: Harvard University Press, 1996).
2. Justin David Suran, " 'Out Now!': Antimilitarism and the Politicization of Homosexuality in the Era of Vietnam." Sibalis, "The Spirit of May '68 and the Origins of the Gay Liberation Movement in France."
3. Geneviève Dreyfus-Armand, Robert Frank, Marie-Françoise Lévy, and Michelle Zancarini-Fournel, eds., *Les Années 68: Le temps de la contestation* (Paris: Editions Complexe, 2000), esp. Part 2. Khursheed Wadia, "Women and the Events of May 1968," in *The May 1968 Events in*

France: Reproductions and Interpretations, ed. Keith A. Reader (New York: St. Martin's Press, 1993).

4. Literature on the *Mouvement de libération des femmes* and French feminism is vast. I have found the following the most helpful: Françoise Picq, *Libération des femmes: les années-mouvement* (Paris: Editions du Seuil, 1993); Annie de Pisan and Anne Tristan, *Histoires du MLF* (Paris: Calmann-Levy, 1977); Association la Griffonne [Martine Bosshart et al.], *Douze ans de femmes au quotidien: douze ans de luttes féministes en France, 1970–1981* (Paris: La Griffonne, 1981); Claire Duchen, *Feminism in France* (New York: Routledge, 1986): Monique Rémy, *De l'utopie à l'intégration: histoire des mouvements de femmes* (Paris: L'Harmattan, 1990). On gay liberation see Jacques Girard, *Le Mouvement homosexuel en France, 1945–1980* (Paris: Editions Syros, 1981); and especially Frédéric Martel, *The Pink and the Black* (Palo Alto, CA: Stanford University Press: 2000); and Michael Sibalis, "The Spirit of May '68 and the Origins of the Gay Liberation Movement in France," in this collection

5. To which Cohn-Bendit replied, "That's what the Hitler youth used to say!" Patrick Seale and Maureen McConville, *Red Flag/Black Flag: French Revolution 1968* (New York: Putnam, 1968), 28–29.

6. Cohn-Bendit, cited in *The Student Revolt: The Activists Speak*, ed. Hervé Bourges (London: Cope, 1968), 78.

7. Mouvement jeune révolutionnaire, "L'Ecoute des étudiants," *Bulletin JR* 2 [n.d.]. Bibliothèque Nationale, 4-LC2–7280.

8. Alain Schnapp and Pierre Vidal-Naquet, *The French Student Uprising, November 1967–June 1968* (Boston: Beacon, 1971), 435.

9. Martel, *The Pink and the Black*, 15–16. Liane Mozère, *Le Printemps des crèches: histoire et analyse d'un mouvement* (Paris: Editions L'Harmattan, 1992).

10. See, however, Roland Gagey, *La Révolution sexuelle* (Paris: L.D. 1968), printed in July of that year. Other movements that considered the sexuality and gender were reformist or associational in nature. See Mouvement français pour le planning familial, *D'une révolte à une lutte: 25 ans d'histoire du planning familial* (Paris: Tierce, 1982). Martel, *The Pink and the Black*, chapter three, for a discussion of the gay organization, *Arcadie.*

11. Hervé Hamon and Patrick Rotman, *Génération: 2. Les années de poudre* (Paris: Seuil, 1988), 106–107. On VLR see also Christophe Bourseiller, *Les Maoïstes: la folle histoire des gardes rouges français* (Paris: Plon, 1996); and A. Belden Fields, *Trotskyism and Maoism: Theory and Practice in France and the United States* (New York: Praeger, 1988).

12. Alain Touraine, *Le Mouvement de mai ou le communisme utopique* (Paris: Seuil, 1968; rev. ed., 1972).

13. Vive la Révolution, *Changer la vie: document politique* (Kremlin-Bicêtre: n.p., 1970), 16.

14. Interview with Roland Castro (May 1999).

15. Several of the articles were reprinted in September 1971 as FHAR, *Rapport contre la normalité* (Paris: Champ Libre, 1971). For the history of the FHAR see Martel, *The Pink and the Black.*

16. *Tout!* 12, April 23, 1971.

17. Christiane, "Pourquoi nous avortons"; "Des filles, et un mec"; Un militant du FHAR, "Vie quotidienne chez les pédés"; Un pédé mineur et devenu joyeux, "Les Mineurs ont droit au désir: 15 Berges"; and Un homosexuel, sale étranger, dangereux communiste, "Le Triangle rose: Lettre ouverte aux hétérosexuels communistes"; Un du FHAR, "Non, on n'est pas des obsedés"; Une du FHAR, "Elles sont unissantes, les filles qui s'embrassent!"; Un du FHAR, "Homosexuels"; Sylvie, "Pas d'accord: Une lettre," ibid.

18. "Le pavé de l'homosexualité dans la mare gauchiste," *Tout!* 13, May 17, 1971.

19. Christian, ouvrier du Livre, "Notre dernier numéro est-il anti-ouvrier?," *Tout!* 13, May 17, 1971.

20. "A trial will only make evident what everyone senses: the decay of bourgeois mores and the new sense of a revolution that aims also to transform daily life." Jean-Paul Sartre, *Tout!*

15, June 30, 1971. On July 16, 1971, the Constitutional Council said that the banning of newspapers by the government was illegal.

21. "FHAR," *Tout!* 13, May 17, 1971.

22. The controversy introduced another element into mounting tensions between male leftists and feminists: race. That theme hovers around 1970s debates on gender and sexuality on the French far-left. Unfortunately, in this essay, the issue of race cannot be treated thoroughly.

23. "Lettre de Mohamed," *Tout!* 14, June 7, 1971.

24. Hélène, "Réponses à la lettre de Mohammed," and Militants du MLF, "Votre libération sexuelle n'est pas la nôtre," *Tout!* 15, June 30, 1971.

25. "Vie et moeurs de la peuplade 'Tuot' ou que vos os pourrissent sous la lune," ibid.

26. Un groupe de filles, "Encore une fois sur Mohammed"; Un du FHAR et de Tout, "Réponse au texte des femmes"; Quelques uns du FHAR, "Bilan," *Tout!* 16, July 29, 1971.

27. Interview with Cathy Bernheim (March 2001). Guy Hocquenghem recounted this weekend meeting in "Femmes et pédés" [November 1972], *L'Après-mai des faunes: volutions*, Preface by Gilles Deleuze (Paris: Grasset, 1974), 190.

28. Bill Marshall, *Guy Hocquenghem: Beyond Gay Identity* (Durham: Duke University Press, 1996).

29. Hocquenghem, *Homosexual Desire* [1972] (Durham: Duke University Press, 1993).

30. Ibid., 87. The "double-bind" theory, popular in much French thought of the 1960s and 1970s, was taken from Gregory Bateson et al., "Toward a Theory of Schizophrenia," *Behavioral Science* 1:4 (October 1956). See Gilles Deleuze and Félix Guattari, *Anti-Oedipus* (Minneapolis: University of Minnesota Press, 1977), 79, 110.

31. Hocquenghem, "Towards an Irrecuperable Pederasty" [July–October 1972], in Jonathan Goldberg, ed., *Reclaiming Sodom* (New York: Routledge, 1994), 241, 244–245.

32. On the positive link between homosexuality and criminality, see Hocquenghem, *Homosexual Desire*, 67.

33. Hocquenghem, "Towards an Irrecuperable Pederasty," 242, 245.

34. Hocquenghem, *Homosexual Desire*, 97–101; "Towards an Irrecuperable Pederasty," 237.

35. Ibid., 235. See also, ibid., 241–42; *Homosexual Desire*, 77, 101, 140.

36. Hocquenghem, "Towards an Irrecuperable Pederasty," 241.

37. Ibid., 242. See also, "Femmes et pédés," 187–190.

38. *Trois milliards de pervers: Grande Encylopédie des Homosexualités*, Special Issue of *Recherches* 12 (March 1973). Collaborators included: Cathy Bernheim, Gilles and Fanny Deleuze, Félix Guattari, Michel Foucault, Jean Genet, Daniel Guérin, Guy Hocquenghem, Georges Lapassade, and Jean-Paul Sartre, among others. The issue was immediately seized by the police, and the journal's director of publication, Félix Guattari, charged with "outrage against public decency." For Guattari's response to the censorship see "Letter to the Tribunal," *Soft Subversions* (New York: Semiotext(e), 1996).

39. Hocquenghem, "Un Transversalisme éhonté" [July 1973], *L'Après-mai des faunes*, 199–200.

40. Hocquenghem, *Homosexual Desire*, 139–140.

41. Bill Marshall and Frédéric Martel are too soft on Hocquenghem's writings on feminism. They are both more dismissive of the "excesses" of 1970s French feminism than they are of Hocquenghem's own distortions. In some sense, they re-write the problematic at another level. Marshall, *Guy Hocquenghem*, 11–12, 93. Martel, *The Pink and the Black*, 98, where he calls Hocquenghem a "radical" on rape who had recovered his "verve."

42. Picq, *Libération des femmes*, 249. Cf. ibid., 235, 241–243. See also Emmanuèle Durand, "Le viol," *Libération des femmes: année zéro*, Special Issue of *Partisans* 54–55 (July–October 1970); and Mai, "Un viol si ordinaire, un impérialisme si quotidien," *Les femmes s'entêntent*, Special Issue of *Les Temps Modernes* 333–334 (April–May 1974). For a long-term view of rape in France, see Georges Vigarello, *A History of Rape: Sexual Violence in France from the Sixteenth to the Twentieth Century* [Paris, 1998] (Cambridge: Polity Press, 2001).

43. Association Choisir/La Cause des femmes, *Viol: le procès d'Aix*, Preface by Gisèle Halimi (Paris: Gallimard 1978), 31. Marie Cardinal, "Le viol est un crime," *Le Monde*, February 3, 1976.

44. Emmanuelle Plas, "Viol: Briser le mur de silence," *L'Unité*, December 3, 1976.

45. Simone de Beauvoir, "Quand toutes les femmes du monde…," *Le Nouvel Observateur*, March 1, 1976.

46. Pia Paoli, "Le circoncision des femmes," *Le Monde*, April 18–19, 1976.

47. Susan Brownmiller, *Le Viol* [New York, 1975] (Paris: Stock, 1976). Marie-Odile Fargier, *Le Viol* (Paris: Grasset, 1976). Roger-Pol Droit, "La fin du silence" [Review of Brownmiller and Fargier], *Le Monde*, November 19, 1976. Cathy Bernheim, "Le viol est pour les femmes, ce que le lynchage est pour les noirs" [Review of Brownmiller], *La Quinzaine littéraire* 251 (March 1, 1977).

48. MLF, "Manifeste contre le viol," *Libération*, June 16, 1976. Christiane Chombeau, "Un millier de femmes ont participé aux 'dix heures contre le viol,'" *Le Monde,* June 29, 1976.

49. "Courrier: En marge de la journée sur le viol: Paroles au masculin 3," *Libération*, June 6, 1976.

50. "Une commission du 'viol' dans le 18è," *Libération*, March 29, 1977.

51. "L'Avocat de son agressor: 'Ce n'est pas la répression qui va améliorer les rapports entre hommes et femmes,'" *Libération*, March 21, 1977.

52. Marie-Odile Fargier, "Un tribunal qui refuse de juger," *Le Matin*, March 22, 1977.

53. The argument of "sexual misery" as a consequence of bourgeois repression was popularized by the widespread attention paid to the theories of Wilhelm Reich. "The sexual misery of the patriarchal-authoritarian society is the consequence of the negation and the sexual representation which characterize it, and which provoke neurosis, perversion, and sexual crimes among all those who are enslaved to it." Reich, *L'Irruption de la morale sexuelle* (Paris: Payot, 1972), 33.

54. Martine Storti, "La 16ème chambre correctionnelle se déclare incompétente," *Libération*, March 22, 1977.

55. Cf. Françoise, "Réponse à Maître Koskas," *Libération*, March 29, 1977: A rapist, "far from revolting against the established order, on the contrary participates in his sexist society, where violence and force are virtues, where murdering masculine sexuality is the norm."

56. Cited in Odile Dhavernas, "Pourquoi les femmes ont-elles le privilège du viol?," *Libération*, April 7, 1977.

57. Michèle Solat, "Les féministes et le viol: 3. Comment lutter?," *Le Monde,* October 20, 1977.

58. "Les cassandres et la sexualité masculine," *Libération*, March 23, 1977.

59. "Une commission 'viol' dans le 18è," *Libération*, March 29, 1977.

60. Hélène Lanive, "'Il faut refuser de se laisser inscrire dans ce cercle où on nous a mises,'" *Libération*, May 20, 1977.

61. To be sure, some radical feminists experimented with vigilante justice [*la justice sauvage*]—punishing perpetrators of violence against women by direct, extra-legal means. Such acts were comparatively rare and, though bearing directly on the debates at hand, will not be examined here.

62. In 1974, Goldman was convicted of the murder of two (female) pharmacists and sentenced to life in prison. At his trial, luminaries of the intellectual-political Left spoke on his behalf. Pardoned in 1976, he was murdered in September 1979. Hamon and Rotman, *Génération* (Paris: Seuil, 1987), 596–603, 657.

63. Pierre Goldman, "Du viol, du bon usgae de la loi, et du désespoir," *Libération*, March 23, 1977.

64. Hocquenghem, "V-I-O-L," *Libération*, March 29, 1977; repr. in *La Dérive homosexuelle* (Paris, 1977).

65. "'Un viol en cache toujours un autre': Une lettre de Mohamed sur le viol et le racisme," *Libération*, April 1977.

66. Josyane Moutet, "Questions à Pierre Goldman," *Libération*, March 28, 1977. See also, Mariella Righini, " 'Nous ne sommes pas des procureurs,' " *Le Nouvel Observateur*, March 28, 1977.

67. Elisabeth Salvaresi, "Ne pas être les violeuses de nos violeurs." Paul Roussopoulos, "Un débat de musée," *Libération*, April 6, 1977.

68. Odile Dhavernas, "Pourquoi les femmes ont-elles le privilège du viol?," *Libération*, April 7, 1977.

69. Thierry Lévy, "La salissure des débats judiciaires," ibid.

70. Brigitte, "Réponse à l'avocat de la défense," *Libération*, May 30, 1977. Cf. Brigitte, "La misère sexuelle n'explique pas tout," *Libération*, September 9, 1977.

71. "La Grande peur des femmes," Dossier in *Le Matin*, September 6–10, 1977; Michèle Solat, "Les féministes et le viol," Dossier in *Le Monde*, October 18–20, 1977. See also, Claudine Hermann, "Le Viol et la violence," *Les Temps modernes*, 375, October 1977; Elisabeth Salvaresi, "Un dialogue de sourdes aux *Dossiers de l'écran*," *Libération*, October 20, 1977.

72. Pierre Leroy, "Instinct et culture" in "Les féministes contre le viol"; Yolande A., "Rompre le mur du silence," *Le Monde*, January 1, 1978; Jacques Ellul, "Le viol et le désir," *Le Monde*, January 3, 1978.

73. Picq, *Libération des femmes*, 242. Martel, *The Pink and the Black*, cites this passage and implies that it was the chief lesson to be drawn from the feminist rape campaign (85).

74. Béatrice Vallaeys and M.C. Husson, "Le Mans: du procès du viol au procès d'un violeur," *Libération*, January 27, 1978. Cf. Laurent Greilsamer, " 'La prison n'est pas une solution,' " *Le Monde*, January 27, 1978; Mariella Righini, "Le prix du viol," *Le Nouvel Observateur*, March 25, 1978.

75. Martine Storti, "Viol: '20 ans, c'est pas possible,' " *Libération*, February 24, 1978. See also Storti, "Des dangers de la reconnaissance du viol sans violence," *Libération*, February 22, 1978.

76. For discussions of the Aix trial and subsequent legislative debates, see Vigarello, *A History of Rape*, 206–214; and Association Choisir/La Cause des femmes, *Viol: le procès d'Aix*. See also Halimi, "Viol: Le crime culturel," *Le Nouvel Observateur*, May 22, 1978; Anne Tonglet and Araceli Castellano, "Insoutenable débat: le vôtre," *Libération*, May 12, 1978; Cathy Bernheim, "Je suis moins désespérée qu'il y a quelques années," *Libération*, May 18, 1978; Monique Antoine, Colette Auger, and Josyane Moutet, "Les avocats et le répression," *Le Monde*, May 4, 1978; and "Contre le viol, la prison?," *Le Nouvel Observateur*, May 29, 1978.

77. The entire episode is recounted by Liliane Kandel, "Sous la plage, les medias," *Est-ce ainsi que les hommes jugent?*, Special Issue of *Les Temps modernes* 391, February 1979.

78. Ibid., 1168.

79. Serge July, "Il est interdit d'interdire, y compris pour les femmes," *Libération*, December 6, 1978).

80. Bruno Frappat, "Féminisme et répression," *Le Monde*, December 6, 1978.

81. Interview with Gisèle Halimi (March 2001).

82. Janine Mossuz-Lavau, *Les Lois de l'amour* (Paris: Payot, 1991); Olivier de Tissot, *La Liberté sexuelle et la loi* (Mesnil-sur-l'Estrée, 1984); Antony Copley, *Sexual Moralities in France, 1780–1980: New Ideas on the Family, Divorce, and Homosexuality* (New York: Routledge, 1989).

83. Interview with Françoise Picq (June 1999).

84. Numerous works on moral panic have been written between Stanley Cohen, *Folk Devils and Moral Panics: The Creation of the Mods and Rockers* (London: Routledge, 1972); and Sonya O. Rose, "Cultural Analysis and Moral Discourses: Episodes, Continuities, and Transformations," in *Beyond the Cultural Turn*, ed. Victoria E. Bonnell and Lynn Hunt (Berkeley: University of California Press, 1999). The entire issue of transgression, on which some moral panic discourses depend, is a vexed one: paradoxically, the transgressor esteems

a violated limit to the extent that he or she finds it worthwhile to break in the first place. Another version of this "Liar's Paradox" with respect to transgression says that the claim "this norm is not binding" can itself be taken as normative. Contrast the discussions of transgression in Martin Jay, "The Limits of Limit-Experience: Bataille and Foucault," in *Cultural Semantics: Keywords of Our Time* (Amherst: University of Massachusetts Press, 1998); and Peter Stallybrass and Allen White, *The Politics and Poetics of Transgression* (Ithaca: Cornell University Press, 1986).

85. Interview with Cathy Bernheim (March 2001).

86. Cf. the comment on sexual misery by Ginnie, "'Il est très difficile d'avoir une attitude tranchée…,'" *Libération*, March 29, 1977.

87. Jean-Marie Domenach, *Une morale sans moralisme* (Paris: Flammarion, 1992).

88. Michel Foucault, "Sexual Act, Sexual Choice" (Interview with James O'Higgins) [Fall 1982–Winter 1983], *Ethics: Subjectivity and Truth: The Essential Works of Michel Foucault, 1954–1984: Volume 1* (New York, 1997).

CHAPTER FOUR

Plus ça Change... *Gender and Revolutionary Ideology in Cuban Cinema of 1968*

EMILY A. MAGUIRE

Ernesto "Che" Guevara said it himself: "Let me say to you, at the risk of seeming ridiculous, that the true revolutionary is guided by great feelings of love."[1] This statement, made in 1965 in the now-iconic essay "Socialism and Man in Cuba" and frequently seen as symbolic of the Argentine doctor's own devotion to revolutionary struggles (Cuban and otherwise), significantly and explicitly connects affect with the political. The revolutionary connects with the revolution emotionally rather than rationally; the motivating force is not so much the head as the heart. Yet while the "love" that he speaks of is ostensibly a love for "the people" as a whole and for the sacred cause of revolution, Guevara's own parenthesis—the revelation that by acknowledging his love he risks "seeming ridiculous"— suggests that gender roles and expectations of masculine performance are intimately connected to the revolutionary enterprise. In fact, it is in this same essay that he coins the term "new man" to describe the kind of transformed individual the Revolution would create.[2] For this "new man," love for the people bleeds over into a love for the project itself; the revolutionary is, in a certain sense, wedded to the revolution, something Guevara suggests later in his essay when he comments that women and families will be part of the general sacrifice to the revolution.[3] Where, then, do other affective relationships fit into this panorama?

This essay turns to one year in particular, 1968, to explore some of the connections between gender, sexuality, and the revolutionary project in Cuba. In many parts of the globe, '68 was a year defined by political struggle: student movements in France, Mexico, Senegal, Great Britain, and

West Germany; Civil Rights struggles and Vietnam War protests in the United States, the contestation of Soviet control in Czechoslovakia and Poland (followed by the subsequent crackdown on this liberalization). In this year of global social and political upheaval, Cuba occupied an exceptional position. It was a third world nation that in nine short years had overthrown a U.S.-supported dictator, undertaken comprehensive measures to redistribute wealth, educate its population, and remake Cuban society; and for many of the students and left-leaning activists engaged in re-imagining society, the Cuban Revolution of 1959 stood as an example of the kind of transformative change they wished to effect. Yet a year after Che Guevara's death in Bolivia, '68 in Cuba was a year of continued consolidation of the political, social, and ideological changes begun in 1959. Even as Cuba stood in solidarity with many of the postcolonial and independence struggles in developing nations, the country began to strengthen its ties with the Soviets (which included eventually supporting the Soviet invasion of Czechoslovakia in response to the Prague Spring).[4] The year 1968 in Cuba also marked the prelude to what has come to be known as the *quinquenio gris*, the "five-year gray period" from the late 1960s through the early 1970s that saw an increase in the censorship and widespread repression of all forms of cultural and artistic expression on the island.[5] It was a year of forging ahead, of continuing to dismantle capitalist systems and ideologies. Yet it was also a year of taking stock, of reconsolidation, of strengthening ideological positions through both political and artistic means. And within the sometimes-contradictory movements of these processes, it was a moment for redefining the "new" revolutionary men and women, and their relationships to both the Revolution and to each other.

It is in light of this backdrop of international upheaval and domestic consolidation (and repression) that this essay turns to an examination of cinema in Cuba in '68. Since the late 1950s, cinema throughout Latin American had been focused on what many of its originators (directors and theorists such as Glauber Rocha of Brazil, Fernando Birri of Argentina, Jorge Sanjinés of Bolivia, and others) termed New Latin American Cinema, a cinema engaged in social critique (particularly of what filmmakers saw as imperialist practices of underdevelopment in Latin American and throughout the third world) and in utilizing film as a form of national popular cultural expression.[6] The conception of cinema as a medium that could (and should) be placed at the service of the people was perfectly in keeping with the new Cuban leadership's ideas about the relationship between cultural production and national identity. Film was recognized as an important cultural medium from the beginning of the Revolution; the Instituto Cubano de Arte e Industria Cinematográfica, or ICAIC, was created in March of 1959, the first cultural decree of the Revolution, and immediately began to train and support Cuban filmmakers.[7] The director

Humberto Solás has said of this period, "[I]t was an intense and interesting moment because the revolution was still very nationalistic and autochthonous, and concerned with affirming its legitimacy."[8] In supporting the creation of a national cinema, the government's intention was that the new medium would produce new cultural products that would both represent and address the "new" nation created by the Revolution.

ICAIC's first films were largely documentaries, but within a year of its founding the Institute was also producing a stream of feature films. '68 saw the release of two particularly important films, each produced by a young ICAIC member: Humberto Solás's *Lucía* and Tomás Gutiérrez Alea's *Memorias del subdesarrollo*, on which this essay will focus. Both of these films directly address the question of political commitment, and do so in ways that foreground the question of gender, sexuality, and their relationship to the Revolution. Solás's *Lucía*, which links the separate stories of three Cuban women at different historical moments, explicitly attempts to chart social change in Cuba through the status of women, symbolically linking the development of female agency to the evolution of Cuban society (and implicitly Cuban freedom from Independence onward) as a whole. Yet as it is portrayed in the film, the social transformation shown as having taken place since the Revolution is revealed to be ambivalent and incomplete at best; as it argues for how gender roles have changed in seventy years of Cuban history, the film also displays the ways in which they have not. *Memorias del subdesarrollo* returns to the question of intellectual participation in the Revolution, choosing as its narrator-protagonist a self-conscious middle-class intellectual who does not seem to fit into the "new Cuba," someone whose relationships with women serve to illustrate both his class loyalties and his stereotypical masculine fantasies. At the same time, the film reveals a society whose very revolutionary outlook is *also* still undergirded by a patriarchal social structure and models of behavior, in which intellectuals (whether bourgeois or revolutionary) are implicitly men, and women only appear as (failed) bourgeois projections. Both *Lucía* and *Memorias* speak to the ways in which other affective relationships (and the gender relations within them) complicate—and sometimes counteract—the revolutionary love that Che emphasizes. The films' failure to resolve these issues, I argue, reflects the sometimes-contradictory impulses and desires produced by the Revolution at this moment.

For the Love of the Revolution: *Lucía*

Lucía, Humberto Solás's sprawling, three-part epic, addresses the question of gender and political participation head-on. The film tells the stories of three different women—all named Lucía—at three key moments in Cuban history: the beginning of Cuba's second War for Independence from Spain (1895), the end of the clandestine fight to overthrow the dictator Gerardo Machado (1933), and an unspecified moment on an agricultural cooperative sometime after the triumph of the Cuban Revolution (identified in the film as 196…). In connecting these three moments, the film hews to a line of thinking, present from the beginning of the Revolution, that the Revolution of 1959 was the culmination of "One Hundred years of Struggle" for Cuban freedom.[9] By focusing on women's relationship to these struggles, it seems to link an increase in female agency to the evolution of Cuba as a nation and its move toward freedom (culminating with the Revolution). While the first two narratives in *Lucía* end in tragedy, the last story, which brings us up to the present day (at least of the film's release), suggests that the Revolution has initiated an era of positive social change.

Solás has stated that despite its three female protagonists, *Lucía* is not a film solely about women: "[I]t's a film about society. But within that society, I chose the most vulnerable character, the one who is most transcendentally affected at any given moment by contradictions and change."[10] A number of critics have argued that the film can be read allegorically: the three Lucías represent the emergent Cuban nation as she struggles to free herself first from colonialism, then from internal oppression, and as she finally fights to throw off the last vestiges of imperialism.[11] Yet by focusing on female characters, it is difficult not to see Solás's film as also positing an evolution in women's freedom in particular, while society changes around them. Rufo Caballero has remarked on the connection in Solás's films between eroticism and a project of nation building.[12] What *Lucía* does more explicitly, I argue, is make visible a direct connection between political engagement and affect. While this implies (like Che's assertion with which this essay opened) that passion is an important part of the political struggle, in the case of all three women, political engagement is always channeled through personal relationships and through their romantic partners. This serves to limit their access to political awareness, and portrays that awareness as still mitigated by men (in particular through romantic relationships), and thus as problematically incomplete.

The most socially constrained of Solás's three heroines, the Lucía of 1895 is someone whose life is almost entirely confined to the closed domestic sphere. An unmarried member of the upper class plantation aristocracy in the city of Trinidad, nearly old enough to be seen as a "spinster," Lucía-1895's days are spent with other wealthy women in a delicate, nearly cloistered feminine domain, rigidly separated from the outside world and the war (for Independence) that has already begun in the mountains outside the city. As Mayra Pastrana has observed, these spaces seem almost to be separate worlds, so rarely do they coincide.[13] The violence of war intrudes only through rumor and gossip, and the stories that do filter into the protected stillness of Luciá's mother's parlor—such as the story of the nun who is raped while trying to aid wounded soldiers—produce a sense of titillation rather than sincere anxiety in the female listeners. Both the camera work and the music enhance the narrative contrasts of these spaces; the soft focus and the popular songs of the interior scenes clash with the sharp (surreal) camera angles and the sometimes-nightmarish atmosphere of the streets.

The film's division of private and public space suggests the ways in which Lucía-1895 is both protected and constrained by her position as an upper-class woman. Her only connections to the outside world, and thus to the political landscape, occur principally through her affective relationships with the men in her life, specifically her brother Felipe, who has sided with the rebels. Lucía doesn't know any specific details of what Felipe does nor of the struggle itself; she only sees Felipe arrive at home, exhausted and dirty, and stay long enough to bathe, grab a clean shirt and a few winks of sleep before disappearing again into the countryside. Lucía supports the fight for Independence because Felipe is involved (and through a vague sense of class loyalty), not because she necessarily understands what is at stake in the conflict. Indeed, her primary concerns are overwhelmingly personal: the need to find love, marry, create an independent domestic life for herself.

Lucía-1895's isolation within this protected domestic space explains why she easily falls for Rafael, the attractive, enigmatic Spaniard who romances her. Charmed by his effusive gestures and his displays of passion, she so desperately craves the attention he bestows on her that she doesn't question his statement of political neutrality, even after she discovers he has a wife and child at home in Spain. Blinded by her desire for Rafael, and willing to defy social convention to experience romantic love (regardless of the cost), Lucía makes plans to run away with him to her family's coffee plantation. In actuality, Rafael is working for the Spanish, and when he and Lucía run away together, their flight leads him straight to the rebel stronghold (as he had known it would). When the Spanish troops that have followed Rafael attack the rebels, Lucía finds herself abandoned on the battlefield. As troops from both sides gallop past her (in a battle that will eventually take Felipe's life), she is literally overwhelmed in the face of the political struggle, unwittingly guilty of initiating the chaos and yet an impotent witness to the violence around her. Her only political act may be the last one in this segment of the film: upon returning to the city, she sees Rafael in conversation with some men and attacks him, stabbing him in revenge for his betrayal and Felipe's death. This violent act can be seen as a kind of liberation, yet it also marks Lucía's descent into madness, as if knowledge itself were too much for her to bear.

Like Lucía-1895, Lucía-1933 also comes from a sheltered, upper class environment, in this case the upper-middle class urban bourgeoisie, yet both changing times and her circumstances allow her to gain more social freedom and political awareness. As the segment begins, Lucía and her mother are sent by her father to spend the summer at their beach house in Cienfuegos, while he stays in the city (with his mistress, it is later revealed). Lucía and her mother lead a life of boredom and idleness, until Lucía falls in love with Aldo, a wounded rebel she discovers hiding in a house down the beach. Aldo and Lucía's romance, clandestine at first, ends with her joining him both physically and ideologically: she moves in with him, gets a job at rolling cigars, and carries out her part in the struggle against Machado.

While Lucía-1895 is never a participant in the political struggle, only a witness to the violence, Lucía-1933 actively takes part in the fight against Machado. She voluntarily joins the working class, taking a job at a cigar factory, where she and her friend Flor help to militarize the other female workers. One scene significantly shows the women marching as a group, shouting political slogans and engaging in scuffles with the police. In another scene, Lucía and Flor use lipstick to scrawl revolutionary slogans on the mirrors of the women's restroom; the beauty products of Lucía's former bourgeois life have been turned into political weapons.

Despite Lucía's active politicization, as Michael Chanan notes, "her liberation as a woman is inevitably constrained."[14] In particular, her personal freedom and happiness continue to be tied to her husband's well-being. The ousting of Machado does not result in lasting political change, as cronyism and corruption continue to prevail. Unwilling to sell-out, Aldo stages a desperate attempt at armed rebellion, and is killed, leaving Lucía a pregnant, grieving widow. The last scene shows her wandering alone by the river in a haze of grief, possibly contemplating throwing herself in. It is as if Aldo were Lucía's link to independence and stability; her increased political awareness and the ties she had formed to a community of other women through the struggle cannot survive his death.

If both Lucía-1933 and Lucía-1895 are restricted by their marginal position (as women) in society and their lack of access to social agency (and/or political awareness), the film seems to suggest that Lucía-196…will provide a marked contrast to this situation. Solás does not give us a concrete date for this final Lucía, thus suggesting both a reading of the Revolution as the significant temporal event (for which everything in the next decade will exist in a kind of temporal coevalness) and creating a sense of contemporaneity for viewers of the film in the year of its release. While the first two Lucías are set in the confining, decadent environs of the city, Lucía-196…moves the action to an agricultural cooperative in the countryside, a space, as Humberto Solás has noted, that was emblematic of the changes the Revolution was bringing to the country and to the lives of ordinary citizens.[15] The first two Lucías came from the landed aristocracy and the urban bourgeoisie respectively; Lucía-196…is a countrywoman, a working class member of the cooperative, a Cuban citizen proudly working in the service of the Revolution.

Except that Lucía is really at the service of her fiancé-then-husband Tomás. A stereotypically dominating, jealous man, Tomás is shown as someone whose ideas of gender roles are outdated, out of step with the changes brought about by the Revolution. (Flavio, the leader of the cooperative, calls him a "mule," and observes that he is just like his father.) Tomás not only keeps Lucía from working once they are married, but is so jealous that he forbids her from leaving the house or entertaining visitors. Lucía attempts to obey Tomás, but her imprisonment stifles her natural drive and energy. One scene shows her putting on make-up, yet the effect is exaggerated and clownish, a parody of the delicate toilette of Lucía-1933. Lucía-196…'s function, the film implies, is as a worker, not as a superficial object of desire.[16]

Things change for Lucía with the arrival of a literacy volunteer from Havana. As Lucía is illiterate, the community leaders order the young man to teach her to read, despite Tomás's vehement jealous protests over having another man in his house. This turns out to be a transformative moment for Lucía. Thanks to the attention of the young literacy teacher, new possibilities for learning and independence open up through reading. At the same time, the young teacher, outraged at the way Tomás treats his wife, urges Lucía to leave him, telling her that she doesn't have to put up with Tomás's treatment, that no woman should be a slave to her husband.

Lucía does leave Tomás, leaving a written note for him that says, "I'm leaving, because I am not a slave."[17] Taking a stand against his physical and emotional abuse, Lucía seems, on the surface, to gain both awareness and agency. Her struggle is also supported by the women in the community, principally Angelina, the wife of the leader of the cooperative, who backs Lucía up when Tomás chases after her and makes a public plea for her to return. Her coming to revolutionary consciousness (and the literacy granted her through the efforts of the revolution) would seem to have given her both an awareness of her own abilities and the confidence to make her own independent decisions.

Two elements of the narrative act to problematize Lucía's achievements, however. The "decolonization" of her consciousness (her *toma de conciencia* as both revolutionary discourse and theorists of New Latin American Cinema would identify it), her gains in knowledge and awareness, are not solely her own: they are still the provenance of masculine space, and her freedom is dependent on being granted access to this space through the help (and mediation) of the male literacy worker. It is also only at his urging that she works up the courage to leave. Most importantly, Lucía cannot entirely free herself from Tomás. As the film ends, she returns to him, telling him she needs to work, but that she also has to be with him: "I've come back because I can't live without you."[18] Her recapitulation, her insistence on the necessity of returning to a relationship that has already been proven to limit her freedom, undercut all of her earlier gains. Despite her increased awareness, her return to Tomás suggests that Lucía cannot do it on her own; to go forward she *must* be connected to a male partner, even if that partner is both potentially hurtful and limiting of her aims as a worker and as a revolutionary. In this sense, Lucía sacrifices her own goals and achievements so that Tomás can make progress toward a new revolutionary identity.[19] This implies that his transformation is more important than hers, that the "new woman" will continue to be a support for the "new man," rather than an independent political actor.

The Intellectual's Guide to Sex: *Memorias del Subdesarrollo*

Solás's film focuses on the political engagement of ordinary individuals, yet throughout the early years of the Revolution the nature of the revolutionary intellectual was the subject of particularly intense debate. The old concept of the intellectual—as educated and elite—smacked of capitalist class privilege; in Cuba's new, classless society, where all were equal, the idea of the intellectual had to be renegotiated. Cuban official discourse in the 1960s sought to reinforce the idea that the Cuban intellectual was one totally committed to the Revolution—"Within the Revolution: everything; against the Revolution, nothing!" claimed Fidel.[20] In keeping with the naming of '68 as "*Año del Guerrillero Heróico*" (The Year of the Warrior Hero), the work of the intellectual was fused into the idea of Cuba's New Man as one engaged in armed struggle. The *Congreso Cultural de La Habana*, held in January of '68, declared that the only kind of person who could be considered a true intellectual was someone who "is ready to take on all risks and for whom the risk of dying while fulfilling his duty does not constitute a brake on the supreme possibility of serving his country and his people."[21] The idea of what an intellectual should aspire to (and what they could say) was thus increasingly limited by official discourse, and by the idea of revolutionary activity as comprised principally of action.

Tomás Gutiérrez Alea's *Memorias del subdesarrollo* explores the conflicts and contradictions inherent in the transformation of this new kind of intellectual. Based on the short novel of the same name by Edmundo Desnoes (1965), Gutiérrez Alea's film focuses on Sergio, a white, upper middle class Havana resident whose family, as the movie opens, is leaving Cuba for the United States. The manager of his family's furniture business prior to the

Revolution, Sergio has stayed in Havana with the idea that he will realize his youthful dream of becoming a writer: "Now I'm going to see if I really have anything to say." Left alone in his comfortable apartment in the formerly upper middle class Vedado neighborhood, he spends his days walking through the city, watching the cityscape (and his neighbors) through a telescope, and occasionally sitting down to tap fitfully at his Remington in what seems to be more a performance of the act of writing than a dedication to the writing itself. His ramblings through his city are nothing so much as the movements of a Baudelairian *flanneur*; he passes by people without interacting with them, moves through crowds without seeming to become a part of the scene. In this way, Sergio often seems to function more as a distanced narrator than as the film's protagonist. Paired with his voiced-over narration, the camera seems to occupy Sergio's perspective as a distanced observer of the people and events going on around him.

Despite his decision to stay, Sergio is conscious that he does not fit into the New Cuba. His inner monologue is a nostalgic rumination on the changes wrought in the Havana that he knew: "Have I changed, or has the city changed?" Given that he has never made a career of writing, Sergio is identified as an intellectual less as a function of his profession than as a result of his class-consciousness, illustrated by his material and aesthetic tastes. He is critical of the ways in which Havana has changed—it now seems like "a provincial backwater"—and his criticism centers on the changes that have separated it from what he sees as its former European sophistication: the closing of exclusive department stores, a preference for Marxist political tracts over literature in the bookstores. Yet his narrative provides moments when this class-consciousness is itself tongue-in-cheek; after declaring in a nostalgic tone that Havana used to be known as the Paris of the Caribbean, he adds, "[A]t least, that's what the tourists and the whores used to call it," as if recognizing that the city may not have been experienced as such by ordinary citizens.[22] His observation, "People seem more stupid everyday," is paired with a shot of him dining with his unapologetically bourgeois friends Pablo and Anita, soon to leave for Miami. Gutiérrez Alea's incorporation of documentary footage at key points in Sergio's narrative further adds to the impression that Sergio has at least some understanding of the political context out of which the Revolution arose. Through his ambivalent commentaries and what Michael Chanan has characterized as a "paralyzed perceptiveness," Sergio thus comes across as both inescapably bourgeois and yet highly aware of the problematic aspects of his position.[23] He is an outsider conscious of his outsider status, a position that allows the viewer the possibility of identifying with his self-doubt.

The film most fully reveals Sergio's class-consciousness through his relationships with women. During the movie Sergio both remembers and interacts with four significant women in his life: Hannah, his first love; Noemí, his cleaning woman, a born-again Christian; Laura, his wife, who has left for Miami, and Elena, a young aspiring-actress with whom he becomes involved after his wife leaves. (The film is, in fact, organized into "chapters" whose titles are the names of these women, another detail indicative of their importance.) Two of these women are no longer actively in Sergio's life at the time the movie takes place. Yet all four women seem to exist for him primarily as memories, fantasies or projections, never as individuals with whom he can connect. These relationships, more than anything, illustrate Sergio's inability to free himself from a patriarchal mindset.

Hannah, Sergio's first love, represents his early missed opportunities for happiness. The perfectly blond daughter of German-Jewish refugees, she moved to New York and ended her relationship with Sergio when he failed to join her there, choosing instead to stay in Havana and run his family's furniture store. Hannah seems to incarnate Sergio's ideal of European intellectual sophistication. Yet his relationship with her never left the realm of adolescent promise, and was never given the opportunity to mature into something real or lasting. His inability to commit to her and leave his life in Havana to remake himself as a full-time writer/ intellectual is symptomatic of the ambivalent position that he occupies in post-Revolutionary Cuba. He may be critical of the situation in which he finds himself, but he seems incapable (or unwilling) to take active steps in any direction.

Noemí, Sergio's cleaning woman, offers him another kind of escapist scenario. When he learns that she is a born-again Christian, he fantasizes about being present for her baptism in the river. Putting himself in the position of the priest, he imagines the two of them embracing in the water, a vision that is plainly erotic and yet (through the action of baptism) simultaneously presents the erotic vision as a rite of spiritual purification. In the film's most significant departure from the novel, Sergio never actually sleeps with Noemí; apart from some gentle flirtation over a cup of coffee, his sexual relationship with her remains at the level of innuendo and daydream. A scene in which he fantasizes about her while touching a picture of Botticelli's Venus humorously places her out of reach and seems to connect her to an image of aesthetic (and perhaps also moral) purity.

Sergio's dreams of what might have been or his fantasies of what might be, as shown in his thoughts about Hannah or Noemí seem to be harmless, if revealing. Yet his more ambiguous and disturbing relationships with Laura and Elena seem almost equally chimeric. If *Lucía* explored the relationship between political engagement and romantic affect, *Memories* makes a more direct connection between the two, as Sergio's ambivalent and disconnected relationships mirror his lack of engagement with the

Revolution. Laura, Sergio's wife, is shown early in the movie leaving for Miami. The viewer sees only a quickly moving sideways shot of her as she turns to board the plane, angrily spurning Sergio's final attempts at good-bye. This gives the viewer an initial impression of her, elegant in a fur hat and coat, but thereafter any representation of Laura in the film is compartmentalized, a disjointed composite formed by fragmented images, traces of her presence. We see her clothes and jewelry, the trappings of the life she has left behind, catch a glimpse of her nude silhouette as she enters the shower, and listen to her voice on a tape that Sergio made of one of their conversations.

The taped conversation between Laura and Sergio, repeated at various points in the film, forms a disturbing background to their relationship. When Sergio plays the tape back for the first time, he simultaneously dresses up in his wife's clothes and jewelry and draws the elements of a woman's face (eyes, nose, lips) on the mirror in lipstick. Sergio's performance as he replays the tape is a kind of transvestism, a taking on of what he lacks, yet it is a distorted performance, given that he does not replicate Laura's feminine appearance but displaces certain elements onto the mirror where they engage with his stockinged face only in reflection. As the taped argument reaches its emotional climax (Sergio has revealed to Laura that he has been taping them), Sergio pulls a pair of nylon stockings over his face. When Laura's now-hysterical voice cries out, "You're a monster!" Sergio's deformed face under the stocking could indeed at that moment be seen as monstrous; its deformation (by means of the stocking, a fundamental element of feminine attire) transforms his cross-dressing play into something more sinister. As Bruce Williams observes, the presence of the mask "positions [Sergio] at once as perpetrator and hostage," aggressor and victim, a description that could equally be applied to the way he feels as a former bourgeois sophisticate in revolutionary Cuba.[24]

Sergio's sarcastic performance of feminine bourgeois superficiality thus highlights the ways in which that which he most desires is also that which he is moved to reject, an inner conflict also expressed in his declaration that Laura is "every day more attractive—more artificial." There is a curious intertextual connection here between what Catherine Benamou has labeled as Sergio's "grotesque (if desperate) parodying of [Laura's] femininity" and the images of one or more of the women in *Lucía* in front of the mirror, particularly the scene in which Lucía-196…applies garish, overdone make-up.[25] In both scenes there is a rejection of the trappings of bourgeois feminine adornment, yet while Lucía-196…seems to scorn this mask in order to privilege the emergence of the real woman beneath, Sergio's performance is a haunting and distorted reconstruction of someone who is no longer there. It suggests that for Sergio the idea of the feminine consists of these material traces, this fragmented performance.

If Sergio seemingly rejects Laura for her bourgeois attraction to superficial beauty and material possessions, one might suppose that in his next romantic relationship he would look for someone different, someone less superficial or perhaps more ideologically committed. Yet Elena, the young woman he picks up outside of the ICAIC offices on *La Rampa* (the Vedado neighborhood's commercial strip) with an invitation to lunch, is far from being a focused revolutionary. An aspiring actress with little education or cultural knowledge, Elena declares upon first meeting Sergio that she wants to "discover herself." Her act falls noticeably flat at the actual film audition Sergio arranges for her (with Gutiérrez Alea himself), but Elena also functions as an actress for Sergio. Dressing up in the chic dresses Laura has left behind, she plays at being the sophisticated, bourgeois object of Sergio's desires. Ultimately, however, Sergio finds her performance unconvincing. He is attracted to her for her youth and naiveté, yet is constantly critical of her lack of sophistication: "I always try to live like a European, and Elena made me feel underdevelopment with each step."[26] Like Havana since the Revolution, Sergio is drawn to Elena more for what she evokes than for who she truly is.

What Sergio seems to be most attracted to in his relationship with Elena is the illusion of control it creates for him. His first meeting with her allows him to play the role of suave sophisticate: "You have beautiful knees; would you care to have lunch with me?" He is the seducer, and Elena's (somewhat feigned) reluctance, as she pushes him away and then pulls him closer, only seems to make the chase more attractive. The scene leading to what we assume is their first sexual encounter extends this play of resistance and domination more strongly, leading some critics to characterize it as a mock rape scene. This play at control backfires when Elena's family actually accuse Sergio of raping Elena. Though he is acquitted, destroys any fantasies he has constructed about Elena, along with his illusion of being in control.

Sergio's unreal and paradoxical ideas about women are a direct reflection of his position in post-Revolutionary Cuba. He wants women to be cosmopolitan and sophisticated, yet he acknowledges that he likes the directness and sensuality of Cuban women: "Here women look you in the eye, as if they would let you caress them with your glance."[27] Similarly, he has chosen to stay in Cuba (indicating that something about the Revolution moves him), yet he cannot change, cannot involve himself. As Henry Fernández points out, "[T]he ony contact [Sergio] makes or tries to make with the people is through observation and sex: literally, he reaches out with his telescope and his phallus."[28] For Sergio, both of these objects are instruments of desire, and yet with both women and the new Revolutionary society of Havana, he often finds himself on the outside looking in. Women are there to be manipulated, as the subjects of fantasy, as something to exercise control over, precisely what he would like to do in a world in which he is not in control and from which he is increasingly distant.

Gutiérrez Alea significantly chooses to set the film in 1962, prior to and during the Cuban missile crisis, a key moment for Cuba in terms of political activity, and a period (like '68) in which the role of the intellectual in the Revolution was publicly questioned and redefined. (In addition to the Bay of Pigs Invastion, 1961 also saw the first public debates over the role of the intellectual, in a conference in Havana that ended with Fidel Castro's famous speech "Words to the Intellectuals.") Sergio, as the figure of the intellectual who does not, cannot, will not, fit in as a New Intellectual, both opens a space for the questioning of this figure, and presents a detailed and critical portrait of a way of thinking and a series of values that the Revolution was actively engaged in trying to reshape. His relationships with women might easily be included as part of this critical portrait, if only other models were available. Though the film critiques Sergio's contradictory behaviour towards women, it does little to counteract (or present alternative perspectives to) Sergio's portrayal of women as weak, hysterical, superficial, or bourgeois. In particular, the space of the intellectual—shown in the film most directly through the formal Round Table held by a group of international writers on the role of the intellectual (a roundtable that, in a kind of meta-narrative turn, features the writer Edmundo Desnoes)—is gendered almost exclusively as male, in terms of both the make-up of the audience and in terms of those who are given a voice. Women are thus objects of the (desiring) male gaze (primarily Sergio's), not speaking subjects, even less thinking revolutionaries.

The only woman who might be an object of sexual desire but who does not appear as part of Sergio's fantasies is revealed in the film's first scene, which shows what appears to be an evening party or gathering of some kind. The film opens in the midst of the spontaneous release of a dance.[29] The camera scans the crowd without really engaging with it, a gaze later to be equated with Sergio's experience, but at this point unidentified. Shots suddenly ring out, but only those next to the fallen man pause in their dancing. As men in military fatigues (the scene's only reference to the Revolution) carry the fallen man away, the dance goes on. The last shot suddenly freezes on the close-up of the face of a dark-skinned dancing woman. Is her wide-eyed stare one of fear, one of surprise, or one of defiance? It is impossible to tell. When this scene is replayed from Sergio's perspective, what stands out is his difference, a difference signaled not only racially (Sergio is one of the few white people in the crowd), but also by his inability to incorporate himself into the dance. Yet this woman is nothing if not involved in this scene. Clearly, the dance has little to do with revolutionary ideology or revolutionary process. Gutiérrez Alea, in an interview with Julianne Burton, has referred to Sergio as "[ending] up like a cockroach—squashed by his fear, by his impotence, by everything."[30] This scene does nothing to redeem Sergio, nor to suggest that there is any more hope for his incorporation into revolutionary society than we might have otherwise supposed. Yet this first scene presents us with a femininity that seems to be both beyond Sergio's control and beyond the boundaries of revolutionary provenance. It forces us to ask, is Sergio squashed by his fear when faced with the Revolution, or by his fear of a part of Cuban society that cannot be contained by Revolutionary doctrine?

Conclusion: Desiring Cuba

Lucía and *Memorias del subdesarrollo* were both released to much critical interest from abroad, at a time when both North America and Europe were anxious to see signs of what was happening in Cuba. Tomás Gutiérrez Alea, in his reflection on *Memorias del subdesarrollo,* remarks that while the film stimulated intense discussions at film festivals such as Cannes and Pesaro, what remains most significant for him is the way in which "it seems to reveal in a most precise and exemplary way the workings of those mechanisms which can be unleashed in the show-spectator relationship and which aid the audience 'to participate in the critique of itself,' as Antonio Gramsci put it."[31] Gutiérrez Alea is speaking, specifically, of the way in which a Cuban viewer of *Memorias,* in identifying with Sergio, might be made to discover his own struggles as a revolutionary.

It is certainly possible that some members of Gutiérrez Alea's audience may have come away from his film with this kind of insight. But his comment, focused as it is on national consciousness-raising (such as the kind going on in Cuba in '68), overlooks the ways in which the Cuban Revolution, as the model and inspiration for so many struggles around the world in '68, was itself an object of desire. For those foreign viewers wanting to taste the success and hope of the Revolution, *Lucía* and *Memorias del subdesarrollo* both offered up examples of positive change: a society with increased agency for women; a place where neither the landed aristocracy nor the idle middle class would be welcome; a place where the intellectual's relationship to society was being redefined. It is significant, then, that both films reject the desire (both national and international) to see the Revolution as a finished achievement, choosing instead to portray it as an ongoing (and sometimes difficult) process. In particular, the female characters in these films, and above all the affective relationships in which they are engaged, show the ways in which women's agency was still limited, whether by the vestiges of patriarchal double standards or by bourgeois fantasies. Paradoxically, these relationships, for all of their obvious limitations (and their sometimes very un-revolutionary affect), are also the audience's access to desire. We may want to condemn Lucía-196…when she returns to her husband Tomás, to see her as betraying her independence and revolutionary ideals. And yet, like the laughing little girl who looks on as the reunited couple kiss one another passionately, it's hard not to acknowledge that at the risk of looking ridiculous, they're guided by great feelings of love.

Notes

1. "Déjeme decirle, a riesgo de parecer ridículo, que el revolucionario verdadero está guiado por grandes sentimientos de amor," in "El hombre nuevo," *Marcha* Montevideo: March 1965. Rpt. Leopoldo Zea, ed., *Ideas en torno a Latinoamérica,* vol. 1 (México: UNAM, 1986), 10.
2. For a more complete discussion of the idea of the "new man," see Ana Serra, *The "New Man" in Cuba: Culture and Identity in the Revolution* (Gainesville: University Press of Florida, 2007).
3. "Los dirigentes de la revolución tienen hijos que en sus primeros balbuceos, no aprenden a nombrar al padre; mujeres que deben ser parte del sacrificio general de su vida para llevar la revolución a su destino; el maro de los amigos responde estrictamente al marco de los compañeros de la revolución. No hay vida fuera de ella." Ibid.
4. Louis A. Pérez, Jr., *Cuba: Between Reform and Revolution,* 3rd ed. (Oxford: Oxford University Press, 2006), 288.
5. There seems to be some debate over the exact dates of the *quinquenio gris.* Ambrosio Fornet, in his recent reconsideration of the period, identifies it as beginning in 1971. ("El *quinquenio gris*: Revisitando el término." *Criterios: Centro Teórico-Cultural.* Ciclo: La política cultural del período revolucionario: Memoria y reflexión [Havana, January 2007], http://www.criterios.es/cicloquinqueniogris.htm). Yet Robin Moore names 1968 as the starting date, one marked by the widespread closing of cabarets throughout the country, and a censorship of artists that ranged from a loss of party membership to being shipped off to the work camps in the countryside. Moore, *Music and Revolution: Cultural Change in Socialist Cuba* (Berkeley: University of California Press, 2006), 104.
6. See Michael Martin, ed., *New Latin American Cinema,* 2 vols. (Detroit: Wayne State University Press, 1997).
7. Michael T. Martin and Bruce Paddington, "Restoration or Innovation? An Interview with Humberto Solás: Post-Revolutionary Cuban Cinema," *Film Quarterly* 54:3 (2001): 4.
8. Martin and Paddington, 5.
9. The beginning of "The One Hundred Years of Struggle" is commonly recognized as the *Grito de Yara,* the first call for secession from Spain.
10. Interview with Marta Alvear, 1978. Reprinted as "Humberto Solás: Every Point of Arrival is a Point of Departure," in *Cinema and Social Change in Latin America. Conversations With Filmmakers,* ed. Julianne Burton (Austin: University of Texas Press, 1986), 150. Interestingly, Solás had also used a female protagonist to deal directly with armed revolution in his first film *Manuela* (1966).
11. See Rufo Caballero, "Erotismo y nación en el cine de Humberto Solás," *Cine Cubano* 167 (January–March 2008): 3–20; Marvin D'Lugo, "Transparent Women: Gender and Nation in Cuban Cinema," *New Latin American Cinema* 2: 155–166.
12. "En Solás la construcción del erotismo se muestra inseparable de la construcción del proyecto de la nación: el erotismo…alcanza a aceitar, a favorecer, la articulación de todo

un proyecto de nación y cultura." Caballero, "Erotismo y nación en el cine de Humberto Solás," 3.

13. Marya Pastrana, "La casa y el afuera en *Lucía*: la vida está en otra parte: ¿Dónde?," *Cine Cubano* 170 (October–December 2008): 26.

14. Michael Chanan, *The Cuban Image: Cinema and Cultural Politics in Cuba* (Bloomington: Indiana University Press, 1985), 233.

15. "Lucía y el tiempo." Supplemental video. *Lucía*, ICAIC: 2006.

16. This is in keeping with Caterhine Benamou's observation that Cuban films of the 1960s and 1970s have generally "tended to construct women as pre-eminently laboring subjects at the expense of their other attributes and their intimate selves." Benamou, "Cuban Cinema: On the Threshold of Gender," *Frontiers: A Journal of Women Studies* 15:1, Women Filmmakers and the Politics of Gender in Third Cinema (1994): 54.

17. "Me voy porque no soy esclaba," *Lucía,* Humberto Solás, dir. (1968). The note is poorly spelled, indicating Lucía's still struggling efforts at writing, and reminding the viewer of what she has accomplished.

18. "He vuelto porque no puedo vivir sin ti." *Lucía.*

19. Adela Legrá, the actress who played Lucía-196… (and who was herself a self-taught countrywoman before Solás cast her in "Manuela"), has disagreed with the films' ending, saying that she herself would never have returned to a man like Tomás. "*Lucía* y el tiempo." Supplemental DVD materials, *Lucía,* ICAIC: 2006.

20. "[D]entro de la Revolución todo; contra la Revolución nada," Fidel Castro Ruz, "Palabras a los intelectuales," June, 1961. Cuban Ministry of Culture. http://www.min.cult.cu/historia/palabras.doc, 10.

21. "[Alguien quien] esté dispuesto a encarar todos los riesgos y para quien el riesgo de morir en el cumplimiento de su deber, no constituya un freno a la posibilidad suprema de servir a su patria y a su pueblo." "Declaración general del Congreso Cultural de La Habana," published in *Vida Universitaria* 206 (1968): 28.

22. "Por lo menos, eso decían los turistas y las putas." Ibid.

23. Chanan, *The Cuban Image: Cinema and Cultural Politics in Cuba,* 237.

24. Bruce Williams, "Memory in Drag: Historical and Sexual Strategies in Tomás Gutiérrez Alea's *Memories of Underdevelopment,*" *Cinémas: revue d'études cinématographique/ Cinémas: Journal of Film Studies* 8, no. 3 (1998): 111.

25. Catherine Benamou, "Cuban Cinema: On the Threshold of Gender," 55.

26. "Siempre trato de vivir como Europeo, y Elena me hacía sentir el subdesarrollo a cada paso." Ibid.

27. "Aquí las mujeres te miran a los ojos, como si te dejaran tocar con la Mirada." Ibid.

28. Henry Fernández, D.I. Grossvogel, and Emir Rodríguez Mangual, "3 on 2: Desnoes, Gutiérrez Alea," *Diacritics* (Winter 1974): 56.

29. Interestingly, this first scene bears some resemblance to *P.M.* the 1961 film by Sabá Cabrera Infante and Orlando Jiménez Leal. *P.M.* was one of the first films to be censured by the Revolution, initiating a fierce debate over both censorship and the role of the intellectual in the Revolution. It is unclear whether this similarity is mere coincidence, or whether Gutiérrez Alea's intends to create an intertextual reference to the issues brought up in the debate over the film.

30. "Tomás Gutiérrez Alea (Cuba): Beyond the Reflection of Reality." Interview with Julianne Burton, 1977. In *Cinema and Social Change in Latin America: Conversations with Filmmakers,* 119.

31. Tomás Gutiérrez Alea, "Appendix: Memories of *Memories,*" in *The Viewer's Dialectic,* ed. Iraida Sánchez Oliva, trans. Julia Lesage (Havana: Editorial José Martí, 1988), 67–85.

CHAPTER FIVE

Africa and 1968: Derepression, Libidinal Politics, and the Problem of Global Interpretation

STEVEN PIERCE

What was the role of Africa in the movements of 1968? At the time it conjured up many images, more perhaps than anytime before or since. Independence continued to come to former European colonies—Equatorial Guinea and Swaziland in that year alone. The "new nations of Africa" was a phrase both trite and exciting. Meanwhile the guerilla leaders of Portuguese Africa, Amilcar Cabral of Guinea-Bissau most notably, were influential theorists of revolution, as well as inspirational figures of struggle against the colonizer.[1] African novels were gaining international audiences and acted both to valorize indigenous cultures and to convince outsiders that Africans had achieved "universal" culture. Excellent universities (Dakar in Senegal, Ibadan and Ahmadu Bello in Nigeria, Legon in Ghana, Makerere in Uganda, Dar-es-Salaam in Tanzania) were becoming important centers of learning. However, in Nigeria a brutal civil war raged, which would make the term "Biafra baby" synonymous with starvation. Military governments ruled much of the continent, and the coups continued—Sierra Leone, Congo-Brazzaville, and Mali as the year progressed. In this grab-bag of images one can discern two dominant tendencies, a continuation of the hopeful postwar narratives of emerging countries and modernization, and an even older story about Africa's violence and brutality.

Africa and 1968: one needs to keep in mind the all-too-distinct histories of African countries and of the ideological appropriation of "Africa" by and for outside interests. Africans played a role in 1968, both as student protestors in many countries and as a place to be invoked as an alternative to Western bourgeois modernity. Africa was a site of struggle and a space of revolutionary hope. In this short essay I take as a point of departure the intricate relationship between the empirical and ideological Africas for that moment, when appropriations were so rich.[2] How did Africa assume ideological importance for foreign political projects in many cases at odds with indigenous systems of meaning, and what does that disjuncture tell us? But there is a deeper challenge Africa poses to narratives of a global '68. Although there *were* student protests, for the most part they were not specifically countercultural, and they did not pose the same challenge to existing norms of gender and sexuality that were being made elsewhere in the world. I argue below that this is because African universities had a very different relation to African bourgeoisies than what existed in countries where countercultures emerged. The very humble backgrounds of the majority of African students (and the absolute necessity of earning degrees in order to attain middle-class status) made students' critiques of bourgeois existence very different from those that pertained elsewhere in the world. This aspect of African class structure combined with a distinctive libidinal economy to provide a striking contrast to movements elsewhere aimed at freeing people from oppressive gender and sexual norms. Ultimately, I argue, these contrasts provide a useful way of complicating triumphalist narrative of the effects of 1968.

Africa in 1968

For most of Africa, 1968 was not so much a watershed as midpoint in the "long" 1960s that stretched from Ghanaian independence in 1957 to the oil shock of 1973. This general trajectory was characterized by decolonization on one hand and by the dangers of dependence on the export of primary products on the other. The paradoxes of 1968 illustrate the overall dynamics of this dialectic. With the exception of the Portuguese colonies of Angola, Mozambique, and Guinea-Bissau and of the apartheid regimes of South Africa and Rhodesia (the latter having unilaterally declared independence in 1965 to avoid liberalization), the advent of majority rule was becoming routinized: no more Camerouns, no more Kenyas.[3] Modernization theory promised industrialization and political development much faster than had occurred in Europe.[4] The revolutionary thought of Sekou Touré, Nkrumah's Pan-Africanism, Nyerere's African socialism, Lumumba's eloquence and courage all provided models for postcolonial political formations and for progressive movements worldwide.[5] But by 1968 Touré's regime in Guinea was increasingly erratic. Nkrumah had been overthrown by the Ghanaian military. Cracks were appearing in Tanzania's socialist experiment. And Lumumba was long dead.

The political problems of independence had obvious causes. It has been argued that one catalyst of decolonization was the European realization that African countries would prove increasingly difficult to rule as popular demands for improved standards of living outstripped the national income of countries depending on the export of primary products. To a certain extent decolonization was simply a process of colonial powers' cutting their losses, and postcolonial reality set in very rapidly. Fluctuations in world commodity prices had brought turmoil to many countries, as their goods commanded lower world market prices.[6] To make matters worse, many states required peasants to sell their crops to marketing boards, which paid low prices and used the profits to aid development projects distant from peasant producers. Social welfare initiatives disproportionately benefited urban dwellers, as did price ceilings for basic foodstuffs. These policies had a net effect of decreasing production of the exports on which African countries depended while impoverishing the countryside.[7] Countries that had been self-sufficient in food were increasingly forced to import staples even as their export revenue plummeted. Meanwhile, a number of the Africa's most important exports—cocoa, groundnuts, palm oil, for example—stagnated.

State apparatuses themselves became enmeshed in postcolonial politics: militaries and bureaucracies were riven by competition engendered by rapid Africanization—enormous promotions had been available to Africans in junior positions when their European superiors departed at the time of independence. By 1968 people in junior positions faced much dimmer promotion prospects and relatively youthful superiors.[8] Thus, for example, the first coup in Nigeria's history was launched by Igbo army majors from the southeastern part of the country, in part disgruntled because northerners had been promoted above them and that their prospect of moving up to colonel was increasingly dim. Even more ominously politics in many countries was increasingly characterized by regionalism, ethnic tension, and winner-take-all competition.[9] Political parties were increasingly associated with one ethnic group or one region. Parties once in power tended to favor their own ethnic and regional bases.

All of these tendencies had been in evidence by the end of World War Two, but after nearly a decade of independence they had catastrophic consequences in many places. By the time of the worldwide economic crisis touched off by the oil shock of 1973, such problems began to appear devastating and inevitable, fatally undermining the coherence of decolonization and development as possible or desirable ends. But in 1968 the process was not yet complete, and thus there were a plethora of Africas available to global progressive movements. Africa proud mother of dozens of glittering civilizations, Africa the victim of colonialism, Africa origin of "Western" civilization, Africa center of revolution, Africa emergent. Center of authenticity, center of innovation, cradle of humanity. Needy recipient of the green revolution. New front in the war between capitalism and communism.

Even if the Africa invoked by progressives worldwide depended upon romanticized notions of decolonization and precolonial history that had only an attenuated relationship to actual events, Africans themselves were critical in formulating images appropriated for international consumption.[10] One aspect of Africa's appropriation in global 1968 is the absence of the countercultural student movement so important elsewhere. Even in instances where students explicitly demonstrated against their governments, such as in Senegal and Ethiopia, their protests are clearly recognizable as traditional left or reformist demands.[11] The channels of Africa's countercultural appropriation were somewhat less direct than simple solidarity. This is not to say that young Africans were politically quiescent in 1968 or that universities were uniformly hotbeds of political orthodoxy. The young were not entirely contented. Students did protest, against oppressive regimes, unpopular university policies, and declining opportunities. They also demonstrated in support of their governments, against neocolonialism and Western cultural imperialism and in support of what they considered to be authentic African mores.

Student Movements

One of the most famous African student protests was the student strike and occupation of the University of Dakar (now Cheikh Anta Diop University) in May–June 1968.[12] Students had been increasingly unhappy over a vast increase in university enrollments, without a concomitant increase in the infrastructure for students. This was coupled in 1967 with increases in university fees and decreases in bursaries, especially to those from well-off families or from Dakar itself. A well-organized students' union had been in existence for several years and entered into talks with the university and the government over student grievances. These negotiations broke down on May 15, 1968, and a strike and occupation of the campus began on the 17th. Negotiations with the university administration over the strike continued until the 28th, whereupon the police surrounded the university, cutting it off from the rest of the city. The next morning they invaded, killing at least one student and wounded at least eighty others.[13] All institutions of secondary and postsecondary education were closed, and foreign students were expelled from the country.[14] The labor unions, however, responded with a general strike, which lasted until June 4. Ultimately, the strikers were able to extract concessions from the government, including an increase in scholarships and the resignation of the ministers of education and the interior. However, President Senghor remained in power, and very little changed fundamentally. Progressive demands, moreover, centered on fees and bursaries, poor living conditions, and unemployment. Their grievances, ultimately, concerned the government's economic mismanagement, corruption, and actions that benefited the elite rather than the masses. Whatever the strikes' successes, this was no dawn of the Age of Aquarius.

A very different mode of youth activism came about in Tanzania at the same time. In October 1968, the General Council of the Youth League of TANU, Tanzania's ruling party, announced that a variety of fashions were antithetical to Tanzania's national culture and would therefore be banned. These included mini-skirts, skin-lightening lotions, wigs, and tight-fitting trousers. Almost immediately, in Dar-es-Salaam, the capital of Tanzania, gangs of young men (many of whom were not actually members of the youth league or TANU) began confronting and beating young women dressed in such styles. Young men dressed in forbidden fashions tended to get off much more lightly.[15] The ruling party engaged in similar activities in Zanzibar, though there the campaign was part of a much longer-term offensive against cinema and other forms of "counterrevolutionary" youth culture, and it targeted males much more directly.[16]

This kind of activism among students and other youth stands in considerable contrast to events in Senegal and elsewhere. Rather than being opposed to the government, activists in Tanzania were members of the ruling party, or at least claimed legitimacy for their actions from youth league exhortations. Moreover, their stated goal was not one of individual self-expression and liberation but rather of achieving freedom from Western imperial control through conformity to a new but nonetheless authentic Tanzanian national culture. Ironically, this effort to discipline the dress of too-Westernized youth went hand in hand with efforts to make disfavored, less Westernized ethnic groups like the Maasai give up their own dress customs and also conform to national norms.[17] Authentic national culture did not allow for cultural authenticity. These efforts by the youth league were not unique. Operation Vijana was one instance among many in which young, politically active men—or at least young men claiming the imprimateur of nationalism—attacked young women for adopting Western fashions and Western sexual mores.[18] In this case, youth activism was not opposed to the government, nor did it directly target the adult elite. By fighting to purge "national culture" of pernicious Western influences, activists were not so much resisting existing power relations within their own countries as they were (at least on the surface) attempting to achieve a more thoroughgoing kind of decolonization.

African youth were sophisticated students of international affairs and were significant contributors to international progressive thought, even if their protests were only very superficially, if at all, countercultural. But this raises an immediate, fascinating series of questions. If youth activism in sub-Saharan Africa was not countercultural, why was the continent different from other places in the world? How, moreover, could African progressive politics appeal to outside student activists if its logic were fundamentally different? What were the structures of feeling that underlay these differences, and how might the particularities of African historical experience be used to elucidate the underlying claims made by the contributors to this volume? In particular, how might the relative unimportance of a counterculture to African youth protest suggest the limits of derepression or queer politics?

Africa's universities were with few exceptions postwar creations. Almost as new were the Western-oriented elites whom they educated. With the exception of elite Africans in South Africa and coastal trading enclaves, the class of Western-educated people who moved into elite government and business positions at the end of the colonial period had only emerged with the intensification of mission education that began with colonial rule in the late nineteenth century. While a tiny group went overseas to earn university degrees and advanced professional qualifications beginning in the early colonial period, the inauguration of African universities after World War Two radically expanded educational opportunities, even as the advent of independence created new positions for members of this nascent elite. The radical expansion of educational opportunities and the burgeoning of elite positions open to Africans presented an unprecedented set of opportunities for people of modest background. A child of peasant background who managed to continue in school could, for a time, hope to become a government minister, an army general, a diplomat, a surgeon. In 1968, most of Africa's university students were not disaffected children of the bourgeoisie. The bourgeoisie was too new for that. Students were often themselves new aspirants to bourgeois status. For many, getting a university degree might ultimately represent security for their entire families. Under such circumstances, turning on and dropping out would have been hideously self-indulgent. The specific character of youth politics arises from this state of affairs.

Class, Family, and Repression

Though there is a danger of homogenizing a continent and jumping too giddily between societal trend and individual biography, it is nonetheless possible to link Africa's lack of counterculture in 1968 to this particular political-economic conjuncture and to a broader logic of familial life in many African societies. It is something of a truism that in Africa wealth has primarily been acquired and consolidated in people rather than in things. Low population densities made labor rather than land the primary bottlcneck to agricultural production. Acquiring a following of dependents whose work one could direct was the prime route to accumulating symbolic and literal capital. Success was marked by being generally accepted as being "big," as holding wealth that could be redistributed to a following. In male-dominated societies, this logic combined with marriage through bridewealth (rather than dowry) to inflect politics between generations of men. Capital could prove almost literally fruitful through enabling marriages (and therefore legitimate births), which created dependents, the most valuable kind of wealth. Junior men were forced to work for senior men in order to accumulate the goods necessary to make marriages of their own and begin the climb toward senior status for themselves.[19] Accumulation of goods enabled further bridewealth payments, giving one access to the labor of new wives and of the children they could bear. Adulthood was measured through marriage and parenthood. Male success was measured through polygamy. Wives, children, and grandchildren were both a mark and a source of wealth. Female accumulation was also possible and in some societies could be supplemented by marriage to another woman and paternity of her children. But in both cases wealth and the desire for wealth centered on relationships to people and depended upon one's ability to control one's dependents.

With the advent of colonialism, junior men found new avenues of acquiring wealth, including that necessary for making bridewealth payments, making paternal control of sons extremely fraught both practically and ideologically. A man desired children who might work for him; the wealth they produced could be used to marry additional wives, to invest in other enterprises, to acquire dependents in other ways, or to pay for one's children's marriages or education. Helping one's children in arenas other than marriage became increasingly important, especially to the extent that it increased children's dependence and their long-term earning potential. An ultimate result of this tendency therefore was an increasing emphasis by many fathers in investing in their children's education. Such investment ultimately might strengthen paternal authority and be repaid manifold. But even as parental investment offered unprecedented rewards, the wealth potentially available through educated children ultimately freed children from dependence on—tangible respect for—their parents.[20] The obligations of educated children to aid their parents were a fairly universal area of concern.

Many students in 1968 faced a potentially heartbreaking set of problems. Great numbers of them were of the first generation of their family to receive university-level education, and in fact many were the first to receive Western education at all, a legacy of the post–World War Two expansion of primary education. Their families had not merely sacrificed greatly to provide them with educational opportunity; rather, the most intimate structures of accumulation and desire that had nurtured them made the success of their educational and work careers of critical importance to entire extended families. While ten years earlier it might have appeared that a university place was a guarantee of lucrative employment and of comfort for an entire family, by 1968 economic and political crisis made this a much dicier proposition. Political activism had immediate stakes and immediate consequences. The young people who made up the youth wings of governing parties like Kenya's KANU were potentially preparing for themselves a place in government, or at least were gaining patrons who ultimately might aid a future career. Those who opposed establishment groups were also engaged in a progressive politics that cannot be considered countercultural. Even if they opposed the status quo, for the most part they were not opposed to prevailing standards of bourgeois domesticity but rather opposed particular regimes, modes of production, or existing ethnic or regional distributions of power.

In effect, African students in 1968—even as their politics and position were drawn ideologically into global '68—did not, explicitly, implicitly, or even symbolically, buy into a paradigm of derepression à la Marcuse.[21] One must be skeptical of the extent to which a Freudian account of repression and the Oedipal drama actually describes the intimacies of the Western bourgeois family, as has been forcefully pointed out by feminists and Foucaultians alike. And of course the debate over whether such dramas could apply outside of Western society is somewhat arid and difficult to generalize.[22] Nonetheless, any sense that youth activism in 1968 sub-Saharan Africa was determined by a desire to break free from the repressive constructs of bourgeois domesticity is belied by the lack of this countercultural derepression. More to the point, the psychoanalytic account of the historical development of kinship after the overthrow of the primal father would suggest that at least Operation Vijana would be best read as an attempt to *create* a regime of Marcusian surplus-repression as a way of achieving authentically African modernity, a kind of psychoanalytic modernization theory. I think this does a certain violence to such youth movements and to African history more generally, slotting them into a somewhat teleological evolutionary progression.

In contexts where the "traffic in women" implicit in kin relations was not simply a matter of women's moving from paternal to husbandly authority, but instead was the key to articulating the relation between wealth in people and wealth in things, the Oedipal drama seems ultimately something of a sideshow.[23] That is to say, in sub-Saharan Africa a child's resentment of the father for blocking erotic access to the mother, and the repression of sexuality that results from it, is likely to be dwarfed in importance by the specificities of the links between marriage, reproduction, and accumulation. Nor could this state of affairs be easily read as an earlier stage in the evolution of kinship before the rise of patriarchal monogamy. Even if African youth movements in 1968 were not countercultural, they did take place in 1968 and should not be taken as different or more primitive. Whatever was at stake in the libidinal politics of Africa's 1968, it was not the overthrow of bourgeois domesticity. Nor was liberation the equivalent of throwing off the restrictive mores controlling sexual relations.

Libidinal politics there were. While the form of movements like Operation Vijana was on the apparent neocolonialism of women's adoption of Western modes of dress and de-Africanizing attempts to lighten skin and straighten hair, there is a more complicated sexual politics at stake. One complaint by young men was that women, in adopting such modes of dress, were abandoning plans of making respectable marriage and instead were positioning themselves to become the mistresses of wealthy, already-established older men. Arguments of this kind were conducted in many idioms—progressive ones like Operation Vijana's, which found female fashions an instance of neocolonialism and reaction, religious ones that found them an instance of women's sinful propensities. Indeed, one can read concerns of this kind as representing an extremely familiar contest between generations of men, conducted in the idiom of female sexual morals and taking as its terrain the tangible symbols of female self-presentation. Public debates over female sexual morality have, across colonial and postcolonial Africa, tended to collapse wide-ranging anxieties over generational conflict, economic change, and class relations into the figure of immoral and improper women.[24] The important point here is that this is a familiar, recurrent form of struggle and does not represent a watershed in libidinal history.

Within the "old" leftism of the students of Dakar and the African authenticity of Operation Vijana, one can begin to discern an implicit query that might be directed at both a neo-Freudian celebration of libidinal derepression prevalent in 1968 and the post-Lacanian and Foucaultian strands of queer theory Cohen and Frazier invoke in their introduction.[25] That is to say, student activism in sub-Saharan Africa does not represent a critique of the libidinal politics of bourgeois modernity, and it does not precisely call into question fixed, dichotomous gender norms. The editors are doubtless right to perceive something very important at stake in the global reach of 1968 *and* to locate it in the production and spread of certain modes of gender and sexual self-expression. The challenge posed to this paradigm by Africa in 1968 does not lie in the fact that Africa is "not Western" or was modernizing but as yet insufficiently Westernized for the counterculture to have had much direct resonance. Rather, it poses in a new form the question of what is at stake in any production of "heterosexual" normativity. Even if the discourses of sexual liberation and self-actualization that made 1968 progressivism novel were inadequate to describe the ultimate stakes of the politics of personhood, Africa cannot be comprehended by a paradigm that simply considers the norm of heterosexual domesticity and its abject others.[26] More to the point, it brings into question whether queer subjectivities could serve to destabilize existing relations of power.

The absence of a widespread counterculture in 1968 Africa, even as Africa was (however partially, erratically, or inaccurately) appearing as progressive inspiration, does not simply demonstrate Africa's position outside or before particular modes of oppressive gender or libidinal norms. Rather, it suggests that we must consider the particularities and contingencies of particular progressive formations, patterns of affective relationships, structures of desire. In this sense, therefore, it is critical to understand the ways in which the particularities of African societies—enmeshed in a particular position within the global order, working through a very particular set of politico-sexual dilemmas—subtended the region's participation in youth movements and therefore cannot easily be incorporated into an analytic developed for San Francisco or Paris. If one also rejects the notion that Africa simply was not "ready" for the counterculture but instead notes that everywhere a critique of economic and libidinal politics drew youthful responses, Africa promises a new set of insights into the politics of personhood that 1968 so urgently challenged.

Notes

My thanks to Claire Breedlove for her loan of materials on Senegal.

1. Amilcar Cabral, *Revolution in Guinea: Selected Texts*, trans. Richard Handyside (New York: Monthly Review Press, 1970).
2. For the purposes of this essay I am excluding student activism in South Africa, which presents a very different set of dynamics due to the profoundly different demographic makeup of university campuses as a direct result of South Africa's status as a settler society and its apartheid government.
3. Bruce Berman and John Lonsdale, *Unhappy Valley: Conflict in Kenya and Africa* (Athens: James Currey, 1992); Richard A. Joseph, *Radical Nationalism in Cameroun: Social Origins of the U.P.C. Rebellion* (New York: Oxford University Press, 1977); David Throup, *Economic & Social Origins of Mau Mau, 1945–53* (Athens: James Curry, 1987).
4. David Apter, *Ghana in Transition*, rev. ed. (New York: Atheneum, 1963); W. W. Rostow, *The Stages of Economic Growth: A Non-Communist Manifesto* (Cambridge: Cambridge University Press, 1960).
5. Patrice Lumumba, *Le Congo, Terre D'avenir, Est-Il Menacé?* (Bruxelles: office de publicité, 1961); Kwame Nkrumah, *Africa Must Unite* (London: Heinemann, 1963); Julius K. Nyerere, *Ujamaa: Essays on Socialism* (Dar es Salaam: Oxford University Press, 1968); Ahmed Sékou Touré, *L'action politique du Parti Démocratique de Guinée* (Paris: Presence Africaine, 1959);

Le pouvoir populaire, 2nd ed. (Conakry: Le Pouvoir populaire, 1969); *La révolution culturelle*, 2 éd. (Conakry: Le Pouvoir populaire, 1969).

6. Samir Amin, *Neo-Colonialism in West Africa*, trans. Francis McDonagh (Baltimore: Penguin, 1973).

7. Robert H. Bates, *Markets and States in Tropical Africa: The Political Basis of Agricultural Policies* (Berkeley: University of California Press, 1981); Frederick Cooper, "Africa and the World Economy," *African Studies Review* 24:2/3 (1980): 1–86.

8. Ibid.

9. Jean Marie Allman, *The Quills of the Porcupine: Asante Nationalism in an Emergent Ghana* (Madison: University of Wisconsin Press, 1993); Richard A. Joseph, *Democracy and Prebendal Politics in Nigeria: The Rise and Fall of the Second Republic* (Cambridge: Cambridge University Press, 1987); Crawford Young, *Ethnicity and Politics in Africa* (Boston: Boston University African Studies Center, 2002).

10. Appiah, K. Anthony, *In My Father's House: Africa and the Philosophy of Culture* (New York: Rowman and Littlefield, 1992); V.Y. Mudimbe, *The Invention of Africa: Gnosis, Philosophy, and the Order of Knowledge* (Bloomington: Indiana University Press, 1988).

11. Michael Watts, "1968 and All That…" *Progress in Human Geography* 25:2 (2001): 157–188.

12. The following account is drawn from Ibrahima Thioub, "Le mouvement etudiant de Dakar et la vie politique Senegalaise: La marche vers la crise de Mai-Juin 1968," in *Les jeunes en Afrique: La politique et la ville*, ed. Helene Almeida-Topor, Odile Goerg, Catherine Coquery-Vidrovitch, and Francoise Guitart (Paris: L'Harmattan, 1992), 267–281; and Momar Coumba Diop. "Student Unionism: Pluralism and Pressure Politics," in *Senegal: Essays in Statecraft*, ed. Momar Coumba Diop (Dakar: Codesria, 1993), 420–469. In cases of divergences between the two accounts, I indicate the source I have used.

13. Thioub, "Le mouvement etudiant."

14. Diop, "Student Unionism."

15. Andrew Ivaska, "'Anti-Mini Militants Meets Modern Misses': Urban Style, Gender, and the Politics of 'National Culture' in 1960s Dar Es Salaam, Tanzania," *Gender & History* 14:3 (2002): 584–607; "Cosmopolitanism and the Production of 'Culture': Urban Style, Gender and the State in Dar Es Salaam, 1930–2000," Ph.D. thesis, University of Michigan (2003).

16. Thomas Burgess, "Cinema, Bell Bottoms, and Miniskirts: Struggles over Youth and Citizenship in Revolutionary Zanzibar," *International Journal of African Historical Studies* 35:2–3 (2002): 287–313; "Remembering Youth: Generation in Revolutionary Zanzibar," *Africa Today* 46:2 (1999): 29–50.

17. See Dorothy L. Hodgson, *Once Intrepid Warriors: Gender, Ethnicity, and the Cultural Politics of Maasai Development* (Bloomington: Indiana University Press, 2001); Dorothy Hodgson and Sheryl McCurdy, eds., *"Wicked" Women and the Reconfiguration of Gender in Africa* (Portsmouth: James Curry, 2001).

18. For a particularly brilliant fictional attack from nearby Kenya, see Ngugi wa Thiong'o, *Devil on the Cross* (London: Heinemann, 1982).

19. Claude Meillassoux, *Maidens, Meal, and Money: Capitalism and the Domestic Community* (Cambridge: Cambridge University Press, 1981); *The Anthropology of Slavery: The Womb of Iron and Gold* (Chicago: University of Chicago Press, 1991).

20. Novels again provide one of the most explicit expressions of this field of concern. See Ayi Kwei Armah, *The Beautyful Ones Are Not Yet Born: A Novel* (Boston: Houghton Mifflin, 1968); Buchi Emecheta, *The Joys of Motherhood: A Novel* (New York: George Braziller, 1979).

21. Herbert Marcuse, *Eros and Civilization: A Philosophical Inquiry into Freud* (Boston: Beacon, 1966).

22. Bronislaw Malinowski, *Sex and Repression in Savage Society* (London: Routledge, 1927); Gananath Obeyesekere, *The Work of Culture: Symbolic Transformation in Psychoanalysis and Anthropology* (Chicago: University of Chicago Press, 1990); Melford E. Spiro, *Oedipus in the Trobriands* (Chicago: University of Chicago Press, 1982).

23. Gayle Rubin, "The Traffic of Women: Notes on the Political Economy of Sex," in *Toward an Anthropology of Women*, ed. Rayna Reiter (New York: Monthly Review Press, 1975), 157–210; Claude Levi-Strauss, *The Elementary Structures of Kinship*, trans. James Harle Bell, John Richard von Sturmer, and Rodney Needham, rev. ed. (Boston: Beacon, 1969).

24. Jean Marie Allman and Victoria B. Tashjian, *"I Will Not Eat Stone": A Women's History of Colonial Asante* (Portsmouth: Heinemann, 2000); Susan Geiger, Nakanyike Musisi, and Jean Marie Allman, eds., *Women in African Colonial Histories* (Bloomington: Indiana University Press, 2002); Steven Pierce, "Farmers and 'Prostitutes': Twentieth-Century Problems of Female Inheritance in Kano Emirate, Nigeria," *Journal of African History* 4:3 (2003): 463–486.

25. Gilles Deleuze and Felix Guattari, *Anti-Oedipus: Capitalism and Schizophrenia*, trans. Robert Hurley, Mark Seem, and Helen R. Lane (Minneapolis: University of Minnesota Press, 1983); Marcuse, *Eros and Civilization*.

26. Judith Butler, *Gender Trouble* (New York: Routledge, 1990); Eve Kosofsky Sedgwick, *Epistemology of the Closet* (Berkeley: University of California Press, 1990).

PART 2

Spirit, Awakenings,
Imaginaries, Beyond '68

Talking Back to '68: Gendered Narratives, Participatory Spaces, and Political Cultures

DEBORAH COHEN AND LESSIE JO FRAZIER

Defining the Space of the Movement

In 2001, we attended a Mexico City conference on twentieth-century student activism, featuring four prominent leaders from the 1968 movement.[1] Student movements, they claimed, were central to Mexico's push toward democracy, a centrality linked to the university as a particular kind of civic space and bringing together those who are—in their words—"informed," "intelligent," and trained to make decisions based on "reason"—all traits commonly associated with middle-class masculinity. We listened, struck by how different these men's narratives were from the stories told to us by women participating in the movement, which we would present later at the same conference.

This essay looks at the convergences and divergences between men's and women's accounts of the movement. We question the focus—inherent in leaders' public accounts as well as most movement analyses—on leaders and the state to understand a struggle that both called attention to state authoritarianism and fostered political participation in a broad sense. We ask why, given the movement's character, have accounts concentrated on its upper echelons and their interactions with the state, eclipsing the impact of base participation. Juxtaposing the accounts of male leaders and female participants breaks open those definitions. It expands our understanding of historical agency and the possibilities for political subjectivity in the movement, revealing the gendered underpinnings of political culture.

Leaders' descriptions of a proper student movement, detailed at the conference, with its masculine qualities of intelligence and reasoned sentiment, disregard the unruly feminine emotion and uncontrolled spontaneity of the masses, which leaders as political vanguard were to mold into a disciplined revolutionary force. Although university students attempted to mobilize diverse sectors of society, the movement's core was still composed of privileged youth destined to assume key positions within the social and political elite. Not surprisingly, then, public narratives of '68 have been predominantly male and elite. This elite male leader version of the movement, we argue, has become the lens through which '68 and subsequent movements have been understood and measured.[2]

Cultural critic Armando Bartra claims there "are many '68s,"[3] yet male leaders' published narratives have reduced this multiplicity to one—one that centers *their* actions, lives, and political visions. While not dismissing the horror of leaders' time in prison, we do suggest that their top-down public narratives have obscured the mass participation that made the movement so powerful and threatening to the state and catapulted its leaders into enduring prominence. In setting male leaders' published accounts against our oral histories of female participants, we challenge the singular version congealed in leaders' public narratives—an official version emerging not in the assemblies and marches of the movement's four primary months, but in the prison. Thus, their narratives mistake the dynamic of *this* space for the movement, effectively erasing the participation of hundreds of the thousands who gave the struggle its unique character and place in recent history.

The spaces of movement, as we understand them, were porous spaces within which social, cultural, and political relations and practices were reconfigured.[4] The actions women recounted primarily took place in "public" spaces—the campus, the street, and the prison—disrupting the automatic labeling of spaces as either male/public or female/private. Women's oral histories—like male leaders' published narratives—reflect their political formation in multiple spaces and the relational aspects of activism that we foreground in this essay, and highlight how political subjectivity is gendered: leadership overdetermined as male and *el pueblo* (understood in populist rhetoric as the beneficiaries of that leadership) as female. This gendered dynamic of political culture has skewed understandings of the '68 student movement precisely because it mapped onto other gendered political tensions—the relationship between leadership and participants.

To unpack this gendering of political culture, we first explore the space of the prison using former leaders' memoirs, arguing that they are the product of, and window onto, the prison and its role in shaping male leaders' positioning as the movement's official spokes*men*. Then, we analyze women's base participation as retold in oral histories we collected. In challenging the leadership-centered approach of previous analyses, we posit their participation as the experiences of a sector that, though defined as "nonvanguard," found ways of participating more in line with the movement's own political convictions. This leadership-centered perspective permeated not only women's understanding of their own participation, but the goals and successes of the movement; and it helped relegate the movement's social and cultural consequences to the realm of the personal-as-nonpolitical, stripping the movement of its complexity and implications.

While we incorporate base participants' words and understandings into our analyses, we do not claim that their movement vision as the "real" one or their experiences as comprising a "women's" perspective. Rather, we challenge a political rhetoric that determines who is and who is not a political actor, and maps the division between leader/political actor and participant/el pueblo onto the space of the movement by highlighting the leader-dominated decision-making bodies as *the* place of politics. Only by questioning a logic that defines certain individuals as political actors and certain spaces as the terrain of political action can we grasp the movement's lasting impact: the links between the changes in formal political practices vis-à-vis the central state and the social and cultural transformations undergone in its aftermath. Our objective is not to debunk men's narratives and supplement this history with women's experiences. Instead, by reading both sets of narratives in relation to one another we gain a different perspective on '68, the spaces in which it was lived, and the kinds of historical subjectivities to which it gave rise.

The Space of the Prison

The Voice of the Leaders

Male leaders' memoirs contribute to a universalist discourse about the movement, in which their experiences represent the entire range of movement participation, and assert the particularity of these men and their roles. By claiming not only the ability, but the right, to speak for el pueblo, leaders situate themselves as not of, but above, el pueblo. They have used this particularity to claim for themselves a heroic masculinity that draws on the "New Man" socialist rhetoric embodied in the figure of "Che Guevara." However, the universalist nature and heroic content of their narratives were more effects of the prison experience than of the four months of mass mobilization. Prison narratives typically cast the prison as a liminal space in which moral positions are constituted and solidified in the context of bodily deprivation. The forging of a collective identity as leaders—which casted them as individual public personalities—is a universal/particular dual positioning granted to male citizenship.

Some writings of leaders and central figures (including Sócrates Campos Lemus, Heberto Castillo, Luis González de Alba, Paco Ignacio Taibo, Gilberto Guevara Niebla, and Raúl Alvarez Garín) were produced during the time of imprisonment or shortly thereafter, while others were written for the movement's twenty- or thirty-year anniversaries.[5] Although the tenor of these narratives changes with time—from 1960s socialist revolutionary rhetoric to a late 1990s one bathed in a language of democracy— these men persistently foregrounded themselves as historical protagonists. The space of the prison overdetermines these accounts by reconfiguring leaders as spokespersons for an entire generation of political activists.

A striking example of the centrality of the prison experience is Sócrates Campos Lemus's account. He opens his account not at some movement originary point, but with a dramatic recounting of the military's march into the Plaza de Tres Culturas. The text then shifts to the actions of leaders in the months leading up to the October 2 climax and their subsequent time in prison. This text, like others, secures the leaders' place in movement history by devoting ample print space to the spaces where men presided: the CNH and the prison. Lecumberri, a panoptic structure lined with individual cells branching off in various directions. In each cell, recounts Gilberto Guevara Niebla, "were four bunk beds and a narrow walkway, which we practically never used since each of us spent [the time] in his bunk." The structure's design had an impact on prisoners' activities. Gilberto continues, we "got accustomed to dialogues from a horizontal position, a great way of having a conversation."[6] While Gilberto and others were physically confined, the prison provided the time necessary for their intellectual and spiritual growth.

While Heberto Castillo found imprisonment overwhelming, he too was able to transcend his confinement and experience intellectual liberation: "I awoke on the second day of confinement with a horrible sensation of asphyxiation. The walls, dirty, damp, putrid, were so close to me that they penetrated my brain, they seared my consciousness making me understand that physical incarceration...brings with it mental incarceration. I understood that my only world...was within myself." This suffering was granted the highest magnitude, changing the prisoners' relationship to the world and to time and space. "In prison, with the passage of time, so slowly, we become lazy, as if our inertia increases as our mass grows. And that which, outside, is left until tomorrow, here it's left for next week."[7] Yet Heberto continued, "in spite of everything, I am free; no one can submit my conscience to prison."[8] Undergirding such descriptions is a

Cartesian separation of mind and body. In the face of bodily degradations, the rational self turns inward—a mapping that leaders inherently drew upon as they linked the prison to the nation. Here the prison is conflated with, and thus condenses, the space of the movement; it is transformed into a space where these men, as political prisoners, express their embodiment of the martyred consciousness of the people from whom these men were brutally separated and who symbolize authentic (and uncontained) passion. Leaders experienced their separation from el pueblo, as the bifurcation of the movement from the nation. Heberto emphasizes this sense of separation: "the real world outside got fatally smaller and also our time. Everything contracted. We, in prison, grew old slowly, at least that's what we thought. Our loved ones grew very rapidly.... To comprehend our reality, we would have had to understand that we were growing old at the same speed as those on the outside."[9] The prison acted as a capsule of space and time set apart from the rest of the world, a utopia of young male homosociality. Leaders sacrificed themselves, through suffering and self-abnegation, in the name of higher ideals.

The Prison: "An Ambivalent Experience"

Prisoners' lives were demarcated by prison walls: damp, dark, dirty walls that penetrated their souls and "seared their consciousness."[10] Nevertheless, this pain, loneliness, and deprivation had another side. As political prisoner Gilberto Guevara explains it, the experience "had two faces."[11] Though no leader would have chosen incarceration, the intensity of that experience produced a very particular sense of community. Although being locked up caused the prisoners much pain, "it yielded an intense interchange of information and judgments; these discussions ended up being very educational. We learned a lot, we had the chance to converse with intelligent and well-informed individuals."[12] Even as bodies were deprived, minds flourished, not unlike a monastic learned society. The time spent behind the walls of Lecumberri provided leaders a physical space to do what they had so much wanted to do: devote themselves to study.

"In Lecumberri, they isolated us," Gilberto said, "they practiced all forms of extortion and violence.... Jail represented an ambivalent experience. In jail you live separated from those you love, from your family, from the spaces in which you've lived, from the University. However, we maintained vigorous connections with the outside world." These connections took various forms. "One was an intellectual connection; the opportunity and possibility of having books and visits from professors ... allowed us to continue growing academically. In this sense, studying represented a form of freedom that articulated everything that happened to us outside of jail.... I wrote my thesis and applied to take my professional exams, but the authorities...refused to let jail be declared a satellite university campus."[13] Gilberto describes the prison as an intellectually liberating space, despite the fact that the state attempted to regulate this liberating potential by refusing to establish the prison as a satellite university site.

Yet, as one of Heberto's comments shows, the liberating potential of the prison was always at risk of contamination from that outside world. "The young prisoners watch, read, and listen all day to the media about how Mexico is drowning in disgrace, that abjection is the best 'virtue' for a man trying to become a [government] functionary, that loyalty is practiced by stupid 'stupids' because they put principles before interests, that love is the motive for mocking, that fidelity doesn't exist, and that lies can be...imposed as long as one has the means to do so." Heberto emphasizes their vulnerability to this corruption: "The young fall easily into the anti-everything...anti-party, anti-TomDickandHarry, anti-love, anti-friendship. In their rejection of all traditional values, the young, inside and outside of prison, have intensified their rejection and repudiation of a system that deceives....[T]hey are against everything." Ultimately, Heberto sympathizes with what he interprets as his younger comrades' confusion, which "is explainable when they know that an imperial giant like the U.S....is spying on countries in Indochina. It is understandable that the young are against everything when they see that high officials, without sweat, say there are no political prisoners, when they hear [President] Díaz Ordaz confirm that 'university autonomy has not been damaged.'"[14]

In this depiction, the prison cell sits between, and acts as an extension of, both the university and the world ripped open by the state's occupation of the campus. The corruption of the outside world—symbolized by the violation of the university, the very space their movement had offered as a model for national reform—heightened leaders' attachment to their own perfection through intellectual transcendence of their physical surroundings. They saw themselves as the moral conscience of el pueblo so easily led astray. Yet the prison space was always at risk: some prisoners could not withstand the stories of corruption and capitalist influence; they were always on the verge of becoming the state's intellectual prey, even though others mobilized the prison's liberating potential to wrest them from the state's unrelenting grasp.

Still, the boundaries of that intellectual liberty were limited by the state, demonstrated by the state's refusal to designate the prison an official satellite campus so that student-prisoners could complete their qualifying exams. The prison became a school for many lessons, one of which was the state-as-father's domestication of these rebellious youths, a substantial number of whom would be reincorporated into the official political party apparatus and the majority of whom would go on to become respectable productive citizens and even professors of subsequent generations.

From the leaders' narratives emerges a constant tension and interplay between restriction and freedom, between deprivation and satisfaction, built upon notions of self-sacrifice for a larger goal. These men became symbolic martyrs, emblems of a movement whose supporters had been slaughtered by state forces in full view of thousands and annihilated again in the government's denials of the massacre. Further echoing Christian symbols and ethos, these leaders turned the other cheek, even as they were renounced as traitors and Communists by the government and forgotten by their following. Yet only through this suffering could their minds transcend the commonness and mortality of their bodies and experience freedom.

Violence and Masculinity

The prison dynamic encapsulated a particular relationship between suffering and thriving that was mediated by the threat of violence constantly hanging over the prisoners' heads. According to Heberto, in an attempt to break a twenty-one-day-old hunger strike, prison officials detained visiting family members.[15] The prisoners defended their heterosexual masculine honor, threatened by the real attack on their women and children. Prison officials, Heberto claims, "instigated the attack of hundreds and hundreds of common prisoners against us, offering them as a prize the booty of our belongings." The common criminals were "armed with sticks, tubes, knives, fists, even machetes, forgotten beings, victims of a society that does not punish crime but poverty." When the attackers entered the part of the prison occupied by the political prisoners, they were met not with resistance, but with "serene" words that "made them realize that we were their victims, not their enemies." "And thanks to that," Heberto states, "they took everything but our lives." Still, it was a terrifying incident: "That night was the worst of all nights: half-naked, lying on the floor on newspapers...surrounded by a multitude of prisoners armed to the teeth, not knowing what happened to many of our compañeros....An aggression like the one we suffered is hardly imaginable...we are completely defenseless against our captors. We know the imminent danger that we run but are incapable of changing it."

The above description evokes several themes. Although these men were walled off from the rest of el pueblo, their separation was partial: in this attack, they were brought face to face with lower-class common criminals, whom they won over even as the threat of violence—implicitly sexualized (naked and prone beneath lower-class men with weapons) and certainly emasculating—challenged these men's roles as historical actors.

Still, through their "serene" words and their noblese oblige in handing over their belongings and yielding to the material desires of those "who had nothing," these men reinforced both their connection to, and separation from, the masses. This meeting of common and political prisoners highlights the perceived differences between them: the political prisoners had more physical possessions than the common criminals; they had committed a crime of more noble action and higher intellect; they acted for the good of all Mexico and had become "the voice of el pueblo."

This incident illustrates the class tension between student and worker, upon which the movement was positioned. The state successfully manipulated the lower-class common prisoners, who were given physical access to the bodies of the movement leaders and egged on with the promise of the leaders' belongings as booty. This served to remind the leaders where their interests lay—not with the working classes, but with a reconfigured state. Also evident in Heberto's account is the constant risk to men's masculine honor. This so-called riot began when the government challenged the prisoners' ability and right to protect "their" women. This subsequent physical attack by lower-class men further compounded the intrinsic dangers of the intensely homosocial prison environment. Perhaps this is why men in their narratives brag about their sexual activities and sexually charged relations with women during the movement, assuring the reader of their securely heterosexual masculinity. Taken together, these narratives depict a prison life fraught with challenges to the students' gender and class identities.

In general, the idea of constant danger and possible death permeates the leaders' narratives. Even as they elevated their minds through intense study and knowledge, their physical bodies faced reprisal for this freedom. Moreover, these men's bodily sacrifice would act as a source of liberation for el pueblo. Although Heberto could have portrayed the leaders as passive victims of the state's wiles, he concluded by reasserting the agency of the political prisoners. While the government was repressing "the voice of el pueblo," he contends that "we will die fighting for the rights of the working people—workers, peasants, small farmers and business people, small industrialists, intellectuals, artists and students. We will die completing our task, understanding that when men die in this way, they are converted into seeds that liberate el pueblo, a pure liberty that will conquer all, despite everything."[16]

Clearly, the prison experience was fraught with fear and uncertainty. We should remember that most political prisoners were young and had little prior experience with physical or psychological deprivation. Interestingly, in their memoirs the men do not articulate their experience as traumatic; rather, they use stories of violence and degradation to demonstrate their heroic fortitude. In using these accounts as primary sources for understanding the '68 student movement, we were struck by the disproportionate weight that accounts of the prison occupied in the texts and the ways in which the trauma of that experience, though unnamed, overwhelm men's narratives of '68, and drown out the earlier events "on the street."

Heroic Masculine Agency

The constant tension that prisoners experienced—between freedom, restriction, and threats of violence—must be filtered through the lens of their place as movement leaders. As leaders and activists, their names were in the papers. They were being followed and they had to take security precautions. They could not go home, slept at safe houses, and could not see their families. Thus, even before their imprisonment, they had experienced a forced separation from society. In prison their separation took on a different form as the institution stripped them of their distinction as individuals. Heberto notes that in prison, "the young prisoners generally don't have outside names. They are called the political prisoners. Not Revueltas, nor De Gotari, nor Rico.... That's how they suffer the contraction of their time and space.... [T]hey don't receive encouragement.... Outside, the great mass of students and...workers don't know them by name, [but] admire them like heroes.[17] Deprived of the names marking their distinctiveness and individuality, they became transcendent symbols of the decimated movement."

Sócrates Campos Lemus's memoir includes both an edited reprint of an article by former leader Luis González de Alba and his own critique of that article. In an article that appeared in a prominent Mexico City monthly magazine, Luis claimed that movement leaders were "the image of chastity and purity," the embodiment of "young honesty," fighting "against the extreme cruelty of the government." Because they were victims and not victors, the activists were "aligned...with the purist of heroes."[18] In grammar school, Luis recounts, students "were told that heroes were the cadets at the Military Academy who defended [Mexico] against invading U.S. troops; in high school, that Hercules was a hero." But in '68, Luis continues, "a representative from the Department of Philosophy and Letters on the Strike Council established that" members of the movements were fighting "honestly against the...madness of the government." Sócrates's critique of Luis's article discards this portrayal flat out as "just ridiculous."[19] Leaders' heroism functioned as the central trope of their narratives: *They* were fighting for truth and openness; faced off against the terrible government, they rallied for a "de-masking of the state, [a] king...naked...before thousands of students."[20] Their desire was not revolution but the opening of political liberties, an end to authoritarianism, and an openness and political transparency that the government would not or could not accomplish."[21]

In the prisoners' telling, the state's betrayal of the nation stands in stark contrast to their own growing capacity to identify with others, culminating in a transcendence of their class position and an even more organic connection to the nation. "In jail I learned to love better. Now I love life more, I love my wife, my children, my friends, my pueblo more. The pueblo that I do not know, the one that works in the fields and the factory. The one that produces riches. This one should be free."[22] This is a romantic vision wherein the prisoners are capable of true sentiment despite being imprisoned by a cold and unloving state-as-father who has betrayed the nation, el pueblo. Through their ability to express this sentiment, through their loss of individual identity, jailed leaders come to stand for the universal; they embody and can speak for el pueblo.

This discourse of heroes and victims, which focuses on leaders' actions, prioritizes a certain relationship between the state and those men defined as movement leaders. It identifies the movement with the actions, ideas, and political strategies of its leaders and defines the space of interaction between themselves and the patriarchal state as its primary arena. The multiple actions of nonleader participants are thus erased, making this movement another in the long line defined through the relationship between the patriarchal state father and its male leader recalcitrant sons. Through his fidelity to the struggle, the son accrues manly honor: "Suffering in prison for [the movement's] goals," in Heberto's words, could "not but constitute a high honor."[23] In other words, these men *became* heroic men— and through this process, *leaders*—ennobled by their experience of suffering and their prison isolation from the movement as a subset of larger society, a society they largely depicted as passive and requiring guidance. This contest between father/state and son/student leader is, in fact, premised on the figuring of society, and the nation in general, as feminine, *the* terrain of patriarchal struggle.

If prison suffering and heroism are organizing tropes that establish these men's status as leaders, these virtues are unattainable to base participants, epitomized by predicament of women activists: not only did few participate at the highest level of the movement, but, more importantly, as women they embody the feminization of the movement/ nation. While men *transcended* their bodies through physical and emotional pain, extending embodied privileges to a universal citizenship that they already possessed as men, women's political agency, in contrast, could not transcend their association with their bodies. Men's agency was never seriously threatened by their subjugation, but, rather, was reconfigured and identified with antiauthoritarian and antiimperialist struggles around the globe. The movement became synonymous with a vanguard that privileged the political strategy and savvy of an inner circle over the actions of thousands. Lost were the actions of highly independent brigades, making this version of '68 closer to other movements of the period. In other words, the experience of a handful of vocal male leaders became *the* movement experience, in direct conflict to broader movement goals of openness and inclusiveness. Although student leaders claimed to be searching for a "collective truth,"[24] in the space of the prison they (inadvertently) solidified their place in the movement and in history as holders of an ultimate and official movement truth. Personal recollections were no longer individual but the experiences of everyone. As Paco Taibo so aptly puts it, "my memories were not [merely] mine."[25] The accounts of specific male student leaders *became* the movement.

Let us be clear: we do not take these narratives to be a transparent window onto the history of men's experiences as political prisoners; rather, we are concerned with the ways that the prison experience overwhelms these memoirs and obscures a broader understanding of the '68 movement. In calling attention to the disjuncture between men's memoirs and the movement's stated goals, our task is not to discredit the male leaders' version of the movement, nor to dismiss the horror of the Tlatelolco massacre or the degradation of the prison experience. Instead, we seek to understand the role of the gendered leadership in relation to base activism, accessed in part through the lens of women's participation.

Women's Agency and the Space of the Movement

Leaders' accounts discussed above, relegated base supporters to an ancillary position while solidifying their own prominence within the movement. Similarly, when we first began to investigate women's participation, we were told by leading historians that women simply had not participated in '68. When, during our first research stint, we interviewed sixty women and compiled a list of twice that many, these findings were discounted with the second standard response facing scholars of women's history—that women's participation had not *really* affected the course of the movement.

Ironically, this stance by (male) historians echoed the feelings of a majority of our interviewees: while they felt that '68 had changed profoundly the course of their own lives, they did not feel that their participation warranted historical study. Instead, we were repeatedly directed to interview La Tita and La Nacha (Roberta Avendaño and Ana Ignacia Rodríguez Márquez), the two women who sat on the CNH. Women's own perception of their participation as insignificant demonstrates how the movement was conflated with its leadership and articulated from a leadership vantage point. This dismissal of their own experiences—in collusion with the dominant perspective—calls for an exploration of the ways in which scholars, state actors, movement leaders, and participants have mutually constructed this movement and the implications of this process. Here we contrast the movement as it congealed in the homosocial world of the prison with the more diffuse and complex array of social, cultural, and political experiences compiled from our oral histories of women participants. Given the feminization of el pueblo in populist rhetoric, women's participation represents a particularly significant component of the movement's base. Examining the participants, their actions, and their view of their actions requires a reconceptualization of the movement and its relation to the people and the state.

Shifting the focus from student leaders to base participants reveals the wider gendered assumptions undergirding not only notions of leadership, but of all political action and agency at the time. Leadership positions were not open to most women. Even though the idea that women could and should play a more visible political role was gaining currency, individual women were too often not considered legitimate political actors. Seen as lacking the skills, political experience, or other qualities deemed inherent to masculinist ideals of leadership (bravery, intellect, courage), they were shut out of highly competitive political positions. This masculinizing of leadership both removes the possibility that real women can *be* political actors and exposes the gendering of nonleaders. Base participation provides a window on to the practices of the movement, practices that constituted a semiautonomous, yet porous, space on the campus and in the street and through which larger sociocultural logics and practices were reconfigured.

The movement was structured to encourage democratic practices. The CNH was composed of representatives elected from each participating school or department, and beneath this formal structure were smaller representative bodies organized by schools and/or departments. While the CNH debated top-level strategies, such as when to hold a large rally or how to react to an attempted police invasion of the universities, the responsibility for organizing and carrying out daily activities was left to the thousands of (primarily) student participants brigades according to school or department. Some brigades were comprised only of young women from all-female schools; others were mixed. As the movement grew, parents and other nonstudents creating support brigades and participating alongside the students. Each brigade was highly autonomous: brigade members decided on the daily activities they would use to take the movement to the streets. The movement's organization thus embodied a participatory mix of direct and representative political practices.

Activists came from a variety of educational institutions: universities, technical institutes, college prep schools, vocational schools, elementary schools. With such a range of institutions, class impacted movement dynamics and helped explain whose participation has been acknowledged and whose is noticeably absent. Class dynamics affected the degree and nature of student participation, which in turn influenced the tenor of the entire movement. The size and gender composition of the student population at any given school also affected participation. Not surprisingly, we found that women from all-girl schools were more likely to have actively participated in strategic and ideological meetings than those from coed schools in mixed brigades. Because the brigades fed into department-level representative bodies, these latter women generally attended coed meetings.

Prior political experience impacted the timing and manner in which participants, both men and women, became involved in the movement. Many of those who were involved from the start had been active in other political and social groups, while others had grown up in politicized families. Many had participated in the Communist Youth or in protests over U.S. policies in Vietnam. Children of European refugees, especially Jews and Spaniards from World War Two and the Spanish Civil War, were often raised in more politicized households. These early activists supplied the movement with much of its initial energy, incorporating participants without prior political experience.

Women often found themselves drawn into the movement through daughters, sons, husbands, or, quite frequently, romantic partners. During daily trips to the market, riding on city buses, or picking up children after school, housewives encountered *brigadistas* making their public pitch. Some mothers and fathers, convinced by their children of the movement's urgency and necessity, came together to form a Parent's Committee in support of their children's movement activities. And after the October massacre, mothers organized groups to provide the prisoners with food and other basic necessities. Primary and secondary schoolteachers, who counted many women in their ranks, were deeply affected by the state repression directed at their young students and at the schools in general. They, together with university professors, organized their own contingent, fueling the movement through internal and external challenges to governmental authority.

Although these interpersonal connections sparked women's initial attraction to the movement, most women committed themselves to the struggle because they believed in its ideals. As Sara Fernández recounted, "I became involved in the movement from the periphery, from a very idealistic point of view." Sara had no prior political experience and adds that her participation "was very romantic, coming out of a great affinity for the principles of the groups that had already formed." Her explanation, in ways reminiscent of leaders' narratives, constructs a gendered dichotomy between intellect/politics/reason and affect/participation/romance. This logic, which made the male leadership and its transcendent post-Tlatelolco massacre bodily suffering synonymous with reason and intellect, already excluded women as *women* from political leadership. It instead incorporated them into the populace, echoing and sustaining the same modernist dualities of spirit/matter and mind/body. Such schema labeled some forms of agency as political and others as nonpolitical, thus scripting the possible protagonists of '68.

This gendered logic, which pervades women's accounts of their participation, also influenced their roles within the movement. Many women volunteered as cooks in the collective kitchens established to feed hungry activists.[26] Mealtimes afforded these women an opportunity to listen to other *brigadistas'* tales of political adventures. Newer recruits found themselves deciding to go, as Susana Rivas told us, "into the streets and learn." As they haggled over fruits and vegetables, they would hold extemporaneous meetings or talk with the market shoppers and venders they encountered. The interchanges that occurred during these moments became a space in which women exercised political initiative. In these forays into the street, women too-often barred access to the formal political arena challenged the definition of the street and politics as (exclusively) male. They pushed beyond the protected, semidomestic space of the university to claim the street and politics—and thus full citizenship—as their own physical space and intellectual domain.

The labor, which provided activists three meals a day, allowed the movement to grow. Mealtimes energized the hundreds of students returning from their activities to food, a place to rest and recuperate, and participate in social exchanges and debates. The laborious tasks of shopping, cooking, and cleaning up, recalled as devoid of significance to the movement and seen as "women's work," were, as Elena Salazar explained to us, important roles: "If you went out in the morning on a political brigade and you returned really hungry, you arrived and ayyyy! What a surprise! The table was nicely set with soup, beans, meat, and vegetables." She underlined the connection between mealtime and forms of productive sociability: "We could talk and exchange our experiences, what we had done that day." While women such as Elena realized the importance of the meal brigades and continued to cook and shop, others felt stymied by the assumption that these were automatically their responsibilities *as women*, and instead challenged these overarching norms. Susana Rivas told us, "Yes, cooking was our role and we did it well. But we also broke with this role. We broke out of our status and called spontaneous meetings in the markets and on the street corners in different neighborhoods."

These kinds of street initiatives are key to understanding the movement's success in garnering support outside universities and secondary schools. In this so-called women's work, young women engaged a world of much broader social relations. Although most women lacked experience talking in front of people, they overcame their initial hesitation. Carmen Torres's brigade intentionally elicited support from the women in the markets. Carmen found that she and her fellow women *brigadistas*—more than the leaders or other men on the ground level—understood how to take the movement beyond the university. In foregrounding women's "greater gift" for "talking with el pueblo," Carmen underscores women's connection to el pueblo (who are, as previously discussed, gendered female). This further feminized her, and like other women activists, defined her and her labors as apolitical, even as she involved herself in highly political activities.

This contact with other women in public places like markets and buses showed women activists that the movement needed to appeal to a broader audience. Activists who were actually on the streets and talking to people translated the leaders' political framework into leaflets and other propaganda that were meaningful to those not (yet) involved, enabling the movement to spread outside the university by leaps and bounds. This propaganda functioned as more than simply a way of communicating with the public. It also fostered a sense of connection between the students and those broader populations, a connection that the students understood in terms of national identity. Women, presumably in touch with their own feelings and having a greater connection *as women* to the masses, became conduits for the exchange between leaders and el pueblo. The need to communicate the movement's political objectives in a widely intelligible medium forced these predominantly middle-class and elite young people to enter into a dialogue with other sectors of society, a dialogue that required them to become competent in other class idioms and to seek the intersections of linguistic communities that could potentially constitute a field they would describe as "Mexican." Yet, although women portrayed their ease of communication with el pueblo in a positive light, their ability to transmit movement ideals was too-often cast not as a political skill but rather a naturalized outcome of their a priori position (as women) as part of el pueblo, also gendered female.

While the majority of women participated at the brigade level and very few in the CNH, some women did become active in individual schools' assemblies, where the nature, purpose, and workings of the movement were debated daily. Many women told us of the vibrancy and enthusiasm that radiated from these various daily assemblies. Other women, however, did not feel comfortable voicing their opinions in the assemblies, citing pressure from their *compañeros* to work quietly behind the scenes. Many women felt inhibited by their lack of prior political experience, although this inhibition was somewhat offset by an increasing awareness of the novelty opportunity for participation that the movement presented. Carla

Martínez noted that for women "to participate was a novelty, because we had never participated in political things before. Our compañeros kept on treating us like inferiors, saying that we didn't know anything, that we couldn't do anything and they could do everything." However, this treatment did not dissuade some women reveling in their newfound capacities for the first time, as Carla continued: "But we began to discover our own abilities and answered: 'Yes, I *do* know and I *can* do these things.'"

Women's political inexperience was not the only challenge they faced in speaking and being heard; as several women reminded us, it was the era of the miniskirt. Male students would wolf whistle loudly at women as they walked by, stood up in class, or tried to express an idea in a meeting. Rosa Bañales was mortified when, at meeting at the male-dominated School of Dentistry, she faced a barrage of whistles and catcalls. "Men used to whistle and shout things at us when we tried to talk. It made it more difficult to talk, to say what was on our minds." Reduced to gendered bodies, these women were once again denied any claim to the mind, intellect, and reason afforded to (male) political protagonists.

The same attitudes that inhibited women from voicing their ideas and denied them full political agency worked to their advantage in other moments. As the conflict between student groups and the state intensified, women mobilized these stereotypes for the movement. Because they were not defined as political actors or seen as threatening to the state, women could infiltrate spaces cordoned off to their recognizably political male counterparts. In full view of the police, they would easily slip in and out of occupied universities and were often assigned to deliver messages or transport activist leaders. Elite young women also mobilized the privileges of class, deploying their family cars or extra apartments to hold meetings or hide people. These upper-class women thus used their social contacts and posture as properly socialized, nonthreatening, young women.

The fateful October 2 rally marked the moment of violent rupture in this narrative of increasing alliance and mobilization. Most leaders were captured and incarcerated after the Tlatelolco massacre, and it appeared as if the government had successfully destroyed the movement. It had instead been pushed underground into a new phase. For many women, these changes did not end their participation, but rather rechanneled their energy into other activities. For three years following the massacre, many continued to honor the aims of the movement by providing logistical support (especially food) for the political prisoners. Raquel Valdez helped organize support networks for prisoners. "Often my friends and I visited the political prisoners," she told us. "The entire leadership of the movement was there. There I established contact with all of the leaders from '68 who were detained and also prisoners from other movements, such as that of the railroad workers, the doctors, as well as the Communist Party. I made a lot of ties…and I…learned a lot."

While Raquel's contact with the prison gave her a new perspective on the movement and politics in general, it also eroded any nascent sense of the importance of her own participation nurtured by the system of individual brigades. Heightened instead was her awareness of the male leaders' centrality to the movement. She learned to frame her role as almost frivolous and carefree: "Those of us outside the leadership lived the movement from the most romantic aspect: activism. We did…what we wanted to do. We assisted the movement without much responsibility beyond taking care of ourselves or own small group. But it was different for [the leaders]." While she and other women were "assisting" with their "romantic activism," ostensibly the leadership was engaged in the real work of the movement. Raquel continued: "I started to know those who had planned all the activities. I also learned about the strategy of the movement through discussions in which they talked about the movement's errors or such-and-such theory, measures that they had adopted. I learned a lot and began to see the movement from their point of view." Raquel not only absorbed a framing of the movement that foregrounded the leaders as the only significant protagonists, she learned to view the movement from leaders' prison-based perspective. This shift away from a movement crafted on the campuses and streets to one congealed in the experience of the prison permeated women's interpretations of their own experiences and what/where the movement really was. That even intensely involved participants reframed the movement from the space of the prison enabled leaders to constitute themselves as leaders, both at the time and in later reflection.

During the prison phase of the movement, women's roles changed, yet they also maintained a certain continuity. Women moved in and out of Lecumberri, visiting political prisoners and organizing collectives to feed them. They provided men with company, physical and otherwise, and helped men maintain their ties to the outside world. In our interview, Gilberto Guevara Niebla recalled the importance of women's solidarity: "There were always compañeras, friends, always with us in prison. And this was wonderful." When later asked to elaborate on the role of prison visitors, he explained: "My [academic] department in particular was very well organized in supporting the prisoners. I can assure you, during those months that we were in prison—think about it—every day, every day, the students sent me provisions, because the provisions that the prison gave us were horrible." He said he received a basket every day for two years. "Do you realize the effort that this entails?…I always felt supported by my student compañeros," he concluded.

Gilberto's narrative is indicative of how men understood women's roles. When asked at the beginning of the interview about women's participation, he acknowledged the value of their solidarity and the constant presence of friends and *compañeras*. Yet later, as he elaborated on the kind of support that jailed leaders received, he labeled duties of feeding the prisoners as work while taking the credit away from women in particular (note the gender shift from *compañeras* to *compañeros*). This labor, so vital to prisoners' survival that it becomes synonymous with all student activism after the massacre, is degendered, even as men continue to link women to their overwhelmingly traditional roles, at the same time they strip this work of its alignment with the particular gendered bodies carrying it out.

Reading Gilberto's statements about the important of women's solidarity against Raquel's description of listening to and learning from the male prisoners points to the relational constitution of leaders and participants. Even before they wrote their memoirs, leaders were able to formulate their particularly leader-centered rendition in front of an attentive audience of jailhouse visitors. Men's ability to position themselves as leaders and spokespeople of the movement required that women's activism be seen as passive, a move that ultimately erased their agency and rendered their labors invisible.

Women's labor, recognized or not, provided the material and emotional support required to construct a homosocial utopic community of suffering in pursuit of knowledge and political/moral integrity. Women not only supplied political prisoners with their daily rations but also donated their professional services as doctors, psychiatrists, lawyers, teachers, and journalists. They publicized the government's brutalit treatment of jailed leaders, galvanizing support for the cause. One aspect of their activism, however, remained the same: they retained a mobility—between home, outside world, and now the prison—not enjoyed by men either during the movement or in jail. During the movement they exploited their "apolitical" standing to pass unnoticed through police barricades and into cordoned-off areas; following the massacre they moved in and out of the prison to feed the needs and desires of the prisoners and relieve a patriarchal state of its responsibilities.

Yet moving in and out of Lecumberri prison was no benign matter for women, for they were often harassed, sexually intimidated, and groped. Thus, women were disciplined for venturing into the realm of the political, experiencing part of the horror of the prison. Aggression against women's bodily integrity served as a way to further discipline male prisoners. While men's own bodily suffering endowed them with spiritual and intellectual transcendence, this aggression bore different fruit for women. The disciplining of women's bodies underscored and solidified their role as objects in male political contests. This juxtaposition of leaders' and women's prison experiences of bodily assault challenges another aspect of the men's accounts of their time in prison: it breaks open the notion of the prison as a strictly homosocial and radically contained space. By looking at the ways women permeated the boundaries of the prison, our reading shows a prison space connected to and shaped by a civic sphere now horribly deformed by state violence.

Both on the street and in the prison, women's ability to cross through barriers impenetrable to men gave them a fundamental role in the movement as mediators and translators between sectors. Yet women's ability to interface between "el pueblo" and "the movement" did not result in recognition—by male leaders and many of the women themselves—of women's political agency. Men's wolf whistles and reminders of women's political inexperience denied women the ability and the right to be heard, stripped them of credit for ideas, and barred them from an active, visible presence in movement decisions. In denying women a voice and defining their participation in terms of silent bodies, women became the embodiment of home and nation. Women's claims to citizenship had to be championed by male leaders. Thus, when women insist on their active role in generating pamphlets and creating speeches in off-campus public spaces, they are claiming citizenship for themselves. Although they acknowledge that their voices were stifled in the struggle's most sacred places—the CNH and various student assemblies—they nevertheless describe practices of articulation that make their participation discernable.

When students occupied the universities, campus spaces were transformed into their political and physical home. In the classrooms, libraries, and cafeterias where men and women had studied economics, philosophy, and mathematics, they now ate, slept, crafted propaganda, and held meetings. The transformation of former classrooms into semidomestic spaces required new logistical arrangements; women's labor underpinned these reconfigurations. Both men and women took turns guarding school buildings against the police; they maintained the sanctity of the movement's home and fragile borders. In so doing, they drew on a pervasive twentieth-century war rhetoric of protecting hearth and home. In this sense, women's presence in the occupied university was not anomalous, but rather necessary in order to regender this space an embattled home front.

Although many universities and secondary schools across the country participated, UNAM came to symbolize the entire movement. This, the country's premier public university, acted as a synecdoche for the nation—a material and imaginary construct that feminist scholars argue is gendered female. Yet while women's presence was critical to the gendering of the occupied campus, women did not see their agency as limited to the campus. In traveling between the campus and other feminine spaces (i.e., the market and elementary schools), in occupying masculine spaces of the street, and in speaking out in these places, women asserted broader possibilities for their own agency and claims to citizenship. Occupying and protecting the campus meant claiming their place as citizens with the power to remake the nation; at stake was nothing less than the possibility of a truly antiauthoritarian Mexico, one in which all members could claim an active citizenship.

Transformations through the Space of the Movement

We now return to one of our original questions: What insight do we gain through examining women's participation, beyond understanding how a previously marginalized group of actors contributed to this massive struggle? We contend that understanding women's participation provides a unique and critical window onto aspects of the movement not previously recognized and forces us to rethink the entire movement and its impact on the deep structures of social, cultural, and political relations, especially for Mexico's middle classes and elites. Women's challenges to the limits on their participation affected broader cultural, social, and political relationships. The movement thus served as a temporally and spatially delimited sphere in which habituated dispositions were reconfigured. It also enabled the reshaping of adolescent rites of passage: especially those pertaining to sexuality, gender roles, and affective ties to home and family. The movement, then, worked as a kind of a liminal space that imprinted participants' social and familial relations.

Intensive involvement in a social movement challenges the rubric of the every day and sets up the possibility of unintended consequences. Spending long hours together generating ideas, debating strategy, and propaganda, and facing physical danger can breed different sorts of relations between men and women, especially where men have historically enjoyed greater political citizenship and agency. The '68 student movement was no exception. While the movement overtly targeted the state, it no less fundamentally challenged social values. This reconfiguration of personal relationships was a common theme in the oral histories we gathered.

Intense interpersonal contact in the context of a volatile political situation helped break down women's existing beliefs about gender. These ruptures went beyond female-male relationships to include a whole spectrum of sexual self-perception and practices—heterosexual, homosexual, and bisexual. Women linked their awakening sexuality to their political awakening. For some women, the implications of adolescent sexual interactions challenged their prior conception of what it meant to be male or female. "We started to question institutions," Angélica continued. "We started to question our own sexual roles." The movement, she felt, "created a great camaraderie between the guys and us. It doesn't mean that they stopped being 'machos' but, rather, that circumstances dictated that we consolidate ourselves into a single force." While Angélica only implicitly linked women's sexual interactions to the possibility of political alliance, in decoupling sex from a future marital project she opened up the possibility of a different sort of intimacy and partnership, one directed—as were their immediate energies—toward the urgent political struggle.

Men and women could now be friends, and not just romantic/sexual partners. Rosa Zamudio recalled how, as the sole female in her brigade, she experienced a new sense of camaraderie with her male companions, a kind of relationship that had been previously denied: "In the movement, my best friends were men.…I had a boyfriend, an architect. He didn't want me to participate. He didn't understand. We broke up because of the movement." Rosa discovered that not only were her interpersonal relationships within the movement taking on different dimensions; they were incompatible with and separate from her outside relationships. She found herself caught between the conventional expectations of her boyfriend and a unique kind of intimacy offered by her fellow activists.

Elena Castillo chose to cultivate her relationships within the movement, despite family opposition. "Women could never go out at night. Every night before the movement started, I was home and couldn't even think of going out after 8:00 P.M." This participation provoked a rebellion against certain familial constraints: "But if you were a member of a brigade, even if you had to be home by 8:00 P.M., you couldn't tell your compañeros, 'Well, I'm going. I have to be home or my mom will kill me.' Instead you said, 'Will you guys take me home?' 'Yeah, we will, but stay a while longer and then we will drop you off.' And our compañeros started treating us more like real partners.…Our lives were transformed."

And, "like real partners," women felt the responsibility of the relatively more equal relationships that were emerging. "Women had a very important role because we participated just like men," Rosa observed. "We shared the risks, because the fact of getting on a bus to distribute propaganda or talk to people meant running the risk that you would be arrested or chased. And both men and women shared that risk equally. The guys had to change…they did change their attitude towards us. Before, they were conquerors. After, they talked about relationships based on friendship, companionship, and solidarity."

While women never completely lost their sense of disadvantage within the movement, their ongoing participation did lessen their sense of inexperience and incompetence. We must, as Luisa Salazar tells us, think critically about this language of equality and that women participated "just like men." Their lives "changed from a situation of feeling inferior to one closer to that of men. The '68 movement was an opportunity for women not to reach the level of men, because that was very difficult, but rather to make a great step towards equality." This statement suggests the profound impact that the movement made on women who participated: as feelings of inferiority and inadequacy dissipated, they saw that they, like their male activists, could play a crucial role in society.

However, the previous statements also hint at the constraints on the movement's transformative potential. Although some women began to see themselves as participating "just like men," others recognized that they still had only partial access to public spaces such as the street. When Elena asked the men in her brigade to take her home instead of heading home by herself, she acknowledged not only threats to her physical safety but women's differential access and freedom of movement. These impending threats worked to discipline women socially and politically, thus fortifying the structures of patriarchal control. Even though Elena struggled against these limits to her participation, she recognized and acceded to the discipline that these constraints entailed. Moreover, by using men's level of participation (as in Rosa's claim that women "participated just like men") as the standard, women reinforce the privilege of men to define normative political agency. Still, for these women, '68—replete with tensions and possibilities—created new possibilities for social relations and, concommitantly, for their own political participation.

These developing interpersonal relationships were predicated on a defiance of patriarchal control in the family home. Women's participation was greatly influenced by their families' reactions. Many families felt threatened by their daughters' activities and feared a challenge to structures of family discipline. When women began outwardly chafing at these constraints, parents—especially fathers—often imposed even stricter measures of control. At the very least, they worried incessantly for their daughters' physical safety. Often, as Gloria Jaramillo relates, this situation of worry and control incited conflict within the family: "[The movement] was a situation in which you lived together with all of your friends. Although the school was women-only, during the movement you were actually living with your compañeras and compañeros who went to other schools." Such behavior "was really scandalous for our parents: first, because their daughter was getting involved in a social movement...where she didn't belong; second, because she might easily rupture the authority of the family." Although Gloria addresses the familial struggle over gender-appropriate behavior, she stops short of examining the ways in which male leaders and participants were asserting themselves as protopatriarchs.

Although some families increased their patriarchal control, others supported their daughters' political awakening and encouraged them to participate in '68. Juanita Alvarez's relationship with her aunt, for example, epitomizes this supportive attitude and its ramifications. Sra. Paredes allowed her niece to use one room in her house for group meetings and for storing printing materials. Moreover, while Sra. Paredes had initially only offered the use of her house, she soon became directly involved in the movement herself.

Thus, daughters and nieces tried to integrate their families into the struggle or, as Natalia Esquivel claimed, young women often "took the movement home," by bringing propaganda home for their parents to read—and hopefully understand it and support them—perhaps even participate themselves. "[Whenever] we had a meeting, a march, we always invited our parents, our friends, friends of our parents." Many parents, including mothers, did become directly involved through their children. These women's ability to "take it home," to link together various places—home, street, university—constituted not only the space of the movement, but, in turn, a terrain of social and cultural change.

Families often treated their politically active sons differently from their involved daughters, allowing sons to participate in certain activities but not daughters. Although women defied these arrangements, they did not yet realize the import of this rebellion against patriarchal authority. Women, for the most part, did not exhibit a conscious awareness of the structural restrictions they faced as women. Neither did young women students reach out to older women outside the university world—for example, in the markets or at elementary schools—on the basis of an explicit vision of common gender interests or even gendered possibilities for communication. Alicia Romero explains that when they went to the schools and the markets, "we didn't have a feminist conception. We didn't go to talk to the women for that reason. Rather, it just made good sense, and there we were well received." Here again we see the naturalization of women's communicative abilities within the gendered political logic—that women are inherently of el pueblo.

Although women did not see themselves as feminists per se, their political participation still challenged authoritarian structures on many levels. Rafaela Morales suggested, "For those of us from secondary schools, we struggled against authority. This contrasted to the focus at the university, where there wasn't this restrictive atmosphere. For us, everything was very limited. In the university they fought more against the authoritarianism of society, of the government." Rafaela continued, "But we from the secondary schools, we saw the fight against authoritarianism that we faced every day—what we faced in the secondary schools. We threw out our uniforms, our sweaters. We shortened our skirts because it was the era of the miniskirt....We fought against the authoritarianism we faced closest to home." In juxtaposing these two particular battlefields in the struggle against authoritarianism, Rafaela connects the battle against the state with the one that waged against school principals and community patriarchs.

For many privileged young women, this experience clarified tensions visible in the wider society. As critic Hugo Hiriart argues, "the merit of

'68 is to have clarified the common political origin of…many authoritarian attitudes."[27] The movement, and the discussions that sprang up around it, oriented these young people politically and gave young women from wealthier and less politically active families a specific political grounding. Such was the case for Monica Larraín. "Before, we didn't have a political formation," she told us. "We started to read, more than anything else, the works of our 'Che' Guevara…. With this explanation, we could relate Che's theory to what we had been living and seeing around us," contradictions that the state had always sought to conceal. This opened up unique possibilities for political transformation. "We felt," said Monica, "that the strategy we had adopted was the only way that we could modify the system in our country and change the conditions of el pueblo. Being convinced of this gave us our passion."

Many women participants saw theirs as a fight for basic human freedoms and against authoritarianism—the same goals as their male counterparts. Said Kati Archuleta, "We fought shoulder to shoulder with the men, and we couldn't see any differences in which ones were our roles and our fights, and which were those of our compañeros. We knew that democracy was for everyone, that the changes were for everyone, and that something [gender] specific didn't exist. We weren't worried about knowing that our lives were different because we were women. That's where the difference lies. In this period, we were androgynous. We were very valiant fighters, equal to any man. We didn't see any differences in what we needed as women or what men needed."

Women, who fought "shoulder to shoulder" with men during the movement, held a vision of themselves as citizens and not merely women political actors. From this conviction comes Kati's basic claim that citizenship could be "androgynous" and nongendered. She did not recognize women's social limitations as citizens. Those insights, for many, would come later.

These last several quotes exhibit a tension between women's highly gendered political experiences and their desire to remove gender from the citizenship equation—the push toward androgyny that Kati alluded to. Given the overdetermination of gendered political subjectivities in 1968, there was no possibility of imagining a specifically "female" citizenship carrying all the rights and privileges of the current ostensibly nongendered citizenship. Hence, the claim of the universal as androgynous provided the only possibility.

In short, women did not see their participation as having explicitly political implications. While they were forced to question gender norms in their personal lives, they did not reconnect this realization to the larger political context of protest: the personal had not yet become political. Nevertheless, women's self-critiques enable us to see how a sense of gendered political agency emerges from sociocultural transformations within women's personal lives. Similarly, the ostensibly political narratives of male leaders were constructed within culturally determined notions of (personal) masculinity. This connection between cultural struggles over gender in women's personal lives and the then-unarticulated struggle over gender in the formal political arena make women's ongoing acceptance of a leader-centered framing of the movement all the more poignant. We must keep on insisting that the personal is political and, moreover, that the political is personal; we must relate questions of political subjectivity to questions of social movements and projects for transformation.

Conclusion: "To Study, Struggle, and Work"

How do we reconcile visions of the movement differing markedly in their description of the struggle yet exhibiting a similar framing of political subjectivity? At the initial conference panel of former '68 leaders discussed at the beginning, the audience was educated about the university as the perfect generative site for social movements and instructed in the life of a proper student. Emblazoned on a wall at the University of Colima, presenter Raúl Moreno explained, is the slogan "to study, struggle, and work," exemplifying the fundamental priorities for a student. Attending college and becoming educated, argued panelist Marcelino Perelló, are not merely individual activities with individual benefits, but instead entail a responsibility to the collective. This vision repudiates the individualism that panel members felt permeates today's students and youth, instead of positing a more collectivist societal vision. Yet this prioritization reflects the specific class and gender perspective upon which leaders grounded and maintained *their* own privileged position.

The ability to dedicate oneself to "study, struggle, and work" requires hidden and unrecognized labor. Just as the jailed '68 activists depended on the largely overlooked labor of visitors for their physical and emotional sustenance, students' idealistic pursuits are subsidized by the necessary but invisible labor of others. If students dedicate their time to studying, struggling, and working, who will feed hungry students returning from class, from night-long strategy sessions, or from daily protests, the very labor upon which the life of the mind is built? In terms of both production and reproduction, these labors are obviously *not* students' responsibility: visible productive labor is usually the responsibility of male heads of household (with children *not* of the middle and upper classes forced to contribute) and reproductive labor generally falls to women, both young and old(er). Thus, a male student's ability to "study, struggle, and work" requires the specific reproductive contribution of women, a contribution made invaluable—and easily forgettable—by its lack of visibility. Constraints of class and gender place these noble activities beyond the reach of the majority of el pueblo. These values, then, best reflect those generated and shared by male leaders in the collective space of the prison, the homosocial intellectual utopia captured in their narratives, in which bodily suffering created a context for transcendent intellectual growth and community.

Women's stories counter the common notion that women "just" cooked or that they did not really participate at all. Their stories instead reveal how deeply involved women actually were and lead us to an understanding of '68 as a broad-based social movement that not only questioned authoritarianism in the formal political arena but also in the domestic sphere. This movement fostered a multiplicity of political practices: semiautonomous brigades, the parliamentary CNH, and the many auxiliary organizations involving parents, faculty, and others. Women's accounts of interactions in homes, markets, and streets point to the attempts to forge connections between this predominantly middle-class movement and the rest of society (in contrast to other student movements, prior and subsequent). More than any political moment since the 1910 revolution, the '68 student movement sought to bring together divergent sectors of society, and this experience forced many women to radically rethink their understanding of who constituted the nation, an insight they would bring to future struggles over labor issues, indigenous rights, the plight of the urban poor, and women's rights.

Any assessment of the impact of '68 must consider social, cultural, and political practices as integral to historical transformations. The story of '68 must be situated in the context of dramatic changes in practices of sexuality and the body, an emerging connection between critiques of domestic and state-level patriarchies, and a broadened sense of the nation in terms of class and ethnicity. Public narratives of '68—by focusing not on the daily activities of the hundreds of thousands of participants in the streets, campuses, and markets, but rather on increasingly volatile negotiations between male leaders and state officials and then the space of the prison— have feminized the movement's base participants (both men and women) and defined them out of the terrain of struggle. Our approach here has been dialectical: taking apart both sets of narratives and recontextualizing them in relation to one another. From male leaders we learn less about the broader political practices and participants in the movement and more about the prison as a key space for the formation of their political subjectivities. From the women, who situate their participation within a broader sociocultural context (despite their general acceptance of the "we-were-not-historical-actors" framing), we get a richer sense of the space of the movement and its transformative potential. Rereading male leaders' narratives against women's accounts, in turn, opens up the possibility of an understanding of men's political lives as specifically gendered.

Arguably, the movement did not have much immediate impact on the formal structure of political life. As critic Michel de Certeau observed about the '68 French student movement, the very connection of university students to dominant political structures offered them a privileged point of critique but ultimately inhibited their ability to craft an original political voice. In '68 Mexico, women's acceptance of a masculine framing of political subjectivity constrained their ability to make the political connections implicit in their narratives. Still, student movements that took place in various countries in 1968 have had enormous purchase on the lives of that generation and on activists in subsequent movements. Taking apart and juxtaposing the accounts by male leaders and women participants within the relevant sociocultural context provides a key to these legacies.

Notes

For more complete references and extended examples, please see our "Defining the Space of Mexico 1968 *Hispanic American Historical Review* (November 2003): 617–660.

1. Seminario Nacional Movimientos Estudiantiles Mexicanos en el Siglo XX, IIB-DGAPA, UNAM, Mexico City, 2001.
2. For an earlier treatment of women's participation, see our "'No sólo cocinábamos…': Historia inédita de la otra mitad de '68," in *La transición interrumpida: México, 1968–1988*, ed. Ilán Semo (Mexico City: Universidad Iberoamericana/Nueva Imagen, 1993), 75–109. See also Eric Zolov's *Refried Elvis: The Rise of the Mexican Counterculture* (Berkeley: University of California Press, 1999) and "Protest and Counterculture in the 1968 Student Movement in Mexico," in *Student Protest: The Sixties and After*, ed. Gerard De Groot (London: Longman, 1998), 70–84; Elaine Carey's, *Plaza of Sacrifices: Gender, Power, and Terror in 1968 Mexico* (Albuquerque: University of New Mexico Press, 2005); and Michael Soldatenko "Mexico '68, Power to the Imagination!" *Latin American Perspectives* 32:4 (2005): 111–132.
3. Armando Bartra, *1968: El mayo de la revolución* (Mexico City: Editorial Itaca, 1999), 139.
4. Pierre Bourdieu, *Outline of a Theory of Practice* (Cambridge: Cambridge University Press, 1999 [1977]).
5. Of these we interviewed (1989) Luis González de Alba, Gilberto Guevara Niebla, and Raúl Alvarez Garín, though for our purposes here we are concerned most directly with their published narratives.
6. Gilberto Guevara Niebla, "Una temporada en Lecumberri," in Bellinghausen, *Pensar el '68*, 136–137.
7. Heberto Castillo, *Si te agarran te van a matar* (Mexico City: Ediciones Proceso, 1998 [1983]), 118, 123.
8. Ibid., 22.
9. Ibid., 118, 123.
10. Ibid.
11. Gievara Niebla "Una temporada en Lecumberri," 135–137.
12. Ibid., 136–137.
13. Ibid., 136.
14. Castillo, *Si te agarran*, 120–121.
15. Ibid., 95–99.
16. Ibid.

17. Ibid., 120.
18. *Nexos,* 189; quoted in Campos Lemus and Sánchez, *'68,* 148, 145.
19. Ibid., 146.
20. Taibo, *68,* 48.
21. Bartra, *1968,* 142.
22. Castillo, *Se te agarran,* 122.
23. Ibid., 42.
24. Ibid., 20.
25. Taibo, *68,* 15.
26. Cohen and Frazier, " 'No sólo cocinabamos,' " 82.
27. Hugo Hiriart, "La revuelta antiautoritaria," in Bellinghausen, *Pensar el '68,* 17–21, 19.

CHAPTER SEVEN

Acts of Affection: Cinema, Citizenship, and Race in the Work of Sara Gómez

SUSAN LORD

The phenomenon of struggle for the vindication of women's rights in Cuba was indisputably linked to the struggle for rights of other social groups; alternative groups, minorities and the socially disadvantaged. These alternative groups continued to be an essential question in the analysis within the system of models of presentation and representation of visual culture. This fact can take place with more or less conscience or feeling of belonging to a determined social group, and with more or less sympathy and compromise with respect to the different political struggles, or the representation that these groups channel.[1]

Dannys Montes de Oca Moreda and
Dayamick Cisneros "Labores Domesticas."

I begin my contribution to this anthology with the above quote because it takes us beyond the affirmative identitarian history of feminism, urging us instead toward the mobile sense of feminism as critical affiliation, signaling how complex and risky "feminist cultural citizenship" may be. The new forms of belonging and engagement available to women in the 1960s in many parts of the world were quickly threatened by national and patriarchal traditions that formed both their context and their subjective terrain. The symbolic burden Cuba bore for most of the freedom-seeking world in the 1960s was amplified in the sphere of race and gender, making

certain images both vibrate with hope and collapse from symbolic satura-
tion. Sara Gómez came to represent this combination of forces: a young,
free, black, beautiful, talented, revolutionary in a miniskirt, with an afro,
holding a camera. This essay is an attempt to understand the difference this
image and the images she made offer us today.

The late-Afro-Cuban filmmaker Sara Gómez is recognized by scholars, filmmakers, and cineastes as having made profound and lasting contributions to Cuban cinema, women's cinema, and postcolonial cinema:
she remains the only woman to have made a feature film in Cuba; she is
one of a very few Afro-Cubans to have made films in the *Instituto Cubano
del Arte e Industria Cinematográphicas* (or ICAIC); her work has inspired a
new generation of Cuban media artists; and her feature film presented
North American and British feminist film critics and theorists with one
of the first "non-Western" films by a woman, thus marking the canon's
shift away from complete eurocentrism. As is well known, Gómez died
of asthma in 1974 before she could complete the editing of *De cierta manera* (*One Way or Another*), the only feature-length film she made after ten
prolific years as a director of short documentaries. The feature was completed by Gómez's colleagues at ICAIC in 1977 and went on to receive
tremendous critical and scholarly attention—and it continues to focus
attention and debate about Cuban culture and society.[2] It is a remarkable film for its portrayal of complex social, racial, and sexual relationships, and for its inventive strategies for giving such relations a mode
of representation adequate to their complexities. The film has, in fact,
become foundational to new Cuban cinema and to feminist film culture.
All of this well-deserved attention given to the feature film has, strangely,
done nothing to encourage distribution and analysis of her earlier short
films inside or outside of Cuba: thirteen documentaries of between eight
and forty minutes in length, addressing a range of themes from Afro-
Cuban musical traditions to autobiography. The exception to the dearth
of distribution in Canada was the festival of new Cuban Film and Video
curated by David McIntosh and Ricardo Acosta for the Euclid Theatre
in Toronto in 1992.

Over the past few years I have been studying Sara Gómez's films in relation to several different contexts and themes: the social and cultural construction of temporality, and the politics of time; as an aesthetic expression
of and engagement with transculturation; and in relation to similar the-
matic and formal strategies in work by women in postcolonial and decolonizing contexts. With these themes, Gómez's work can be seen as initiating
aesthetic reflection on the gendered transcultural conditions that see the
power and authority of tradition and the self-certainty and promises of
modernity in tension and in doubt. This encounter renders an especially
complicated yet productive space for the appearance of women as agents of

social change and cultural expression. For, as traditional culturally specific gender roles and temporal realities are threatened by the standard time of modernization and commodification, the gains and losses brought by the encounter between tradition and modernity become tangible and available to critique and reflection. The appearance of this "new woman" as an agent rather than symbol depends upon collectivities and new formations of social relations. This describes precisely the project expressed by Gómez and the Revolutionary context in which she worked.

Gómez's films are consistently about experiences of belonging and marginalization "today" such as these are a result of long and deep cultural histories that inform each other across the colonial divide. Unlike her colleagues at ICAIC, she did not make films about the "past" of racial identity. Particularly attentive to the status of women and the role of machismo, and Afro-Cuban culture and enduring racism, the films also address how marginalization is a cultural problem for the revolution's political aim to unify a people, a popular culture, and a nation. Thus, rather than repeat the binary formation of margin versus center, the films adjust the frame so as to take up the radical claims for a new society based in cultural difference and expressed through popular democracy. Most of the documentaries present a view of participation as that which is practiced fundamentally as critical engagement. I have written about *Mi Aporte/My Contribution* as one of the best examples of the extent to which Gómez's filmmaking and the social subjects of those films together embody feminist, radical, participatory democracy (thus participating in the larger project in modernity of the democratization of culture).[3]

For the occasion of this publication, I wish to consider the work in relation to three somewhat different but intersecting fields of emerging research and historical understanding: citizenship, cities, and cosmopolitanism; Youth Culture and the 1960s; and Black Power and the African axis of decolonization. The themes intersect through the paper, rather than being sequentially presented. The paper pivots on a film Gómez made in '68: *En la otra isla*, a film about the dream of belonging and about affective solidarity on the Isla de la Juventud (then called Isla de pinos). This site and its experiment of being Cuba's currency-free communist zone in the mid-1960s, a world ruled by young people, where women were central organizers, embodies many of the dreams and failures of the larger Island's experiments that come in the post-'68 grey years.[4]

The contexts that shaped ideologies of gender, race, and ethnicity in Cuba, before and after the revolution in 1959, are pressing historical realities for Gómez as a social subject, as a filmmaker, and as a revolutionary. Her connection to international women's movements and intellectual projects deserves particular attention. She worked with French filmmaker Agnés Varda in 1963 when Varda came to Cuba; and she was interviewed

by the late French writer and filmmaker Marguerite Duras; she worked
inside ICAIC during a period of its most intense cosmopolitanism; she was
a member of group that studied ethnography and black history; she read
Franz Fanon (a quote from *Wretched of the Earth* forms the epigraph of Una
isla para Miguel); was in the stream of Black Power; and walked Havana
with Jamaican novelist Andrew Salkey and Trinidadian poet John La Rose
upon their arrival for the 1968 World Cultural Congress of Havana. Of
her, Salkey writes in his fascinating *Havana Journal*:

> Sarita, in her very early twenties, has eight important documenta-
> ries to her and ICAIC's credit.... She gave the impression of going
> dynamically ahead of her field, and yet both John and I wondered
> if she wasn't just a little too imaginatively vital and aspiring for the
> confines of the cultural blockade and its aftermath in Havana which I
> had, so far, very narrowly peeked at since my arrival. In her conver-
> sation we both spotted a mind about to "crash," if their wider con-
> cerns weren't allowed maximum room for exploration, comparative
> criticism and development.... The artist is *not* dictated to in any way,
> Marcos and Sarita mentioned from time to time. The artist works in
> a culturally "permissive" Havana; this is the tone of the declaration
> drawn from Sarita's statements....[5]

Six years after this encounter, at the age of thirty-one, Sarita died, leaving
behind two children, two husbands, loving friends and comrades, thirteen
documentaries, a feature film, and an image of utopia.

In his article, "Ruin and the Other: Towards a Language of Memory,"
Teshome Gabriel writes a text very close to the way Walter Benjamin
thinks about history. Gabriel writes about cultural memory, cross-cultural experience and diaspora, about what happens when we encounter a
text, story, image, and so on that no longer has present tense in everyday
life. He says that the ruin is as much in our heads, that the thing—the
object—conjures memory, which is always a ruin: scattered, buried, invisible. Rather than restoration, to understand the ruin as ruin, as a recognition of what's been lost, is primary to the utopian imaginary. Gabriel's
description of cultural memory holds a double meaning when considering
certain documentary practices from a historical moment that was itself
so intensively imagined through documentary: Cuba in the first decade
of the revolution.[6] We can also advance Fernando Ortiz's theory of transculturation as a means by which to understand how cultural difference
fractures the time of modernity. By elaborating her life and work through
these considerations of a utopian imaginary for history within an international lens, we may come to a deeper understanding of Gómez as a social
subject of both Cuba and the world.

Theoretical Background

The particularity of ethnicity, race, and gender identity is, as has often been discussed, inconsistent with the synthesizing and equalizing task of the revolution. Gómez's work consistently refocuses the unfinished work of the popular struggle for social change. In doing so, however, she also represents Afro-Cuban traditions as a historical and material culture that is embodied in everyday life. Cultural memory is thus represented in the present tense, subject to social, political, and subjective revisions. The reframing of Afro-Cuban culture does not function within the tradition of salvage ethnography; rather, it is presented as a problematic but rich and complex living culture, long subject to historical time, and brought into dialogue with revolutionary aims.

In documentary cinema and in the history of ethnography there are various ways to overcome the "orientalism" of the traditional anthropological gaze. The *cine rescate* (the Latin American version of the ethnographer's salvage documentary) is precisely not about entombment or preservation against the time; the intention of this mode is "to bring history alive" (Chanan) and to fold this history into the now-time of the nation—with the nation being a revolutionary project. *Cine rescate* differs substantially from the "necrology" of salvage ethnography that performs rescue missions on "dying cultures"; following Jacqueline Loss's use of Amy Fass Emery's "fables of intimacy"[7] to discuss the testimonio, we can say that Sarita at times produces "fables of intimacy" that authorize her to speak of the Other not as detached social scientists, but as Selves intimately involved with the Others she represents. But at other times she is inside the process known as "native ethnography," and is informed by feminist practice of "consciousness raising"—where the social subjects and the ethnographer are the same. This mobile form of engagement, of the dynamic relation between self and other, provides her with an ethical mode, which is unavailable to the "fabulists" or the anthropologists. The degree of self-reflexivity we find in her films is consistent with this radical "autoethnographic" practice. The moments of interactive/reflexive subjectivity, such as the young boy mugging at the camera at the beginning of *Una isla para Miguel* or in the playful exposure of the camera in *Iré a Santiago,* extend to more developed forms such as that which takes place in *Mi Aporte* when the filmmaker enters the frame as a participant-observer. She puts herself in the frame, as we will see at the end of this essay, in acts of giving over/up directorial power to a collective imaginary.

From that freeze-frame at the beginning of *Memories of Underdevelopment* to Giral's *María Antonia* the female Afro-Cuban identity functions as an especially powerful sign of the violence of the history of the colonial encounter that undergirds cultural difference—an image not necessarily subsumable within the narratives of Cuban national or revolutionary identity. Nor, I should state, are the significances the same, or even similar, across these examples. The changing and contested value of this figure is testimony to its affective, political, and aesthetic power. In the main, the figure of the Afro-Cuban woman is deployed as the lynchpin, the punctum, in the national, revolutionary, and gendered visual allegories of oppression and decolonization. "She" becomes the significance-saturated figure for the revolution. However, the weight of this meaning simultaneously introduces an aporia or at least a crisis in signification to allegories of oppression and decolonization. And, this signifying crisis can become problematic insofar as the figure becomes hypostatized as the abject subaltern—a spatial figure, timeless and iconic. With Sergio Giral's *María Antonia*, we are confronted with a spiritually, socially, and sexually abject woman in the 1950s, who after many attempts to be healed through sex or through the Santaría priest, is brutally murdered by her lover. The violence of the content is met with a "violent" rhythm in editing. María dies at a Santaría altar, and then with an invisible edit on sound is "reborn" in postrevolutionary times. The combination of transcendence and progress, of cyclical time and monumental time, of the immeasurably old and the "now time" of revolution, provides the film with that "subtle beyond" of temporal borderlines that animates desire, a desire for a radical futurity: that blindspot in the frame of modernity. As impressive and important as these images are for considerations of race, gender, and revolution, I wish to argue that Sarita's work begins new politics of time for the image of the Afrocuban woman, one that places her in the frame of citizenship and history, rather than as spatial, iconic, and timeless. As Emily Maguire argues in this volume, a director such as the late Humberto Solás makes "visible a direct connection between political engagement and affect. While this implies (like Che's assertion with which this essay opened ['Let me say to you, at the risk of seeming ridiculous, that the true revolutionary is guided by great feelings of love.']) that passion is an important part of the political struggle, in the case of all three women, this passion also serves to limit their access to political awareness, and portrays that awareness as still controlled by men, in particular through romantic relationships." To such a problematic, Gómez said to Marguerite Duras in '68: "As time goes by, we are less of a polite, aesthetic, static, sexual and passive object."[8] For her, love offers not a romance but a world.

Gómez's Work in the Context of Citizenship

In 1989, *Cine Cubano* published a special issue on Gómez. Of the ten articles and reminiscence written by filmmakers, colleagues, and family, two (other than a translation of Michael Chanan's text) make more than passing reference to the documentaries.[9] The 1998 issue of *Cine Cubano* published in anticipation of the fortieth anniversary of the revolution, and of ICAIC, offers numerous archival documents, reprints of past issues, and a celebration of the life and work of Alea, who had recently died. The pages of the issue are filled with photographs, stills, testimonies. In contrast to the 1989 issue, however, there is not one single mention of Gómez. There are a couple of passing references to the feature film, but not a single still or commemorative statement appears. What happened in these ten years to bring such an erasure to her memory? My provisional and tentative answers are that in the 1990s she was claimed as an "ethnic" filmmaker within and outside of Cuba, as well as the fact that she remains the only woman to have made a feature within ICAIC signifies a persistent gender inequality within the Film Institute. In times of crisis, states shrink their public spheres and close their borders—and some of that history concerns me here. As well, however, Sara Gómez's films from the 1960s can teach us important lessons about citizenship today.

Today we live in a world wherein more people than ever before do not belong to the nations in which they live—diasporas, the flows of populations across borders, exiles and nomads, refugees. Those without franchise, without the voting rights that constitute the main artery of citizenship, live alongside the largest ever block of enfranchised nonvoters ever seen in the West—Obama notwithstanding. The loss of faith we see in formal political modes of citizenship, borne out of the constricting of public life and the takeover of public culture by private interest, is met by an expanding cultural citizenship. Citizenship practices have outstripped their formal political/statist forms and now take place through cultural discourses, practices, institutions, and economies.

The profound shift in the way art is taking place in the context of globalization is notable in the relationship between art and everyday life, between artists and political life, and between artists themselves. Globalization changes the nature of capital, the way in which national governments govern, and the experience of everyday life. George Yudice, in *The Expediency of Culture: Uses of Culture in the Global Era*, argues that culture in the era of globalization is a resource. For Yudice the expediency of culture is destructive and productive for social justice, citizenship, and histories: on the one hand everything is commodified, including local cultures for export, and on the other the new expediency has enabled new expressions of global citizenship and responsibility. On the one hand, "culture is being invoked to solve problems that previously were the province of economics and politics," and on the other "the reciprocal permeation of culture and economy, not just as commodity—which would be the equivalent of instrumentality—but as a mode of cognition, social organization, and even attempts at social emancipation, seem to feed back into the system they resist or oppose."[10] The changes in the meaning of art—its value, function, and publicity—take place when the images, stories, and histories from which it draws are part of a global culture industry and part of a political trade in symbolic power. One of the most significant forms of this shift in the production and dissemination of art can be seen in the way artists create connections to other artists across localities. Through shifting and mobile forms of collectivity and connectivity, artists are negotiating the social and political failures of nations, generating new forms, reappropriating cities, and transversing borders. Arjun Appadurai maintains that terms like "international civil society" do not capture the mobility and malleability of those creative forms of social life that are localized transit points for mobile global forms of civic and civil life.

In the introduction to *Culture and Citizenship*, Nick Stevenson suggests that one of the key aspects of cultural citizenship is the deconstruction of the notion of the citizen traditionally associated with liberalism's civil society.[11] "Questions of 'cultural' citizenship," Stevenson argues, "therefore seek to rework images, assumptions and representations that are seen to be exclusive as well as marginalizing."[12] Iris Marion Young and Chantal Mouffe are two feminist political theorists who have offered a radical politics of difference as an alternative to liberal/statist versions of citizenship that seemingly imply a specific institutional modification of the universalistic conception of citizenship. The main type of argument is that across a wide range of contemporary social struggles—from the movements of ethnic groups to feminism—can be found the demand to have the distinctive characteristic of one's group acknowledged. In this "radical pluralism argument" the cultural fragmentation of citizenship is seen not as a danger, but as a positive advantage. They argue that the universality of citizenship in the sense of inclusion and participation for everyone stands in tension with the other meaning of universality embedded in modern political ideas: universality as generality and universality as equal treatment. Thus, the idea of citizenship as expressing a general will tending to enforce a homogeneity in practice excludes groups judged not capable of adopting the general point of view. Second, according to such an approach, where differences in capacities, culture, and values exist among groups but some are privileged, strict adherence to a principle of equal treatment tends to perpetuate oppression and disadvantage. As Young writes,

> The attempt to realize an ideal of universal citizenship that finds the public embodying generality as opposed to particularity, commonness versus difference, will tend to exclude or put at a disadvantage some groups, even when they have formally equal citizenship status.... Different social groups have different needs, cultures, histories,

experiences, and perceptions of social relations which influence their interpretation of the meaning and consequences of policy proposals and influence the form of their reasoning.[13]

An increasing number of theorists argue that citizenship must take account of these cultural differences. Accordingly, these groups can be integrated into a common culture only if we adopt a notion of "differentiated citizenship." This means that members of certain groups could be incorporated into the political community not only as individuals but also through groups, and their rights would depend, in part, on their group membership. This type of theory offers something important in the age of displacement, but also as a way of thinking about the history of struggle.

Artists in the Americas and many parts of Europe and Asia have diversified their practices through new media to both resist and take advantage of new global economies, forming new kinds of translocal partnerships with artist communities around the world. Such connectivities are creating possibilities for grassroots politics and reorienting and enriching the expressive order of collective life in certain parts of the world. While we live inside these flows of culture and capital, we need to inform our practices not just across localities but across temporal horizons as well.

And so, while the world Sara Gómez worked in during the 1960s in Cuba appears a stark contrast to this current condition I describe, there are points of connection from which we can draw valuable lessons and insights: in the role culture played in the making of citizens, the global imaginary permeating the era, intensification of cosmopolitanism, the connections people made across previously unbridgeable differences, and the transformation of the citizen from that of being a function of nation to an active participant in the making of the nation through culture, and affective solidarity.

In the 1960s the renewal of citizenship in these forms was being realized in various parts of the world at the same time, beginning in a sense with the Bandung Conference of 1955 where the nonaligned third world met to create the possibility for a decolonized world—a decolonization that dismantles a political and economic system *and* a psychological system. W.E.B. DuBois wrote to those in attendance at the Asian-African conference (as he was unable to attend): "Let the white world keep its missionaries at home to teach the Golden Rule to its corporate thieves. Damn the God of slavery, exploitation and war."[14] Dedicated to the elimination of "colonialism and the color line," the Bandung Conference redrew a map of the world that connected Indonesia to Algeria to Harlem to Paris to Havana. The political work of decolonizing and reterritorialising the world had to happen alongside the reformation of culture and psyche. We could say that the dream of Africa, the imagined Africa, animated this consciousness for Cubans, consolidating an historical narrative of liberation struggles, with Martí's "¡Seamos moros! [Let us be Moors]" echoing across the revolutionary landscape to Fidel's 1966 appeal to join the Organization of African Unity as an "overseas African country" because "African blood flows in the veins of half of the Cuban people."[15]

As Albert Memmi and Franz Fanon so powerfully argued, under colonialism, racism is internalized by both colonizer and colonized; thus decolonization must be transpersonal and transnational; and the prerequisite of transnationalism is not nationalism but "national consciousness": it is "the only thing," Fanon writes, "that will give us an international dimension.... because the building of a nation is of necessity accompanied by the discovery and encouragement of universalizing values," "it is at the heart of national consciousness that international consciousness lives and grows."[16] The role of culture is utterly essential, then. Aime Cesaire's call to "invent new souls" requires the work of culture, of the informed, critical imagination—the work of artists and intellectuals. These writers of decolonization were, of course, being read and debated in Havana throughout the 1960s, alongside Che, Trotsky, Malcolm X, and others.

This global consciousness born out of a national consciousness that made Algeria the model spread to the Black Nation, the Indian Nation, Quebec—the sovereign nation—and, of course, to Cuba. While the campesino's role was essential for the building of national consciousness, these radical nation-building projects took place in and through cultural institutions in Harlem, Havana, Montreal, Algiers, Paris, and so on. It was through the cultural transits and transmissions of film, pamphlets, art, music, and, of course, books that student movements and workers were finding their ways to each other—cracking the ice of the Cold War with their rejection of a world based on two powers.

Let us begin at the end. At the end of Sara's work, an end that is really a beginning or *en medias res*. The final image she left with us: Mario and Yolanda taking it to the street.

As authors with diverse conclusions about race and the 1960s have shown, and as I will review further on, the 1960s in Cuba offered a critical public sphere for an intelligentsia but there were limits: they had to be willing not to speak about enduring racism in Cuba, although the public discussion of racism was encouraged when discussing that which came with American imperialism. By the early 1970s the critical public sphere was narrowing further. It is into this space and time that Yolanda and Mario take their argument—they take it to the streets. And what is their argument? It is an argument about revolutionary citizenship, and it is conducted in the acoustic space of unequal culpability, with a *trove* playing out this final scene, demarcating the limits tradition continue to make, with lyrics about women's culpability.

In all of Sara's films, windows and thresholds or doorways speak volumes—they are spaces of emergence. They are interior frames that function to mediate or create a density of mediation by which to literally "see" the emergence of a new subjectivity. In *Mi aporte*, women are often at thresholds; in *De cierta*, the privacies of race and gender enter the class-less streets as the grey years were restricting the spaces of civil society. We need here to pause over this very point. If, as I am arguing, Sara's films are about the expansion of the public space through the citizenship practices of cinema, we must review what we mean by the notion of civil society, especially for Cuba at that time.

Desiderio Navarro, of Casa de las Américas, wrote these words in the year 2000 about role of critical intellectuals (of whom he includes artists) in the 1960s: "For the majority of the revolutionary intellectuals—but not for the majority of the politicians—it was clear that their role in the public sphere should be one of critical participation. Around '68, intellectual critical intervention in the public sphere made itself felt with considerable strength and from diverse political positions. The relative monologism dominant for years thanks to spontaneous political consensus and, to some extent, self-censorship motivated by the danger of manipulation of information by the enemy, was broken by isolated intellectual voices that called into question narrow or broad aspects of the revolutionary process, or even the whole of it.... [These] were some of the factors that contributed to intellectuals being seen by many politicians as untrustworthy fellow travelers, and even as a potential oppositional political force."[17]

Navarro's account does not look at the issues of race, racism, and Afro-Cuban cultural forms, but it does provide an argument for the role of critical culture in the expansion and progress of the revolution. The civil society operated in the universities, cultural organizations such as ICAIC, and through the newly established (CFN) National Folkloric Ensemble, UNEAC, as well as less formal spaces. Recognizing that many things changed very quickly, let us just say that these organizations, these cultural institutions, created fora for the public discussion of issues of race.

In his book *A Nation for All: Race, Inequality and Politics on Twentieth-Century Cuba*, Alejandro de la Fuente argues that the importance of identification with nonwhite people increased as tensions between the U.S. and Cuban governments escalated *and* at the same time the internal discourse about Santaría, race, and racism was being deflected through the spectacles of folkloric cultural expression and institutions in the 1960s. "The lack of a public debate about race and racism facilitated the survival and reproduction of the very racist stereotypes that the revolutionary leadership claimed to oppose."[18] While an important moment had been lost, the efforts to promote African roots of national culture were not meaningless, exposing Cubans to a different vision of themselves and their nation. Within ICAIC there were three black filmmakers (Sarita, Nicolás Guillén Landrián, and Sergio Giral) whose work has been marginalized for a host of complex reasons that are not primarily racist but the consequence is that the cinematic efforts to decolonize consciousness through work on race were not inward looking. Instead, the efforts were outward looking and part of the anti-imperialism of films such as *NOW.*

This linkage of racism and imperialism functioned at the political levels as well, as Fuentes notes, from 1959—when the government sponsored, all-expense paid tours of African Americans—to Fidel's visit to Harlem through to the agreement to harbor Black Liberation Army member Assata Shakur after her 1979 escape from jail. According to de la Fuente, the discussions that took place in the 1959–1960 period were broad and public, following Fidel's public condemnation of racism and his support of a broad discussion of race in the media. "The environment was propitious enough for some Afro-Cuban intellectuals to bring into the public sphere issues and cultural expressions that had been traditionally hidden or demeaned and 'black things'"—such as Santaría and Abakuá. Journalist Gaston Aguero and writer Walterio Carbonell published arguments about the direction the revolution should take regarding black culture, racism, and identity. Carbonell's argument was in accord with the arguments found in Fanon and later in many Black Power writers: the culture of the slave-owners could not be that of revolutionary Cuba; rather it was necessary to create a new "historical consciousness" that gave Africa and its descendants the place they deserved in the formation of the Cuban nation.[19] He despaired, writes Fuente, over the inability of some revolutionaries to free themselves from the influence of what he termed the "bourgeois conceptions" of culture with regard to race.

While it is true that some institutions took up the historical contributions of Afro-Cubans to the development of Cubanidad, few voices were heard discussing the contemporary problem of racism after *P.M.* According to film scholars who are clearly friends of the revolution, such as Michael Chanan, the banning of *P.M.* is cited as an error in judgment, a defensive act in the midst of the Girón invasion. He argues that it was the images of decadence, which presented a disrespect for the seriousness of the times, for the soldiers fighting, for the country's future. Others more critical of the revolution's ideological turn cite the ban of *P.M.* as the first of the restrictions on intellectual and artistic life that would lead to the international break with leftist intellectuals cited above by Navarro. But is there another way to interpret the coincidence of these two silences—of *P.M.* and of discourse on racism? Alfredo Guevara in conversation with Michael Chanan said, "it showed a world inhabited by mainly the black and mulatto lumpenproletariat. Obviously it wasn't made out of any feeling of racial discrimination, but the presentation of these images at this time was nonetheless questionable." Interpreting his remarks, Chanan writes, "it presented black people in roles associated with the state of oppression from which they were in the process of liberation."[20] Hence, the story of *P.M.* is more than a story of the censorship of a film that coincidentally has black content; it is a story about the struggle over how to tell the story about race.

Within the same year, from Giron on, black activists, organizations, scholars, and cultural workers found their public sphere shrinking rapidly—de la Fuente writes that 170 black organizations were shut down in 1961. It has been written that in 1967, shortly after the visit of Stokely Carmichael and before the 1968 World Cultural Congress of Havana (to which several leading Afro-Cuban figures were not invited), a group of black political and cultural figures—with Afros and the fire of Black Power activism on their tongues—approached the government to address the concerns of Afro-Cubans. Among them were Sara Gómez, Nancy Morejón, Nicolás Guillén Landrián, Walterio Carbonell, Rogelio Furé. Minister Llanusa Gobels labeled their appeal seditious. Walterio Carbonell's book was "seized" and he was jailed. Nicolasito was jailed. Doing a proper historiography of this period is better left to another time.[21] My reason for mapping this out is because it delineates a moment when the potential of working through the racism of Cuban identity was truncated by an as yet-undeveloped self-understanding of "national consciousness." If the official public sphere cannot support the work, then the citizenship practices of artists, cultural workers, and intellectuals become all the more vital.

William Rowe and Vivian Schelling make a case for understanding popular culture in Latin America in the following way: "When popular culture is defined not as an object, a meaning or a social group, but as a site—or, more accurately, a series of dispersed sites—then it generates a principle of opposition to the idea…of the national body as a single body."[22] What is "popular" and what is "folklore" in Cuba after the revolution presents an interesting problem for Afro-Cuban identity. The early work of the revolution saw marginalized popular traditions gain centrality and authority in the project of building a new national culture. These dispersed sites of cultural practice, rooted in tradition but transformed by revolutionary purpose, did permit the previously marginalized cultures to participate in the project. However, the retrenchments brought about internally, ostensibly as a response to the United States's continual aggression, saw those local cultural traditions of religious connotation and ritual value musealized as "folklore" and then housed in national institutions. According to Rowe and Schelling, Cuban socialism thus repeats the enlightenment-modernity trajectory of educating "the people" as a unified body away from what is seen as mere superstition and irrationalism.

Gómez's work marks this shift as a double-danger. First, when musealized as "folklore"—as a "distanced past", a sign of underdevelopment—the problematic ritualized orders of a patriarchal governance (such as Abakuá) are reproduced/repeated within social relations. Not subject to historical transformations—to coeval temporal creation and communications with other institutions—the religious practitioners are thus not subjects of history. The second danger is that given that these folkloric practices are *Afro*-Cuban, this marginalization remarks a racial difference on top of an already historically repressed group. Hence, Gómez' films seek to reframe these cultural practices as popular subjects of and to history. History, however, is not accorded a single formation of monumental or revolutionary time; for Gómez the specificity of cultural memory requires that the revolutionary narrative be dispersed and popular.

Locations

Finally, "Una ciudad de cartón."

These words are spoken inwardly by Sergio, the main character in Tomás Gutiérrez Alea's film *Memories of Underdevelopment*, as he traces the Malecón with his telescope from his apartment balcony. As one moment in his running interior monologue about the changes in and his alienation from the space, place, history, and social relations of Cuba one year after the Revolution, Sergio's statement reveals one of a kaleidoscope of views that comprise the Malecon as a space of representation. Arguably the foundational film of post-1959, *Memories of Underdevelopment* returns in the final scene to the Malecon from uptop Sergio's apartment at a peak moment in the Cuban Missile Crisis: the roadway is thick with military vehicles. Between these two images, Sergio is a flanuer/anthropologist, whose mobile gaze maps the city and produces space coextensive of his class, race, and gender.

Joined with these considerations are the citizenship practices of urban (auto) ethnography in the 1950s and 1960s. When we look at Gómez not just relation to her colleagues in Cuba (particularly Nicolás Guillén Landrián and Santiago Álverez) but in relation to international networks being mobilized by the decolonizing projects and new social movements, we find a series of connections to black power, the left bank film projects, feminist organizing, and newsreel film—which combine to remap the city as a space of world citizenship and localized histories.

Much has been written about the Italian neorealist influence on Cuban cinema. Instead, I draw your attention to the tradition of the urban ethnographer such as we see in Jean Rouch and Edgar Morin's important film *Chronicle of a Summer*, Chris Marker and, of course, Agnés Varda's films, as well as the Quebec filmmakers, such as Michel Brault, who was instrumental in the making of Rouch's *Chronicles of a Summer* (Rouch was close to and worked with Michel Leiris, who came to Cuba as the leader of the French delegation of leftist artists and intellectuals in the late 1960s). This network of urban ethnographers created an aesthetic by which to express locality and urban life inside the movement of an emergent global and decolonized consciousness.

Sarita's *Iré a Santiago* wasn't about *going* to Santiago; it was about Santiago de Cuba. It is about the street, and cinema's reflection on and recording of public life and cultural memory. *Crónicas de mi familia* isn't just about her family, it is about the locatedness, the urban genealogy of cultural history; *Y tenemos sabor* is at once an Ortizian ethnography of *son* and an urban soundscape. The final argument in the street in *De cierta manera* meets the demolition at the beginning: the city as the space of contestation, love, and citizenship practice. The liminal spaces between home and street in *Mi aporte*; between work and street; the spaces of argument—a public space. The urban ethnographer goes to La Isla de la Juventud where people have gone *from* the city. She doesn't interview campesinos or pineros— she interviews youth who had become homeless (in a variety of ways) in Havana.

Cinema-making is a citizenship practice; but it is so in the material- ity of the representation—the carving out of representational space, a publicity in which to engage in the question of belonging and to create national consciousness. Cinema has, since Vertov and Eisenstien, had a very self-conscious role to play in the production of the imaginary of "the new man"; and, with even more force through "the magic of Hollywood style," the extension of the imperial imaginary. The "third cinema" debates and manifestos that were mounted through the 1950s and 1960s project of decolonization and anti-imperialism aimed themselves squarely and directly at the decolonization of consciousness (*la toma de consiencia*) with statements such as these by Solanas and Gettino:

The decolonization of the filmmaker and of films will be simultaneous acts to the extent that each contributes to collective decolonization. The battle begins without, against the enemy who attacks us, but also within, against the ideas and models of the enemy to be found inside of each one of us. Destruction and construction. Decolonizing action rescues with its practice the purest and most vital impulses... People are witness to a constant astonishment, a kind of second birth. They recover their early simplicity, their capacity for adventure. The cam- era is the inexhaustible expropriator of image-weapons; the projec- tor, a gun that can shoot 24 frames per second.[23]

The coming together of the avant-garde projects of estrangement and shock with the uses and misuses of Fanon in the writings and rhetoric of this movement creates an interesting set of historical vectors and contesting temporalities, and a great deal of metaphor that has yet to be fully researched. The quote above is from the Argentinian filmmakers' Fernando Solanas and Octavio Getino's 1969 manifesto "Towards a Third Cinema: Notes and Experiences for the Development of a Cinema of Liberation in the Third World"; it begins with a quote from Fanon: "we must discuss, we must invent." The Solanas and Gettino manifestos and film projects, such as their *Hour of the Furnaces,* were emerging out of national contexts and were intended to mobilize what Fernando Birri called "sublife" into "life."

This transformation, to return to the beginning, depends not just on a political reterritorialization of land, economy, and power but upon an imaginary for the Other, a plentitude of attention to that which has previously robbed them of their potentiality and particularity. The role of consciousness-raising films was central for feminist and antiracist movements, for they offered an affective vocabulary and an image of collective overcoming. And Sara was the first to develop an aesthetic that brought this consciousness-raising practice together with decolonizing language of "third cinema." Sara refuses to use the camera as weapon; rather, it used as a mirror of affection. "She does not try to teach us," writes Gerardo Fulleda León, "she grasps, listens, shows.... There are no slogans or ideological sermons, so fashionable at the time," adding that, *Crónicas de mi familia* "is a cinematographic poem that takes [the woman's] authenticity out of the trunk, where all black families have wanted to hide all our false aspirations, our mediocre existence and our little human miseries as miserable evils that we cannot show. Sober and bitter way of building our dignity, of being what we are."[24]

Rebellion and *Rebeldes*

Julio Garcia Espinosa made a film entitled *The Young Rebel,* about the training of a young man to become a disciplined revolutionary, to think with his head and not his sex. Much could be done about this film in particular for the way in which it genders and whitens revolutionaries and represents the condensation of discipline in the body, but for today I want to slide it in to the discussion of the way the revolution was understood in terms of youth culture. And beside it I wish to place two other sets of images: the literacy campaign and the Isla de pinos. The images of the literacy campaign, especially Manuel Octavio Gómez's remarkable *Historia de una batalla,* give citizenship to young black girls and women. And there are few images from the period more exhilaratingly hopeful than a teenage black girl wearing a military uniform and armed with the alphabet. Sara's *En la otra isla* begins with the images of young women working together in the fields of the Isla de Pinos; it then proceeds to give us portraits of specific youth—their differences and particularities attended to very carefully by Sara.

La Isla de Pinos and the documentaries Sarita made about it in the late-1960s, present a twofold promise: on the one hand, the previously marginalized groups (young, female, black, poor) will not just work for or benefit from but will *make* the revolution; and, on the other, these "Pioneers of the future" will themselves become the ageless face of the Revolution. She began a trilogy of ethnographic documentaries but completed only two: *En la otra isla* and *Una isla para Miguel,* both in '68. She also made a documentary about the history of the Island for the popular encyclopedia series of ICAIC. The earlier two are ethnographic documentaries (excellent examples of direct cinema) about the Island's most recent inhabitants: thousands of people under the age of thirty-five who arrived in waves over the first seven years. The intention was to populate the Island, which had been abandoned by other governments. Some of these youth were sent to study, work, and develop as revolutionaries; others arrived as *brigadistas* to help after Hurricane Alma destroyed great portions of a fertile and productive agricultural area, where previous waves of immigrants (including Japanese) made farms or worked for American orchard owners. And others, the subjects of Gómez's documentaries, were sent to because they were perceived to be in need of reform, because their values were in contradiction with the values of the revolution: sexuality, religion, long hair, and marginalization due to race or abandonment.

To end, then, I wish to discuss a segment from *En la otra isla* that works as my touchstone, an image upon which all three of my themes hang. In it Sara interviews a young black man about his desires to be an opera singer. She listens and she waits and she gently probes him to speak his difference. This beautiful two-shot performs an equalization of relations between filmmaker and subject. The two-shot in cinema is the conversation shot, one wherein the gaze is not the property of either of the filmed subjects. In mainstream fiction, the two-shot can be used as a surveillance shot, as an image of intimacy or privacy, as a moment in a cessation of power dynamics. In documentary, the two-shot is used as a sign of interactive or reflective practice on the part of the filmmaker, as an equalization of the planes of power between the social subjects of the documentary or between the documentarist and her subject. In a two-shot the screen is democratized, perspective is forgone in favor of frontality. There is, however, for the viewer a sense of listening in, of a privileged p-o-v. There is an intimate conversation, a vulnerability to which we are invited to listen, to attend, and possibly to protect or take care of that which we hear. This is qualitatively different from another type of two-shot used in documentaries around the same time, the two-shot of the voyeuristic directors such as Fredrick Wiseman where the intimacy is really a privacy. Participating instead in the verité networks that move between the streets of Montreal, Paris, Algiers, and Havana, Sara is in the picture in *En la otra isla*, not just on an equal plane aesthetically but also ethically—this picture is a moment of autoethnography: a young black man, a young black woman; an opera singer, a filmmaker; brought to this moment of vulnerability with each other through the near unspeakability of race. In the dialogue, in Sara's waiting for him, even as he wants her to speak for him, she is his mirror and interlocutor, to whom he can speak shame of race. To bring it out, into the public world, a world not owned by any, a world shared by all.

Notes

This essay was originally written and presented at the colloquium *Sara Gómez: Imagen Múltiple* held in Havana from November 1 to 3, 2007. Thanks to the organizers of the colloquium for their invitation. This essay could not have been written without the love and conversation about matters Cuban that I have enjoyed with Paul Kelley, Karen Dubinsky, María Caridad Cumaná and Scott Rutherford. This research was supported by funding from the Social Sciences and Humanities Research Council of Canada.

In writing about race in Cuba, I have found the vocabulary very dynamic and limiting. The discourses of race that are invoked by "black" both overlap and differ substantially from those invoked by "Afro-cuban." While I occasionally use "black," "Afrocuban" is preferred in part because of the historical period I am referring to in this essay—where race, nation, and heritage were in a process of transformation by the revolutionary context.

1. Dannys Montes de Oca Moreda and Dayamick Cisneros Rodriguez, "Labores Domesticas," in *Labores Domesticas: Versiones Para Otra Historia De La Visualidad En Cuba: Genero, Raza Y Grupos Sociales* (Cuba: Galeria UNEAC (Pinar del Rio, Cuba), Galeria Telepinar (Pinar del Rio, Cuba), Central Provincial de Artes Visuales (Pinar del Rio, Cuba), 2004).

2. Here are a few sources, primarily in English, where Gómez's feature film is discussed. Catherine Benamou, "Cuban Cinema: On the Threshold of Gender," *Frontiers: A Journal of Women's Studies* 15:1 (1994): 51–75; Julianne Burton, "Film and Revolution in Cuba: The First Twenty-Five Years," *New Latin American Cinema: Volume Two: Studies of National Cinema,* ed. Micheal T. Martin (Detroit: Wayne State University Press, 1997); Michael Chanan, *Cuban Cinema* (University of Minnesota Press, 2004); *Cine Cubano* 127 (Special issue on Sara Gómez) (Sumario 1989); Catherine Davies, "Modernity, Masculinity and Imperfect Cinema in Cuba" *Screen* 38:4 (Winter 1997): 245–259; "Reply to John Hess," *Screen* 40:2 (Summer 1999): 208–211; Julia LeSage, "One Way or Another: Dialectical, Revolutionary, Feminist," *Jump Cut* 20 (May 1979): 20–23; Zuzana Pick, *The New Latin American Cinema: A Continental Project* (Austin: University of Texas Press, 1993); B. Ruby Rich, "An/Other View of New Latin American Cinema," *Iris: A Journal of Theory on Image and Sound* 13 (Summer 1991): 5–28.

3. Susan Lord, "Temporality and Identity: Undertaking Cross-Cultural Analysis of Sara Gómez's Documentaries," in *Women Filmmakers: Refocussing,* ed. Jacqueline Levitin, Judith Plessis, and Valerie Raoul (Vancouver: U.B.C Press, 2002).

4. Author in conversation with the late Leida Oquendo in Havana, March 2004. Oquendo was an anthropologist and a close friend of Sara Gómez. She was among that group of Communist Youth who went to the Isla de Pinos, "with the feeling that with the experiment

we undertook, we carried a great burden—that of the entire future of the revolution upon—our shoulders."

5. Andrew Salkey, *Havana Journal* (Pelican Books, 1971), 27–28.

6. Teshome Gabriel, "Ruin and the Other: Towards a Language of Memory," in *Otherness and the Media: The Ethnography of the Imagined and the Imaged*, ed. Hamid Naficy (Langhorne, PA: Harwood, 1993).

7. Jacqueline Loss, "Global Arenas: Narrative and Filmic Translation of Identity," *Nepantla; Views from the South* 4:2 (2003): 317–344. Amy Fass Emery, *The Anthropological Imagination in Latin American Literature* (Columbia: University of Missouri Press, 1996).

8. Sara Gómez, interviewed by Marguerite Duras in Havana. [1968?] From the Gómez file at the ICAIC Cinemateca archive.

9. Haydee Arteaga, "Recordar a Sara" and Gerardo Fulleda León, "Una Reina Desoida," *Cine Cubano* 127 (Special issue on Sara Gómez) (Sumario 1989).

10. George Yudice, *The Expediency of Culture: Uses of Culture in the Global Era* (Durham and London: Duke University Press, 2003), 25 and 28.

11. Nick Stevenson, ed., *Culture and Citizenship* (London: Sage, 2001), 2–4. On cultural citizenship see Toby Miller, *The Well-Tempered Self: Citizenship, Culture, and the Postmodern Subject* (Baltimore and London: Johns Hopkins University Press, 1993); Engin Isin and Patricia Wood, *Citizenship and Identity* (London: Sage, 1999); Seyla Benhabib, *The Claims of Culture: Equality and Diversity in the Global Era* (Princeton: Princeton University Press, 2002); Engin Isin and Bryan Turner, *Handbook of Citizenship Studies* (London: Sage, 2002); and Toby Miller, *Cultural Citizenship: Cosmopolitanism, Consumerism, and Television in a Neoliberal Age* (Philadelphia: Temple University Press, 2007).

12. Stevenson, ibid.

13. Iris Marion Young, "Polity and Group Difference: A Critique of the Ideal of Universal Citizenship," *Ethics* 99 (January 1989): 250–274; See Ernesto Laclau and Chantal Mouffe, *Hegemony and Socialist Strategy: Towards a Radical Democratic Politics* (London: Verso, 1985); and Chantal Mouffe, ed., *Dimensions of Radical Democracy* (London: Verso, 1992).

14. W.E.B. Du Bois, "The Bandung Conference," *Writings in Periodicals Edited by Others* 4 (Millwood, N.Y.: Kraus-Thomson Organization, 1982), 237–247.

15. Fidel Castro, cited in Carlos Moore, *Castro, the Blacks and Africa* (Centre of Afro-American Studies/University of California), 251.

16. Franz Fanon, *The Wretched of the Earth* (New York: Grove, 1968), 45–48; 197; 94. Thanks to Sean Mills for his work on this theme.

17. Desiderio Navarro and Alessandro Fornazzari, "In Medias Res Publicas: On Intellectuals and Social Criticism in the Cuban Public Sphere," *boundary 2* 29:3 (Fall 2002): 187–203. A lengthier extract gives a fuller sense of his argument and the history of this moment: "On the other hand, in relations with foreign intellectuals an analogous political heteroglosia appeared: a large part of the foreign leftist or progressive intelligentsia (primarily Western European and Latin American) criticized the revolutionary government for its approval of the 1968 invasion of Czechoslovakia by the troops of the Warsaw Pact and for the 1971 detention of the Cuban poet Heberto Padilla. In January 1968, on the occasion of the Cultural Congress of Havana, the intellectual workers of the world, and of Europe in particular, were exalted for intervening in the public sphere with protests and combative mobilizations in favor of causes such as Cuba's position during the October missile crisis, Che's guerrilla movement, the Vietnam struggle, the black people's movement in the United States, and so on, in contrast with the limited or nonexistant public support given to such causes by the world revolutionary avant-gardes, parties, and political organizations. But, soon after the above-mentioned criticisms in 1971, within that intelligentsia a 'mafia' of 'false intellectuals' was discovered and described as 'petit bourgeois pseudo-leftists of the capitalist world who used the Revolution as a springboard to win prestige among the peoples of the underdeveloped countries,' and who 'attempted

to permeate us with their debilitating ideas, to impose their styles and tastes, and even to act as judges of the Revolution'…[Declaration, 1971]. [By 1971] all of a sudden, for most politicians, the intellectual appeared as a real ideological Other who was publicly interpellating them on extracultural matters of national politics. That appearance, along with the knowledge of the role played by Czech intellectuals in the Prague Spring and the growing influence of the Soviet sociopolitical and cultural model in its Brezhnevian stage of 'Restoration,' were some of the factors that contributed to intellectuals being seen by many politicians as untrustworthy fellow travelers, and even as a potential oppositional political force."

18. Alejandro de la Fuente, *A Nation for All: Race, Inequality and Politics in Twentieth-Century Cuba* (Chapel Hill and London: University of North Carolina Press, 2001), 290–337, passim.

19. Ibid., 287.

20. Chanan, *Cuban Cinema,* 133.

21. It needs to be said that this history is contested. During interviews I recently conducted in Havana, many of my participants were unwilling or unable to recall these events. Equally impressive was the fact that several happily recalled the fact of the World Cultural Congress, but details were not forthcoming. The literature on race in Cuba is blossoming beyond the fairly polarized positions held previously. For a view of the polarized debates, see http://afrocubaweb.com. For further reading of recent works, please see: Tomas Fernandez Robaina, *Cuba: Personalidades en el debate racial* (Cuba: Editorial Ciencias Social, 2007); Esteban Morales Domínguez, *Desafíos de la problemática racial en Cuba* (Fundación Fernando Ortiz, 2007); "The New Afro-Cuban Cultural Movement and the Debate on Race in Contemporary Cuba," *Journal of Latin American Studies* 40 (November 2008): 697–720; and a new documentary on race, *Raza* by Erick Corvalán Pellé (Cuba 2008). Of course, to this we must add the culture of and literature about rap because they address the complexities of the discourse on race.

22. William Rowe and Vivian Schelling, *Memory and Modernity: Popular Culture in Latin America* (London: Verso, 1991), 2.

23. Fernando Solanas and Octavio Gettino, "Towards a Third Cinema," in *Movies and Methods: An Anthology*, ed. Bill Nichols (Berkeley: University of California Press, 1976).

24. Gerardo Fulleda León, "Sara Gómez: Una obra cinematográfica para la reflexion sobre la memoria popular." Lecture delivered at the International Symposium "Popular Memory and Changes" in Ascona, Switzerland, April 1–May 1, 1998.

CHAPTER EIGHT

The "Burning Body" as an Icon of Resistance: Literary Representations of Jan Palach

CHARLES SABATOS

In '68, Czechoslovakia's attempt at widespread political reform, which became known as the "Prague Spring," attracted worldwide attention. Under the leadership of Alexander Dubček, who famously described the movement's aim as "socialism with a human face," the regime allowed a level of freedom (including a virtual end to press censorship) that had not been seen since the Communist rise to power twenty years earlier. However, these developments were brought abruptly to an end by the Soviet-led Warsaw Pact invasion of Czechoslovakia that August. While the first weeks of the occupation inspired widespread public protests, opposition had gradually broken down by the beginning of the following year. On January 16, 1969, twenty-year-old university student Jan Palach set himself on fire in Prague's Wenceslas Square in protest against the growing Czech apathy toward the occupation. He succumbed to the burns three days later, leaving behind a letter that he signed "Torch Number 1." This event was a traumatic turning point that both shocked the Czechs, who had been withdrawing into stunned passivity, and unified them; his funeral in Prague drew thousands of mourners and became a major demonstration of anti-Soviet sentiment. As one man, waiting in line to see Palach's coffin, lamented, "What a country we live in! Where the only light for the future is the burning body of a young boy."[1] By the end of that year, thousands of Czechs and Slovaks had gone into exile, and all calls for reform had been effectively silenced, but Jan Palach became a symbol of national defiance until the end of Communist rule in 1989.

As a symbol of national sacrifice, Palach echoes a deep tradition of martyrdom in Czech history, epitomized by the early religious reformer Jan Hus (who was burned at the stake as a heretic).[2] For Ladislav Holy, "By setting himself alight [Palach] was attempting metaphorically to set fire to the nation. By making the ultimate sacrifice he was trying to move people to make a lesser sacrifice for the common cause."[3] Palach's death marked the end, not the beginning, of significant resistance to the occupation, but his memory inspired the successful protests that led to the end of the Communist regime twenty years later. In itself, this tale of a national martyr is nothing out of the ordinary for the smaller countries of Eastern Europe, historically caught between more powerful nations. What is exceptional is Palach's emergence as an icon of resistance on both sides of the Cold War–era ideological divide. Beginning almost immediately after his death, Jan Palach inspired numerous literary representations, which cross cultures and genres but share a crucial concern with the violence enacted upon the body by political forces. By calling attention to Palach's "burning body," these writers (in Michel Foucault's terms) "expose a body totally imprinted by history and the process of history's destruction of the body."[4] The reaction from writers in the West during the 1970s established him as an image of the "violated" Czech nation. During the final decade of Communism in the 1980s, the memory of Palach had faded in the West but was still very much present for Czech and other East European writers. After the two decades in which Palach's memory was officially taboo in Czechoslovakia, he was enshrined as a Czech national martyr in the post-Communist period. For the younger generation, however, the meaning of his sacrifice has become increasingly remote, even as it continues to inspire tragic acts of imitation.

Jan Palach was born in August 1948, less than six months after the Communist Party took control of Czechoslovakia, and was raised in a small town east of Prague.[5] While he came from a middle-class background (a political liability during the Communist period), he himself was part of the earliest generation who had grown up entirely under socialism. His father, who died when he was thirteen, inspired his deep interest in Czech history. Palach was initially denied entrance to the Philosophical Faculty of Prague's Charles University and entered the Economics University instead, but two years later he reapplied and was accepted as a history student.[6] In 1967 and '68, he went as a student worker to the Soviet Union, and in fall '68, he also traveled and worked in France (which gave him firsthand experience of both Eastern and Western Europe). Upon his return, he became increasingly politically active, although it has not been proven that he was part of a group, as his note claimed (and as the name "Torch No. 1" implied). In a letter written to one of the leaders of the student protest movement only two weeks before his death, Palach had urged that they occupy the national radio station, concluding with the provocative postscript: "January '68 began from above, January '69 can begin from below."[7]

Palach's final act was likely inspired by the self-immolation of Buddhist monks protesting the U.S.-supported South Vietnamese regime in 1963.[8] However, as Kieran Williams points out, Palach "was not, as is commonly claimed, protesting the invasion, nor was his act anti-Soviet or anti-socialist," and his self-immolation "was not an act of desperation but of hope that the defiance of August could be revived."[9] Palach's final letter was not directed at the Soviets but at the Czechoslovak authorities, calling for an end to the censorship that had been reinstated after the invasion and protesting the distribution of the newspaper *Zprávy*, printed by the occupiers and collaborators. The Italian writer and filmmaker Pier Paolo Pasolini similarly observed, in an article written shortly after Palach's death, that his "protest was not anti-Communist. It demonstrates, on the contrary, to what level of idealism a young Communist, born and raised in a Communist world, can be driven. An idealism which allowed him to commit an act worthy of an ancient age; of a modern Vietnamese saint."[10] Even while rejecting a simplistic anti-Soviet interpretation of Palach's deed, Pasolini suggests that it is alien to modern European culture, a reaction later echoed by such writers as Milan Kundera. However, other Czech men followed Palach's example in the months after January 1969, notably the high school student Jan Zajíc, who also set himself on fire on Wenceslas Square and left a farewell note in the form of a poem dedicated to Palach, signed "Torch No. 2."[11]

Even before he was buried, Palach's body had already become an important symbol for the Czech nation; the sculptor Olbram Zoubek secretly entered the hospital where he had died and made a death mask. After Palach's funeral, the Square of the Red Army Soldiers, in front of the Charles University Philosophical Faculty, was renamed Jan Palach Square, replacing an official symbol of freedom (the liberators of Prague from the Nazis in 1945) with the new national hero (an unofficial victim of the "liberation" of '68.) After a short time, the name was officially changed back. Palach was first buried in Prague's Olšany cemetery, and his grave was later decorated with a sculpture by Zoubek, which was quickly removed and destroyed by the authorities. So many people visited the grave that Palach's body itself was taken away, cremated, and finally reburied in his native town of Všetaty. In the place of his former grave, the authorities buried an obscure woman, but although the name and even the body had been changed, the site remained a place of pilgrimage, which visitors decorated with candles and flowers.

Palach's deed challenged a deep-rooted national tradition of self-preservation, as described by Josef Korbel, "when this passion for freedom and social justice and the will to survive are suddenly opposed…survival becomes the first law."[12] Defying this passive tradition, the playwright Václav Havel sent an open letter to Alexander Dubček (then still in public office) and urged him not to repudiate the Prague Spring reforms. Adopting a genuine resistance to the occupation would make Czechs and Slovaks "realize…that no political defeat justifies complete historical skepticism as long as the victims manage to bear their defeat with dignity." Havel concludes with an ambiguous allusion to the young national martyr: "Your act would place before us an ethical mirror as powerful as that of Jan Palach's recent deed, though the impact of what you do will be of longer duration."[13] Soon after Havel's appeal, Dubček was removed from his position, expelled from the Communist Party, and fell into obscurity. Yet Palach remained as a lasting symbol of what the Czechs and Slovaks had lost. As Eugen Steiner explains, Palach's death "kindled a flame in the consciences of the Czech and Slovak people and indeed the peoples of the whole world."[14] Nineteen Slovak students went on hunger strike with the declaration: "This act has marked an absolute frontier, an absolute value in the face of which all reality crumbles—here I stand, my whole personality, my hands, my lungs, my eyes, my burning body, I, a living man, I cry NO in the face of the inhuman reality which burns up the truth…"[15] This may be one of the earliest evocations of the "burning body" of Palach as a call to political resistance.

Silence and Action: The Western Literary Response

The complicated transformation of Palach from a "burning body" to a metaphorical "flame" illustrates the concept of the imaginary body, which Moira Gatens describes as "those images, symbols, metaphors and representations which help construct various forms of subjectivity."[16] Noting that since the ancient Greeks, "only a body deemed capable of reason and sacrifice can be admitted into the political body as an active member," Gatens focuses on the way that gender affects this ideological construction of the individual body, suggesting that "the modern body politic is based on an image of a *masculine* body which reflects fantasies about the value and capacities of that body."[17] Thus the representations of Jan Palach's "sacrifice" cover a variety of "forms of subjectivity," but all of them illustrate Gatens's suggestion that gender be understood "not as the effect of ideology or cultural values but as the way in which power takes hold of and constructs bodies in particular ways."[18] Palach's self-immolation is most striking for the many ambiguities it opens up:

self-destruction is the ultimate sacrifice, yet it is also a passive form of protest that does not reflect traditional notions of masculine heroism.

Some of the earliest literary reflections on Jan Palach's deed came from poets. Miroslav Holub's poem "The Prague of Jan Palach," which was published in Prague within days of the student's death, describes "a statue without the torch" and "a torch without the statue."[19] Holub, who had written two travel accounts about the United States, particularly New York, alludes to the Statue of Liberty by transforming the student's "burning body" into the torch itself. Despite Palach's drastic call for freedom, however, the world had reacted with silence.[20] Another Czech poet, Óndra Łysohorský, draws a clear parallel between Palach and Jan Hus in the title of his "Ballad of Jan Palach, Student and Heretic." The "dead philosophy student" speaks louder than the Czech government, whose "words are swept on the rubbish heap of history." Palach, by contrast, "acted at once. And for ever."[21] In contrast, the American poet David Shapiro in his 1971 poem "The Funeral of Jan Palach," focuses less on the student and more on the mourning of his mother: "My son, my beloved son, / I never thought this possible..."[22] Shapiro himself was a student leader in the '68 protests at Columbia University, yet in this work, his emphasis is less on the bold action of his Czech contemporary and more on the effect upon those left behind. For all three of these writers, Palach's actual burning body has been replaced by an imaginary body, a metaphor for sacrifice in both East and West.

Alan Burns and Charles Marowitz's play *Palach* was produced at the experimental Open Space Theater in London in 1970. *Palach*'s main characters are a nameless middle-class family (identified only as "Dad," "Mum," "Boy," and "Girl") along with a priest and a "chorus of students." The stage is broken into four sections and the characters move back and forth between them, speaking to each other without any real communication. The dialogue is a pastiche from a variety of sources, ranging from Shakespeare to recorded transcripts of official Czechoslovak Radio news reports. Much of the play's action consists of the Boy trying to make some sense out of Palach's death, while the others go about their daily routines:

MUM: It was to do with a political thing, wasn't it? It was political. I know it was...rather sad at the time.

GIRL: I've just washed my hair, and I can't do a thing with it!

BOY: Even sadder than why he did it was the fact that he did it to impress upon our memories—

MUM: Your hair used to be so beautiful when you were a child.

BOY: And I've discovered that he...failed. He didn't impress anyone. We only remember something sad.[23]

Finally, the Boy's increasingly desperate attempt to convey the meaning of Palach's death is interrupted by the other family members, as well as the Priest, chanting banal advertising slogans:

> *BOY:* To commit suicide, and at the same time to be there, afterwards—
> *PRIEST:* An Omega does so much more than tell the time!
> *BOY:* —to witness the shock or the pain—
> *PRIEST:* If you want television in every room: go Panasonic!
> *BOY:* —or even the glee—
> *PRIEST:* Get a new tart with amazing Esso Voltpak!
> *BOY:* —that your suicide produced on all those tentacular bonds—
> *PRIEST:* Trust Gold Leaf—
> *BOY:* —which link an individual to his family—
> *PRIEST:* —to taste good!
> *BOY:* —his girl-friend, or his wife... The sacrifice acquires a mythical or religious dimension. The theme recurs: the enlightened person is not just dead to the world, but has actually consumed himself, and this consuming of self is explicitly compared in certain texts to combustion, to destruction by fire.[24]

The Boy's reflections on Palach's "consuming of self" is ironically juxtaposed with the material consumption eagerly pursued by the other characters. In the final scene of *Palach*, all five characters begin to speak one by one, and continue unceasingly until all of them are speaking at the same time. The Boy, who is the last to speak, begins to recite Palach's actual letter listing his demands. His words are overshadowed not only by the voices of the other actors but by noise made by the group of students, and he runs up to each of them, trying to make himself heard, until he finally gives up and sits down in the audience. Burns and Marowitz end on this rather bleak note; with all of the distractions of modern society, the meaning of Palach's "consuming of self" quickly fades away, leaving only a vague feeling of "sadness" among the general public. By "consuming himself," the Boy becomes "enlightened" in a way that is not open to his sister, fussing over her hair, or his mother, preoccupied with keeping her children happy. In both Czechoslovakia and the West, the political hopes of '68 have been betrayed by those who have placed physical pleasures over spiritual liberation. Although the play is opposed to the consumer culture of the West, it privileges the young male body (symbolized by the sacrifice of Jan Palach) as the primary "active member" of society—just as the Western media and advertising have done.

The 1973 play *Jan Palach* by the German author Erwin Sylvanus features seven characters, including Palach's mother and sister, but Palach himself (as if his body has been "dissolved" by historical events) never appears on stage.[25] *Jan Palach* was later produced as an opera with accompaniment by the Austrian composer, Luna Alcalay. In the staging of the play, "dialogues occur in which only one character speaks...reacting to a silent character and to the situation through a mimed response."[26] Sylvanus's ingenious method of portraying Palach as "imaginary," through the reactions of the other characters, shows the national repercussions of his act without sacrificing the human, personal aspect of this tragedy. Part one of *Jan Palach* portrays the uncertainties of life under the increasingly solid power of the Soviet occupation, and narrates the events leading up to Jan's decision. It begins with a scene featuring Jan's mother on a train: "Keep out of politics, I told him. No, mother, he said. One cannot always remain silent. I can still hear him. One cannot always keep quiet."[27] In this context, of course, Palach is indeed silent; the audience can only hear him through the repetition of his words by the mother. Palach's act is observed in the following scene by a black-market moneychanger: "He's running toward the statue of St. Wenceslas. Running...He's just standing there. And standing. And dousing himself. Dousing himself very quickly. And...no...no! He is burning. Flaming! Flaming! A young man. Like myself. (*Very slowly he lights his cigarette.*) Damn it, I can't pray. Or help. And can't do it with him." The most dramatic moment of the play—the destruction of Palach's body—is thus seen only through the words of this eyewitness. A moment later, the Mother, giving her ticket to the train conductor, takes a scarf she is knitting for Jan out of her bag: "Especially now in winter, he needs his scarf...I don't want him to freeze. He shouldn't freeze."[28] At the end, Palach has become a "light" of freedom shining into the darkness of political oppression, yet the play manages to avoid reducing him to a mere symbol. Through such humble details as the mother knitting a scarf that her son will never wear, or the cynical moneychanger lighting a cigarette within sight of the young man in flames, the reader or viewer perceives a painful sense of loss for a young, promising life taken away for no reason. Rather than reducing the political message of the event, this brings it more sharply into focus, and highlights the complex balance of strength and vulnerability that Palach's "burning body" represents.

Palach's deed influenced Latin American writers as well, such as the Argentinian novelist Ernesto Sabato. The narrator of Sabato's *The Angel of Darkness* (1974) reflects that "maybe writing was a necessity for people like him, people incapable of such absolute acts of passion and heroism.

Because that kid had set himself afire one day in the middle of a square in Prague, and Che Guevara, and Marcelo Carranza—none of them had needed to write."[29] While some people in the West saw writers as figures of resistance, Sabato suggests that writing is only an inadequate substitute for more "absolute acts" such as Palach's. A more extensive meditation in Spanish on Jan Palach is by the Cuban poet Angel Cuadra, a member of the underground movement UNARE, whose aims he described in a 1963 essay: "It is the first time that in a country under the communist system a group of intellectuals, of poets, all together under one fighting banner, takes up the spontaneous, voluntary and heroic act of creating a written work directed against the governing regime and generated by actions due to that government."[30] This manifesto seems to anticipate the important role of writers and intellectuals played in Czechoslovakia during the Prague Spring. Cuadra's *Violent Requiem for Jan Palach,* which he wrote while imprisoned in 1972, is divided into ten sections. The first four are comprised of highly symbolic imagery, and the first description of Palach appears in Section Five, who is portrayed as dreamy, bookish, and "anonymous." However, at the beginning of Section Seven, Cuadra describes the destruction of Palach's body and the emergence of his name into history:

> You didn't have a weapon
> except your sudden and desolate skin under the stars,
> and your blood, like a silent river
> under the outrage and the infamy and the disgust....[31]

In this stanza, which illustrates Palach's transformation from an unremarkable individual to a universalizing force of his society, his books and dreams have been replaced by vivid (almost Christ-like) images of his vulnerable skin and his streaming blood. This imaginary body is clearly not that of a warrior, however, since Palach has no weapon but himself. Palach's transformation from a living human being to a symbolic name is highlighted in the end of Section Nine, when he is metaphorically described as a "bonfire" into which people toss words that have lost their meaning, including "self-determination," "coexistence," "internationalism," and "peace." The end of Cuadra's poem returns to "the earth of Olšany," and adds an allusion to "songs behind the night" and "music, that goes on washing off the dust with which stars soil themselves." It concludes with a "lit name...encountered/between the unnameable lips with which your town sings." Palach, more than a man, has become a name that evokes music, while his fatal flame overcomes earthly power by reaching out toward the universe, light, and the stars.[32] His "burning body" has become a symbol of the temporary defeat of the Czech striving for freedom.

Words and Memory: Palach's Legacy in Eastern Europe

Through the 1970s and 1980s, Palach's self-immolation was eerily echoed across Eastern Europe, most often by young men such as the Lithuanian student Romas Kalanta in 1972.[33] In some cases, such as Kalanta's, their "burning bodies" became symbols of sacrifice for their own oppressed nations, but none other than Palach gained widespread fame across cultural and ideological boundaries. What is more surprising is that Palach's deed was not even the first such protest against the Soviet occupation of Czechoslovakia. In September '68, a fifty-five-year-old Polish man named Ryszard Siwiec had set himself on fire in the stands of Warsaw Stadium. The radio announcers reporting live from the stadium completely ignored the event, and although it was witnessed by thousands of people, it went largely unreported by foreign media.[34] Even if his political message had been expressed more clearly, and the event had gained broader coverage in the West, Siwiec was less likely to be appropriated as a hero figure than Palach. Even Tadeusz Konwicki's 1979 novel *A Minor Apocalypse,* which alludes specifically to both Palach and Kalanta, avoids direct mention of Siwiec. As the middle-aged narrator approaches the Warsaw Palace of Culture, he prepares to set himself on fire:

> A certain Czech and a Lithuanian had preceded me on this path which led to a Buddhist monk's pyre. And people of various races, languages, and religions had walked that blazing path before them. Why is solitary suicide a pitiful act? And why is a public suicide performed with all the majesty of ritual an Ascension to heaven? Why is a solitary death at one's own hand a sinful violation of divine law, and a death witnessed by others a victorious challenge hurled at God?[35]

Siwiec's deed, despite thousands of spectators, was essentially a "solitary death" without a clear purpose. As a Pole (whose death contradicted the Polish self-image of manly resistance) he was less directly symbolic of the "Prague Spring." As an older, married man who left a widow and several children behind, he could not simply be seen as an idealistic youth whose only responsibility was to the truth. While it is not likely that Siwiec directly inspired Palach (since the former's deed was almost unknown in Czechoslovakia until after the latter's death), these two acts by men from these traditional "brother nations" form an intriguing counterpoint: both are protesting the same invasion, but the older man's death is forgotten, while the student in Prague is immortalized as an international icon of resistance.[36]

In the contested territory of Eastern Europe, the concept of "nation" is one that must be constantly "ensured," as Katherine Verdery explains, "through culture, heroic deeds, and qualities of the spirit: the realm of men."[37] The gendering of territory as feminine "makes [territorial] boundaries like the skin of the female body, fixed yet violable, in need of armed defense by inevitably masculine militaries."[38] Verdery cites a Romanian nationalist text from the 1980s, entitled "Patriotism—A Vital Necessity": "Love, any love, raises up and purifies, and love of country … gives another meaning to everything…transforming the adolescent into a hero, as has so often happened, as will happen again, and as ought to happen." This passage draws a clear connection between patriotism and youthful heroism, but even more remarkable is the following metaphor: "Romania is my natal land, the land of my dreams…it is the land with the name of a girl and the fiery soul of a fiery man!"[39] The erotic personification of the nation is perhaps not so unusual, but the land portrayed here is clearly androgynous, simultaneously "girl" and "man," complicating the object of the poet's desire. With his creative yet self-destructive deed, Palach simultaneously symbolizes the masculine "realm" of "heroic deeds" and the violated feminine "territory" of the Czech nation.

During the 1980s, although references to Palach began to diminish in the West, the "torch" of his memory was passed to the East, where it remained a taboo topic.[40] The dissident writer Eva Kantůrková, who had spent several years in prison, analyzed the ethics of Jan Palach's death in a 1989 *samizdat* essay. Although she judged that "Jan's deed missed its moment [and] greatly overreached the people at whom it was aimed," she attested to its lasting relevance: "Palach's freely chosen death, it seems to me, has also given dignity to those people who were slaughtered like cattle, the luminousness of his deed meeting their misery."[41] Despite Palach's physical suffering, Kantůrková feels that his death is genuinely a "sacrifice," freely chosen and dignified, unlike the millions killed by the Nazis. However, like Václav Havel's letter to Dubček twenty years earlier, her essay seems to underestimate the lasting power of Palach's "deed." Her emphasis on the individuality of Palach's sacrifice provides an insightful contrast between his "burning body" and the victims of the brutal German occupation thirty years earlier. Daniela Hodrová's novel *In Both Kinds* (1991), set in an apartment just across from the Olšany cemetery where Palach was buried, begins with one of these victims: a young Jewish woman committing suicide to avoid deportation to a concentration camp. In her chapter "Nation," Hodrová draws a direct link between Palach and the Czech nation, but suggests an ambiguous reaction to Palach's deed: "I am the [nation]. I have fallen into a new Egyptian captivity…I have my revolutions and my heroes. One of them went up in flames on a pyre that he'd made himself—between the National Museum and Main Grocery Store…I am the [nation], disillusioned with my revolutions and invasions, as well as with my burnt offerings."[42] Although Hodrová's "nation" refers to Palach as a "hero," its "disillusionment" with its tragic history emerges in the more ironic reference to him as a "burnt offering" (which implies an unwilling victim, such as a sacrificial lamb, and even alludes to the millions who died in the Nazi camps).

The ambivalence of Palach's deed is reflected in an ambiguity in the Czech language. In his essay collection *The Young Man and Death,* the philosopher Karel Kosík distinguishes between the positive and negative connotations of the word *obět'* (both "sacrifice" and "victim" in English). This interpretation restores Palach's deed to its proper place in Czech history:

> Through his sacrifice, the son takes over the obligations which the fathers neglected, but does not make claims at reward or honor. His act is a tear, a break, a caesura, which will always continue to disturb, irritate and provoke productive disputes about the meaning of life. The young man's death implores. It is only seemingly a denial of the famous saying: young men should work for their country, not die for it. In reality, it amplifies its power, because it shows the limits of normal situations.[43]

Although this passage asserts the "disturbance" that Palach's act continues to provoke, Kosík actually smooths over the ambiguity of his self-destruction, by reestablishing him as a dutiful "son" of the nation.[44]

Milan Kundera is best known for his novel *The Unbearable Lightness of Being* (1984), which explores the connection between politics and the body (a major theme through all of his work) and brought the "Prague Spring" back into the Western popular consciousness. His earlier novel *Life Is Elsewhere,* as Květoslav Chvatík explains, "ends with the great metaphor of time, the metaphor of fire, announcing the end of the era of revolution in Europe, the border of Palach."[45] In this novel, Kundera foreshadows the death of his protagonist, a naive young poet, suggesting that "the act of dying has its own semantics, and it matters how a man dies, and in what element." He continues with a comparison of Hus and Palach:

> Jan Hus and Giordano Bruno could not have died by the rope or by the sword; they could have died only at the stake. Their lives thus became the incandescence of a signal light, the beam of a lighthouse, a torch shining far into the space of time. For the body is ephemeral and thought is eternal, and the flicker of fire is the image of thought. Jan Palach, who . . . drenched himself with gasoline in a Prague square and set his body afire, would have been less likely to succeed in making his cry ring out to the nation's consciousness as a man who had drowned.[46]

In a different piece, Kundera suggests that Palach's deed overshadows the other national traumas of modern Czech history: "Not the world war, not the concentration camps, not the Stalinist terror but the burning body of Jan Palach filled me with a sense of the apocalypse." He warns that despite the frequent temptation to compare them, "Jan Palach, an adolescent, bore no resemblance to Jan Hus, one of the great intellectuals of the fifteenth century... The example of Hus, burned as a heretic, is difficult but not impossible to follow. To imitate the other Jan is inconceivable." He claims that at "the terrible moment of January 1969," the Czechs "saw the history of their country as if in fast motion: like the passage between two flames, the one that burned the body of Jan Hus and the one that burned the body of Palach. With the first, their country appeared on the scene of Europe, with the second, it disappeared from it."[47] In his 1984 essay "Paris or Prague," Kundera also treats Palach's deed with notable ambivalence: "The fire which Jan Palach lit with his own body in January 1969 to protest against the fate which had befallen his land (his desperate act, it seems to me, is as foreign to Czech history as the ghostly sight of Russian tanks)— that fire brought a period of history to a close."[48] As in his influential essay "The Tragedy of Central Europe," also written in the early 1980s, Kundera describes the Soviet occupation as the death knell for Western culture in his homeland. In all of these references, Kundera emphasizes the horrifying image of Palach's "burning body" as lying beyond the normal limits of national identity. The Russian poet Joseph Brodsky, arguing against Kundera's claims, also alludes to Palach: "Western civilization and its culture... is based first of all on the principle of sacrifice, on the idea of a man who died for our sins... It's too early to bid farewell to Western culture, even in Prague, if only because of Jan Palach, the Czech student who immolated himself publicly in January 1969 as a protest against the Russian occupation."[49] While they are ideologically opposed in their views of history and culture, the one point upon which these two East European exile writers can agree is the lasting significance of Palach's deed, whether as a sign of the end of Western civilization or of its resilience.

Another Czech novelist, Libuše Moníková (who emigrated from Prague to West Berlin after '68 and wrote only in German) used her own experience of exile for a metaphorical exploration of the connection between nation, resistance, and the body. Most of her novels contain explicit references or implicit allusions to Palach as a recurrent symbol of Czechoslovakia's subjugation within the Soviet empire.[50] Moníková was in a cinema on Wenceslas Square, literally within a few meters of Palach, at the time of his self-immolation. "If he would have cried out," she notes, "I could have heard his scream."[51] *The Façade: M.N.O.P.Q.* (1987), the only one of her works currently translated into English, features a character based on the real-life sculptor Olbram Zoubek (called Olbram Maltzahn in the novel.)[52] Most of Part One of the novel takes place in a small Czech town, where Maltzahn and several other artists are painstakingly restoring the historic façade of the castle. They are visited by a group from a nearby collective farm, whose bookkeeper bears a surprising resemblance to Alexander Dubček:

> Watching him walk away, Maltzahn remarks to Podol, "At least he's still alive. All that's left of Palach is the death mask I was able to make."
>
> "Have you ever known a politician who would set fire to himself?" Podol is too old a hand to be impressed by a deposed party functionary.[53]

Dubček (who was then living in relative obscurity) is also sometimes seen as a victim of the Soviet occupation—even Kundera describes him in sympathetic terms in *The Unbearable Lightness of Being*. For the jaded middle-aged Czechs of Moníková's *Façade*, however, Dubček is still just a "functionary" whose personal sufferings cannot be compared to the ultimate sacrifice of the young martyr Palach.

The artists are later joined by a young archivist named Nordanc from Luxembourg. After moving to Prague with a Czech lover in '68, Nordanc decides to stay after the invasion, even after his lover has left the country. Although doubly marginalized as the only non-Czech and only gay man in the group, Nordanc also identifies closely with Jan Palach's deed, and even witnessed its immediate aftermath, as he describes to one of the artists, Podol:

> "I started down Wenceslaus Square in a kind of daze, and a few steps ahead was a small group of people standing around a piece of paper nailed to a tree: 'A half hour ago a young man burned himself to death here; his name is unknown.'...A few days later I was coming back from work...about forty people were walking down the street carrying a sign: Jan Palach Died of His Burns Today...Then they dug him up, Palach I mean, stole the body one night, so that there'd be an end to all the candles and the silent crowds at the grave...Overnight, people started calling Red Soldier's Square, in front of the School of Philosophy, Jan Palach Square...after a few weeks, it all stopped again. But to this day, the most beautiful square in Luxembourg is called Jan Palach Square."
>
> "I didn't know that. I don't know much about Luxembourg."
>
> "I even have a picture of it. Wait, here it is." Nordanc pulls a color photo from his cupboard: he is leaning, slim and laughing, against a wall, above him the name Jan Palach.[54]

Through Nordanc's story, two young Czech men (the departed lover, and the unseen hero) blend into a narcissistic figure of desire (the photograph from Luxembourg emphasizes his own self-identification with Palach). In the scholarship on Moníková's work, *The Façade* (with few major female characters) has been relatively overlooked, and Nordanc has received little critical attention (despite his anomalous role as the only gay character), but one possible key to interpreting his character is through Jan Palach.[55] Both Nordanc and the author are voluntary exiles, who moved across the Iron Curtain for emotional rather than political reasons (Moníková for her West German husband, the Luxembourger for his faithless Czech). Like Moníková herself, Nordanc was in a cinema on Wenceslas Square (even watching the same film, the 1964 Japanese *Onibaba*) at the moment of Palach's self-immolation. Perhaps Nordanc, who enters this all-male artistic group marked by sexual difference, is a transgendered alter ego of Moníková herself, slyly confronting the often misogynist Czech literary world from her seemingly marginalized position in exile.

While Moníková uses Nordanc to satirize the somewhat masochistic identification of Western Europeans with "Eastern Bloc" suffering, she also demonstrates Palach's genuine function as an icon of resistance far beyond the Czech context. In Part Two of the novel, the group travels to Siberia en route to Japan. When an oncoming blizzard prevents their flying onward, a young Russian named Oleg leads them to a cabin where they can wait out the snowstorm. However, after they are trapped together for several days, tempers flare and Podol begins to blame the Russian personally for the Warsaw Pact invasion:

> "Have you ever heard of the 'intervention' in Czechoslovakia in '68?…And Jan Palach…do you know the name?" Oleg shakes his head; his eyes are set hard, his eyelids half closed.
>
> "Back off!" Orten pulls Podol away.
>
> "Who is Jan Palach?" Oleg follows them.
>
> "He was a student, about your age, who set himself on fire to protest your help! And there were others, Jan Zajíc…"
>
> "I didn't know any of this! I swear. No one did!…We didn't have any idea! We were fifteen years old!"
>
> "They sent soldiers that age, too," Podol replies.

Intimidated by the Czech's hostility toward him, Oleg runs away from the group, but Nordanc runs after him and has the last word. When he returns to the cabin alone, Nordanc tells the others: "[Oleg] asked me if people know about Jan Palach in Luxembourg. I told him that we'd named a town square after him. The Czechs weren't allowed to do that in their own country."[56] Thus the "imaginary body" of Palach has inspired an alliance between the Czechs and the West—as well as a symbolic victory over the Soviets in the heart of Siberia.

Another use of Jan Palach as an international icon can be seen in Dubravka Ugresić's 1988 novel *Fording the Stream of Consciousness,* set at an international writers' conference in Zagreb. A Croatian and an American are drinking toasts to various writers and cultural figures, culminating in the Beatles, when they are suddenly interrupted by a Czech writer, who proposes Jan Palach. Because Zdražil (the Czech) does not speak English, Pipo (the Croatian) is ironically forced to toast Palach's memory in Russian, their only common language: "'I drink, you drink...*pyom za Jana Palacha!*' said Pipo, straining to bring back the Russian he had learned in elementary school. '*Ponimaesh?* Understand? To Jan Palach!'...Zdražil smiled sadly. Even though his nerves had calmed down, he was on the verge of tears out of sympathy for the Czech martyr."[57] Even as she places the image of Jan Palach in the foreground, Ugresić emphasizes the Czech writer's almost hysterical lack of self-control (he is later shown naked, crying, on a toilet), symbolizing the Czech nation's lack of control over its own destiny since '68.

In the short story "Desires, the Erotica of Communism," by the Bulgarian writer Ivailo Dichev, Jan Palach takes on a specifically sexual significance (although his function as a figure of desire is bitterly ironic.) For Dichev's narrator, the best way to show solidarity with the Czechs after the Soviet invasion is through a freedom that parallels the sexual liberation practiced by hippies, students, and other social rebels in the West: "As a sign of protest, we organized mass gatherings all over the country where we participated in promiscuous sexual acts...Among the forms of our taking the law into our own hands were the most amazing objects: belts, whips, desecration of holy sites, and of course orgasms." This liberation comes to an end with Jan Palach's death, which reduces the sexual festivities to the hopelessness of masturbation:

And in spite of everything, one fine day, they broadcast the news that the Czech student Jan Palach had doused himself with petrol and burned like a torch in the centre of the city. Then, filled with furious powerlessness, I set off toward Party Headquarters in order to masturbate so that the splashes would reach the star on top and everything would collapse and end.[58]

Dichev's defiance of power through public sexuality attempts to challenge "history's destruction of the body" through a bodily destruction of history. Palach's "burning body" outshines the glowing star of Communism, despite the narrator's feeling of powerlessness.

In January 1989, a week before the twentieth anniversary of Palach's death, Václav Havel received an anonymous letter, supposedly from a group of students who identified with Havel's activity in the Charter 77 dissident movement. The letter claimed that "in the afternoon of January 15, 1989, a human torch will once more blaze alongside the horse in Wenceslas Square." In a public address broadcast on Voice of America, Radio Free Europe, and other media, Havel urged the sender not to follow through with this plan. "It is an appalling tactic never to be repeated. After all, before his death, Palach himself appealed to his friends to try to understand his action as a plea for a life of dignity, and something not to be repeated."[59] While no copycat incident occurred in 1989, the Palach anniversary did have a significant political impact when authorities prevented representatives of Charter Seventy-Seven (including Havel) from delivering a speech in Palach's honor on Wenceslas Square. This event marked an increasing boldness among those resisting the regime, and a stronger sympathy among the general public for their activities.[60] Martin C. Putna's novel *Kniha Kraft* (*The Book of Kraft,* 1996) recounts the tensions and hopes surrounding the Palach anniversary from the perspective of a student (too young to remember '68) who attends underground seminars and contemplates religious conversion: "Some lunatic wrote a letter to Havel saying that he wants to repeat [Palach's deed]. I disagreed with this pious act from the beginning. It still strikes me, I can't help it, as a glorification of suicide...Yet I did the only thing I could, that is, I prayed that everything would turn out all right." As Putna's narrator notes, observing the beating of demonstrators on the square, "It was already clear that for a long time now it hasn't been Palach at stake." [61] In November, the "Velvet Revolution" led to the rapid and peaceful fall of the Communist regime, and less than a year after the "Palach Week" protests of 1989, Havel had become President of Czechoslovakia.

As Aviezer Tucker observes in his analysis of the Czech dissident movement, "Free and available information enabled the free competition between ideas that destroyed the spirit of totalitarianism even while its body was still rotting slowly."[62] While Tucker does not mention Palach, it is clear from his metaphor that the "burning body" of the Czech student outlasted the "rotting body" of the regime he had resisted. Had he lived until the end of Communism, Palach would still only have been in his early forties, younger than many of the dissidents who had taken leading roles in the new government (which itself was considerably more youthful than the Communist regime). In fact, unlike most of the other national icons across Eastern Europe, Palach could be seen, even in 1989, as forever young.

Reason and Sacrifice: The Ambiguities of Martyrdom

Palach was only one of many figures across the region who had been buried in unmarked graves or had died in exile during the Communist period
and had been officially ignored by the ruling regimes. Soon after the revolution, Jan Palach was reburied in his original grave in Prague. Discussing
"the political lives of dead bodies," Katherine Verdery suggests that such
renewed attention to the graves of such national figures served "to institute ideas about morality by assessing accountability and punishment...to
redefine the temporalities of daily life...and thereby to reconfigure the
communities people participate in," during the deep uncertainties of
the immediate post–Communist period.[63] In the peaceful setting of the
Olšany cemetery, where Habsburg-era tombstones are decorated with
quaint gilded inscriptions, Palach's grave stands out: the full-sized, starkly
abstract sculpture by Olbram Zoubek, representing his disfigured body,
lies prone upon the marble slab, while his name (carved along the bottom)
is at first glance almost invisible. Even as Palach's remains were returned
to Prague, his "imaginary body" was reinstated at one of the most youthful spots on the Prague cityscape: the square in front of the Philosophical
Faculty was once again named after him, and his inconspicuous monument on the front of the university building features a replica of his death
mask by Zoubek. Looking down Kaprova Street from one corner of Jan
Palach Square, one can see the birthplace of a Prague native who was
famously obsessed with the destruction of imaginary bodies: Franz Kafka
Square. A memorial to both Palach and Zajíc was also installed near the
site of their self-immolations on Wenceslas Square.

The flood of Czech publications in the 1990s on previously taboo subjects included several books on Palach. The memoir *A Light at Dusk* (1994)
by Palach's history teacher Miroslav Slach creates an intimate if idealizing
portrait from the perspective of someone who not only knew the young
man well, but was in some ways a substitute father figure. The Czech
national tragedy is personalized through the grief of Jan's widowed mother
Libuše, "who received letters from around the world, celebrating the heroic
deed of her son Jan, squares and streets of world capitals were renamed
after him, abroad they built memorials to him, wrote poems, perhaps even
books about him...But no one could bring him back to her."[64] Visiting
Libuše Palachová for the first time since her son's death, Slach also presents
a striking moment of confrontation with Palach's "imaginary body." Left
alone in his former student's empty bedroom, he looks through the books
(including two that he had lent Palach) and newspaper clippings (including those about Buddhist monks who had set themselves on fire in protest
against the war in Vietnam): "I sat down at Jan's desk. It was difficult for

me. Such a beautiful and pure boy. Why did everything have to happen the way it did? History is sometimes basically cruel."[65] This tragic family symbolizes the nation: the son's body, destroyed by history, has "kindled a flame" of conscience around the world, but the solitary figure of the Czech mother is left to fulfill the traditional feminine role of mourning and remembrance. An interview with Slach and his wife Blažena on the thirtieth anniversary of Palach's death in 1999 reveals Slach's hagiographic tendency: after explaining that Palach read the Old West novels of German author Karl May (featuring "red Indians who suffered bravely and bore pain without letting anybody know about it"), he adds, "And he liked sports—" At this moment, Blažena Slachová (only slightly older than Palach, and also one of Slach's former students) interrupts him: "No, he didn't. He was a bookworm...I knew Jenda [Jan] pretty well. He was dark-haired and handsome, but in a soft way because he didn't exercise that much."[66] The attempt to create a more "manly" Jan Palach has been thwarted by his own contemporary, whose memory of his physical "softness" intrudes on the construction of the immortal "imaginary body."

In the post–Communist period, the culture of consumption has grown rapidly, even as job security has dropped sharply. While prostitution has exploded across the region, the Czech Republic has become a focal point for male prostitution and pornography.[67] Many young men, with few options in a time of growing economic disparity, are willing to sell the only thing available: their bodies. The Irish writer Desmond Hogan's novel *A Farewell to Prague* ironically pinpoints the discrepancy between the "imaginary body" of resistance and the economic realities of the early 1990s: "[T]here are little photographs of Jan Palach and Jan Zagik [*sic*] stuck on telephone kiosks. 'Let us never forget boys,' a poster says outside the Hussite Church...[On Wenceslas Square] under the Air France sign, a male prostitute waits. He has one gold tooth."[68] Hogan's intentionally comic omission of the definite article from the memorial poster perhaps unintentionally suggests that while Palach and Zajíc are remembered, a whole generation of "boys" is in the process of being forgotten. The body (beaten, imprisoned, exiled, or even killed) is no longer a symbol of Czech resistance, but has become just another commodity for Western consumers in search of "the exotic" at bargain prices.[69]

When Havel finished his final term as Czech President in 2003, the election for his successor had a living connection to the "burning body" of Jan Palach. One of the main candidates, Jaroslava Moserová, was a burn specialist who was one of the last people to see Palach alive. The aftermath of this highly contested election (in which Prime Minister Václav Klaus defeated Moserová after three rounds of voting) also carried tragic echoes of Jan Palach.[70] A day before Klaus was sworn in as President, an eighteen-year-old student named Zdeněk Adamec set himself on fire on Wenceslas Square, and died less than an hour later. In his farewell note (which he began optimistically, "Dear citizens of the whole world!") Adamec referred to Jan Palach, criticized the current state of national and international affairs, and called himself "Action Torch 2003."[71] On the first day after the suicide, the Czech press mentioned its possible political aspect, but by that weekend (with unexpected echoes of the Communist regime's attempts to discredit Palach in 1969) media coverage focused on the student's connections with illegal groups over the Internet, as well as his abnormal dependence on his mother. Such an adolescent could not be "transformed into a hero," much less a national sacrifice. With tensions high in the Middle East, the incident received little notice in the international press, despite Adamec's avowed hope to address "the whole world." An article that appeared in the *New York Times* the following week quotes Jaroslava Moserová's assertion that "the situation in the country is not the same as it was" in 1969, although she adds that "there is a great feeling of despair arising among young people today."[72] Disturbingly, Adamec's death apparently inspired a resurgence in self-immolations: at least four other Czechs (including one woman) attempted suicide by fire in March and April 2003. However, with the growth of global terrorism, the spectacle of violent self-destruction has become almost commonplace, and the 2003 suicides were perceived as a perverse trend far removed from Jan Palach's original act of resistance.

Moserová's autobiographical monologue "Letter to Wollongong" is a description of Jan Palach's death by a surgeon who treated him in his final days and was later interrogated about her role in the incident. Written in the form of a letter to the speaker's brother, who emigrated to Australia, it focuses on resistance and submission to the Communist regime after '68. "You know," she tells him, "we, as a nation, didn't lose when the armies invaded…no, *we lost the moment we gave up.* That's why you left. *You saw it coming,* and that's why *he* did what he did…He set himself on fire in January 1969, because people were not only giving *up,* they were giving *in,* and that, of course, is much worse."[73] Even in the work of Moserová, who had direct contact with Palach's disfigured body in his final days, the physical image of the student fades into the background. Her contrast between "giving up" (which implies outward cooperation with the regime, but passive resistance) and "giving in" (suggesting full cooperation with the system) emphasizes the importance of resisting in the traditionally feminine "private sphere" even when the broader "public sphere" has already been lost. Moserová seems to suggest that the most lasting symbolism of Palach's "burning body" is for those who left Czechoslovakia after '68, yet it is the female narrator, sacrificing her freedom to remain in the "political body" of the state, who offers the truest resistance to the regime.[74]

The first full-length portrayal of Jan Palach in Czech fiction is Lenka Procházková's *Full Sun: The Story of Jan Palach* (2008). This novel, which presents the final months of Palach's life, from the Soviet invasion to his death, is divided into five parts: three are narrated in the third person from Palach's perspective, while two are presented as Palach's own diary entries. It includes "documentary" materials such as photographs from the period of the Soviet invasion, and the full text of the influential Prague Spring manifesto "Two Thousand Words" by Ludvík Vaculík.[75] By fictionalizing Palach's experiences, Procházková humanizes him, particularly in the portrayal of his relationship with his mother:

> "Did you bring [the mushrooms]?" she asked, turning from her sewing machine.
>
> "What? No…They're not growing. Turn on the radio!"
>
> "Did something happen?" […]
>
> "Mom, later, all right?"
>
> The reception was good, but the news wasn't. There had been shooting in the streets of Prague that afternoon […]
>
> "Can I talk now?" she asked meekly.
>
> "I'm sorry," he leaned over and kissed her hair. "I'm terrible!"
>
> "You're unhappy. Maybe…you should have a girlfriend. That would help."[76]

Like all of the writers who have represented Jan Palach in literary form, however, Procházková cannot provide a real answer to the question: what inspired Jan Palach to commit his unthinkable deed? She suggests in one of the "diary" sections (although there is no proof that Palach actually knew about Siwiec) that Palach heard about Siwiec's self-immolation from a Polish student he met in Paris: "A nightmare…Such things aren't done in Europe. Only in Vietnam. But there monks burn themselves. Buddhists…I imagined it. A normal person cannot do such a thing. But where are the limits of normality?"[77] In her afterword to the novel, Procházková explains her motivation for writing the novel, particularly her desire to preserve Palach's memory for those too young to remember the atmosphere of his times. She quotes extensively from interviews she had conducted with university students in 1988, whose knowledge of Palach ranges from vague to wildly inaccurate. For many of her readers twenty years later, the memory of the Prague Spring and the invasion is even more remote than it was for students in the late Communist period. She concludes by comparing Palach's radical deed to the passivity of most of the nation:

> while Jan Palach deliberated and acted like a man (a politician, strategist and soldier in one individual), society behaved like a woman, the

mother of the family, who instinctively defends her other endangered "young." She seems not to perceive that this passive, hopeless and tearful protection jeopardizes, for a long time, (!) that whole endangered homeland.[78]

Through his deliberation and action (his "qualities of the spirit" and "heroic deeds," as Verdery suggests), Palach attempts to lead his nation to freedom, but its maternal instinct of protection (like Korbel's "will to survive") actually threatens its future. Procházková's comparison echoes Moira Gatens's critique of the "imaginary body," implying that "reason and sacrifice" is an individual, masculine quality in contrast to the collective, feminine passivity of Czech society.

In 2008, French Prime Minister Nicolas Sarkozy officially offered the Czech Republic an abstract memorial to Jan Palach, showing a body surrounded by flames, created in 1969 by the late Hungarian sculptor András Beck. This gesture revived the sense of Palach as an international symbol of Czech resistance across national boundaries. Nonetheless, officials in Prague rejected the gift, stating that the sculpture should remain in France. The mayor of Mělník, where Palach had attended school, promptly suggested his own town as an appropriate site for the memorial, which was approved by the French authorities. The dedication ceremony for Beck's sculpture was held in Mělník on the fortieth anniversary of Palach's death in January 2009. The occasion was also marked by such events as an exhibit in Prague and a seminar at Charles University, yet the displacement of Beck's "burning body" sculpture from its intended setting in Prague to a small park in a provincial town symbolizes Palach's increasing marginalization from his former role as an icon of resistance. With the Czech Republic now integrated into the European Union and rapidly becoming an "ordinary" Western country, it seems that Jan Palach is no longer a torch of freedom burning through the darkness of oppression, but has been reduced to a candle flickering in a corner of the Czech national memory.[79]

Notes

1. Alan Levy, "Miroslav Slach: Remembering Jan Palach," *Prague Post* (January 13, 1999): B2.
2. Robert Pynsent has described Palach not only as part of the "Czech martyr complex" but as "a solar deity of a kind," whose memory was kept alive for twenty years "like the memory of Christ in the disciples between Good Friday and Easter Day." See Pynsent, *Questions of Identity: Czech and Slovak Ideas of Nationality and Personality* (Budapest: Central European University Press, 1994), 209.
3. As Holy notes, "Palach's death directly evoked Hus's betrayal by foreigners and the inspiration of a movement in which the Czechs played their most significant role in Europe ever.

It was these two particular connotations of Hus's death which gave a particular meaning to Palach's death and made him a symbol of resistance to the post–'68 regime." Ladislav Holy, *The Little Czech and the Great Czech Nation* (Cambridge: Cambridge University Press, 1996), 44–45.

4. Michel Foucault, *The Foucault Reader,* ed. Paul Rabinow (New York: Pantheon, 1984), 83.

5. The most complete biography available is Jiří Lederer, *Jan Palach: Zpráva o životě, činu a smrti českého studenta* (Prague: Novinář, 1990); first published in German as *Jan Palach* (Zurich: Unionsverlag, 1982). No full-length biography or study of Jan Palach has been published in English. See also the thesis by Rebecca A. Forest, *Torch: The Changing Views of Jan Palach's Self-Immolation in Prague* (Fairfax, VA: George Mason University, 2006).

6. Entrance to the humanities departments such as history, in particular, was often determined according to the student's political background rather than academic qualifications.

7. This letter was only discovered by historians almost forty years after Palach's death. See Petr Blažek, Patrik Eichler, Jakub Jareš et al., eds. *Jan Palach '69* (Prague: Univerzita Karlova, 2009), 600–602.

8. Several Americans had also died by self-immolation in sympathy with the Vietnamese, such as Norman Morrison in front of the Pentagon.

9. Kieran Williams, *The Prague Spring and Its Aftermath: Czechoslovak Politics, 1968–1970* (Cambridge: Cambridge University Press, 1997), 189–190.

10. Pier Paolo Pasolini, *Il caos* (Rome: Editori Riuniti, 1979), 129. For more on Pasolini's last play, which is set in Czechoslovakia and alludes to Palach, see my previous article, "The Burden of Ideology: Pasolini as Czech Poet in *Bestia da stile*," *Slovo* 15 (Spring 2003): 73–86.

11. Kurt W. Treptow, *From Zalmoxis to Palach: Studies in East European History* (Boulder: East European Monographs, 1992), 130.

12. Josef Korbel, *Twentieth-Century Czechoslovakia: The Meanings of Its History* (New York: Columbia University Press, 1977), 253.

13. Václav Havel, *Open Letters* (New York: Knopf, 1991), 42–43.

14. Eugen Steiner, *The Slovak Dilemma* (Cambridge: Cambridge University Press, 1973), 208. Steiner's inclusion of the Slovaks is notable in view of the post–1968 attempts by the Communist authorities to win Slovak loyalty by portraying the Prague Spring as a strictly Czech affair.

15. Ibid., 210–211.

16. Moira Gatens, *Imaginary Bodies: Ethics, Power and Corporeality* (London: Routledge, 1996), viii.

17. Ibid., 23, 25.

18. Ibid., 70.

19. Miroslav Holub, *Intensive Care: Selected and New Poems* (Oberlin: Oberlin College Press, 1996), 37.

20. Other Czech poets who wrote about Palach included Josef Kainar ("May I Be Delivered from Pain") and Josef Šimon ("…pyre…"). See Jiří Holý, *Writers under Siege: Czech Literature since 1945* (Brighton and Portland: Sussex Academic Press, 2008), 122–123.

21. Óndra Łysohorský, "Ballad of Jan Palach, Student and Heretic," in *Against Forgetting*, ed. Carolyn Forche (New York: Norton, 1992), 436. As a poet writing in the minority dialect of Lachian (between Czech and Polish), Łysohorský had faced considerable repression from Communist authorities.

22. David Shapiro, *A Man Holding an Acoustic Panel* (New York: Dutton, 1971), 30. This poem was later the inspiration for an opera by Connie Beckley in 1990, as well as a pair of sculptures by John Heyduk, exhibited at Prague Castle in 1991.

23. Charles Marowitz, ed., *Palach*, in *Open Space Plays* (New York: Penguin, 1971), 207–208.

24. Ibid., 218.

25. Erwin Sylvanus, "Jan Palach," in *Stücke* (Frankfurt: Suhrkampe, 1980).

26. Martha Mehta, "Luna Alcalay's *Jan Palach*: An Introduction," *Cross Currents* 8 (1989): 267.

27. Ibid., 270.

28. Ibid., 278.

29. Ernesto Sabato, *The Angel of Darkness* (New York: Ballantine, 1991), 6–7.

30. Angel Cuadra, *The Poet in Socialist Cuba* (Gainesville: University Press of Florida, 1994), 143–144.

31. Angel Cuadra, *Requiem Violento por Jan Palach* (Miami: n.p., 1989.) (The work is not paginated.)

32. Musical compositions were among the earliest artistic responses in the West to Jan Palach's suicide, including a "Requiem per Jan Palach e altri" in 1969 by Giampaolo Coral, and an arrangement of "Funeral Music for Jan Palach" in 1970 by Walter Mays.

33. Petr Zídek, "Palachova zkratka na cestě do dějin," *Lidové noviny* (January 10, 2009): 1.

34. *Hear My Cry* (*Uslyszcie mój krzyk*), a 1991 Polish documentary about Siwiec, shows how his deed challenges national and gender identities. One eyewitness suggests that had Siwiec set himself ablaze during the Polish president's speech some time earlier, his act would have been seen as overtly political, but by doing so in the middle of a folk dance, his act was reduced to absurdity. An acquaintance of Siwiec in the documentary compares his self-immolation to a woman defending herself from rape (echoing the same gender ambiguity seen in Verdery's discussion of national borders). Yet a woman who witnessed the suicide says that it had "the same significance as a train accident."

35. Tadeusz Konwicki, *A Minor Apocalypse* (Chicago: Dalkey Archive Press, 1999), 226.

36. In 1983, the Polish artist and political refugee Wiktor Szostalo presented his "Performance for Freedom," in which he wore a sign saying, "I am Jan Palach. I'm a Czech, I'm a Pole, a Lithuanian, a Vietnamese, an Afghani, a betrayed you. After I burn myself a thousand times, perhaps we'll win." See Szostalo's home page, http://www.wsart.com/performance/jan_palach/freedom.html, accessed January 2009.

37. Katherine Verdery, "From Parent-State to Family Patriarchs: Gender and Nation in Contemporary Eatern Europe," *East European Politics and Societies* 8:2 (Spring 1994): 242.

38. Ibid., 248–249.

39. Ibid., 246.

40. A poem dedicated to Palach even appeared in a Russian emigré journal: see Eduard Nekrasov, "Jan Palach," *Kovcheg* 3 (1979): 1.

41. Eva Kantůrková, "On the Ethics of Palach's Deed," in *Good-bye, Samizdat: Twenty Years of Czechoslovak Underground Writing*, ed. Marketa Goetz-Stankiewicz (Evanston: Northwestern University Press, 1991), 177.

42. Daniela Hodrová, *Podobojí* (Ustí nad Labem: Severočeské nakladatelství, 1991), 120, cited in Robert Porter, *An Introduction to Twentieth-Century Czech Fiction: Comedies of Defiance* (Brighton: Sussex Academic Press, 2001), 165.

43. Karel Kosík, *Jinoch a smrt* (Prague: Hynek, 1994), 30, cited in Libuše Koubská, "Same Age, New Generation," *New Presence* (January 1999): 9.

44. See also the 1969 essay by Jinděich Chalupecký, "Smysl oběti," in *Tíha doby* (Olomouc: Votobia, 1997).

45. Květoslav Chvatík, *Svět románů Milana Kundery* (Brno: Atlantis, 1994), 69.

46. Milan Kundera, *Life Is Elsewhere* (New York: HarperPerennial, 2000), 293–294. *Life Is Elsewhere* was the last novel Kundera wrote in Czechoslovakia; it was originally published in French in 1973. The Czech original mentions Jan Hus but not Palach; Kundera added the latter while thoroughly revising the French translation of the novel in the 1980s.

47. Milan Kundera, "Esch Is Luther," afterword to Carlos Fuentes, *Terra Nostra* (New York: Farrar, Straus, Giroux, 1976 [afterword copyright 1983]), 779–780.

48. Milan Kundera, "Paris or Prague?," *Granta* 13 (Autumn 1984): 19.

49. Joseph Brodsky, "Why Kundera Is Wrong about Dostoevsky," *New York Review of Books* (February 17, 1985): 31.

50. The names of several of Moníková's characters allude to Palach, including the female tram driver Jana in her first novel *An Injury* (*Eine Schädigung,* 1981), which is dedicated to him. Although Palach is not mentioned in the text, the novel focuses on physical violence with political overtones (Jana is raped by a policeman, and she kills him in retaliation). The protagonist of Moníková's second novel, *Pavane for a Dead Princess* (*Pavane für eine verstorbene Infantin,* 1983) is named Francine Pallas, alluding to both Palach and Franz Kafka.

51. Libuše Moníková, *Prager Fenster* (Munich: Hanser, 1994), 113.

52. Květoslav Chvatík's review of *The Façade* dwells on Palach at length, explaining that he and Moníková were students at Charles University at the same time and "could have been class-mates;" he also claims (writing twenty years after Palach's death) that "today few people of the younger generation in Prague know [Palach's] name, and the way he looked has been completely forgotten." See Chvatík, "*Fasáda* Libuše Moníkové," *Listy* 18:3 (1988): 105.

53. Libuše Moníková, *The Façade: M.N.O.P.Q.* (New York: Knopf, 1991), 30.

54. Ibid., 152–53.

55. For example, Helga G. Braunbeck's otherwise perceptive study refers to the novel's "four male picaresque heroes." See Braunbeck, "The Body of the Nation: The Texts of Libuše Moníková," *Monatshefte* 89:4 (1997): 495.

56. Moníková, *The Façade*, 290–291.

57. Dubravka Ugresić, *Fording the Stream of Consciousness* (Evanston: Northwestern University Press, 1993), 55.

58. Ivailo Dichev, "Desires: The Erotica of Communism," in *Description of a Struggle,* ed. Michael March (New York: Vintage, 1994), 192.

59. Jan Vladislav, ed., *Czechoslovakia: Heat in January 1989* (London: Centre for the Promotion of Independent Czechoslovak Literature, 1989), 62.

60. The Czech novelist Bohumil Hrabal describes the hopes and tensions of early 1989 in his essay "The Magic Flute," in the collection *Total Fears* (Prague: Twisted Spoon Press, 2001), 9–22.

61. Martin C. Putna, *Kniha Kraft: Ein Bildingsroman* (Prague: Torst, 1995), 50.

62. Aviezer Tucker, *The Philosophy and Politics of Czech Dissidence from Patocka to Havel* (Pittsburgh: University of Pittsburgh Press, 2000), 169.

63. Katherine Verdery, *The Political Lives of Dead Bodies: Reburial and Postsocialist Change* (New York: Columbia University Press, 1999), 127.

64. Miroslav Slach, *Světlo v soumraku* (Prague: Gloria Kyjov, 1994), 64.

65. Ibid., 67. (The Czech "*čistý*" means both "pure" and "clean," suggesting physical as well as spiritual purity.)

66. Levy, "Miroslav Slach," B2.

67. Several documentaries (treading uncertain ground between empathy and voyeurism) have explored the dangerous world of young Czech male prostitutes; one of them is aptly titled *Body without Soul.*

68. Desmond Hogan, *A Farewell to Prague* (London: Faber, 1995), 114–115.

69. See also Matti Bunzl, "The Prague Experience: Gay Male Sex Tourism and the Neocolonial Invention of an Embodied Border," in *Altering States,* ed. Martha Lampland (Ann Arbor: University of Michigan Press, 2000), 70–95.

70. The Czech Republic does not have direct elections for its president, who is elected by the Parliament.

71. "Nelíbí se mi dnešní svet, psal sebevrah," *MF Dnes* (March 7, 2003): A3.

72. Peter S. Green, "Student's Suicide Leads Czechs to Bout of Soul-Searching," *New York Times* (March 12, 2003).

73. Jaroslava Moserová, *Letter to Wollongong* (n.p., 1993), 3. Manuscript courtesy of the Czech Centre, London.

74. For another testimony by a medical witness to Palach's final days, see Marie Vojtová, *Proč jsem nemluvila* (Trebíč, 1996).

75. While this manifesto is one of the most important documents of protest from '68, it also illustrates the complex relationship between the political and the personal in Procházková's work: Vaculík was not only a major leader of the Prague Spring, but also her former lover.

76. Lenka Procházková, *Slunce v úplňku: Příběh Jana Palacha* (Prague: Prostor, 2008), 89.

77. Ibid., 124–125.

78. Ibid., 266.

79. My research in Prague was conducted while at the Institute for Czech Studies in fall 2002, supported by a fellowship from the American Councils for International Education and the U.S. Department of State, Program for Research and Training on Eastern Europe and the Independent States of the former Soviet Union. I would also like to thank Jonathan Bolton, Madelaine Hron, and Jitka Malečková for their helpful comments on various drafts of this essay.

CHAPTER NINE

Ambiguous Subjects:
The Autobiographical Situation and
the Disembodiment of '68

MICHELLE JOFFROY

On October 2, 1968, while Mexico City prepared to host the '68 Summer Olympics, government tanks patrolled the city's main streets, and "hundreds (some estimates say thousands) of students were massacred in Tlatelolco...their bodies...burned or dumped in the ocean."[1] The popular student movement was effectively silenced, symbolically "disappeared" on the bodies of the dead and missing.

Historically, the massacre marked the culmination of over a decade of civil protest in the name of cultural, political, educational, and economic reform. And though some critics maintain "what actually happened during the summer of 1968...is more a matter for historians than for students of literature," others point to the dominant, indeed indispensable, role that literature has played in documenting and dramatizing the crisis.[2] In fact, Tlatelolco and the events of the summer of '68 have inspired more than thirty novels, commonly referred to as the *novela del 68* (novel of 68). As Gonzalo Martré argues, "[literary works] at that moment, and since then, represented what journalists, mortified by their conventional self-censorship, would not chronicle in the pages of history."[3] In the wake of those "missing" bodies, it is arguably to this literary body that we have looked for a narrative of that "ghost that sweeps across Mexico."[4]

As framed within contemporary Mexican social and cultural studies, the '68 student movement articulates a disjuncture in the State's historical narrative, which can now be divided into the roughly twenty-year period of political and economic stability *pre-'68* (the so-called Mexican miracle), and the subsequent political crisis and unmasking of the *true* Mexico, *post-'68*.[5] The student movement, and the government's violent repression of it, succeeded in disarticulating the PRI's (*Partido Revolucionario Institucional*) mythical narratives of an institutionalized democratic revolution, disrupting the coherence of a narrativized national, political, and cultural stability. Among the perceived political consequences of the student movement are post-'68 electoral reforms, the period of "democratic openness" of the Echeverría presidency (1970–1976) and the formation of oppositional leftist political parties as a challenge to PRI dominance.[6] The cultural implications of the student movement are perhaps even more far-reaching, inasmuch as it served as precursor and referent to subsequent regional cultural movements of the 1970s and innovative forms of popular urban organization beyond the limits of official state political parties.[7] The movement can thus be read as a catalyst precisely for the construction of alternative revolutionary bodies, spaces, and social agency beyond official state formations.

Unlike previous popular movements, the '68 student movement succeeded in galvanizing divergent sectors of Mexican society, not as one voice making a single demand, but rather as a multiplicity of discourses coalescing in a resounding rejection of an authoritarian Mexican state.[8] The movement and its violent repression effected a profound reconsideration of citizenship in relation to processes of democracy, cultural autonomy, and political action. In fact, in the aftermath of '68 Mexican intellectuals began to openly interrogate the state's own historicizing practices, as well as its relationship to imperialism within and beyond its borders. And literary intellectuals in particular, as noted above by Gonazalo Martré, interrogated the diverse political, social, and cultural meanings of '68.

It was in the context of a ruptured national, political, and cultural narrative of a revolutionary and democratic Mexican state that the *novela del 68* initially engaged the theoretical and philosophical questions of the representation of history, culture, and state subjects, through the overt critique and deconstruction of representational practices, as revealed in autobiographical metafictional texts. Autobiographical and testimonial accounts of the events of '68 emerged almost immediately following the massacre at Tlatelolco and the subsequent imprisonment of movement leaders. From such first-person "insider" narratives the *novela del 68* articulated the male experience of '68, from the perspective of those whom the movement empowered.[9] To the extent that a male perspective dominated from 1969 to 1982, however, the novels of '68 were traditionally read as the literary articulation of a masculine identitarian movement whose privileged intellectual male subject encompassed all possible readings and meanings of '68. Thus, while in the context of the movement these revolutionary autobiographical subjects "embodied" the ghosts of the silent and missing, and thus deconstructed a cohesive pre-'68 Mexican state and its stable subject formations, in a textualized post-'68 the male autobiographical "I" reproduced a specific masculine self whose own ideological, gender, and sexual coherence elided any potential subjective discontinuities.[10] In these early autobiographies the male body became the site for imagining the "I" of '68, effectively reproducing—at the level of sex and gender—the pre-'68 Mexican state as inscribed on a coherent and cohesive masculine citizen's body. My project, then, is to overtly examine the dynamics of sex and gender in women's novels about '68, precisely because sex and gender have traditionally been overlooked, or rendered invisible, as specific categories for the analysis of power relations in both the production and the reading of these texts.

In this essay I argue that María Luisa Puga's 1983 novel, *Pánico o peligro* interrogates the gendered imaginaries of 1968 and ultimately suggests a reading of the "I" of '68 beyond traditional, coherent binaries of sex and gender. *Pánico o peligro* is a response not only to the historical referent of the '68 student movement, I argue, but also to the textual event of the *novela del 68*, specifically because through its protagonist Susana, the novel establishes a critical dialogical relationship to the repesentative autobiographies of the *novela del 68*. This dialogical relationship is marked by a pronounced interrogation and reconfiguration of the textualized male subject of '68, through the strategic narrative device of autobiographical simulation, in which the autobiographical project itself is reoriented away from the self who writes and toward the construction of a self who reads. This strategy integrates not only a "metaliterary" conversation with the *novela del 68* by privileging the reader's position in the production of the text's—and history's—meaning, it also pursues a "cultural conversation" about the restrictive gender constructions of 1968 that haunt a post-'68 Mexico.[11] Ultimately, I propose, the novel opens a new site for imagining cultural actors and political subjectivities that challenge, disrupt, and disarticulate the dominant narratives of the Mexican '68.

When the "I" Speaks: Autobiography and '68

With the 1982 publication of Martha Robles's *Los octubres del otoño: biografías clandestinas*, the masculine narrative "I" of '68 experiences its first displacement in a novel that suggests the possibility of discourses critical of '68 emerging from the marginalized spaces of post-68 Mexican society. The titular reference to narrative subjects constructing alternative biographies of the Mexican '68 suggests an intertextual relationship with the early authoritative autobiographies, and establishes the referent of the textualized '68. In doing so, the novel articulates its own "worldliness": its always and already being enmeshed status in relationships to the author, the reader, historical situations, and "to other texts."[12] María Luisa Puga, I would argue, goes even further than Robles in articulating the text's worldliness by positing not only an alternative female narrator of '68, but an autobiographical "I" who explicitly interpellates and simultaneously resists the authoritative masculine subject of the early autobiographies of '68. In addressing her notebooks to an unnamed *tú* who configures '68, Puga's narrator imagines a '68 whose ambiguous body is beyond the fixed/fixable categories of male and female subjectivity. By refusing to textually "embody" *tú*, Susana resists the reproductive and repressive function of the earlier masculine "body"/"I" '68.

Pánico o peligro consists of twelve notebooks written sometime around 1979 by Susana, a twenty-seven-year-old legal secretary, and addressed to *tú*, Susana's current lover. Structurally, *Pánico o peligro* resists strict generic categories, instead integrating a number of genres: diary, journal, history, autobiography. Simultaneously revealing elements of all these, it nevertheless resists containment in any one of them. The unifying force in the novel is Susana's attempt to read and "tell" her self in the context of a complex social reality. Thus, the text is dominated by a specific situation that privileges Susana as both subject and object of the text.[13]

Critical scrutiny of *Pánico o peligro*'s first person narrative has resulted in an almost unanimous consensus about the feminist dimension of the novel and its grounding in the feminist practice of autobiographical writing.[14] Shifting the theoretical perspective away from a one-to-one correlation between author and text, and toward the fictionalization of the autobiographical act, I argue that it is Susana—and not María Luisa Puga—who is engaged in an autobiographical project. Susana is read, in my analysis, as a fictional character. Her processes of self-telling and interpretation of reality, in this setting, are literary representations, fictionalizations of autobiographical writing. Read, then, as a *simulation* of the autobiographical situation, the novel articulates a fictional autobiography and meta-literary text that comments on the processes of autobiographical writing and on the construction of a subject/self in dialogue with a specific cultural context. Furthermore, I propose that as the implied reader of the notebooks, *tú*'s textual/structural specificity (and, significantly, *tú*'s bodily ambiguity) exposes a process in which Susana's autobiographical subjectivity is explicitly constructed in reference to an acknowledged reader. That this reader configures an imagined "I" of '68—as I will argue below—reveals the construction of a post-'68 subjectivity always and already in critical dialogue with the historical and literary "bodies" of '68. And to the degree that Susana confers a bodily ambiguity, an openness, on *tú*, the novel reveals as well the potential for dialogue with a '68 constrained neither by historical time nor restrictive categories of sex and gender.

The Autobiographical Situation and the Reading Self

Viewed through the lens of classical autobiography theory, the early autobiographies of '68 articulate the paradigmatic autobiographical self: "the subject who has had to pay the price of world-habitation for access to itself." Quite literally, because of their status as political prisoners, the subjects of the early autobiographies constructed themselves narratively from a space of isolation and withdrawal from society. A paradigmatic example of this autobiographical self emerges in Luis González de Alba's 1971 autobiographical novel *Los Días y los Años*. In this novel, as Rubén Medina has eloquently noted, fiction and testimonial autobiography are combined in de Alba's construction of a self who systematically distances himself from all sectors of the political spectrum except his own political organization. Ultimately this self is one whose objective is to legitimize the leadership role of the *Consejo Nacional de Huelga* (the National Strike Committee) and to "affirm his political independence and ideological purity in contrast to the traditional Left."[15] While this narration of self posits the theory that only those narratives of '68 produced by participants in the student movement are "true" and that official government versions are not, it also isolates the self from any other potentially competing versions. This gesture, then, results in the actualization of that traditional autobiographical self whose identity can only be narrated in isolation from a complex world that may problematize his own theories of self and reality. The markedly heterosexual male body of de Alba's autobiography, I would argue, suggests as well a limited and ideologically isolating imaginary that forecloses the possibility of alternative constructions of sex and gender identity.

Susana, conversely, represents an alternative autobiographical self, a subject who "inhabits" the world through acts of reading and interpretation, and thus reorients the starting point of autobiography away from the private act of a self writing to the public or "cultural act of a self reading."[16] This shift not only privileges reading in the novel as constitutive of identity formation—by grounding Susana's post-'68 identity in specific kinds of reading acts—it also emphasizes '68 as a textual referent itself and suggests, in the affirmation of Susana's reading "I," the imperative for rereadings of '68's dominant (male) narratives and subjectivities. Ultimately, the metafictional critique highlights the role of extratextual readers, their identities, and their potential roles in the configuration of '68.

Reading happens at two points in the novel's simulated autobiographical situation: "by the autobiographer who, in effect, is 'reading' his or her life; and by the reader of the autobiographical text." Thus, though *tú* is structurally invoked as the text's reader, Susana, the "writer" also occupies the position of the reader, because "reader" identifies a position and not a person.[17] Furthermore, reading takes place within the parameters of concrete, recognizable social and historical situations. This self who reads, be it the autobiographer or the other reader(s) of the text, is the "*displayed self*," that is, the self "who speaks, who lives in time, and, by virtue of living in time...can thus experience the inter-and transpersonal grounds by which personal identity becomes possible."[18] What this implies, not merely for Susana but also for *tú*, is the cultural persistence of '68 in the construction of political subjectivities in post-'68 Mexico. The construction of a displayed autobiographical self, I argue, disarticulates the "hidden self" brought forth in classical autobiography and contests the totalizing force of the male "hidden selves" of the foundational autobiographies of '68. Simultaneously, the explicit interpellation of an ambiguous *tú* suggests a symbolic "outing" of the hidden—and haunting—selves of '68 who potentially exist beyond the gendered imaginary of the textual '68.

In *Pánico o peligro* Susana's autobiographical impulse, that which compels her move from "life" to "text," is manifested in her effort to confront the problem of temporality and somehow recuperate a lived past in the present reality—specifically a loving and intimate relationship with *tú*. This impulse to read her past so as to construct a self in the present— always bearing in mind that this present acknowledges the specific past of '68—resides at the intersection of the multiple ideological discourses of gender, class, race, ethnicity, and sexuality that construct Susana's subjectivity. On the first page of the first notebook Susana poignantly describes her own attempts at reading her life and her place in the world from the double writer/reader position that the autobiographical process suggests, juxtaposing two distinct reading sites: her memories of the past and the actual physical spaces that she knew as a child. "Remembering it now, I miss it...it hurts, well, I wouldn't want to live it again, but I do notice how I seek out certain smells, street corners, lights. I've gone back to Jalapa Street many times and the building is still there, older, more run-down; it saddens me...because I no longer find myself there."[19] Though Susana utilizes both memory and physical space as texts in an effort to narrate the meaning of her past, the definition of who and how she was, she ultimately is not able to easily "read" those meanings in either text. It is also painfully clear that she cannot "find" or locate herself in that past or in the texts (in this case the old building on Jalapa Street) that she reads. That she continues to write about, and in effect read her life despite these initial difficulties suggests that Susana is willing to confront some of the conflicts posed by reading a past that produced but ultimately does not reflect her. In the context of her overt interpellation of *tú* and the specific past of '68, this suggests, theoretically, a reading self who also interrogates that particular history's textual exclusions.

Throughout the novel Susana identifies specific incidents in her life that place her in a direct confrontation with reading as a problematic, not transparent, act. In this way, Susana's autobiographical perspective is shaped by her own resistant, oppositional, and contestatory reading acts. The self-as-reader that Susana represents is constructed in the context of her small circle of girlfriends, and specifically in resistance to Lourdes. As she notes in the very first notebook, Lourdes was "the most daring one...who was curious about everything." Of herself she writes, "Lourdes called me the gawker."[20] Susana thus establishes an oppositional relationship to Lourdes, which is sustained throughout the novel and forms the basis of an autobiographical perspective that resists specific kinds of reading acts: reading as an activity limited to texts and textuality—as embodied by Lourdes; reading as an uncritical assimilation of master texts that reproduce state subject formations—as embodied by Mateo; and reading as an exercise in theoretical abstractions—as embodied by Arturo. Susana narrates her self, always in the context of her direct interpellation of *tú*, from the contestatory perspective of a reader who interrogates precisely what constitutes a text and where its meanings and subjects are located.

In the case of *Pánico o peligro*, Susana's direct interpellation of *tú* also makes available for scrutiny the ways in which the reader exerts influence over the representation of self in autobiography in general and in Susana's notebooks in particular. Although never named or described physically, some aspects of *tú*'s history and identity are delineated in the novel, woven obliquely into the narrative as a parallel or point of (self) reference directly linked to Susana's history. Because Susana insists on invoking *tú*'s history, *tú* is revealed as the "silent" partner that is never named in traditional autobiographical writing, but whose power and influence are nonetheless exerted over the writing process.[21] *Tú* influences what I earlier described as the autobiographical impulse by virtue of a particular set of expectations, ideological perspectives, and discursive positions. *Tú*'s role as reader in the novel, then, becomes essential to its production of meaning, as the novel reveals the dynamic interaction between readers, texts, and the construction of the autobiographical "I."

Though Susana's representation of *tú* is not straightforward or direct, we are able to develop a sense of *tú*'s personal history, especially in relation to '68 and Tlatelolco. Early in the novel Susana refers to the years 1964–1965 and imagines *tú* as a seventeen-year-old who was "finishing high school." Three or four years later, in '68, *tú* would have been a twenty or twenty-one year-old. Thus, while Susana was on the cusp of that generation who experienced Tlatelolco and the student movement firsthand (recalling that she was fifteen when the massacre occurred), *tú* is unquestionably part of that generation. Therefore we can locate *tú*, the explicit reader of Susana's autobiography, in the context of '68 and the generation of left-wing political activists it produced.

The specific relationships that *tú* establishes with political and class identities are also discernible from Susana's representation. Politically *tú* is integrated into a university union, is an active contributor to political criticism in journals such as *Unomásuno*, and is active in left-wing Central American political solidarity activities. *Tú*'s political identity, manifested in activism, is rooted, in fact, in a worldview that has been shaped by a generational identity: "Sometimes, when you talk about 'your generation,' about what you believed in 'your day'…well, I envy you. You talk in this way of belonging to something that is completely unfamiliar to me."[22]Again, Susana makes an oblique reference to the generational politics of the youth who experienced '68, the violence of Tlatelolco, and its cultural and political aftermath. At the same time, it is evident that *tú*'s social position and professional life—*tú* is a party leader in an unnamed, leftist political party—result from a worldview and ideological perspective that have been shaped not just by oppositional politics but by class privilege as well. "I had never heard anyone talk about their past like you. Remembering yourself like that, as if nobody but you existed. Is that what it's like to be born into a certain class? What does it mean to you now? Is it about fighting for everyone's right to what you had? Is that what we call equality?"[23] Here, Susana openly questions a privileged, upper class model of revolution and social change predicated on a limited scope of subjectivities. Significantly, Susana takes *tú* to task for suggesting that revolution and social change are predicated on the reproduction of a limited and particular set of experiences.

Finally, *tú*'s representation of reality, at the level of discourse, is referred to as Susana critiques *tú*'s tendency to use language as a means of constructing and defining reality. From Susana's perspective, *tú*'s discursive position is one that limits interpretive possibilities because it is so fixed by rigidly defined categories of what constitutes political discourse: "I know that when you say 'the working class' you honestly think you know what you're talking about. You even talk about its 'recovery.' Ultimately, being a leftist means, to a great extent, *talking* like one."[24]As the designated reader of Susana's autobiographical notebooks, *tú*'s history and identity not only play into any possible personal response to the notebooks, but also directly influence the ways in which Susana tells and identifies herself. In *tú*, then, we have a reader who is both an internal and an external element in the autobiographical situation. *Tú* is implicated in the autobiographical impulse insofar as *tú*'s interpellated presence brings Susana to a moment of confrontation, or crisis, with her self and her history. Furthermore, *tú*'s presence/absence, along with Susana's desire to make her past available for reading in their present relationship, is what brings Susana to the moment of textualization.

Given the amount of information we have, we are able to imagine *tú* within specific contexts: that is, the generation of '68, left-wing politics, the upper middle class, and "progressive" sociopolitical discourse. The seeming "rhetorical" function of *tú*, then, is undercut by actual specificities of identity and what they represent in post-'68 Mexico. *Tú* actually functions as the external historical referent of '68 and its persistence in contemporary Mexican reality. From this perspective the autobiographical situation simulated in *Pánico o peligro*—a narrative situation influenced and shaped by the interpellated presence of '68—clearly establishes a contemporary dialogue with the early autobiographical texts of the *novela del 68*—authoritative narratives propelled and shaped by the potential disappearance of '68.

Positing *tú* as the historical referent of '68, as well as an integral structuring element in the production of meaning in the novel, I would argue that Susana is narrating her self, and constructing a cultural and political subjectivity, in response to the trace of '68 as it is revealed in *tú*'s identity. But beyond that, she clearly adopts a resistant and critical position in her reading of *tú*. This reading exposes limitations in *tú*'s—and '68's—political imaginary on two specific counts. Susan challenges *tu*'s/'68's "reproductive" model of social revolution—"Is it about fighting for everyone's right to what you had? Is that what we call equality?"—as well as *tú*'s/'68's limited revolutionary vocabulary—"…being a leftist means…talking like one." Significantly, Susana does not reject *tú* (or '68) wholly, but instead seeks a means of bringing *tú*'s history to meaningful relevancy in her life story—it is love for *tú* that, after all, compels her to write and narrate herself in dialogue with *tú*'s particular history. Susana's persistence, despite the potential discontinuities or limitations of *tú*'s political identity articulates, ultimately, the ways in which '68—as a particular set of limited readings and political identities—must also be reimagined, interpellated on the basis of its relevancy to other subject positions and cultural histories. To the extent that Susana interrogates the dominant modes of representing and reading *tú*, she is also suggesting the possibility of alternatives to ways of reading '68.

What I propose is that in *Pánico o peligro* María Luisa Puga opens up the possibilities for reading both the historical "I" of '68 as well the *novela del 68*. Susana's emphasis on the mechanisms of reading and narrating—reflected on one level in a displayed self who problematizes specific reading acts, and on another level in the interpellation of her reader—focuses attention on the fact that '68 has become a text to be read and interpreted, and that the meanings of that text are produced in a dynamic relationship between readers and the discontinuities, ambiguities, and contradictions of the text. I am not suggesting that '68 is merely a text without a connection to an objective reality. Nor am I arguing that Puga suggests this in the novel. What is at issue, though, is the fact that all historical events eventually are subjected to textuality, and that the experience of the historical "reality" will be, for many, limited to the ways in which, and by whom, those texts are read—and that these processes are always about power. If, in response to the presence of '68, as traced in an ambiguous *tú*, Susana rejects certain restrictive models of reading and proposes more open alternatives, this suggests that implicit in the novel is a possibility for broadening the traditional readings of '68.

Reading Ambiguity and Discontinuity:
Disembodying the "I" of '68

Throughout the novel Susana insists on the contradictions and complications inherent in the human experience that disrupt the purest theoretical models of both reading and subjectivity. Throughout the novel she refers to her own deficiencies, as well as the debilities of people in her life for whom she cares, without condemning or rejecting them. Instead of insisting on "perfect texts," Susana attempts to integrate the contradictions, limitations, and inconsistencies of these people from a perspective that ultimately contextualizes them in a complex reality. In this gesture Susana highlights her difference vis-à-vis the isolated male "I" of the early autobiographies of '68, with their implicit—and at times explicit—ideological and gendered purity. Susana moves about the world, reading not only in textual spaces, but often turning deliberately to a window, a marketplace, a photograph for an alternative to the confines of texts.

Susana engages not only alternative sites for reading but also alternative models. From her perspective, certain models of reading are sanctioned and privileged in ways that limit the potential for a broader or more complex understanding of what texts are and what '68 was and is. Significantly, these sanctioned models are "embodied" in the novel by specific identities: by Lourdes, who interprets reading as activity limited to texts; by Mateo, Susana's summer lover, who enacts reading as an uncritical assimilation of master narratives that reproduce state sanctioned subject formations; and by Arturo, another lover who converts reading into an exercise in mere abstraction, wholly disengaged from material reality. The alternative models for reading that Susana proposes throughout the novel ultimately advocate for a shift away from the limits of text and abstract theory to the broader forums of experiential knowledge and theories that include openness, ambiguity, difference, and contradiction as a closer reflection of reality. Ultimately these models reveal the possibilities for more relevant ways of reading '68 in a contemporary Mexico.

Thus when Lourdes recommends that Susana read the novel *One Hundred Years of Solitude*—in an unabashed project of "educating" Susana about her political and historical identity—Susan is put off by the novel's density of language, by the basic lack of space for engaging with the text or imagining herself as implicated in it. "I started reading and didn't understand a thing. I honestly tried, but I couldn't do it. I would look out the window, listen to other people's conversations. They would inspire me. They sounded like the habits of the everyday world."[25] In the novel's place Susana proposes the bus window and the street market as sites for reading that emphasize encounters and interaction with real people whose experiences are not subjected to the exigencies of textual style. From Susana's perspective, it could be argued that in this alternative model a reading of '68 is still available experientially beyond the boundaries of the page, in the stories of those who lived it, and not solely in the stories of those who, for various reasons, had access to the means of producing a "readable" text.

Similarly, her questioning of Mateo's master narratives suggests that cultural and political identity is much more fluid than what is implied in historical chronologies.[26] When Mateo discovers Susana reading the novel Pedro Páramo he readily approves. "'Very important,' he said, 'to understand History.'"[27] However, her experience of the novels of the Mexican Revolution—those that Mateo insist she read to understand history—is inscribed to a much greater degree by the voices of these novels' characters and their marginalized status. "If I found these books interesting and comprehensible it was because I felt that the people in them were the same as the people I met everyday. People on the streets [of San Blas]....But I wasn't understanding history. I wouldn't have been able to give him a chronology of the Revolution. In those books I saw and felt people. [I remember] the novel told by a woman, about a town that speaks its memories. I remember the crazy man who lived with prostitutes...I remember her voice...the shuttered houses."[28] Thinking about '68, Susana's readings suggest that its historical meaning might also be found in those marginalized voices that are not necessarily expressed in the sanctioned narrative histories of '68. It is not an outright rejection of historicity but rather an insistence on linking the readings of the historical past—specifically through the memory of the individuals who inhabit the text—to a present that is simultaneously being read.

Finally, Susana's oppositional stance toward Arturo's theoretical abstractions—readings that ultimately reject the complex reality toward which they are directed—suggests that '68 should be read not from within the confines of theoretically pure models, but rather with a grounding in the complex reality that produced it. When Arturo—who has "opted out" of the university system in pursuit of a more authentic experience of Marxist theories—actually confronts the "real" world, he is thoroughly frustrated by its disorderliness. Susana recalls the day when she and Arturo are having lunch in a small restaurant along with a group of laborers, who are seated at a nearby table. As Arturo attempts to explain "something about the modes of production, the laws of the marketplace," he is continually interrupted by the workers' boisterous music and their loud drinking and conversation. Finally he abruptly leaves the table and complains loudly to the cashier, "give me the check. It's impossible to talk in here; it's worse than a bar." As Susana wryly summarizes it, "it bothered him that the workers hadn't allowed him to reflect on class struggles."[29] To the extent that she rejects Arturo's model of reading, Susana suggests an alternative model in which difference and at times contradiction must be relevant factors that ground "stable" theoretical practice in a "disorderly" material reality.

Clearly, reading acts are central to Susana's construction of an autobiographical self, in terms of defining her relationship to *tú* '68, her self, and her world. And while I have argued throughout this essay that Susana's interpellation of *tú* is simultaneously an interpellation of '68, *tú* is not the only "reading" that Susana has of the student movement and the massacre at Tlatelolco. In fact, Susana's first encounter with '68 was through a newspaper story that Lourdes read to her and their friend Lola in the days immediately following the massacre—when the three girls were roughly fifteen years old. Though the "events" were taking place in the very city where she lived, Susana's initial experience of Tlatelolco was, ironically, mediated by its textualization. While Susana acknowledges that she had seen other newspapers in the past, this one she "truly" saw. "There it was, with pictures of the men murdered at Tlatelolco. Lourdes brought it: look, she said…the rows of dead men. While we were hanging out, look what was going on. I remember the look of horror on Lola's face; Lourdes's voice. The photograph. Lourdes read the article aloud but I hardly heard it, I just saw death. I saw those dead men, so many of them."[30]

Nevertheless, as the preceding passage emphasizes, the "text" of Tlatelolco itself, the actual narrative of the events, was subsumed by the photographs that accompanied the article. To a similar degree, the horrific meaning of the massacre is contained in the look on Lola's face and in the sound of Lourdes's voice—as opposed to the narrative itself. Tlatelolco and '68 are "read" and "remembered" by Susana, not in their textuality, but rather in their figurative "embodiments": in the bodies of dead men, on the faces and in the voices of young women. Susana's resistance to texts is revealed in this initial reading of '68, wherein its "meanings" are constructed beyond the limits of the page. Furthermore it is significant that, while Susana makes explicit the historical, cultural gaze on the male body as a site for constructing '68's meanings, she simultaneously resists the demarcation of that body as the only site: Lola and Lourdes enact as well, the novel suggests, possible sites for Susana's construction of '68 and its meanings.

As I have suggested throughout this essay, the reader—that is, the role as opposed to an actual person designated as *the* reader—and reading as a cultural act occupy privileged positions in *Pánico o peligro*. Susana represents an autobiographical "I" who differentiates herself critically from the male "I" of '68 embodied in the early autobiographies of the *novela del 68*. She simulates the process of constructing an autobiographical subjectivity grounded in acts of engaged, resistant readings—of reality and of actual modes of reading—that contrasts with the isolated writers and "hidden" subjects of the earlier autobiographies. Through the construction of a subjectivity actively engaged in the cultural act of reading Susana also makes overt the process of self-construction as a dialogue between the self and potential readers through the interpellation of a specific reader, *tú*. *Tú*, as I have argued, represents as well a specific historical and political identity—'68—and thus highlights the ways in which readers and cultural and historical dialogues inflect the construction of meaning in the text. I would argue, then, that the novel's emphasis on both the reader and alternative reading acts necessarily evokes the role of extra-textual readers, their subject positions, and identities, and their interaction with both the text and reality beyond its pages. The novel ultimately provokes an entire set of questions relevant to the production of meaning and of the histories of '68 as enacted in the interaction between readers, texts, and reality.

Unlike the male embodiment of '68 in the early *novela del 68*, Susana's interpellation of *tú*/'68 is not imagined or constructed on any specific body. This *tú* is physically ambiguous, disembodied, made available for imagining beyond the restrictive limits of specifically male or female bodies. The novel evokes an "I"/subject of '68 imagined in a space of ambiguities that rejects reproduction of a singular and prescriptive subjectivity. This *tú* resists containment in strict sex and gender categories, suggesting disembodiment as a resistance to the dominant male body of '68. Disembodiment, then, as a strategy for reading and producing meaning, also suggests the potential for thinking and imagining sex and gender beyond the limits of specific bodies, as well as beyond the limits of dominant modes of resistance. *Tú*'s disembodiment—another way of thinking about the "ghosts" of '68—allows us to imagine a '68 that, however conflicted, interrupted, or disrupted (i.e., not ideologically pure), nevertheless persists as a referent in the construction of contemporary resistant subjectivities. Ultimately '68 persists as a potentially relevant and meaningful referent for other kinds of resistances, without necessarily imposing a restrictive reproduction of its own limited (historically male and heterosexual) "subject" of resistance.

At the same time, *tú* occupies and reflects the position of the extra-textual reader and makes available for scrutiny the ways in which readers' identities and subjectivities participate in the production of meanings in a text, and ultimately, of reality. By positing *tú* as a physically ambiguous reader, the novel opens up, rather than restricts space for multiple readers, from multiple subject positions and identities, to produce the meanings of '68. The opening up of the reader's subjectivity necessarily produces questions about readership, meaning, and resistance. For example, what would it mean for a queer body, a female body, an indigenous body to occupy the space of the reader? In what ways would the specificity of those subjectivities, those histories, those political and cultural agencies inflect and produce new meanings of '68 itself as well as its political and cultural legacy? By disembodying the reader, refusing to define its physical limits, the novel forces us to consider who reads '68, who participated in a produced '68, who gets imagined as '68, and how '68 can be read in a contemporary cultural moment. What would it mean to imagine '68 as a queer/female/indigenous revolutionary subject? Disembodying '68 does not mean rejecting or denying the existence of the bodies of '68—it means resisting the reproduction of privileged bodies that obscure at best and prevent at worst the reading of other bodies that also mean '68. I would argue that the novel's privileging of conflicted and disrupted reading models, as well as of an ambiguous and expansive reading subject, compels us to read '68 beyond the limits of its traditional bodies, to continually reimagine it as a site for the construction of political and cultural agents of resistance in a specific past as well as in an imagined future. If '68 is a ghost that still sweeps Mexico—and I would argue that it is—*Pánico o peligro* suggests the usefulness of ghosts, of the persistent disembodied spirits that lend themselves as spaces for reading the bodies the rest of us still inhabit into the social texts of contemporary political and cultural struggles.

Notes

1. Diana Taylor, *Theatre of Crisis: Drama and Politics in Latin America* (Lexington: University of Kentucky Press, 1991), 55.
2. Martin Stabb, "The Essay," in *Mexican Literature: A History*, ed. David William Foster (Austin: University of Texas Press, 1994), 330.
3. Gonzalo Martré, *El movimiento popular estudiantil en la novela mexicana* (Mexico: UNAM, 1986), 2. This and all other translations mine.
4. José Revueltas, "Un fantasma recorre Mexico," in *México 68: Juventud y revolución*, ed. José Revueltas (Mexico: Ediciones Era, 1978), 79–84.
5. See Sergio Zermeño, *México: Una democracia utópica* (México: Siglo 21 Editores, 1978) and Sara Sefchovich, *México: País de ideas. País de novelas: Una sociología de la literatura mexicana* (México: Grijalbo, 1987).
6. See Rubén Medina, "Ayer es nunca jamás: Continuidad y ruptura en la narrativa mexicana del 68," *Revista Crítica Literaria Latinoamericana* 21:42 (1995): 207–218.

7. Jean Franco, *Plotting Women: Gender and Representation in Mexico* (New York: Columbia University Press, 1989).

8. See Sergio Zermeño, *México: Una democracia utópica* (México: Siglo 21 Editores, 1978).

9. See especially Gilberto Balam, *Tlatelolco: Reflexiones de un testigo* (Mexico: Talleres Lenasas, 1969); Luis González de Alba, *Los días y los años* (Mexico, Ediciones Era, 1971); José Revueltas, *Tiempo de Hablar* (Mexico: Ediciones Era, 1970); Herberto Castillo, *Libertad bajo protesta* (Mexico: Ediciones Era, 1973); and Horacio Espinosa Altamirano, *Toda la furia* (Mexico: Editorial Reportaje, 1973).

10. Recent work by cultural historians has begun to deconstruct the male-centered histories of the Mexican '68, and literary historians as well have argued for greater scrutiny of the male identitarian politics of the *novela del 68*. See Deborah Cohen and Lessie Jo Frasier, "Mexico 68: Defining the Space of the Movement, Heroic Masculinity in the Prison and 'Women' in the Streets" (this volume) and Cynthia Steele, *Politics, Gender, and the Mexican Novel, 1968–1988: Beyond the Pyramid* (Austin: University of Texas Press, 1992). In addition, as Elaine Carey noted in a personal communication, despite the heteronormative representation of masculinity in *Los días y los años*, Luis González de Alba went on to become one of the founders of the Mexican gay rights movement.

11. See Danny J. Anderson, "Cultural Conversations and Construction of Reality: Mexican Narrative and Literary Theories After 1968," *Siglo XX/20th Century* 8 (1–2): 11–30. Anderson's extremely helpful article discusses the ways in which *Pánico o peligro* participates in extratextual cultural conversations in post-'68 Mexico. His discussion of these cultural conversations allows us to think beyond a finite set of textual propositions, and, in fact, helped me to understand the discourses of '68 as part of an ever changing and fluid set of broader cultural conversations.

12. Edward Said, *The World, the Text, the Critic* (Cambridge, MA: Harvard University Press, 1983), 157.

13. Aralia López-González argues that since women have historically been silenced by a "rational," patriarchal discourse that denies them historical, individual, and social subjectivity, contemporary Mexican women writers have had to respond transgressively in order to subvert what she calls "el discurso monológico institucional." Aralia López-González, "Dos tendencias en la evolución de la narrativa contemporánea de escritoras mexicanas," in *Mujer y literatura mexicana y chicana: Culturas en contacto, II*, ed. Aralia López González, Amelia Malagamba, and Elena Urrutia (Tijuana: El Colegio de la Frontera Norte, 1990), 21. One manifestation of this "contradiscursive" response is the positing of the female in the text as both subject and object of her own discourse, a tactic employed by Susana in *Pánico o peligro*.

14. Kristine Ibsen notes that "Many trends characterized—and criticized—as 'women's writing' during the last two decades, such as the integration of popular culture and peripheral discourse, are affiliated with the wider set of literary tendencies associated with the equally debated term 'postmodernity.' More specifically, the use of autobiographical elements and the reinscription of historical discourse seen in several of these texts also forms part of a generalized trend in contemporary Mexican literature" *The Other Mirror: Women's Narrative in Mexico, 1980–1995*, ed. Kristine Ibsen (Westport: Greenwood Press, 1997), 10.

15. Medina, "Ayer," 210.

16. Janet Varner Gunn, *Autobiography: Toward a Poetics of Experience* (Philadelphia: University of Pennsylvania Press, 1982), 8.

17. Gunn, *Autobiography*, 22.

18. Ibid., 8.

19. Puga, *Pánico*, 7.

20. Ibid., 12.

21. Sidonie Smith, *A Poetics of Women's Autobiography: Marginality and the Fictions of Self-Representation* (Bloomington: Indiana University Press, 1987), 49.

22. Puga, *Pánico*, 169.
23. Ibid., 191.
24. Ibid., 196.
25. Ibid., 23.
26. For a discussion of how master narratives remain a persistent dimension of literary and cultural texts "because they reflect a fundamental dimension of our collective thinking and our collective fantasies about history and reality"; see Frederic Jameson, *The Political Unconscious: Narrative as a Socially Symbolic Act* (Ithaca: Cornell University Press, 1981).
27. Puga, *Pánico*, 55.
28. Ibid., 97.
29. Ibid., 183.
30. Ibid., 20.

CHAPTER TEN

The Spirit of May '68 and the Origins of the Gay Liberation Movement in France

MICHAEL SIBALIS

Interpretations of May '68 in France have been many, varied, and contradictory.[1] While no one disputes that the so-called "events"—the riots, strikes, and demonstrations that almost toppled the Gaullist regime—amounted to more than an ordinary crisis, most analyses point to their ultimate failure to change French politics or society in any meaningful way. Even so, an entire generation has defined itself (and been defined by others) in terms of its relation to May '68, and much of France's political history over the subsequent forty years can be written as the story of this generation's itinerary: the (rare) fidelity of ex-militants to their youthful ideals or, more commonly, their (reputed) betrayal of their principles for American-style or Thatcherite economic liberalism or for François Mitterrand's brand of socialism.[2] Over the decades, the rebellious youths who took to the streets in '68 and challenged authority have accommodated themselves to the status quo. As Henri Mendras cynically but perceptively observes, in the end the radical tendencies that emerged from '68 "had as their principal result the opening of a new political and cultural space within which the new rulers served their apprenticeship to become leaders. This new generation of leaders then took its natural place within the existing institutions against which it had fought." Mendras recognizes only one permanent consequence of May '68: a weakened respect for traditional authority and an expanded sense of individualism that together transformed sexual behavior and public attitudes toward sexuality.[3] In short, May '68 brought about a "moral revolution" in France, not a political or social one.

The French student uprising, like the 1960s "youth revolt" elsewhere in the world, accelerated a broad cultural shift that was essentially generational in origin. May '68 was, as one of its leaders put it two decades later, "the act of a generation" motivated by "the desire for a radical break with the values, norms and institutions of the established order."[4] This had profound implications for sexuality, sexual identity, and gender relations: "The overthrow of the value systems—under the circumstances, the taboos—of the French with respect to sexual relations and the status of the sexes was all the more violent because in 1968 the representative system codified by legislation, custom and their artistic transcription had not perceptibly changed for about a century."[5] And yet, although many 68'ers advocated (and even indulged in) free love—albeit hardly to the extent fantasized by prudes, one of whom wrote that "[at] the Sorbonne, in May 1968, people made love on heaps of file cards"[6]—the overall attitude of the students to sex and gender remained surprisingly conventional. Leftist women have described their male comrades as no less misogynist than other Frenchmen: "We did the cooking, made the sandwiches, looked after the guys.... We were the revolutionaries' maids...."[7] As for homosexuality, asked twenty years afterward what students had thought about it in '68, Daniel Cohn-Bendit, the best-known student leader, admitted that "we didn't really worry about those problems. It was [only] in the 1970s that there occurred the growth of what we call 'specific movements': the women's movement, the homosexual movement, taking into consideration sexuality in all its forms."[8]

Even if male students were largely indifferent or hostile to emergent feminist demands, "whatever their age, whatever their itinerary, [French feminists] belong to the same political generation, the one for which May '68 was the founding event."[9] The same was true of gay militants. In 1985, a gay activist described the contemporary French "homosexual movement" as "this natural child of May '68 and of the great student protests of the 1960s."[10] One gay publication, using the metaphor of the "Big Bang" that began our Universe, termed May '68 (in English no less!) "le Pink Bang."[11] Of course, French homosexuals had not waited until '68 to begin pressing their demands. There were two earlier but abortive attempts to publish politically oriented homosexual periodicals—*Inversions* (1924–1926) and *Futur* (1952–1956)—and several homosexual associations were formed in the 1950s, most notably the immensely successful Arcadie, founded and led by André Baudry.[12] But the gay movement that began in France in '68 and flourished in the following decades represented a new generation with new ways of thinking and acting. It was a generation hostile not only to the French establishment, but also to its "homophile" predecessors.

The homophile movement of the 1950s–1960s was worldwide, with centers in the United States, Switzerland, the Netherlands, and France.[13] Homophiles disliked the word "homosexual" for stressing sex rather than love. They were often middle-class, with conformist, even conservative values. André Baudry, the public face of the French homophile movement, was a former seminarian and philosophy teacher, who founded and edited the monthly homosexual review *Arcadie* (1954–1982), which sold at least ten thousand copies a month. In 1957, he established the Club Littéraire et Scientifique des Pays Latins (Literary and Scientific Club of the Latin Countries), a social organization (often also called Arcadie for short) that held dances, sponsored lectures, and promoted and defended the rights of France's homosexuals. Born in 1922, Baudry was only twenty to twenty-five years older than the students of May '68, but that was enough to make their views worlds apart. Often attacked for his authoritarianism, conservatism and preachy Catholic moralism, Baudry propagated a normalizing and assimilationist ideology. He argued that public hostility to homosexuals resulted from their outrageous and promiscuous behavior; homophiles would win public approval and the good opinion of the authorities if they showed themselves to be discreet, dignified, virtuous, and respectable.[14] In 1956, for instance, Baudry wrote that "the French homosexual should do everything to present himself in a favorable light." Denouncing "the superficial way of life" of those who frequented "bars, cabarets and other disreputable places," he urged that homophiles "educate homosexuals to appreciate the danger and futility of [this lifestyle]."[15] As late as May 1982, when he dissolved his movement and retired to Italy, Baudry still insisted that "the homosexual must live in the society within which he finds himself" and condemned American gays and gay liberationists for their "excesses." "They make me want to vomit," he declared; "I pray...that this never reaches France."[16]

Baudry's reluctance to offend public sensibilities derived in part from his awareness of the hostile attitude toward homosexuality predominant in the Fourth Republic (1946–1958) and early Fifth Republic. France was one of freest countries in the world for homosexuals—the state had decriminalized same-sex activity between consenting adults in private as long ago as 1791–but in the post–1945 era, the government, the medical establishment, and the media promoted the values of social conformity and family life, which many homosexuals themselves internalized as shame.[17] Discreet bars and clubs were allowed to operate, especially in Paris (where a police ordinance nonetheless forbade men to dance together), but the police used laws against public indecency to harass and entrap those homosexuals who picked each other up in parks and around street urinals. A decree by the collaborationist government of Marshal Pétain in 1942 had reintroduced into French jurisprudence the insidious distinction between "natural" and "unnatural" sexual acts by criminalizing "shameless or unnatural acts" committed by an adult with a minor (under twenty-one) of the same sex. General de Gaulle's provisional government reaffirmed this law in February 1945, so that it remained on the books after the Liberation. In July 1960, parliament voted a law that included a clause (dubbed the "Mirguet amendment" after the deputy who proposed it) categorizing homosexuality as a "social scourge" along with alcoholism and prostitution, and authorizing the government to take measures to check its spread. The law was primarily symbolic, but on November 25, 1960, the cabinet used its authority under the amendment to double existing penalties for acts of public indecency when these involved homosexuals.[18]

This was the context within which the French gay liberation movement made its appearance in the streets and cafés of the Latin Quarter and in the hallways and classrooms of the student-occupied Sorbonne. Its initiator was Guillaume Charpentier (a pseudonym used here at his request) (born December 1938), a student of French literature, who was at the time preparing for the *agrégation* (an annual competitive examination qualifying the candidate to teach in the secondary school system) while working as a *pion* (proctor) in the Lycée Saint-Louis, a secondary school across from the Sorbonne. Although Charpentier's activities in '68 have left almost no documentary trace, they can be reconstructed in some detail from the interviews that he has given over the past twenty years.[19]

Charpentier participated in the student protest in the Latin Quarter from the very first day (May 3, 1968), but, as he recalled in 1988, it was about two weeks into events that he and a fellow proctor, Stéphane (a pseudonym), concluded that "we are getting to spew out all our frustrations—university, intellectual, etc.—within the framework of this sort of student revolution at the Sorbonne, but our basic problem...is sexuality.... There were vaguely committees...for sexual liberation, but nothing explicitly homosexual." Sitting at a table at the Café L'Écritoire on the Place de la Sorbonne, the two young men made eight handwritten placards in the name of the *Comité d'Action Pédérastique Révolutionnaire* (Committee for Revolutionary Pederastic Action or CAPR), which they then posted along the quadrilateral of hallways around the Grand Amphitheatre of the Sorbonne. Asked in 1988 why they had used the word "pederastic" rather than "homosexual," Charpentier explained that "we were fascinated by...young adolescents...[but] we were also speaking about homosexuality [in general]." (*Pédéraste* has been commonly used in France since the mid-eighteenth century to designate any man who engages in same-sex relations, with no implication of intergenerational sex. In abbreviated form [*pédé*] the word is an insult, equivalent to "fag" or "poofter.")[20] Today, Charpentier even more explicitly rejects any suggestion that the CAPR advocated pedophilia. By "pederastic," he and Stéphane meant "a practice...as old as the world, illustrated by, among others, the great works of our contemporary literature from Gide to Montherlant" and accepted moreover by the Greco-Latin and Arabo-Muslim civilizations. They also adopted the term for its shock value and "to exorcize the quasiracist insults of which we were the victims."

The text of their poster survives only because Pierre Hahn, a gay journalist, took the time to copy it down and later published it, although he amputated a reference to "the old reactionary marchionesses" of Arcadie (Hahn was himself a member):[21]

> Troubled and deeply moved by the civil and police repression exercised against all erotic minorities (homosexuals, voyeurs, masochists, orgies), the Committee for Revolutionary Pederastic Action denounces the restriction of amorous possibilities that is prevalent in the West since the appearance of Judeo-Christianity. Examples of this odious repression are not lacking; you have them before your eyes at every moment; the sketches and graffiti in the toilets of the Sorbonne and elsewhere, the beating up of homosexuals by the police or by backward civilians; the keeping of police records [of homosexuals], and in general the submissive attitude, the downcast eyes, the cringing behavior of the typical homosexual; the broken careers, the loneliness and the clandestinity that are the lot of all erotic minorities. For one glorious Jean Genet, [there are] a hundred thousand shamefaced pederasts, condemned to unhappiness.
>
> The CAPR launches an appeal for you, pederasts, lesbians, etc...., to become conscious of your right to express freely your options or your amorous particularities and to promote by your example a veritable sexual liberation that the so-called sexual majorities need as much as you do....
>
> (One man in 20 is a fag; among a world population of 4 billion, that makes 200 million fags). NO LONGER LOVE AND DEATH. BUT LOVE AND LIBERTY.

This was not the only student manifesto to denounce the social constraints placed on sexuality, to defend the rights of "sexual minorities" and to call for a "sexual revolution," but it was the only one explicitly to mention homosexuality.[22] It expressed a deeply felt dissatisfaction with the homosexual condition in postwar France. Homosexuality may have been legal, but only a few men (like the writer Jean Genet, cited in the manifesto) dared to flaunt their sexual orientation. The police still kept homosexual venues under surveillance, compiled files on individual homosexuals and taunted (even brutalized) the men whom they arrested. The popular press stigmatized homosexuals and lesbians as pathetic at best

and as abnormal monsters who preyed on children at worst. There were
gay and lesbian bars (at least in Paris), but drinks there were expensive, certainly too costly for the average student or worker. As the CAPR's manifesto noted, most French homosexuals coped by accepting their lot with
resignation or by living secretive (today we would say "closeted") lives.[23]
Charpentier remembered the situation this way in his 1988 interview:

> There was a silence about [homosexuality], we were frustrated at
> not being be able to talk a bit about it.... We went out to the Fiacre,
> which was a classic nightclub where in the evening we could cruise,
> we could pet and possibly meet somebody or find a lover...but we
> went a lot to the street urinals, they were the major cruising sites
> at the time,...and then also to the public parks, etc. etc. We called
> it..."shamefaced homosexuality"...because it was ultimately a
> somewhat clandestine homosexuality. ... But we were frustrated by
> this absence of [public] discourse.

And yet the CAPR made no concrete proposal beyond stating that homosexuals had a right to their sexuality, should talk more openly about their
lives and ought to "promote by example a veritable sexual liberation" that
would somehow free heterosexuals and homosexuals alike.

Joseph Lovett, who met Charpentier as a student in Paris in 1966, remembers him as intellectually "dazzling" and "mesmerizing." Lovett was especially impressed by "the intensity of [Charpentier's] politics, which came
out of his life experience."[24] Charpentier himself attributes his radicalism
to both his "proletarian" background and his sexual orientation, which
together estranged him from the dominant values of French middle-class
society: "I felt doubly outcast as a fag and as one of the people," he declared
in 1988. His parents were domestic servants rather than factory laborers,
and he developed a lifelong hostility to the upper classes from seeing them
bossed about by their employers. Although Lovett remembers Charpentier
as a Marxist, by 1968 there were other even more significant intellectual
influences on him. As he explained in 1988, "you restructure a new [polit-
ical] discourse" from "scraps." In the case of his sexual politics, these were
scraps of Herbert Marcuse and Wilhelm Reich, who influenced others of
his generation, but also a recently translated book on "erotic minorities"
by Dr. Lars Ullerstam, who argued that the so-called sexual perversions
"allow considerable chances to achieve human happiness" and were "in
themselves good and therefore ought to be encouraged." Claiming that
"sexual deviations," including homosexuality, incest, exhibitionism,
pedophilia, and sadism, were "fully legitimate methods of satisfying the
sexual urge, fully equal to heterosexual coition," Ullerstam called for an
end to "the society of sexual privilege."[25]

Charpentier's expectation that the CAPR and its "new discourse" would find favor with the revolutionary students and their leaders was rapidly disappointed: "I dreamed that this idea…would set something in motion," he said in 1988, but "it didn't take." In one typical incident, recounted by Charpentier in 2001, the future novelist Philippe Sollers dismissively said to him: "What, you haven't read Freud? He explains your problem, which is neither political nor revolutionary, but personal."[26] Reflecting on the failure of his ideas to find any echo in May '68, Charpentier today argues that they were quite simply out of place in a student revolt that spoke a "freudian-marxist jargon":

> The perhaps clumsy but spontaneously transgressive emergence of this taboo question of "love between boys"…totally contravened the commonly accepted revolutionary verbiage…of the children of the French bourgeoisie of May '68. In the context of the [political] catechisms of the day, even the libertarian ones, our modest discourse was unclassifiable, heretical and impossible to assimilate.

Charpentier believes today that he and Stéphane were able to formulate their new and different analysis only because "we were not prisoners of these marxist-leninist discourses, which dismissed 'our problem' outright as an abnormality and a 'marginal deviance.'…Our references were instead Gide, Montherlant and Genet."

A poll of university students across France taken in 1966 concluded that they "understand [homosexuality] as a sickness, and they seem full of compassion for the sick person."[27] Students at the Sorbonne in '68 did not see homosexuality as an issue worthy of their attention, nor were they particularly well disposed to the homosexuals in their midst. "Henry," who was eighteen years old when he occupied the Sorbonne in May '68, later remembered: "One of the leaders of a leftist group took my virginity. I was somewhat his 'girl.'…I was told to keep my mouth shut about our sexual relations. Which did not keep me from speaking about homosexuality within my group. I was kicked out."[28] Guy Hocquenghem (1946–1988), who concealed his own homosexuality while serving on the Sorbonne's Occupation Committee in '68, before eventually emerging as the emblematic gay militant of the 1970s, later wrote: "The Occupation Committee at the Sorbonne worried about the presence of homosexuals around the toilets. It risked 'discrediting' the movement; at the very moment that we thought we had reached the heights of liberation of all possibilities, there were still aspects of our lives that we were not allowed to display."[29]

It is therefore not surprising that the CAPR's first eight posters were torn down within hours, apparently by decision of the Occupation Committee. This was undoubtedly the second Occupation Committee, elected by a general assembly of students on May 17. The first committee, dominated by the anarchic "Situationists," was replaced that day by one made up of Leninists, Trotskyists, and Maoists, "people who had specific responsibilities, and knew that you cannot say and do just anything...." As a result, in the occupied Sorbonne there was "at one and the same time freedom of speech and necessarily restricted action, without which you would fall into liberal individualism."[30] Claims that Hocquenghem himself was involved in removing the CAPR's posters, however, are almost certainly unfounded. Hocquenghem later said that he had been unaware of the CAPR in '68: "I learned about it only three years later."[31]

Charpentier and Stéphane stuck up ten new posters the next day and this time the Occupation Committee left one or two in place by a stairwell near the toilets and leading up to the Quinet and Michelet lecture halls. They also mimeographed their text as a flysheet that called on interested students to meet with them in the Sorbonne. They distributed five hundred copies in the Sorbonne courtyard, in front of the Odéon theater and in the streets of the Latin Quarter, particularly near the public urinals. Many closeted students seemed "terrified" to be handed the flysheet, and forty years later, Charpentier is still bitter when recalling how one student, today a celebrated gay activist, "pretended not to know me so as to avoid taking the flysheet that I was holding out to him."

Meetings of the CAPR were sporadic and informal, discussions vague and rambling. "We were rather timid," Charpentier commented in 1988, "awed by our own undertaking; we stammered out a few analyses, in short we simply defended our poster."[32] Over a two-week period, Charpentier and Stéphane hung about the Sorbonne, speaking with those students who stopped to read their poster or who showed up after seeing their flysheet; sometimes they squatted one of the classrooms. As Charpentier explained in 2008,

> Our committee...remained more or less unknown, consciously ignored, although several times we tried to mobilize people with an appeal posted on the doors of the Quinet and Michelet lecture halls: we waited in these classrooms, people came, hesitated, waited around, discussions began but no collective political will to elaborate appropriate emancipatory discourses emerged from these groups.

Since the CAPR had no real existence, it evaporated once the agitation of May–June '68 died down. A year later, Charpentier left for the United States. But, as the (gay) sociologist Daniel Defert has observed, the May events were important for homosexuals because of "the fantastic discussions that took place everywhere" and because "the boundaries between private life and public space were shifted. The elements of private life became political issues."[33] Within a few years, the spirit of May '68 that the CAPR embodied had changed forever the mood and direction of the homosexual movement in France. After May '68, André Baudry's reluctance to challenge the status quo appeared outdated and his political line ineffectual. As one of his many critics has put it, "Try talking about 'dignity' and 'morals' to the children of the barricades and of the permissive society!"[34] In Guy Hocquenghem's analysis, the CAPR marked a decisive shift from "a movement defending and justifying homosexuality" (Baudry's homophile movement) toward a "homosexual struggle" that accepted homosexual orientation as a fact of life requiring neither explanation nor justification and that rejected the idea that homosexuals should assimilate into society as it existed and accept the dominant social values.[35] In Françoise d'Eaubonne's pithy phrase, flung at Baudry in the early 1970s, "It's not a matter of integrating the homosexual into society, but of disintegrating society through homosexuality."[36] In other words, gay radicals believed that homosexuals had to transform society if they were ever to live freely; and, more than this, that their sexual orientation made them a socially disruptive force and was therefore in and of itself politically subversive. "Our ass-holes are revolutionary," quipped Hocquenghem.[37]

Three years passed between May '68 and the establishment of a radical gay organization, the *Front Homosexuel d'Action Révolutionnaire* (Homosexual Front for Revolutionary Action, or FHAR).[38] On March 10, 1971, a small group of lesbians and gays disrupted a live radio broadcast animated by Ménie Grégoire on the "problem" of homosexuality. The protesters— among them, Guillaume Charpentier—went on to found the FHAR that very evening. They were soon holding general meetings every Thursday evening at Paris's School of Fine Arts. The publication of their manifesto in a special edition of the Maoist newspaper *Tout!* (April 23, 1971), coordinated by Guy Hocquenghem, attracted new recruits and attendance at their weekly meetings grew into the hundreds. Most new recruits were men, however, and the women, exasperated by an ambient misogyny, began deserting the FHAR.[39]

The link between May '68 and the FHAR was explicit. One gay activist described the FHAR as "this ripening of shame into anger, which was able to emerge politically [only] in the aftermath of May '68."[40] Another observed that "[t]he spirit of May '68 had rooted itself deeply among a number of young intellectuals [and] students," and that even the FHAR's oldest participants, like Daniel Guerin (born in 1904) and Françoise d'Eaubonne (born in 1920), "had in common with the youth of 1968 the rejection of bourgeois ideals and of Marxist political cant."[41] For a third, the FHAR was "the child of May '68.... The spirit of May '68 was still very much alive... [and] we applied one of its most apt slogans: everything is political."[42]

The lesbians who founded the FHAR came to the gay movement via May '68 and the subsequent feminist movement.[43] Many of the men had also participated in May '68, but several were also directly influenced by the American gay liberation movement. Guillaume Charpentier arrived in the United States in June 1969, just in time to witness the Stonewall Riots in New York City. He stayed in the West Village with his old friend Joseph Lovett, who remembers that Charpentier "was quite exhilarated by the buzz of revolution—especially gay revolution—which infused the air of NY at the time. He bemoaned the fact that nothing was happening in Paris."[44] Charpentier spent some fifteen months in America, teaching French and attending gay liberation meetings in New York and Los Angeles. "I learned everything in the United States," he later remarked,[45] which is an odd comment by the man who had already tried to launch radical gay militancy in France. In 1988 he described his time in America as an "apprenticeship" that taught him how to mobilize homosexuals politically and to stage a protest with slogans: "while finding again what I had clumsily tried to formulate in the CAPR at the Sorbonne,...I americanized my experience of liberation." Back in Paris in October 1970, Charpentier was soon in regular contact with other gay and lesbian radicals. He joined with them to storm the podium at Ménie Grégoire's broadcast and to found the FHAR. Indeed, it was most likely he who gave the organization its name.[46] Gilles Châtelet, another FHAR activist, had also taken part in student protests in May 1968 ("In '68, I did what everybody did, I followed the movement," he later commented), but did not discover gay militancy until a sojourn in California in 1969 ("France, in comparison, was a provincial asteroid"). Back in Paris, he attended meetings of the FHAR as "a way of finding again the ambiance of the United States."[47]

Even so, the FHAR's rhetoric owed more to '68 than to America. It denounced "fascist sexual normality," "sexual racism," and the "heterocops" who enforced the sexual status quo.[48] Sexual liberation was part and parcel of a more general revolutionary project: "The total liberation of everybody, the goal and object of the revolution, implies the liberation of homosexuals as much as that of workers, women, or oppressed peoples."[49] The FHAR explicitly recognized its debt to the May events:

> Unfortunately, until May '68, the revolutionary camp was one of moral order, inherited from Stalin. Everything there was gray, puritanical, deplorable....But suddenly, that clap of thunder: the May explosion, the joy of living, of fighting....Dancing, laughter, celebration!...And so, faced with this new situation, we homosexuals in revolt—and certain among us were already politicized—discovered that our homosexuality—to the extent that we could affirm it in the

face of and against everything—made us into authentic revolutionaries, because in this way we called into question everything that was forbidden in Euro-American civilization.... Don't doubt it: we want the *annihilation* of this world. Nothing less.... The freedom of everybody, by everybody, for everybody is in the offing.[50]

This quotation (from 1971) is typical of the FHAR, whose language remained deeply rooted in the idiom of '68.

The FHAR's rhetoric and consciously provocative tactics offended not only its inevitable enemies on the Right, but also its potential allies on the Left. Leftists generally still regarded homosexuality as a "bourgeois vice" of which the virile proletariat was naturally free unless corrupted by the decadent middle class. Jacques Duclos, secretary of the French Communist Party, once upbraided FHAR militants: "You pederasts—where do you get the nerve to come and question us? Go get treatment. The French Communist Party is healthy!"[51] Trade unionists, Socialists, Communists, Maoists, or Trotskyists all looked askance at the gay liberationists from the FHAR who joined their annual May Day march in 1971. The transvestite (and sometimes transexual) *gazolines*—no more than about a dozen members of the FHAR, but always an obstreperous presence—won the FHAR public attention but no sympathy. "For us, political action meant wearing makeup, going down to Barbès [an Arab district in northern Paris] or the Café de Flore [in the Saint-Germain-des-Prés quarter] in bathing suits, and tottering on high heels with hair on our legs," one former *gazoline* has recalled with some embarrassment.[52] They represented, in exaggerated form, the dominant mood at the FHAR, which rejected leaders (indeed, the very principal of leadership) and refused to fix precise goals or adopt a specific program, so that weekly meetings at the School of Fine Arts soon deteriorated into anarchy. Many of the men drifted away from the pointless debates in the auditorium to go hunting for sexual encounters in the hallways and upstairs classrooms. "It was chaos," Gilles Châtelet later recalled, "permanent sleeping around."[53]

All of this detracted from the FHAR's effectiveness and ability to persuade. In later years, some former FHAR activists came to recognize that their youthful exuberance had led them astray: "to a great extent we let ourselves be carried away by the flood-tide of the ideologizing, revolutionary and marginalizing movement that characterized the infantile phase of this homosexual movement."[54] Guy Hocquenghem summed it up best: "The FHAR always maintained an irresponsible side, an inability to think strategy."[55] When the police moved in at the request of the administration of the School of Fine Arts to expel the FHAR from the premises in early 1974, the movement had long ceased to have any political significance.

The mid- to late 1970s witnessed a gradual shift of the gay movement toward pragmatic reformism, which included the formulation of specific demands for equal rights and political lobbying to obtain them. The gay world was also changing and emerging into the open, with the expansion of gay commercialism and an explosion of bars and nightclubs, especially in Paris, first along the Rue Sainte-Anne in the 1970s and then, from about 1979, in the Marais district (still today the city's "gay ghetto"), but also in many other large towns and cities.[56] The gay press prospered, especially *Gai Pied*, which began in 1979 as a monthly political newspaper advocating political and social change to improve the life of gays only to evolve into a glossy weekly magazine that catered to gay consumers by glorifying a youthful and costly "gay lifestyle" centered on bars, nightclubs, bathhouses, tourism, and fashionable clothes.[57]

The *Groupe de libération homosexuelle* (Group for Homosexual Liberation, or GLH) straddled this transition period. Created in late 1974, the GLH attempted to build a national network to bring together both Parisian and provincial homosexual groups. Internal dissensions fragmented the GLH into three factions in December 1975. The most successful of these, with perhaps one hundred Parisian members at its peak, was the GLH-PQ (PQ stood for *Politique et quotidien,* that is, "Politics and Daily Life"). The GLH-PQ took a radical political stand inherited from May '68 and the FHAR: "No socialist revolution without sexual revolution; no sexual revolution without socialist revolution."[58] But it recognized all the same that the times had changed, declaring in 1976 that whereas "our first cry of revolt isolated itself through uniquely provocative practices," the GLH-PQ now "participates…in the anti-capitalist struggle alongside the labour movement all the while fighting against the direct or indirect repression of which homosexuals are the victims."[59] The members of the GLH-PQ were still 68'ers at heart, but they understood that real progress for gays required a practical program and political allies on the Left.

For the journalist Jean-Luc Hennig, this amounted to a new start: "Nothing to do with the FHAR…: no, it's something more structured, aiming to carry out specific actions, a real movement." He pointed out that whereas members of the FHAR had mostly been students, the GLH brought together junior executives, teachers, clerks, and young workers, many of whom (although he did not suggest this) were likely the FHAR's student members now grown up. They wanted an organized movement, patterned after American gay liberation, that could fight against both daily harassment and the more systematic (and more subtle) institutionalized discrimination that victimized gays.[60]

The GLH-PQ kept the gay cause in the public eye and drew the attention of both press and politicians. It staged the first autonomous protest demonstration by homosexuals in Paris on June 25, 1977 (this was the city's first Gay Pride parade), laid a wreath every April at Paris's memorial to the victims of Nazism and persuaded journalists to publish articles sympathetic to the gay movement. It also—much more in the FHAR's spirit of provocation and impudence—launched commando raids to disrupt one radio broadcast by two homophobic sexologists (January 1976) and another by André Baudry (February 1976), and smashed the windows of a Paris café that had thrown out two men for kissing in public (November 1977).[61]

Two events in early 1978 that marked the GLH-PQ's apogee were also its swan song. The first occurred in January 1978, when the GLH-PQ organized a film festival at La Pagode movie theater in Paris. On the evening of 27 January, a squad of neofascists attacked the theater, assaulted the audience, and ran off with the cashbox. The next evening, outraged activists protested outside the gay bars along the Rue Sainte-Anne in an attempt to precipitate a French version of New York's Christopher Street Riot. The police dispersed them and made arrests.[62] The second event was the candidacy of four gay militants in two Parisian constituencies in the March 1978 legislative elections under the political label: "Homosexual Difference." One militant group explained at the time: "We [gays] don't have any program, we are only asking for the suppression of discriminatory laws.... The point is for us to show ourselves openly."[63] The candidates won only a handful of votes, but attracted considerable publicity, which was the purpose of the exercise. A number of French intellectuals, including Simone de Beauvoir and Marguerite Duras, signed a petition defending their candidacy on the grounds that "they are posing the problem of the repression of homosexuals by the Penal Code and by existing police and psychiatric practice."[64] And yet, by then the GLH-PQ was falling apart, with frequent complaints about "petty leaders" competing for power.[65] In the spring of 1978, the GLH-PQ fractured into "neighborhood groups," most of which soon disintegrated as well.

Delegates from gay groups across France met in Lyon in November 1978. No formal program emerged, but there was a manifest determination to work together to defend their "democratic rights."[66] The result was the *Comité d'Urgence Anti-Répression Homosexuelle* (Emergency Committee against Homosexual Repression, or CUARH), which emerged at the first Summer Homosexual University, a gathering of gay activists at Marseille in July 1979. The CUARH adopted a federal structure in order to coordinate the activities of gay groups across the country.[67] A declaration of principles in March 1980 declared: "It has taken the movement ten years for us to begin seriously defending homosexuals and lesbians!" The CUARH laid claim to "a pragmatic approach." It fostered contacts with the press, trade unions, and political parties and lobbied for an end to discrimination as "the most effective way to change the conditions of life that are imposed on us."[68]

The most striking evidence of the CUARH's commitment to participate in the political process was the decision, taken in September 1980, "to campaign during the [forthcoming] presidential election in order to oblige the candidates to speak out publicly about anti-homosexual discrimination. This is so that homosexuals and lesbians will at last become a political force to be reckoned with in this country."[69] The CUARH organized a massive political demonstration by at least ten thousand men and women in Paris on April 4, 1981, three weeks before the presidential elections, to "affirm loud and clear [...] that we demand that all candidates take a clear public position for the satisfaction of our demands."[70] Whether or not there was in fact a "homosexual vote" in 1981 remains open to debate.[71] Whatever the reality, however, gay militants and to some extent the Socialist Party believed that homosexuals, either by voting for the Socialist candidate, François Mitterrand, or by abstaining from voting for his rival, the centrist Valérie Giscard d'Estaing, helped put Mitterrand over the top in the second round on May 10, 1981 and subsequently contributed to the Socialists' winning a parliamentary majority in the legislative elections in June. "The victory of F. Mitterrand," crowed the CUARH, "gives us hope and opens [new] perspectives."[72] Jean Boyer, one of the CUARH's founders, later commented: "We understood then that the knell had definitively rung for the small '68-style ideologizing groups that were concerned with hardly anything other than fighting with each other....Another direction has been taken."[73]

This direction, with many gay activists campaigning for Mitterrand and then petitioning his government for reform, dismayed other activists who stayed more faithful to their youthful ideals. For them, Mitterrand's election heralded the death of the revolutionary spirit of May '68 and of the FHAR. Alain Sanzio, for example, wrote that "13 years after [May '68] [the radicals] celebrated, they believed, their victory, without knowing that they were burying their illusions to enter into modernity." May 1981, he argued, meant the end of "the crazy hope of changing one's life, of those millions who once [in 1968] believed that they were living in the Year One," that is to say, at the start of a new and very different era.[74] According to Sanzio, "gay militancy, the only one of the great social movements of the 1970s to have survived into the 1980s, is now moribund." The CUARH had committed a fundamental error by turning radical gay liberation into "a classical protest movement."[75]

Hocquenghem was even more polemical in his critique of this reformist tendency. As early as 1980, he had witnessed with disdain the appearance of gay activists whom he called the "new fags" and who, instead of challenging the law, sought legal protection for gays.[76] He despised those homosexuals and heterosexuals who rallied to "Mitterrand the First" (as he called the president) in the name of political pragmatism.[77] "This stand," according to Keith Reader, "derives its polemical force from his conviction that what the 'May generation' now see as the maturity of realpolitik is simply an infatuation with power—the power they sought to overthrow in '68 and, now that it lies with the 'court' of Mitterrand, [they] brazenly covet at the cost of any ideological or artistic integrity."[78]

Ironically, then, as Hervé Liffran of the CUARH remarked, the election of Mitterrand "struck a heavy blow to the militant [gay] movement" because the Socialist government's satisfaction of certain (minor) demands "allayed the militants' mistrust [of politicians]."[79] But the increased public visibility and social acceptance of gays in France and the parallel development of a thriving gay subculture in Paris (and to a lesser extent in other French cities) made political activism seem irrelevant. As a British journalist noted in 1985, "Walk around the streets of Les Halles [in central Paris] and you'll see hundreds of pretty young post-hunks...who identify themselves much more with the [gay] subculture of Le Marais than with any gay movement."[80] What possible appeal could gay militancy have for the young, who no longer felt oppressed and wanted only to enjoy the pleasures of the new gay lifestyle?[81]

Twenty years after May '68 French homosexuals had apparently come full circle: apolitical in the 1950s and 1960s, revolutionary from May '68 into the late 1970s, politically pragmatic in the early 1980s, and once again apolitical throughout most of the 1980s. During the 1980s, however, gays were also developing a strong sense of community, centered on bars, clubs, and bathhouses, but also on gay associations of every sort, from hiking clubs to choirs. The AIDS crisis eventually rekindled militancy and roused this community to fight for new rights, including the *Pacte Civil de Solidarité* (Civil Solidarity Pact, or PaCS), which instituted civil partnerships for gay (and straight) couples, passed by parliament in November 1999.[82]

May '68 may have been the starting point of this process, but today's militants, who publish periodicals, lobby politicians, and run for public office (Parisians elected an openly gay mayor in April 2001) owe far more to the pragmatic traditions of the CUARH than to the radicalism of the CAPR and the FHAR. The history of gay liberation in France confirms the irrelevancy of May '68 to French politics—activists achieved little until they turned their backs on radical, anarchic protest and accepted the need for pragmatic politicking—while underlining its real significance as a moral, sexual, and gender revolution. The May events failed, but the spirit of May transformed how French gays regarded themselves and eventually how the wider society looked upon and treated them.

Notes

1. Philippe Bénéton and Jean Touchard, "The Interpretations of the Crisis of May/June 1968," in *The May 1968 Events in France: Reproductions and Interpretations*, ed. Keith A. Reader (London: St. Martin's Press, 1993), 20–47.

2. Hervé Hamon and Patrick Rotman, *Génération*, 2 vols. (Paris: Seuil, 1987–1988); Elizabeth Salvaresi, *Mai en héritage: 14 portraits, 490 itinéraires* (Paris: Syros, 1988); Jean-Pierre Le Goff, *Mai 68: L'héritage impossible* (Paris: La Découverte, 1998).

3. Henri Mendras, *La seconde Révolution française 1965–1984* (Paris: Gallimard, 1988), 288–290, 300–301, 310.

4. Henri Weber, *Vingt ans après: Que reste-t-il de 68?* (Paris: Seuil, 1988), 71–72.

5. Pascal Ory, *L'entre-deux-Mai: Histoire culturelle de la France, Mai 1968–Mai 1981* (Paris: Seuil, 1983), 185.

6. Pierre Emmanuel, "Pour en finir avec la femme-objet," *Preuves* 18 (Summer 1974): 41.

7. Évelyne Rochereux, "Sous les pavés, l'espoir," *Lesbia* 171 (May 1998): 25–26. See also Reader, *The May 1968 Events*, Chapter Six: "Women and the Events of May 1968."

8. Yann Alba, "Daniel Cohn-Bendit: Le charme ravageur de la révolution" (interview), *Gai Pied Hebdo* 242 (November 1–7, 1986): 40–42.

9. Françoise Picq, *Libération des femmes: Les années mouvement* (Paris: Seuil, 1993), 44.

10. Hervé Liffran, "La lente levée d'un black-out," *Le Matin* (September 23, 1985): 5–6.

11. "Mai 68: Le Pink Bang," *3 Keller* 38 (May 1998): 8–16.

12. Olivier Jablonski, "The Birth of a French Homosexual Press in the 1950s," in *Homosexuality in French History and Culture*, ed. Jeffrey Merrick and Michael Sibalis (New York, London, Oxford: Haworth, 2001), 233–248.

13. David S. Churchill, "Transnationalism and Homophile Political Culture in the Postwar Decades," *GLQ* 15 (2008): 31–66.

14. Julian Jackson, *Living in Arcadia: Homosexuality, Politics, and Morality in France from the Liberation to AIDS* (Chicago: University of Chicago Press, 2009); Jacques Girard, *Le mouvement homosexuel en France 1945–1980* (Paris: Syros, 1981), 39–80; Frédéric Martel, *The Pink and the Black: Homosexuals in France since 1968*, trans. Jane Marie Todd (Stanford: University of Stanford Press, 1999), 55–60.

15. André Baudry, "The Homosexual in France," in *Homosexuals Today: A Handbook of Organizations and Publications* (Los Angeles: ONE, 1954), 120.

16. André Baudry, "Des homosexuels sous condition" (interview), *Gai Pied* 38 (May 1982): 12.

17. Georges Sidéris, "*Folles*, Swells, Effeminates, and Homophiles in Saint-Germain-des-Prés of the 1950s: A New 'Precious' Society?," in *Homosexuality in French History and Culture*, ed. Merrick and Sibalis, 219–231.

18. Michael Sibalis, "Homophobia, Vichy France and the 'Crime of Homosexuality': The Origins of the Ordinance of 6 August 1942," *GLQ* 8 (2002): 301–318; idem, "Mirguet, Paul," in *Who's Who in Contemporary Gay & Lesbian History: From World War II to the Present Day*, ed. Robert Aldrich and Garry Wotherspoon (London and New York: Routledge, 2001), 285–286; Janine Mossuz-Lavau, *Les lois de l'amour: Les politiques de la sexualité en France (1950–1990)* (Paris: Payot, 1991), 233–240.

19. Charpentier gave a first interview under the pseudonym "Guy Rey" to Jean Le Bitoux and Jacques Vandemborghe in 1988: "Mai 68, dans la Sorbonne occupée" and "FHAR, Le témoignage," *Mec Magazine* 1 (March 1988): 30–33; *Mec Magazine* 2 (April 1988): 30–32; it is republished in Jean Le Bitoux, *Entretiens sur la question gay* (Bézier: H&O, 2005), 81–92. I have used the original tape-recording, graciously provided by Jean Le Bitoux, which differs slightly from the published version. Charpentier gave a second interview under his real name in 2001: "Le sacerdoce de l'activiste," *Têtu* 54 (March 2001): 97–99. I interviewed Charpentier a third time in Paris on July 30, 2008.

20. Jean-Claude Féray, *Histoire du mot pédérastie et de ses dérivés en langue française* (Paris: Quintes-feuilles, 2004).

21. Pierre Hahn, *Français, encore un effort: l'homosexualité et sa répression* (Paris: Jérôme Martineau, 1970), 197.

22. See two manifestos by the "Nous sommes en marche" committee, in Jean-Louis Brau, *Cours, camarade, le vieux monde est derrière toi! Histoire du mouvement révolutionnaire étudiant en Europe* (Paris: Albin Michel, 1968), 296–301.

23. See Sidéris, "*Folles*, Swells, Effeminates"; Martel, *The Pink and the Black*, passim; Jackson, *Living in Arcadia*, passim.

24. Author's telephone interview with Joseph Lovett, November 30, 2008. Lovett is today a filmmaker in New York City.

25. Lars Ullerstam, *Les minorités érotiques* (Paris: Jean-Jacques Pauvert, 1965); quotations are from the English edition, *The Erotic Minorities* (New York: Grove Press, 1966), 43, 148, 161.

26. See Philippe Sollers, *Un vrai roman: Mémoires* (Paris: Plon, 2007), 106–108, for his own recollections of '68, which do not mention this incident.

27. A.G. Clout, "L'enquête chez les étudiants français," *Presse Université France: Bulletin* 72 (May 23–29, 1966): 12–14.

28. Quoted in Pablo Rouy, "Vive le matérialisme histériiiique!," *Gai Pied Hebdo* 319 (May 5, 1988): 82.

29. François Paul-Boncour, "La Révolution des homosexuels" (interview with Hocquenghem), *Nouvel Observateur* 374 (January 10–16, 1972): 34. See also Guy Hocquenghem, "Subversion et décadence du mâle d'après-Mai," *Autrement* 12 (February 1978): 159.

30. "La Sorbonne occupée: Entretien avec Madeleine Rébérioux," in *Mai 68: Les mouvements étudiants en France et dans le monde*, ed. G. Dreyfus-Armand and L. Gervereau (Paris: La Découverte, 1988), 159.

31. Martel, *The Pink and the Black*, 382, note 5; Roland Surzur, "Les premières lueurs du Fhar" (interview with Hocquenghem), *Gai Pied Hebdo* 319 (May 5, 1988): 31.

32. A novel by Dominique Fernandez, *L'Étoile Rose* (Paris: Grasset, 1978) gives a fictionalized version of the CAPR that plays fast and loose with the facts and provides a highly inaccurate description of the meetings, which conflates later events from the 1970s with '68. A recent film, "Ma Saison Super 8," directed by Alessandro Avelis (2005), dramatizes the events in fictionalized form; here the founder of the CAPR is a twenty-ish student named Marc.

33. Daniel Defert, "Quand la sexualité est devenue un enjeu politique" (interview with Éric Lamien), *Ex aequo* 18 (May 1998): 30.

34. Pierre Fontanié, "La Mort d'Arcadie," *Homophonies* 20 (June 1982): 22–23.

35. Guy Hocquenghem, *Le désir homosexuel* (Paris: Jean-Pierre Delarge, 1972), 101–102.

36. Françoise d'Eaubonne, letter in *Gai Pied* 44 (November 1982): 3.

37. Guy Hocquenghem, "Towards an Irrecuperable Pederasty," in *Reclaiming Sodom*, ed. Jonathan Goldberg (New York and London: Taylor & Francis, 1994), 236.

38. For the history of the FHAR, see Michael Sibalis, "Gay Liberation Comes to France: The Front Homosexuel d'Action Révolutionnaire (FHAR)," in *French History and Civilization: Papers from the George Rudé Seminar*, vol. 1, ed. Ian Coller, Helen Davies, and Julie Kalman (Melbourne: George Rudé Society, 2005), 267–278, available online: http://www.h-france.net/rude/2005conference/Sibalis2.pdf.

39. Girard, *Le mouvement homosexuel en France*, 81–111; Martel, *The Pink and the Black*, 13–31. On lesbianism and the FHAR: Marie-Jo Bonnet, *Les rélations amoureuses entre les femmes* (Paris: Odile Jacob, 1995), 332–340.

40. Jean Le Bitoux, "Le groupe de libération homosexuelle (1975–1978)," *La Revue h* 5/6 (Spring/Summer 1998): 43.

41. Francis Lacombe [Franck Arnal], "Les années lumières," *Gai Pied Hebdo* 460 (March 7, 1991): 54–55.

42. Alain Prique, "L'Herbe folle de mai 68," *La Revue h* 2 (Autumn 1996): 32.

43. "Mais quand reviendra-t-il le joli mois de mai?" (interviews with lesbian militants), *Lesbia* 171 (May 1998): 22–29.

44. E-mail from Joseph Lovett to the author, October 1, 2008.

45. Quoted in Martel, *The Pink and the Black*, 18.

46. Or so Charpentier claims. Two others have made claims to naming the FHAR: Laurent Dispot, "Aventuriers de la liberté," *Gai Pied Hebdo* 460 (March 7, 1991): 60; and Françoise d'Eaubonne, "Le FHAR, origines et illustrations," *La Revue h* 2 (Autumn 1996): 21.

47. Gilles Châtelet, interviewed by Anne Rousseau, in "Le Pink Bang," 12.

48. FHAR, *Rapport contre la normalité* (Paris: Éditions Champ Libre, 1971), 11.

49. Bibliothèque Nationale de France, 4-WZ-10838, "F.H.A.R. Y a-t-il une misère à la Cité Internationale?" (mimeographed flysheet, 1972).

50. FHAR, *Rapport contre la normalité*, 43.

51. Martel, *The Pink and the Black*, 25.

52. Ibid., 27.

53. Interviewed in "Le Pink Bang," 12.

54. Jean Boyer, "Le mouvement homosexuel dix ans après," *Rouge* (July 3–9, 1981): 23.

55. Guy Hocquenghem, *L'après-mai des faunes* (Paris: Grasset, 1974), 189, 199.

56. Michael Sibalis, "Paris," in *Queer Sites: Gay Urban Histories since 1600,* ed. David Higgs (London and New York: Routledge, 1999), 30–36.

57. Jan Willem Duyvendak and Mattias Duyves, "Gai Pied after Ten Years: A Commercial Success, A Moral Bankruptcy?," in *Gay Studies from the French Cultures,* ed. Rommel Mendès-Leite and Pierre-Olivier de Busscher (Binghamton: Haworth, 1993), 205–214; Franck Arnal, "The Gay Press and Movement in France," in *The Third Pink Book: A Global View of Lesbian and Gay Liberation and Oppression,* ed. Aart Hendriks, Rob Tielman, and Evert van der Veen (Buffalo: Prometheus, 1993), 38–45.

58. Gilles Santis [Pierre Hahn], "Entretien avec le groupe de libération des homosexuels," *Don* 2 (February 1976): 6–13; Le Bitoux, "Le groupe de libération homosexuelle"; idem, "The Construction of a Political and Media Present: The Homosexual Liberation Groups in France between 1975 and 1978," in *Homosexuality in French History and Culture,* ed. Merrick and Sibalis, 249–264; Philippe Bataille, "Le mouvement homosexuel français: Exclusion ou rupture?" (unpublished Mémoire de maîtrise, Université de Lille-I, Institut de Sociologie, 1984–1985), 53ff.

59. Collectif du GLHPQ, "L'homosexuel: l'autre?" *Tribune socialiste* (June 25, 1976): 20.

60. Jean-Luc Hennig, "Naissance d'une autre histoire de l'homosexualité," *Libération* (June 24, 1975): 4.

61. See Le Bitoux, "The Construction of a Political and Media Presence."

62. Olivier Jablonski, "Les Festivals gais et lesbiens de cinéma en France en question," *La Revue h* 5/6 (1998): 8–13; Jean Le Bitoux, "Notre Christopher Street," *3 Keller* 16 (October–November 1995): 32–33.

63. Christian Colombani, "Deux candidats homosexuels à Paris: A visage découvert," *Le Monde* (March 12–13, 1978): 6. There were two candidates and two alternates.

64. Quoted in Le Bitoux, "The Construction of a Political and Media Presence," 258.

65. Michel, "En réponse à Philippe" (letter), *Man* 2 (1979): 41–42.

66. Alain Sanzio, "Rencontre plurielle des comités homosexuels," *Rouge* (December 24, 1978): 9.

67. Girard, *Le mouvement homosexuel*, 173–181.

68. Jacky Fougeray, "Une étrange rencontre," *Gai-Pied* 8 (November 1979): 5; Jacques Girard and Françoise Renaud, "Une tribune libre de CUARH-Paris," *Gai-Pied* 12 (March 1980): 7.

69. "Présidentielles," *Homophonies* 1 (November 1980): 6–7.

70. "A Paris le 4 avril: Marche nationale pour nos droits et libertés," *Homophonies* 2 (December 1980): 5; "Marche nationale," *Homophonies* 3 (January 1981): 5; "La longue marche des

homosexuels" and "Le ghetto c'est foutu, les homos sont dans la rue," *Le Matin* (April 5–6, 1981); "Marche nationale," *Gai Pied* 24 (March 1981): 1; "La marche triomphale" and "Notre préférence," *Gai Pied* 26 (May 1981): 1–2.

71. See F. Edelmann, "Le vote des homosexuels," *Le Monde* (May 12, 1981): 12; and Jean Cavailhes, Pierre Dutey, and Gerard Bach-Ignasse, *Rapport Gai: Enquête sur les modes de vie homosexuels en France* (Paris: Éditions Persona, 1984), 130–138. Didier Marie, "Existe-t-il un vote gay?," *Rebel* 4 (April 1993): 61–64, dismisses the "gay vote" as "a legend."

72. "Après le 10 mai!" *Homophonies* 8 (June 1981): 3.

73. Jean Boyer, "Le CUARH et Homophonie: Six années de militantisme gai," *Masques* 25–26 (Spring/Summer 1985): 87.

74. Alain Sanzio, "Que reste-t-il de nos amours?" *Masques* 25–26 (Spring/Summer 1985): 10.

75. Alain Sanzio, "Splendeurs et misères des gais 80: Une page tournée," *Masques* 25/26 (Spring/Summer 1985): 57–58.

76. Guy Hocquenghem, "Mais qui sont les 'nouveaux pédés'?," *Libération* (May 31–June 1, 1980), 7.

77. Guy Hocquenghem, *Lettre ouverte à ceux qui sont passés du col Mao au Rotary* (Paris: Albin Michel, 1986), 14, 197.

78. Reader, *The May 1968 Events*, 114–116.

79. Hervé Liffran, "Débout les gars, reveillez-vous!," *Gai Pied Hebdo* 116 (April 21–27, 1984): 16.

80. Alex Taylor, "A Gay's Gaze," *5 sur 5* 20 (April 1985): 54–55.

81. See comments by Eric Lamien, "Exit la militance," *Gai Pied Hebdo* 352 (January 12, 1989): 58–59.

82. On 1980s militancy see "Militantisme homo: Du naufrage à la renaissance," *Gai Pied Hebdo* 301 (January 2–8, 1988): 9. For the reaction to AIDS: Martel, *The Pink and the Black*, 187–359. The second French edition of Martel's book has an excellent addendum on the struggle for the PaCS: Martel, *Le Rose et le noir: Les homosexuels en France depuis 1968*, rev. ed. (Paris: Seuil, 2000), 593–663.

AFTERWORD

MICHELE ZANCARINI-FOURNEL
(TRANSLATED BY DEBORAH COHEN
AND LESSIE JO FRAZIER)

I thank the editors for inviting me to comment. I see this as a transcontinental exchange in the spirit of reciprocal dialogue and knowledge. Lately I have been calling for a sociopolitical history—rather than the French form of cultural history where studies of gender and sexuality are usually situated—to foreground the force of events, engagements, and political ruptures called '68. Explaining this call to unite the two strains requires a brief synopsis of French interpretations of '68 with attention to what can be obscured by apparently similar terms in their uses on both sides of the Atlantic given serious disjunctures between the two continents in ways of thinking about questions of sexualities, race, and class.

A quick tally of these disjunctures: Judith Butler's *Gender Trouble* was translated into French a full thirteen years after its publication in the United States, meaning that queer theory only very recently became of interest in France; postcolonialism is a concept less than ten years old in our country; and gender is a term officially prohibited by the French State—indeed, on July 22, 2005, the *Official Journal of the French Republic* published official recommendations regarding improper uses of the word gender because "extension of the application of gender is not justified in French." Nonetheless, the term gender is still used in French social sciences; we could not give it up. Thus, we in France are working as outlaws in linguistic illegality.

In French 1968 as doxa and an "event" is told as a political, institutional, and social defeat, but a cultural victory. However, diverse sources have made it possible to write a history contrary to that conveyed in the media, one that analyzes its deep impact on the lives of ordinary people. Its impact is characterized not so much by a notion of "event" as by what I call "The 68 Years." A notable contribution in this direction has been made by exploring the expression of female subjectivities through the study of radio (Anne-Marie Sohn) and television (Marie-Francoise Levy). In French scholarship, the history of women and gender in the 68 years has been explored especially around questions of work and of activism—trade union, political, and feminist. But, despite the strengths of this work, missing were questions of the body, forms of engagement, as well as gendered representations. Fanny Gallot revisited the topic of work through the idea of the "attack of nerves," considered typically female, and its representation—in particular, cinematic—as starting point of resistances to the trade union and factory order. This gendered history, which concerns women as well as men and is attentive to power relations, thus pays attention to perceptions, trajectories, and practices of actors by exploring new sources—televised and filmic images, oral talks, correspondence, private diaries, autobiographies—to restore the expression of individual and collective experimentation and the direction and consequences of these actions.

To say that 1968 was the moment of sexual revolution is now as trite as saying that "second wave" feminism was born in 1970. Yet we must revisit the expressions, chronologies, forms, and places of 68 collective mobilization—while keeping in play both the individual and the national—to understand how ordinary individuals subverted standards of gender and helped spark a transformation of the social and political institutions, such as the couple, the family, the school, or the state. Modes of intervention and the paths of actors before and after 1968 make it possible to analyze the articulation of the various movements and the political feminist and homosexual claims born from or following the events of May–June 1968. The study of gender also makes it possible to examine how the *mise-en-scene* of the bodies was upset during the time and how changes in the gender order transformed the whole social body in the 68 years.

The history of masculinities is only starting to emerge in France, inspired in part by the work of English and American scholars. The work of Julian Jackson invites us to understand the ways in which the members of the Arcadie movement (which emerged in 1954) lived their homosexuality and how, after 68, its principal leader, André Baudry, was confronted by a budding militant homosexual movement. Todd Shepard (using activist writings on Alegerian struggles) invites us to take into account the beginnings of a sexual register into politics, discerning, as his work does, traces of the Algerian War through a gendered analysis of the generation of young men exposed to the event and their resulting relationships with their families, their sisters, and their wives. Moreover, using this lens reveals the extent to which May 68 threatened to emasculate France, a phenomenon that might explain why the right and anticolonial extremists found common ground in the crisis of May–June.

Beyond traditional histories of militant organizations, research on women's groups illuminates forms of feminism traveling such unlikely routes as Tupperware parties, where the revolution in plastic made possible new forms of direct sales that transformed the gender order for ordinary women residing far from the intellectual coteries and regular meetings of the Latin Quarter. During the 1970s, home direct sales created space for the formation of circles of sociability between women, diffusing feminist ideas and practices through these budding capillaries (Catherine Achin and Delphine Naudier).

Moving from the study of groups, militants or otherwise, to look at women themselves and their friendships and sexualities, Anne-Claire Rebreyend meticulously studies autobiographies to consider what constitutes a "liberated woman" in the context of feminist-inspired principles, constraints, and emotional realities. To live this "sexual release" remains tied to the loss of one's virginity without awaiting marriage, a connection that becomes clear by juxtaposing men's and women's speeches on the topic. Sexual initiation, at times cast as devoid of emotion, still represents an obligatory passage: for boys, to reach the status of "man" and for girls, that of "liberated woman." In theory, the sexual revolution, as it was preached, meant equal access for girls and boys to sexuality and pleasure, but in fact, it was gendered, bringing different possibilities and implications for young men and young women. Moreover, the sexual revolution itself became a common mantra in the student scene. Militants reproached fellow militants for not being fully liberated, while an activist's unconventional behavior, perceived as an invitation, could in an extremely rare instance end in rape. Sexual revolution entailed not only the authorization—even demand—to sleep with whomever you desired, but also the duty to enjoy sex. Girls, especially, were labeled repressed, though the call to liberation also touched insecure boys, who, while not derided as were girls, were also pressured by this demand. Yet girls alone carried the risk of pregnancy, which impeded their sexual freedom. Access to contraception, though legalized in 1967, was far from easy for minors to acquire before 1974 and abortion remained illegal for an additional year. By the early 1970s, pregnancy outside marriage, however, started to be tolerated, more so in the city than in the countryside.

The arrival of children usually pushed couples to marry and stabilized a division of roles close to the existing parental model. The ideal of the couple and the family preserved the love myth, often seen as a counterpoint to discourses of sexual revolution and its dream of more emancipated women. In the 1970s, there was an idea that a couple, too absorbed in itself, undermined love little by little—as in *Beautiful of the Lord,* Albert Cohen's famous novel published in 1968; whereas now a couple must be comprised of two autonomous individuals, possibly involved in contingent relations—indeed, Simone de Beauvoir and Jean-Paul Sartre constituted the model couple for the 68 generation. What has changed, then, is that women, though dissatisfied with their relationships, were less easily resigned than their mothers to a sexually and emotionally disappointing marriage, a change for which the rise of women's liberation as a public discourse was responsible.

Don't get me wrong, rejecting a homogenizing cultural history that dissolves not only the events themselves, but also specific, national, local, and individual aspects by rejecting differences is not to refuse to take culture into account. Rather, drawing on an anthropological notion of the creation of shared meanings as giving direction to individual lives and the collective order, I suggest that bodily attitudes, clothing, food practices, ritual or festive practices, and sexuality all belong to the realm of culture. A cultural history of objects—for example, how a particular fabric becomes a miniskirt, or unisex trousers like jeans—can articulate with an approach that simultaneously takes into account events, social differences, and aspirations for freedom.

Thus, we must see radical cultural transformations as potential instruments of political change, obliging us to reconsider the place of culture in politics. Feelings and emotions—the affective component—also play a crucial part in political engagement. Political engagement is not only a question of rational calculation, nor the mere expression of frustrations. Instead, each period of political upheaval has been accompanied by a redefinition of the relationship between culture and politics. We can see the transformation in this relationship when we examine gender and sexuality, more specifically, when we situate gender and sexuality at the center of the 68 years.

INDEX